D1074363

GRAND STRATEGIES

GRAND STRATEGIES

LITERATURE, STATECRAFT, AND WORLD ORDER

CHARLES HILL

Yale
UNIVERSITY PRESS
New Haven & London

Copyright © 2010 by Charles Hill.
All rights reserved.
This book may not be reproduced, in whole or in part, including illustrations, in any
form (beyond that copying permitted by Sections 107 and 108 of the U.S. Copyright
Law and except by reviewers for the public press), without written permission from
the publishers.

Designed by Mary Valencia.
Set in Simoncini Garamond type by Duke & Company, Devon, Pennsylvania.
Printed in the United States of America by Sheridan Books, Ann Arbor, Michigan.

Library of Congress Cataloging-in-Publication Data
Hill, Charles, 1936–
Grand strategies : literature, statecraft, and world order / Charles Hill.
p.   cm.
Includes bibliographical references and index.
ISBN 978-0-300-16386-5 (cloth : alk. paper) 1. Diplomacy in literature. 2. International
relations in literature. 3. Diplomacy—History. 4. International relations—History.
5. Politics and literature—History. I. Title.
PN56.D55H55 2010
809′.933581—dc22

2009049442

A catalogue record for this book is available from the British Library.

This paper meets the requirements of ANSI/NISO Z39.48–1992 (Permanence of
Paper).

10 9 8 7 6 5 4 3 2 1

To *NT*

CONTENTS

WORKS DISCUSSED IN THIS BOOK

GRAND STRATEGIES

PROLOGUE:
BOOKS OF THE RED CHAMBER

L ate on the morning of February 21, 1972, I listened at my desk in the American Embassy Saigon to Armed Forces Radio Vietnam's relay of an announcer describing the arrival of President Nixon in Beijing. I had been a Foreign Service "China watcher" through the horrendous years of the Great Proletarian Cultural Revolution, when Chairman Mao sent thousands of young Red Guards out to burn books and put an end to China's traditional culture. After my diplomatic reporting on the Cultural Revolution I had been assigned to wartime Vietnam under a general instruction to look for indications that China might intervene, as it had when Mao ordered human-wave attacks which seized nearly all the Korean Peninsula from American forces in early 1951. For more than two decades, American strategists considered themselves engaged in a colossal struggle against revolutionary communism, an ideology bent on destroying and replacing the established international state system of world order. Now here were Richard Nixon and his chief adviser, Henry Kissinger, presenting themselves to the "Great Helmsman" of the People's Republic of China.

In the manner of dictators, Mao suddenly summoned the two Americans to his private residence in the sequestered Chungnanhai compound next to the Forbidden City. Kissinger later described Mao's study in his memoirs: "Manuscripts lined bookshelves along every wall; books covered the table and the floor, it looked more like the retreat of a scholar than the audience room of the all-powerful leader of the world's most populous nation."

The few unfrequented bookshops left in China offered little else but the writings of Mao and Marx and Lenin. But here in his lair, Mao had hoarded all the great texts his heart desired. He knew them well, and marked them up. ("If you don't put your pen in action, it cannot really be considered reading," he had said.) *The Outlaws of the Marsh* (or *The Water Margin*), a tale of bandits in rebellion against oppressive lords, inspired him, and classical Chinese poetry too, much of which concerns matters of war and statecraft; Mao inflicted his own considerable poetic output on the masses. But what are we to make of Mao's love for the huge eighteenth-century novel *The Dream of the Red Chamber,* which he boasted of having read five times? He fended off questions by claiming that the novel "showed feudal China in decline"; but far from revolutionary, *The Dream of the Red Chamber,* replete with the stratagems of an array of girls swirling around a romantically individualistic young man in search of experience and pleasure, all in a marriage plot, has as many examples of statecraft and diplomatic intrigue as the novels of Jane Austen.

What are dictators, generals, and strategists looking for in the books they keep around them or carry with them? Certainly Mao was not made a better person by his extensive reading in classic texts. The works considered in this book address the conundrums of statecraft in ways which may be used for good or ill by people in power. Inhumane leaders have made use of humane letters; the Nazis cultivated the arts. But admirable underlying principles of statecraft can be found in nearly all the texts considered here.

Alexander the Great carried the *Iliad* with him on his eastern conquests, keeping it, Plutarch said, with a dagger under his pillow, "declaring that he esteemed it a perfect portable treasure of all military virtue and knowledge." Prior to sainthood, Thomas More read Roman poets and playwrights. Queen Elizabeth I read Cicero for rhetorical and legal strategy. Frederick the Great studied Homer's Odysseus as a model for princes. John Adams read Thucydides in Greek while being guided through the "labyrinth" of human nature by Swift, Shakespeare, and Cervantes. Abraham Lincoln slowly read through Whitman's *Leaves of Grass* and was changed by it. Gladstone, four times prime minister under Queen Victoria, wrote volumes of scholarly commentary on Homer and produced vivid translations—the best kind of close reading—of Horace's *Odes.* Lawrence of Arabia, who wrote himself into history as a fictional character leading Arab tribes in revolt against the Ottoman Turks, carried Malory's *Morte d'Arthur,* if not in his camel's saddlebags then in his head.

Through long nighttime transatlantic flights on the secretary of state's aircraft, when most passenger cabin lights were out and the sound of a deck of cards being shuffled was heard from the press corps seats far in the back, one reading light was always still on. Paul Nitze, the arms control strategist and negotiator, would be reading Shakespeare. Nitze was the only statesman who spanned the Cold War, from being "present at the creation," in Dean Acheson's words, to the day the red hammer-and-sickle flag was pulled down from the Kremlin. Nitze read Shakespeare, he told me, for the plays which interwove principles of statecraft with the foibles of the human condition. On one flight to Moscow, Nitze was struggling through *Cymbeline,* a work of excruciating plot complexity, bearing, as Auden said, the marks of a late work: obscurity, strangeness, and a certain indifference to its effect on the public. Nitze saw in its portrayal of the ancient Roman-Briton struggle a crucial moment in world history. The play recalls the *Aeneid,* in which Trojans and Latins fight for empire yet in the end accept a political-cultural accord. But what must they give up to get peace? Nitze related this to his once famous "walk in the woods" near Geneva in 1982 with his Soviet counterpart Kvitzinsky, a step toward the end of the Cold War which was made into *A Walk in the Woods,* the 1988 Broadway play.

Nitze would probe one intellectual dimension after another in search of aids to his thinking about the vagaries of statecraft. When explaining how the United States needed to approach the USSR, Nitze described a diplomatic version of Niels Bohr's principle of complementarity: "Light can be both wave and particle at the same time"; the United States would have to be adversarial and accommodating at the same time. But then Nitze would return to a literary reference, quoting F. Scott Fitzgerald: "The test of a first-rate intelligence is the ability to hold two opposed ideas in the mind at the same time and still retain the ability to function."

"Two things" were never enough for Nitze; he wanted more expansive examples; a favorite was the literature of fishing. Our 1960s-era Boeing 707 could not fly from Europe to America without refueling, always at Shannon. As Nitze looked out of the taxiing aircraft at the bright green Irish landscape fingered by dark water, he recalled that in the days of piston-engine DC-8 stops here, there always was time to get off the airfield to "wet a line and kill a salmon." Nitze seemed to consider literature, angling, and diplomacy as so obviously interlinked as to require no explanation. Izaak Walton's *The Compleat Angler* and Thoreau's version of Walton in *A Week on the Concord and Merrimack Rivers* were noted. Years later, I shared Nitze's sense when I read, in Gore Vidal's novel of the fifth century B.C., *Creation,* a Cathayan version of a *Compleat Angler* scene. When Baron K'ang sends an agent to neutralize Confucius, he finds the sage wearing an old quilted robe, sitting cross-legged on the damp riverbank: "Confucius proved to be a master angler. Once a fish had taken the hook, he would ever so delicately shift the line this way and that; it was as if the line was moved not by a human hand but by the river's own current. Then, at precisely the right moment, he would strike."

But how to get the hook into the quarry in the first place? And at what risk? And how to avoid getting hooked? (Baron K'ang never hooked Confucius.) For these "ungraspable phantoms" of statecraft, Nitze had to read *Moby-Dick.*

The great matters of high politics, statecraft, and grand strategy are essential to the human condition and so necessarily are within the purview of great literature. Tolstoy's *War and Peace* treats them directly. What has not been much recognized is that many literary works read and praised for insights on personal feelings, such as Jane Austen's *Emma,* possess a dimension wholly apt for statecraft—in Emma's case, the gathering and misanalysis of intelligence.

The literary works arrayed here form a logic chain across the centuries to illuminate ideas and actions affecting world order. Each text explored in these pages illuminates one or another facet of the centuries-long process leading to the current world order, providing ways, old and new, to think about it, literature above all being a supreme way of knowing. Classical works delve into diplomacy and strategy prior to the state, then consider how the formation of states called forth structures for international interaction—often unstable or oppressive, acquired and maintained at great human cost.

The plan is to introduce these ideas in more or less the order in which they become salient issues in statecraft. Starting with use of stratagems, intelligence, and diplomacy and proceeding through core concepts such as the tension between divine and secular legal orders, the awakening of national consciousness and identity, the variety of forms of polity, the nature of war and its impact on society, the book is intended almost as a primer of statecraft and its essential ideas.

On the most profound level, and one of urgent significance today, the texts examined here reveal across time the construction and critique of the modern international state system, launched in 1648 with the Treaty of Westphalia, which ended the religion-inflamed Thirty Years' War and which by the mid-twentieth century had become the recognized system through which states on every continent had agreed to conduct their official interactions. But by the opening of the twenty-first century, the system had deteriorated from within and was assaulted from without by yet another violent, ideological world-spanning movement. This book throws a new angle of light on the foundation stones of world order, their weakening condition, and what needs to be done.

Perhaps most profoundly through literary lenses, "America" as a new idea for the world revealed layers of meaning, mainly in a democratic direction, for the project of constructing a modern international system.

The Enlightenment as the tutelary spirit of modernity produced both the idea of reasoned progress and the revolutionary movements that would aim to destroy and replace the emerging international state system. The novel, rising in accompaniment to the modern age, reveals this momentous dichotomy.

By the mid-twentieth century, the Westphalian system had by adoption or imposition reached every continent to establish diplomatic, legal, commercial, security, and narrative mechanisms. While not amounting to anything approaching world governance, something of a moral order took form in which state, community, and individual aspirations could interact among disparate peoples.

None of the premodern "world" systems devised within the various regions of the world proved able to cope with the destabilizing forces of modernity. The expansion of global exploration and consciousness required a new conception, grounded in agreed procedures and resistant to substantive, religious, or ideological dominance. The genius of the 1648 Westphalian system—the basis for today's international order, such as it is—was its one big "hedgehog" idea: that there must be many "foxes," organized through agreed procedures, to accommodate human diversity. Literature reveals the sources and motivations behind acceptance of the state as the basic unit of world affairs, and explores answers to the next question: what form of governance could best serve a state's people? As seen here, only literature lasts, while history requires constant revision.

For some decades now, the international state system has been deteriorating, intellectually disparaged from within and assaulted by a series of rival systems from without. But literature, once paramount as a way of knowing, was evicted from its place in the pantheon of the arts by popular cultures of entertainment sometime in the late mid-twentieth century, and statecraft has suffered from the loss. Today, both the state order and literature are under assault. Whether the present international system can be shored up and repaired or must be transformed, statecraft cannot be practiced in the absence of literary insight.

Statesmen have looked at literature not only as another source of strategic insight but as a unique intellectual endeavor. Of all the arts and sciences, only literature is substantially and methodologically unbounded. Literature's freedom to explore endless or exquisite details, portray the thoughts of imaginary characters, and dramatize large themes through intricate plots brings it closest to the reality of "how the world really works." This dimension of fiction is indispensable to the strategist who cannot, by the nature of the craft, know all of the facts, considerations, and potential consequences of a situation at the time a decision must be made, ready or not. Literature lives in the realm grand strategy requires, beyond rational calculation, in acts of the imagination.

Dante, in the final canto of *Paradiso,* sees God as a book. The leaves of a notebook—*squaderna*—telling of people, chance happenings, and their consequences, are scattered around the world, but God, the poets know, has bound them into a single volume. In Henry Wadsworth Longfellow's translation:

> I saw that in its depth far down is lying
> Bound up with love together in one volume,
> What through the universe in leaves is scattered;
> Substance, and accident, and their operations.
> All interfused together in such wise
> That what I speak of is one simple light.

Dante immediately gives a literary example: Neptune, startled by a shadow moving across the ocean floor, looks up to see the ship *Argo* skimming the sea's surface, Jason and the Argonauts bound on the first international intervention, to Colchis to strive to win the Golden Fleece. This is literature: the interruption of the light reveals the light, which was not understood because perfect. Imperfection—the conflicts, stratagems, and surprises of world affairs—can convey an ineffable, transcendent sense of things. Clausewitz called it the *coup d'oeil:* an integration of experience, observation, and imagination that "constructs a whole of the fragments that the eye can see." Imprinting it "like a picture, like a map, upon the brain." The approach is like a poet's, involving the quick recognition of a truth that the mind would ordinarily miss, or would perceive only after long study and reflection. Oswald Spengler, at the end of *The Decline of the West,* a kind of tome-poem, praises something similar, the sense possessed by a judge of "horseflesh." A statesman requires such a sense, but in every category of life literature can capture the multifarious whole.

This is all the more necessary in our time because of the hegemony of the social sciences, particularly political science, which by self-definition must confine itself to a narrow band of problems capable of scientifically replicable solutions—leaving the biggest questions beyond its reach. There is as well in the field of literary studies the supposition that high politics and strategy are at best incidental and somewhat suspect subjects for literature. If a great book takes up such themes, those do not constitute the source of its greatness, which must lie elsewhere.

So the argument of this book is that the world should recognize high political ideas and actions of statecraft as aspects of the human condition that are fully within the scope of literary genius, and ones that great writers have consistently explored in important ways. They were not simply using political circumstances as a background for their characters' dramas but were instead thinking deeply and significantly about the ideas themselves. The great authors not only reveal themselves aware of statecraft, some are themselves strategists, exploring ideas fundamental to statecraft and international order.

To be more specific about why literary insight is essential for statecraft, both endeavors are concerned with important questions that are only partly accessible to rational thought. Such matters as how a people begins to identify itself as a nation, the nature of trust between political actors or between a government and its people, how a nation commits itself to a more humane course of governance—all these and many more topics dealt with in this book—can't be understood without some "grasp of the ungraspable" emotional and moral weight they bear. A purely rational or technocratic approach is likely to lead one astray. A virtue of the books examined here is that, while not slighting rational thought, they manage to convey the inchoate aspects of affairs within and between states to attentive readers.

To put it as Paul Nitze would, in a "logic-chain," it is that 1) statecraft is protean, incessantly assuming different forms and presenting new predicaments beyond the ken of established methodologies; 2) some of the greatest classical texts—the *Iliad,* the *Aeneid*—deal with such challenges through their unboundedness, intertwining what would later be labeled as history, theology, psychology, literature, and philosophy before those modern disciplines were formalized; 3) literature, however, largely has remained unbounded, able to probe realms of statecraft which other disciplines have placed off-limits; and 4) some major works conventionally catalogued as nonfiction have jumped over methodological walls to become "fellow-travelers" of literature. This is why no apology is given for those books read here which commonly have been catalogued under history, law, or philosophy, rather than literature. Almost every truly great work of "nonfiction" has achieved its extra level of superiority by soaring above and beyond factual analysis. Kant's *Perpetual Peace* is an imagined story of mankind's political development over eons; Thucydides' *Peloponnesian War* is an epic "ring composition" transcending history; T. E. Lawrence's *Seven Pillars of Wisdom* is a novel traveling under the cover of autobiography.

In this book, literature shows its relationship with statecraft to be reciprocal. Literature informs leaders whose actions may later become the stuff of literature. One might say that the Trojan War was fought in order to supply material for the *Iliad,* and the *Iliad* transmogrified resurfaces in Joseph Conrad's novel *The Rescue:*

Shaw stifled a yawn. "Women are the cause of a lot of trouble," he said dispassionately. "In the *Morayshire,* I remember, we had once a passenger—an old gentleman—who was telling us a yarn about them old-time Greeks fighting for ten years about some woman, the Turks kidnapped her, or something. Anyway, they fought in Turkey, which I may well believe. Them Greeks and Turks were always fighting. My father was master's mate on board one of the three-deckers at the Battle of Navarino—and that was when we went to help those Greeks. But this affair about the woman was long before that time." "I should think so," muttered Lingard, hanging over the rail and watching the fleeting gleams that passed deep down in the water, along the ship's bottom.

1

CLASSICAL ORDERS

Look at Rembrandt's *Aristotle Contemplating the Bust of Homer*. What is he contemplating? How to convey the matters of war and peace, of strategy and humanity, found in Homer's *Iliad* and *Odyssey* to Aristotle's pupil Alexander. Homer's face and sightless eyes give no clue. Aristotle's gaze is off into space. His right hand touches Homer's head, while his left fingers the chain that carries a pendant engraved with the head of Alexander the Great, whose expression we cannot make out. We can imagine the thoughts and words of Homer running like an electric current up to and through the mind of Aristotle, then down into the mind and actions of the conqueror of the world.

Aristotle would use the *Iliad* to teach the first principle of statecraft: diplomacy and power are indispensable and must be used, for best effect, in tandem. Diplomacy precedes the state, and with the use of power may create the state. The *Iliad* is the first of key texts through which classical Athens and Rome probed the foundations of international order.

DIPLOMACY PRECEDES THE STATE:
THE EMBASSY TO ACHILLES

Homer's epic of war between assembled Greek warriors and the citadel of Troy reveals that diplomacy precedes the state and is natural to the human condition. Everyone practices it in some form, from "signaling" to making concessions, to "getting your way without force," to coercive diplomacy.

The origins of the formal diplomatic role run deep into the classical past and the link between theory and practice. The word *theoros* meant something like "to travel far to observe a situation and report back" and was applied to an ambassador or envoy sent for example to the oracle at Delphi: "The *theoros,* then, went to the source of truth to bring back the words of the god to the political authorities of his *polis* and was expected to render a full account of what he had heard and seen."[1] Reporting accurately and completely was essential so that words and facts—theory and practice— were of a piece. The "Embassy to Achilles" portrays that unity violated.

The *Iliad* is "the poem of force," which makes its focus on diplomacy all the more vivid.[2] Nine years into their siege of Troy, the Greeks have come to that moment when Agamemnon, prompted by a false dream sent him by Zeus, believes that the next assault he orders will cause the city to fall. But first Agamemnon foolishly decides to test his soldiers' loyalty. The war is hopeless, he declares. We'll never take the city. Run to the ships, and we'll sail for home.

But instead of valiantly standing fast, the troops break and run from the battlefield. Ordered by Athena to stop the Greeks' self-induced stampede, Odysseus seizes Agamemnon's royal scepter, beats some of the soldiers with it, and restores order. Then Thersites steps forward, an ugly, twisted lowlife figure, the only one in the Greek ranks described as less than impressive in mind and body. In a sneering, mocking voice, Thersites denounces Agamemnon for unjustly taking the spoils of war: women and gold. Thersites' condemnation echoes the charges made earlier by Achilles when Agamemnon pulled rank in order to take Achilles' girl-prize. (Two girls had been taken captive by the Greeks. One, the daughter of a priest of Apollo, was given to Agamemnon, the other to Achilles. When the priest demanded that his daughter be returned, Agamemnon refused, leading Apollo to strike the Greeks with pestilence. Agamemnon relented but demanded Achilles' girl as recompense. This brought on "the anger of

Achilles"—the theme of the epic.) But whereas Achilles spoke as a noble warrior dishonored, Thersites speaks as a rabble-rouser, a common man challenging the inequality imposed by the warrior system. Thersites agitates for the army to go home as a rebellion of the masses.

Odysseus does not deign to refute what Thersites says; he beats him with the scepter, the troops laugh, and the moment passes. But when the ruling class is in conflict with itself, as Achilles is with Agamemnon, a popular uprising and a more egalitarian politics may be imagined.[3]

The collapse of the Greek cause is imminent unless Achilles can be persuaded to return to the battlefield. Diplomacy becomes essential. Agamemnon yields to Nestor's advice to send an embassy to Achilles, to urge him to return to the battle line. Agamemnon will agree to return the girl to Achilles and swear that she has not been violated. Moreover, Agamemnon will give to Achilles gold, horses, and a daughter in marriage with a dowry of seven cities. Nestor selects Phoenix, Ajax, and Odysseus as his envoys. Heralds will escort them, and a prayer will be offered to Zeus, all to convey that this is an official mission. Phoenix, an old friend of Achilles, is sent ahead. When the *Iliad* began, Agamemnon had declared that if he must relinquish his girl-prize, he would take a girl from either Achilles, Ajax, or Odysseus. Because the latter two had been insulted as well, they would be the right ones to send to Achilles. The choice of Odysseus as lead negotiator had to be weighed against his reputation as "a man of twists and turns." He would be a clever bargainer; on the other hand, he might not report back reliably.

Agamemnon's detailed instructions to his ambassadors end with the demand that Achilles bow down to Agamemnon as "the greater man." Thus the gifts are an expression of Agamemnon's power, not a peace offering to Achilles. The mission is flawed from the start.

Book 9 reports "The Embassy to Achilles" in dialogue, as an act in a staged play. The ambassadors find Achilles playing his lyre for his companion Patroclus. Achilles is delighted to see them:

> Welcome! Look, dear friends have come our way—
> I must be sorely needed now—my dearest Friends
> In all the Achean armies, even in my anger.

Odysseus speaks first: "All hangs in the balance now." If Achilles will not return to the fray, "then it will be our fate to die in Troy." Odysseus calls upon Achilles to think of his comrades and relent. He then presents Achilles with what diplomats today would call a "package" of material benefits and full recognition of his dignity. Odysseus follows his instructions by repeating the king's offer word for word: riches, women, honor, and "seven citadels," which will honor Achilles like a god. However, Odysseus disobeys the first rule of ambassadorial conduct by omitting Agamemnon's demand that Achilles bow down to him. Homer does not point this out to us; we have to recall Agamemnon's original instructions to his envoy. Odysseus must have realized that omitting that demand offered the only hope of success for the mission.

Achilles' reply is by turns wistful and furious. He praises Odysseus as a "great tactician," but scorns him for his duplicity: "I hate that man like the very Gates of Death / who says one thing but hides another in his heart." Achilles then questions the heroic warrior code and calmly says that tomorrow he and his men will leave the war and sail for home. "Watch, my friend . . . and you will see my squadrons sail at dawn." He advises all the Greeks to do the same and repeats the antiheroic, war-rejecting declarations of the rabble-rouser Thersites, but from an elevated social class.

In fury, Achilles denounces every point in Agamemnon's proposal conveyed by Odysseus and sets out his famous "choice": either a short life and fame or a long life in obscurity at home; he is ready for the latter. He tells the delegation to return to Agamemnon and report his reaction.

Phoenix intervenes. In the rambling disquisition of an old man, he tries to play on Achilles' emotions with stories from the past. Casually he tells the tale of a grievance he once held to make the point that it is time for Achilles to put his grievance behind him. Then he tells the story of the boar of Calydon inside-out, to try to awaken Achilles to his terrible isolation.

Phoenix's line of argument pits one tenet of the warrior code against another. Achilles has justified his actions on the grounds of the dishonor done to him when Agamemnon demanded his girl-prize. Phoenix raises another part of the code: when the one who committed the dishonor appeals to the one dishonored, it is wrong to turn down the appeal. To do so will bring "ruin" down on the one who will not relent. He shows Achilles the cost of disobedience to order, no matter how arbitrary the order may seem.[4]

Achilles seems softened by the long speech of Phoenix. Instead of repeating his intention to sail for home in the morning, Achilles tells Phoenix:

You stay here and spend the night in a soft bed
Then, tomorrow at first light, we will decide,
Whether we sail for home or hold out here.

The third member of the team, Ajax, slow in speech and mighty in battle, had not been expected to speak. He stands and says to Odysseus: we have failed; let's leave. Still looking at Odysseus, Ajax vents his anger on Achilles. Turning to speak to him directly, Ajax bluntly sums up the code that Achilles is violating: guest-friendship ("here we are under your roof," Ajax says); accepting suppliants (when an apology is made, you must accept it); and the love owed your comrades (who will die if Achilles does not return to the fray).

Odysseus's demarche has failed, yet something in Phoenix and Ajax's approach may have had an effect. Achilles seems not to relent, but watching the exchange silently has been Patroclus, Achilles' companion, as what Adam Smith would call "the impartial spectator." The reaction of Achilles' own side will affect his position. The importance of direct, face-to-face negotiations comes with the eye contact observed by the three envoys when they see that Achilles

gave Patroclus a sharp glance, a quiet nod
. . . a sign for the rest to think of leaving quickly.

Although the embassy has failed to persuade Achilles to accept Agamemnon's offer and return to battle, something nonetheless has been gained.

Achilles had said he would not decide until morning whether to give up the war and sail home. Odysseus, however, reports to Agamemnon that Achilles

has no intention of quenching his rage.
He's still bursting with anger, more than ever—
he spurns you, spurns all your gifts.

Here Odysseus reports the reaction he received from Achilles, but says nothing about the shifting, introspective, conditioned comments and decisions made by Achilles in response to the presentations of Phoenix and Ajax, certainly matters of some significance. Odysseus has violated two fundamentals of diplomacy. He has not followed his instructions, deciding on his own to try to make his mission succeed by conveying all that Agamemnon proposed except the demand that Achilles submit openly to Agamemnon as his superior. And he has not reported back to Agamemnon accurately.

Odysseus showed himself a great commander, in the Iliadic sense, when he saved the Greeks from a debacle following Agamemnon's foolish test of his troops. He was chosen as Agamemnon's ambassador to Achilles because of his "Odyssean" qualities for "tact"—as a tactician. Odysseus has a diplomat's useful quality of "creative dissembling" but does not know its limits. It is strange that the crafty Odysseus—a man on whom nothing was lost—was oblivious to the change in Achilles' demeanor. Like too many envoys, Odysseus was following his own agenda.

What if Odysseus's edited version had been accepted by Achilles? Achilles would have returned to the war to be confronted with Agamemnon's demand that he "bow down" to Agamemnon as "the greater man." We can imagine that Achilles would have tried again to kill Agamemnon. Athena would have to intervene again. The will of Zeus would be affected, and chaos would follow.

Michel de Montaigne, in one of his early essays, "A Tricke of Certaine Ambassadors," describes what had become a diplomatic commonplace. In reporting back to the king, ambassadors "dissembled the chiefest part unto him" instead of fulfilling the duty "truly and exactly to set downe things as they were, and in what manner they succeeded." To prevent such distortions, Montaigne noted that the kings of Persia would "mince the instructions given to their Agents and Lieutenants so small that in the least accident they might have recourse to their directions and ordinances."

This is not satisfactory either, and Montaigne knows it. To be effective, ambassadors do not merely execute, "but frame and direct by their own advice and counsel, the will of their master." They need leeway to distill, classify, clarify, and shape the essence of their mission.

This and surrounding diplomatic conundrums would be taken up eventually through the creation of career diplomatic corps in the service of sovereign states within an international system.

FROM BLOOD FEUD TO STATE: THE ORESTEIA

The story of how the world came to be so thickly populated with states has hardly begun to be told.

—*David Armitage, The Declaration of Independence: A Global History*

To speak on behalf of the state has not been a comfortable assignment in recent times. Lenin called for the state to be "smashed"; if the state continued to be necessary after the revolution and under the Dictatorship of the Proletariat, it would soon "wither away." Stalin created the state as an all-dominant totalitarian monster. In American politics, the right warns against statism as the enemy of freedom; the left favors government but fears the state's designs on civil liberties. Feminists declare it to be "male" and so by definition illegitimate. Anarchists and libertarians oppose the state altogether.

Aristotle, though, seeking the sources of human society, found the state, or city-state or *polis,* to be a fact of nature. As "the political animal," man would find his true vocation in ruling, and being ruled in turn, in the state. For Hegel, the state was the objective form of the universal law, the very incarnation of the "spirit of the world"; it was not possible to speak of historical life outside of or before the state. In opposition to Saint Augustine's certainty that the earthly city (*civitas terrena*) is a disfigured version of the City of God (*civitas divina*), Hegel declared the state to be "the divine idea as it exists on earth." All this notwithstanding, it seemed to be stating the obvious when in 1970 a scholar of the medieval origins of the modern state said that "Today we take the state for granted."[5]

We do not take it for granted anymore. Globalization is said to have eroded sovereignty to a point where the state must be considered an obsolete form of governance. Political scientists have called it fallacious to think that polities existing before the Industrial Revolution, or the Electronic Revolution, or Globalization, or some other cutoff point can be spoken of as "states." The state to them is a modern creation whose time is about up. Many of the entities we see around the world today are "failed states," or supranational units, or Islamic states, or "market states," "kleptostates," "petrostates," "propaganda" states: degenerate versions of the state in the nineteenth-century sense, and not to be compared to the polis or other polities of the premodern past.

This last approach does not hold up; there are fundamental commonalities between the states of millennia before and those around us today. Granted, the nature of the state is hard to grasp, but unless it is understood in a classic way, we cannot shore up the contemporary state or understand that there is no replacement for it.

Aeschylus's great trilogy the *Oresteia* locates civilization's origin in the creation of the state. The drama tracks the aristocratic house of Atreus, disintegrating under a curse that demands revenge down the generations until Orestes, in Athens, is the central character in a transition from the primeval cycle of revenge to civil society based on judicial order.

The line that is crossed, from precivilization to civilization, has at least six concepts of continuing importance. The first is the shift from the family as the seat of governance to the *state.* Private interests, however essential to human flourishing and societal productivity, may not overtop the *public* good. Status, largely related to family or clan, would in progressive societies shift "from status to *contract.*"[6] Personal and family honor, when calling for "taking the law into your own hands," gives way to *justice,* administered publicly. To administer justice properly, the integrity of the *process* must be maintained; regardless of the substance of the case, an ill-prepared court case must be dismissed even though the wrongdoer goes unpunished. Finally, there is *marriage* as an institution of civilization: "Therefore shall a man leave his father and his mother, and shall cleave unto his wife: and they shall be one flesh."[7] Status or kin relationship is superseded by contract: the marriage vows.

The line between primeval and civil society is clear on all these points in the *Oresteia,* and all are visibly contested today in parts of the world where civil society has not taken hold or has slipped backward.

"When I read the *Oresteia,* I receive the uncanny impression that Aeschylus somehow precedes Homer in time, if only because the cosmos and the gods seem more archaic, less rational, even than they do in the *Iliad.*"

—*Harold Bloom*

In a course called "International Ideas and Institutions," I asked the students how many had read the *Oresteia.* About half raised their hands. "How many have been to Mycenae?" Maybe ten had seen the high-seated citadel of King Agamemnon in northeastern Peloponnesus, near the Aegean Sea. Perhaps not surprising. The *Oresteia* is the only complete trilogy extant from the great age of Athenian drama, and its intricately woven plots touch upon most major themes of Greek literature. Above all, the trilogy represents the moment of transition from prestate society to a polity we may recognize as statehood.

There is a curse on the House of Atreus, so ancient as to be traced back to the gods. Among mortals it begins with the betrayal of marriage and proceeds through cannibalism and murders.

As you approach Mycenae, the road passes by the beehivelike tomb of Agamemnon. Looking up to the high, heavy hill, you are struck by how difficult it is to see where the fortress, designed for security above all, actually is.

Once through the Lion Gate and into the palace precincts, you see a starkly steeper hill looming over Mycenae's walls. You can visualize that night when the play opens. In a dramatic way familiar to us from the way Shakespeare echoes Aeschylus's model, watchmen, ordinary soldiers, are muttering to each other about the return of King Agamemnon to his queen, Clytemnestra. Signal fires have been lit, glowing points linking the sea islands to the east to Ilion's shore. The Trojan War is over. The Greeks have won.[8] Their commanding general, Agamemnon, is on his way home.

Tension shrouds the night. The war against Troy has raged for ten years, but a bloody act at the very outset that enabled the Greek ships to sail is now recalled in the minds of all Mycenaeans.

When warriors from all over Greece assembled at Aulis to sail against Troy, the ships were windbound in harbor. For the expedition to proceed, the goddess Artemis required the sacrifice of Agamemnon and Clytemnestra's daughter Iphigenia. The dilemma pits Agamemnon the commander of the Greeks against Agamemnon the head of his household. Public responsibility and morality are at odds with private. Agamemnon has Iphigenia put to death to placate the goddess, and the winds carry the flotilla on to Troy. The family curse of the Atridae is now bound up with the fate of all the Greeks.

The curse on the House of Atreus represents the ancient and established form of justice: blood revenge. Each kin-murder demands that another murder be committed in turn. Agamemnon's father, Atreus, and his uncle Thyestes had been rivals for the rule of Argos, a rivalry exacerbated by Thyestes' adultery with Atreus's wife.

Feigning a desire for reconciliation, Atreus invites Thyestes to a feast at which the main dish served to his brother is the cooked flesh of his children. When Thyestes discovers what has been done to him, he pronounces a curse on the House of the Atridae. Agamemnon's sacrifice of his daughter Iphigenia carries the curse into another generation.

When Agamemnon returns to Mycenae, he is welcomed home by his queen, Clytemnestra, who invites her war-hero king to approach ceremonially on a red carpet. The king demurs; the queen insists; the Chorus moans in foreboding. Agamemnon does as Clytemnestra bids. Soon thereafter she appears standing over her husband's body, having taken blood revenge for the murder of her daughter. The Chorus now invokes Orestes, the son of Agamemnon and Clytemnestra, as the next to act out the curse.

In the second part of the trilogy, Orestes returns to Mycenae, where he meets his sister Electra, who questions the code of blood vengeance. But Orestes knows that his duty is to avenge his father by killing his mother. Matricide would be the worst act of all, deepening the curse of the house even more.

Orestes knows that the Furies—ancient earth-god creatures who oversee primeval justice—will pursue him if he does not kill Clytemnestra. Despite great misgivings, Orestes murders his mother. The Chorus sings of pity, but the code demanded her death.

At the opening of the third play, *The Eumenides,* the Furies have pursued Orestes to the Temple of Apollo at Delphi. For the Furies, Orestes' matricide is a blood crime, and he himself must be killed in revenge. Clytemnestra's murder of Agamemnon was not, according to the code, of such magnitude because he was not kin to Clytemnestra, merely her husband. The Furies rage against Apollo (the old earth gods against the sky gods, who largely have replaced them) for protecting Orestes. Apollo, however, asserts that law is higher than blood revenge as a matter of justice. Thus marital contract is more sacred than the status of kinship. Orestes flees to Athens and takes refuge in the temple of Athena on the Acropolis.

Athena intervenes to decide which form of justice will prevail. Orestes' case will be heard by a jury. The case pits heaven against earth. The new gods, with Apollo as their spokesman, will defend Orestes; the old earth gods, the Furies, will prosecute him.

The outcome is a hung jury, but Athena casts the deciding vote.[9] The outraged Furies threaten to pitch Athens into civil war. Only when Athena invokes Peitho, the goddess of persuasion, do the Furies relent and accept an honorable place in Athens as the Eumenides ("The Kindly Ones"). Rhetorical advocacy creates the political space essential to law and order. This case marks the shift from the state of nature's anarchy to the order of civil society.[10] Justice will be carried out not by individuals on behalf of families or clans, but by the state. Irrevocably, capital punishment will from this point forward be a matter for the state to decide in accordance with open procedures centered on the jury. This makes the death penalty the foundation stone of civilization, for only when a victim's kin are convinced that the state will exact justice in response to murder will they entrust that power to the state. The state may make capital punishment extremely rare, but to abolish it would undermine that contract between the people and their government. Revenge is replaced by the rule of law, which must include at least the possibility of imposing the death penalty for capital crimes. John Locke would later make clear the foundational importance of this compact. The rights that individuals cede to the state are revocable if the government fails to perform the responsibilities entrusted to it. But the right to punish under the law is not revocable, but "wholly given up."

The blood feud has continued to exist in places where full state sovereignty is lacking. It appears vividly in Mark Twain's *Huckleberry Finn.* Huck asks, "What's a feud?" Buck explains, "A feud is this way: a man has a quarrel with another man, and kills him; then that other man's brother kills *him;* then the other brothers, on both sides, goes for one another, then the cousins chip in—and by and by everybody's killed off, and their ain't no more feud. But it's kind of slow, and takes a long time." The feud Huck asks about is between the Grangerfords and the Shepherdsons. These are portrayed not as precivilized brutes but as wealthy grandees, sartorially elegant and devoted to chivalric manner, yet they continue to slaughter each other for an original cause neither can remember.[11]

At the bar in the country club of Rochester late one evening we were discussing the Middle East today. An old hand long involved in commerce and trade in the Arabian Peninsula and Persian Gulf area summed it up: "It's all clans." The eons-long struggle between the blood feud way and the civil society of statehood is fully alive there, as well as in Afghanistan and other parts of the Middle East. The clan puts the substance of a problem above all else; the state is concerned with process—to ensure that all are treated equally and fairly, even if it means that some wrongdoer may go unpunished because of a procedural flaw in the case. The state focuses on the public good; the clan cares most for its own private cause. The state is committed to administer justice; the clan is sensitive to its honor. The state recognizes and enforces contracts; the clan may deal in something akin to contract, but hierarchy or status counts for more. Sir Henry Maine, the Victorian legal historian, summed up the course of all civilization in these terms: "From status to contract." Today in the Middle East, Africa, and elsewhere, the state's essentials—process, the public good, justice, and contract—have lost ground or been abandoned.

So in the *Iliad* we see diplomacy, the central element of statecraft, practiced before anything like the state we know exists. In the *Oresteia* the state comes into being to replace the blood feud as the source of justice and the foundation of civilization. The next stage will be the need to shape an international system of states, a network of Greek city-states with their leading polities of Athens and Sparta as vividly narrated by Thucydides in *The Peloponnesian War*, "a manual for statecraft." Somewhere in this procession the "Socratic Revolution" takes place: the warrior ethic of Achilles at Troy is superseded by the civic ethic of Socrates in Athens.

Most Near Eastern relations were empire-to-empire; the Greek *poleis* and their interactions seem very like modern states. Neither were they successful empires nor did they develop effective mechanisms of international relations beyond Hellas itself. Permanent peace among so many independent states was unrealistic, but Thucydides shows them achieving a layered—political, economic, and security—set of pacts and arrangements that, in the best of times, adhered to the profound fiction of "the equality of states." They were most successful in the conduct of their international relations in "their impressive record of interstate arbitrations, which stand in comparison only with that of nineteenth-century Europe and America."[12] The modern international state system may be viewed as similar to that of the small Greek society of states in the sixth and fifth centuries B.C. Both involved broad moral agreements, respect for multiple sovereignties, concern for the balance of power and other means of maintaining international peace and security, and diplomacy as the lubricant of it all.

Thucydides was a natural text for the strategists of the Cold War because it could be read, superficially, as regarding the accumulation of military power as the sole determinant of statecraft. The standoff between the United States and the Soviet Union seemed to reflect the characters of ancient democratic Athens and oligarchical Sparta. Key factors in that bipolar contest, such as economic productivity or intercontinental ballistic missiles with calculable "throw weight," were readily reckoned into a quantitative net assessment. Secretary of State George C. Marshall spoke openly about the Cold War as a version of the Peloponnesian War, although he did not really understand that ancient conflict. Brainy members of the

State Department's Policy Planning Staff, who grasped Thucydides' text very well, wrote Peloponnesian War insights into American foreign policy in the 1950s.

Thucydides really came to town when Henry Kissinger joined President Nixon in the White House. Kissinger had taught Thucydides in GOV 800 at Harvard, and soon National Security Council staffers and Foreign Service officers who never had read the work were quoting the Athenians in "The Melian Dialogue": "The strong exact what they can; the weak concede what they must," the motto of Cold War realists.

A classic text can be defined as one that each generation reads in its own way to fill its particular need, each finding something new in it. There was more to Thucydides than the crude doctrine of realism and Kissinger knew this perfectly well. Thucydides is more astutely read as a critique of Realpolitik. As a manual of statecraft, the work takes the reader across the entire range of factors, none of which the statesman can risk neglecting: the economic base of the state, the legal framework, diplomacy, national character, leadership and its flaws, rhetoric and language, the public and the private in tension, the certainty of the unexpected blow. All these are treated in Athens's rise and reprised in Athens's momentous fall.

Thucydides is called the first objective historian, but later historians of the Peloponnesian War of 431–404 B.C. find many ways to quarrel with him, as do political scientists. Historians have the pleasure of dealing with all the facts known to all the participants of any past event, but the statesmen of the time must make decisions when knowing only a small portion of what is happening. The political scientist, trying to get replicable results, must focus on a narrowly defined corner of an event and on a few key variables. In contrast, the statesman must attend to the multiplicity of variables: everything counts. Neither historians nor political scientists can deal with the complexity of true strategy and statecraft. Thucydides does so because his narrative is literature, and literature does not restrict itself. It can say anything that needs to be said.

The frontispiece to Thomas Hobbes's translation of Thucydides depicts—vividly, as do many title page illustrations of early modern books— the elements of the international state system of ancient Hellas. It shows the two states: on one side Sparta under Archidamus, a hoary, traditional figure wearing a crown. Drawings above and below show Sparta as a land-based military power, governed by oligarchy (*oi aristoi*). A Doric column in the background indicates the male principle of national character: stern, spare, wary, unrelenting. Opposite is Athens under Pericles, in his prime and modern in appearance. The drawings depict a naval power, governed by the people through direct democracy (*oi polloi*). This side's column is Ionic, representing the lighter, swifter, innovative female principle. In the center of it all is Thucydides, holding his book, asserting that it will be "a possession for all time."

We need not go far into these pages to recognize that the confrontation is set within an international system for the Hellenic world: Sparta and its network of alliances, the Peloponnesian League, versus Athens, which has transformed the Delian League, a defensive alliance against Persia, into its own naval empire. The two Greek powers had fought each other sporadically from 460 to 445. They then forged the "Thirty Years' Peace," which in 432 was jeopardized by a seemingly minor revolt in a one-goat town in the far northwest corner of Greece, Epidamnus. The town appeals to its mother state Corcyra but is rejected. It then turns to Corinth for assistance and gets it. This puts Corcyra and Corinth at odds. The former appeals to Athens for help, citing Corinth's rising naval strength as a threat to Athens itself. Athens ponders the legal, commercial, and strategic stakes and decides what great powers almost always decide: to get "partially involved," by offering Corcyra an alliance, but with significant reservations attached. Corinth then puts pressure on Athens by stirring up trouble in Potidaea, an Athenian dependency. Athens retaliates by imposing a trade embargo on Megara, which mattered economically to both Corinth and Sparta. The reader can see elements of an international state system at work: treaties, trade, sanctions, the balance of power, and an escalating confrontation moving through phases that could illustrate Samuel Huntington's *The Clash of Civilizations.*

The scene then shifts to "The Debate at Sparta," where the Corinthians call upon the Spartans to get involved before Athens's accumulation of power reaches the point where nothing Sparta does can stop it. The Corinthians harangue the Spartans, trying to goad them out of their typical sluggish caution. The disparate national characters of the two powers are contrasted. "There is promptitude on their side," they tell the Spartans, "against procrastination on yours; they are never at home, you are never from it. . . . One might truly say that they were born into the world to take no rest themselves and to give none to others."

The literary genius of the scene is glowing. Not long ago a company of professional actors from Manhattan were brought to Yale to perform it as a one-act play. The actors did not understand the story and so played all parts, as actors like to do, as angry, shouting Shakespearean kings. Directed well, the drama not only is packed with ideas but also is funny. The Athenian ambassadors present, after watching the Corinthians try to shame the Spartans into action, play to Spartan propensities as well, but by engaging their cultural inclinations: "Take your time" in deciding, the Athenians say, a line made for a thespian with a comic gift.

Turning serious, the Athenian envoys then reveal in a line just how complex and "modern" is the international system they share with Sparta: "While it is still open to us both to choose aright, we bid you not to dissolve the treaty, or to break your oaths, but to have our differences settled by arbitration according to our agreement."

The Spartans then decide within the context of their own system, a kind of executive branch–legislative branch policy debate. King Archidamus speaks at length (an un-Spartan thing to do) to argue for delay (very Spartan). A representative of the ephors, a kind of board of counselors, replies laconically (Spartans are supposed to be men of few words) but argues in favor of going rapidly to war (very un-Spartan). The ephor wins the argument. Thucydides has silently conveyed to us that in matters of war, peace, and national character, style often wins out over substance.

This Congress at Sparta in 432 could have been one in the series of the "Conference System" put in place by the greatest diplomat of the nineteenth century, Prince Metternich. Emerging from the 1814 Congress of Vienna following the Napoleonic War, Metternich's system called for conferences to convene whenever differences arose among the Great Powers which might lead to war and the collapse of the overall international system. Here, too, would be one of Thucydides' appeals to Henry Kissinger.

The Spartan decision did lead to war, a war that proved too much for Athenian democracy (a lesson that led the American Founding Fathers to design a very different kind of democracy, specifically to avoid Athens's flaws). The final disaster came with the Athenian people's swift decision to launch the Sicilian expedition. There, at Syracuse, in a night battle in which the Athenian forces fell into disarray, even losing their password, they revealed how much of their national character and purpose had been lost— caught up in what later would be called the doctrine of realism, seeking power above all else. Pericles in his Funeral Oration, the greatest speech in history, had told the people that their sons would fight for Athens because the Athenians would forever honor their fallen heroes. But at the end of his book, Thucydides writes: "The victorious Syracusans now picked up their wrecks and dead, and sailed off to the city and set up a trophy. The Athenians, overwhelmed by their misfortune, never even thought of asking leave to take up their dead or wrecks, but wished to retreat that very night." When my colleague John Lewis Gaddis taught at the Naval War College in Newport, Rhode Island, Thucydides was a core text of the curriculum. In that post–Vietnam War year, the book was almost too much for that class of officers to bear. In the past few years it has been read against the background of the war in Iraq.

RECONSTITUTING THE STATE

Late in the Second World War, two British statesmen exchanged thoughts on their reading of Xenophon's *Anabasis* (otherwise known as "The March Up Country" or "The Ten Thousand"). Leo Amery, secretary of state for India, wrote to Field Marshall Sir Archibald Wavell, imperial viceroy. Amery had been rereading the *Anabasis* and found it "full of sound remarks" on generalship and "on the tactics of moving an army of heavy foot-sloggers through country full of enemy cavalry or mountain catch-'em alive-oes." Wavell wrote back that he had found Xenophon "most extremely dull" when he first read him at school "since no-one troubled to explain to me what Xenophon was doing or even what country he was in; and I connect him mainly with rather unenlightening statements of the number of *parasangs* [a Persian distance of about 3.4 miles] he traversed daily and how he made camp. If only I had had a master who had told me something of his remarkable exploit and of his tactics, I might have taken a livelier interest in it than I did. I have since been over quite a good deal of the country which he covered in his march [Mesopotamia, or today's Iraq]."[13]

These two notables in the last years of the British Raj, which soon would force two new states into being, India and Pakistan, would have seen something else in Xenophon's book: the creation of a polity under difficult and dangerous conditions—after a major war had caused social collapse.

Of the great texts that "every schoolboy used to know," Xenophon's *Anabasis* is now little read though enduringly famous for the cry of "*Tha-*

latta! Thalatta!"—"The sea! The sea!" What was it that every schoolboy knew? That ten thousand soldiers from all over Greece, after the devastating Peloponnesian War, signed on as mercenaries to fight for Cyrus in a Persian struggle for power that went wrong. Finding themselves in Mesopotamia without a patron, with many of their generals slaughtered, and menaced by enemies on all sides, the Ten Thousand decided in the fall of 401 B.C. to march north to the Black Sea and then sail westward home to Greece. They chose Xenophon the Athenian to lead them, following him across rivers and mountains, through deserts and snows, in the face of barbarian assaults all along the way.

Lawrence of Arabia said that Xenophon had been of more value to him in his desert campaign than his formal study of Marshal Foch's *Principes de guerre.* When the Turks surrendered and Lawrence raced through a driving sandstorm down to Aqaba on the Red Sea and splashed into the water, if *Thalatta, Thalatta* was not on his lips it was in his thoughts.

Because the Peloponnesian War has shattered the Greek polity, there is a sense that the expeditionary force is little more than a randomly assembled band of brutes selling their services in desperation for pay. Their "march up-country" is an *Iliad* (or Babyloniad) with no heroes and no worthy purposes. No sacrifices to the gods are recorded.

When their employer Cyrus is killed at the battle of Cunaxa, north of Babylon (on the future site of Baghdad's Saddam Hussein International Airport), the Greeks, no longer mercenaries, come alive vividly. When the Persian king's forces close in on them, they sing the paean and they charge. Suddenly the text is filled with the names of the Greek fighters. They begin to debate vociferously about their next course of action. Here, as Xenophon steps forward, an Odyssey begins. The polis wracked by the Peloponnesian War is forged anew as the soldiers vote for their leaders, debate their policies, form committees to oversee logistical requirements, and solidify their political community through one crisis after another.

Xenophon comes into focus after the Persian general Tissaphernes treacherously lures five Greek generals and twenty captains to a conference where they are seized and slaughtered. The Ten Thousand choose Xenophon as leader. The murder of their chief generals was not a disaster. Experienced as citizens of democratic polities, the soldiers were ready to debate and decide by voting on new commanders and new courses of action.

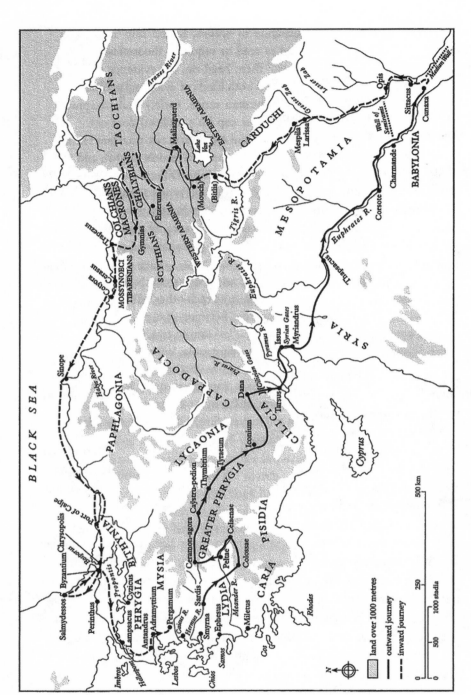

Figure 1. The route of Xenophon's army, 401 B.C. Robin Lane Fox, *The Long March: Xenophon and the Ten Thousand* (New Haven: Yale University Press, 2004)

And so the Greek cohort carries out a military retreat, which John Ruskin called "more honorable than a thousand victories."[14] During their retreat, the Ten Thousand shape themselves into a polis on the march, they change their form of "government" through the classic cycle of rule by the one, kingship (when unity was the priority), to rule by the few (the elite officers corps when expertise was needed), to rule by the many, the "body politic" of the soldiers themselves (when full commitment by the entire corps was imperative). Significantly, they decide much by a "show of hands." While the state is the fundamental entity, different forms of state governance may arise in sequence. Ultimately the Greeks employ the best form, democracy. Thus Xenophon anticipates Churchill's pronouncement that "democracy is the worst form of government except for all those other forms that have been tried from time to time."[15]

> When the men in front reached the summit and caught sight of the sea there was great shouting. Xenophon and the rear guard heard it and thought there were some more enemies attacking in the front. . . . So Xenophon mounted his horse and, taking Lycas and the cavalry with him, rode forward to give support, and, quite soon, they heard the soldiers shouting out "The sea! The sea!" and passing the word down the column then certainly they all began to run, the rearguard and all, and drove on the baggage of animals and the horses at full speed; and when they had all got to the top, the soldiers with tears in their eyes, embraced each other and their generals and captains.

The sight of the sea was taken by the troops as proof that they had survived the march through the most deadly territory and were now truly on their way home. At Trapezus on the Black Sea they demanded ships so that they might sail back to Greece, "stretched out at my ease on deck, like Odysseus," a reference to Odysseus carried home to Ithaca on a Phaeacian ship.

At this point, when it would seem that the *Anabasis* is near its end, Xenophon's text is in fact hardly past the halfway mark. The polis meets to consider the matter. Xenophon's problems as leader are far from over. His strategy must adjust to the new situation. On the return leg, the polity progressively falls into factionalism and disarray. New adventures befall them, but the tone is not the same. The polis is still in being, but the atmosphere has turned acrid. The soldiers hold an inquiry into the past conduct of their generals, a very Greek thing to do, but not good for the solidarity of an army still in difficult straits. Charges of brutality and arrogance are brought against Xenophon, but his rhetoric gains him a reprieve.

When they reach a remote colony of the Greek city of Megara, the troops want to extort money from the people. Xenophon opposes this, and the dispute splits the army into three groups, each making its own way onward. As Xenophon's text ends, the Ten Thousand again sign on as mercenaries, to fight in Asia Minor. Geographically, politically, and morally, the *Anabasis* has come full circle.

Both Xenophon's epic and Plato's *Republic* take up the matter of how a new political community is formed out of catastrophe, the result of the Peloponnesian War, which destroyed the Athenian empire.[16] There is a sense of postwar hopelessness. Both Socrates and Xenophon go *down* to a physical and political low point; then both struggle to go *up* through the difficult process of creating a new polity.

Socrates, in Plato's *Republic,* intellectually attempts to design a new polis. The result is repulsive, perhaps an ironic demonstration of how pure intellect in its search for political utopia can produce a tyranny that would drain humanity of its capacity for virtue. Xenophon takes another route, literally the road of an actual army on the march. His polis emerges not from theory but from practice.[17] The Ten Thousand achieve a new polity that works—but once they are safe from the Persians their political unity collapses. The result is a return to the low and disgraceful starting point of the saga. *Anabasis,* like Plato's *Republic,* shows the limits of politics.

The poet-classicist A. E. Housman surely had Xenophon's Ten Thousand in mind when he wrote "Epitaph on an Army of Mercenaries."

> These, in the day when heaven was falling,
> The hour when earth's foundations fled,
> Followed their mercenary calling
> And took their wages and are dead.
> Their shoulders held the sky suspended;
> They stood, and earth's foundations stay;
> What God abandoned, these defended,
> And saved the sum of things for pay.[18]

Housman's poem compels the reader to consider that world order requires hard actions beyond the realm of personal morality. The meter moves at a slogging pace, the soldiers doing what they signed on to do, with no ennobling talk about valor or sacrifice. "They took their wages and are dead," calls forth Romans 6:23, "the wages of sin is death." By conventional judgment their fighting is a sin, but Housman knows more is involved. The poem heaps scorn on those who, safe abed at home, look down on mercenaries who, like Atlas, hold the sky on their shoulders to safeguard the foundations of world order. There is a profound if troubling truth in Housman's lines, but he does not go on to probe Xenophon's greater message: that these soldiers took up their unwanted role when their state had collapsed, and re-created a statelike polity by democratic means even as they kept others safe.

Simply to recognize the elemental reality of the state, and the lack of an alternative form of polity, is no small matter. Of equal importance is the international order in which the state functions.

The Trojan War began the formation of the Greek nation. The Persian War saved it. The Peloponnesian War tore it and its international system apart.

Principles for managing an international system on the grand scale come forward with the rise of Rome, with its *civitas Romanum sum* and *Pax Romana*. A conversation on this across centuries takes place in literature through the interlocking stories of Homer's *Iliad* and Virgil's *Aeneid*.

THE TROJAN HORSE: FROM STRATAGEM TO WORLD SYSTEM

In 1506 an astonishing sculpture was dug up on the Esquiline Hill: a heroic figure in a death struggle with huge, hideous serpents. Flanking the hero were two boys also in the coils of the snakes. It appeared to be the work by the Greek sculptor Agesander's studio at Rhodes described by Pliny the Elder. Although it clearly depicted Laocoön, the priest of Poseidon who warned the Trojans against the gift horse built by the Greeks, a great controversy arose over the meaning of the sculpture. Scholars declared it a Roman work, perhaps a copy of a Greek original. Bought by Pope Julius II and installed in the Vatican, it would become one of the best-known works in all of art history. Modern political cartoonists turn to it on a predictable basis: Nixon in the coils of his tapes; Bush in Iraq menaced by a Sunni snake and a Shia snake.

In the 1500s the controversy concerned the depiction of Laocoön. His writhing body and agonized expression were in contrast to the serene

Figure 2. Laocoön and his sons, by the studio of the sculptor Agesander.
Vatican Museums; photo © BigStockPhoto, reprinted by permission

Greek sculptured faces. They also seemed at odds with Roman stoicism. To
Byron, in *Childe Harold,* the face combined a "mortal's agony / with an immortal's patience blending." No, said Shelley, it is "an upraised countenance
of despair, and appeals with a sense of injustice"—that is the predominant

and overwhelming emotion—yet there is "a nobleness of expression, and a majesty that dignifies torture."[19]

The story of the Trojan Horse is one of the most famous in history, so it often baffles first-time readers of the *Iliad,* who ask when the Trojan Horse part will appear. It's not there, which does seem odd for the great epic of the Trojan War. The story does come up in Homer's *Odyssey,* when the wandering Odysseus asks a bard to sing about it. Even there, the story is told only a very rudimentary way. Laocoön is not mentioned. The full tale emerges only in the great Roman epic, Virgil's *Aeneid,* when, in book 2, Aeneas tells Dido the story of Troy's fall under the final Greek assault. The Trojan Horse story is a flashback from Aeneas's then-current narrative, and commentators have not probed very deeply into it, at least not from our angle of interest.

The Trojan Horse is a case in grand strategy. As introduced by John Dryden in his 1697 translation of the *Aeneid,* still the best in English:

> The Greeks grew weary of the tedious War:
> And by Minerva's Aid a Fabrick rear'd,
> Which like a Steed of monstrous height appear'd.

On the divine level, the Trojan War was fought between, on one side, Venus, the mother of Aeneas (she had been chosen the most beautiful by the Judgment of Paris), and Neptune the sea god, and their adversaries Minerva and Juno, who were furious with the Trojans because Paris, a Trojan, had decided against them.

The Trojan Horse does not appear in the *Iliad* because that poem ends with Achilles killing Hector and then relenting by returning Hector's body to his father, King Priam of Troy. Now time has passed. Achilles is dead, killed by Paris's shot to his heel. There had been, apocryphally, a running dispute between Achilles and Odysseus (Ulysses) over whether to make force or guile the basis of the Greek strategy. With Achilles dead, Ulysses—the man of twists and turns, skilled in deception—prevails. So the Greek strategy post-Achilles will be deception. The Trojans knew, or should have known, that with the great warrior Achilles dead, the Greek siege of Troy could never succeed by force of arms. They should have been expecting the Greeks to turn to a strategy of guile. They weren't. This was the first in a series of Trojan failures to understand what was going on. Why? Was it a case like Pearl Harbor, when the Americans could not tell the difference between signals and noise?

We know from Homer that Athena (Minerva) and Odysseus (Ulysses) have a relationship of friendly rivalry, a contest of which is the more clever. It looks as if Minerva came up with the wooden horse trick. Ulysses, of course, will claim credit for the stratagem and actually design its implementation.

So the Greeks, as Dryden's translation puts it, fabricate a huge wooden steed. Then they take ship, as though giving up the war. But instead of sailing home to Greece, they go to the offshore island of Tenedos and hide their fleet there. The Trojans, so long besieged, unbar their gates and come out to look at the now-deserted Greek camp. Laocoön comes out as well and shouts to the Trojan crowd:

> O wretched Country-men! What fury reigns?
> What more than Madness has possess'd your Brains?
> Think you the Grecians from your Coasts are gone,
> And are Ulysses' Arts no better known?
> This hollow Fabrick either must inclose,
> Within its blind Recess, our secret Foes;
> Or 'tis an Engine raised above the Town,
> T' o'erlook the walls, and then to batter down.
> Somewhat is sure designed; by Fraud or Force;
> Trust not their Presents, nor admit the Horse.
> (Beware of Greeks bearing gifts).

Laocoön is a priest of Apollo (the background, not explicit in the *Aeneid,* is that Laocoön had angered Apollo by marrying and fathering children despite his celibacy vow—and made matters worse by lying with his wife in the presence of a shrine of Apollo). Laocoön has just been elected by the Trojans to be their priest of Neptune (a post that changes hand each year). As he runs out to warn the Trojans against the horse, he declares that everybody knows Ulysses is a deceiver: either Greek soldiers are hidden inside the wooden horse or it was made so big in order to be used as a siege engine to overtop the walls of Troy. Then, to demonstrate the validity of his warning, Laocoön takes action:

> Thus having said, against the Steed he threw
> His forceful spear, which, hissing as it flew,
> Piercéd through the yielding Plancks of jointed Wood,
> And trembling in the hollow Belly stood.

Note that Laocoön is not acting in his role as priest or seer. He is saying directly to the Trojans that Ulysses has a record of trickery, so don't fall for this one. And he is acting directly by throwing his spear into the side of the horse, which produces the sounds of rattling weapons and groans from the Greeks hidden within. So evidence from the past and a demonstration at that present moment support Laocoön's warning:

Enough was said and done, t'inspire a better Mind

Why didn't the Trojans take the warning? Because the outcome was *fated,* says Aeneas to Dido. There are big issues here; we think of Tolstoy's philosophy of history as described by Isaiah Berlin in *The Hedgehog and the Fox:* the "great man" is nothing; history inexorably takes its own course. In the *Odyssey,* the hero made the Trojan Horse ploy a success. In the *Aeneid,* when the horse is at the gate, where is Aeneas? The hero is Laocoön, and we shall soon see what happens to him. If Laocoön's warning had been heeded, Troy would not have fallen. Here we have to think of Milton's *Paradise Lost* and the realization of "the fortunate fall." If Troy had not fallen there would have been no Rome, no Western civilization, no United States of America as we have known it. The difference between Homer's *Iliad* and Virgil's *Aeneid* is stark. The great Homeric hero is indispensable; Aeneas is the unhero who must align himself with the forces of history in order to serve his people and the larger cause of world order.

Now comes the *implementation* of the Greek strategy of guile. A Greek soldier is captured and brought to Troy. He has let himself be captured in order to tell the Trojans a phony story. He says his name is Sinon and that the Greeks abandoned him. (We know that the Greeks, as a free and unregimented lot, have not yet developed a sense of national coherence and patriotism; they have a reputation of producing traitors and defectors, so *this* evidence from the past the Trojans seem to take seriously.) Sinon says that Ulysses, in one of his typical schemes, slandered Sinon's patron in the Greek command, and Sinon consequently fell from favor. Sinon threatened revenge, which only led Ulysses to accuse him of treason and call for him to be executed. So, Sinon says, if you Trojans kill me, it will please Ulysses immensely.

This of course makes the Trojans, who already feel pity for Sinon ("Unknowing as we were in Grecian Arts"), only want to hear more. So, Sinon tells them, the Greeks, tired of their unsuccessful siege of Troy, had long ago resolved to give up the war and sail home, but were blocked by rough seas and unfavorable winds. So they sent an envoy to the oracle at Delphi. She pointed out that when the Greeks ten years before had decided to sail to Troy, they had been thwarted by bad weather, and that only a human sacrifice (Agamemnon's sacrifice of Iphigenia) had caused the wind to shift in their favor. So, said the oracle, they must do likewise in order to get home from Troy. Ulysses then got the Greek priest Calchas to choose Sinon as the victim. Sinon fled, he says, and

> Hid in a weedy Lake all Night I Lay,
> Secure of Safety when they sail'd away.

Here we begin to sense the appearance of serpent images and sounds: Laocoön's spear "hissing" through the air. Sinon's name with its snaky sound. Sinon lurking in concealment on the edge of a lake. The Greek strategy is snakelike. Troy's King Priam asks Sinon directly:

> But truly tell, was for Force or Guile,
> Or some Religious End, you raised the Pile?

Sinon, the gifted liar, says it was religious. Because Ulysses had stolen Minerva's image from her temple (the Palladium), the Greeks had built this great wooden horse in tribute to her, to assuage her anger. This will please Minerva, Sinon says, and she will soon help the Greeks return here to continue the war against Troy. If you Trojans violate the horse, Minerva will turn even more harshly against you. If you were to take the horse inside your walls to protect it, then you Trojans would prevail over all Greece. That's why, Sinon explains, the Greeks built the horse so large that it would not fit through your city gates. Although Sinon knows the horse is made of pine, he in passing refers to it as made of maple. This adds authenticity to his claim to have been a victim of the Greeks, cast out, and not part of their plot to take Troy by guile. Yet Sinon knows quite well that it is made of pine. This, it must be admitted, is guile indeed: a complicated and persuasive story. Sinon has presented a brilliant falsehood and made it plausible by embedding in it some facts known to the Trojans from their own experience or widely accepted reports.

To ward off the threat, the Trojans have Laocoön, Neptune's priest, sacrifice a steer to propitiate the god.

> When, dreadful to behold, from Sea we spy'd
> Two Serpents rank'd abreast, the Seas divide,

And smoothly sweep along the swelling Tide.
Their flaming crests above the Waves they show,
Their Bellies seem to burn the seas below; . . .
Their nimble Tongues they brandish'd as they came,
And lick'd their hissing Jaws, that sputtered Flame.

The serpents seize and begin to devour Laocoön's two children. Laocoön rushes to save them but the snakes attack him; he roars and bellows in agony. The serpents kill them all and slither off to the shrine of Minerva, where they coil around the feet of the statue of the goddess.

The Trojan witnesses to this horror declare that Laocoön was doomed to die because he had called the wooden horse a fraud and struck it with his spear. The serpents thus were Minerva's revenge. So the Trojans, following Sinon's false advice, vote to bring the horse inside their walls, believing that to do so will give them the upper hand against the Greeks. Because of the size of the horse, the Trojans have to break open their own walls in order to make a hole big enough to get it through. This is somewhere around step six or seven in the Greek scheme. The Trojans by this point had to have believed seven levels, and about four subcategories, of Greek lies *before* the point of their construction of so large a horse comes into play. So the Trojans knock down their own walls and put wheels on the horse's feet, and it slides snakelike into Troy.

The rest is history. The Greek fleet slides snakelike toward the Trojan shore *tacitae per amica silentia lunae* (secretly under the benign silence of the moon). The Trojans sleep soundly. Sinon secretly unlocks the pine bolts of the trapdoor of the Horse, and down a cable slide Ulysses and the Greek soldiers.

Their Forces join
T'invade the Town, oppress'd with Sleep and Wine.

Aeneas then tells Dido at great length of the horrendous battle that raged as the Greeks stormed through Troy and set it aflame. Wandering among the burning ruins, Aeneas finds himself alone when

The graceless Helen in the Porch I spy'd.

She is hiding there, snakelike, in the temple of Vesta, a goddess of fire, fearing death whichever side finds her, Greek or Trojan. Aeneas is about to kill her when Venus, his mother, appears to him to say

Not Helen's Face, nor Paris was in Fault,
But by the Gods was this destruction brought.

In other words, all this was fated to happen; nothing could have prevented it. So under Venus's guidance and protection Aeneas takes his household gods—the *lares et penates*—and, bearing his father and leading his son, Iulus, makes his way out of ruined, flaming Troy. His wife Creusa follows, but falls behind and is lost. Aeneas rages through the streets trying to find her until she appears, a ghost, and tells him that she too is fated to be left behind as he, father, and son wander until

Then, after many painful Years are past,
On Latium's happy Shore you shall be cast:
Where gentle Tiber from his Bed beholds
The flowry Meadows, and the Feeding Folds.
There end your Toils: And there your Fates provide
A quiet kingdom, and a Royal Bride.
There Fortune shall the Trojan line restore;
And you for lost Creusa weep no more.

The literary triad of ferocity, deceit, and fire comes in the repeated images of serpent and flame (the red flickering snake's tongue). Death and rebirth merge in a single transforming event. The serpent, a symbol of guileful deceit, is also a symbol of rebirth, as a snake sheds its skin and emerges anew. So Troy will be reborn as Rome.

As a final symbol, after the serpentine Greek strategy of guile has set Troy ablaze,

Strange to relate, from young Iulus Head
A lambent Flame arose, which gently spread
Around his Brows, and on his Temples Fed.

The flame around the head of Iulus (that's Iulus as in Julius Caesar) will later appear around the head of Caesar Augustus and Oliver Cromwell in Andrew Marvell's ode and even around the head of America's epic poet of democracy Walt Whitman (in "Crossing Brooklyn Ferry").

This is the start of the *translatio imperii,* the movement of empire ever westward in the cause of universal peace: to a *Pax Romana, Pax Brittania, Pax Americana.* As Yale's Bishop Berkeley would poetically declare,

Westward the course of Empire takes its way.

So it was all fated, predestined. We are familiar with that all across history. Fate or free will? If God knows all that will happen, how can we have free will? But if free choice by the individual is required for salvation, then how can it be fated? The answer always is: free will exists even when all is predestined. Even Tolstoy, who says we have *no* influence over history, portrays Marshall Kutuzov as making sound strategic decisions because he *senses* the course of history. This is Clausewitz's *coup d'oeil*. If you have that sixth sense, you can size up the situation at one glance and decide how to incorporate it, or not, into your grand strategy.

The Greek grand strategy at the outset was not impressive. Marriage and *xenia* had been violated when Paris took Helen away. But to launch an expeditionary force to lay siege to a far-off citadel was far from promising. You would be away from your base. Your long logistic line could not be maintained and you could not easily live off the invaded land for long. As Clausewitz would later teach, the defensive position would have the stronger hand. What were the Greek assets? Achilles the best fighter and Ulysses/Odysseus the best schemer. But Achilles was always a problem, and after ten years of war he was killed. That left three options: 1) Continue the siege with no hope of success; 2) Quit the war and go home; 3) Try something else: a stratagem of deception. Given the wily Ulysses as an asset, option 3 was the clear choice.

Surely the Trojans would anticipate something like this; they knew about Ulysses and his reputation for stratagems. So a plausible—indeed ingenious—context had to be concocted in order to throw the Trojans off the trail:

1 A defector/traitor with an explanation for his turncoat decision: he had lost favor with the inner circle of leadership. This would be believable because the Greeks, a nation lacking unity, were always squabbling and defecting.
2 A second layer of narrative that certainly was true: the Greeks were weary after ten years of war and wanted to go home.
3 A third level, perhaps most compelling of all to the culture of the time and place. Everyone knew that the Greeks at the start of the war had had to sacrifice one of their own, Iphigenia, in order to get favorable winds to carry their fleet to Troy. So the false story that the Delphic oracle required them to carry out another human sacrifice in order to

get favorable winds to carry their ships home from Troy instantly made sense to the Trojans. It made the war into a "ring composition." (In fact, the whole tale Aeneas tells Dido is a contest, ring-composition-style, of sacrifices, six or seven in sequence, like a game of musical chairs, to see which side's sacrifice wins at the end.)

4 Fourth, the Greeks would sacrifice the defector because, after all, he already was out of favor. This gave added credibility to his story.

5 To all this was added another dimension, also based on a known fact: that Ulysses had made off with the palladium of Minerva (the shrine-image in her temple). So it seemed to make some sense that, to ensure that Minerva would not in anger thwart the Greek plan of withdrawal, they had constructed a giant wooden horse and dedicated it to her. And to make sure that the Trojans would not take the horse for their own and thereby shift Minerva's favor to themselves, the Greeks had built it so large that it could not be fit through the gates of Troy. (Here is something like Br'er Rabbit's briar patch ploy: fervently assert what you desperately do *not* want to happen in order to make sure it *does* happen.)

Here then is the new strategy designed by the Greeks:

- it replaces a problematic and unsuccessful earlier strategy;
- it takes full advantage of the Greeks' strongest remaining asset;
- it provides a comprehensive story line which their opponents would be eager to adopt;
- it is anchored in previously known facts about Greeks;
- it is in accord with previous assumptions about Greeks;
- and it is shored up by appropriately related religious practices.

All points are covered: individual, societal, divine; historical, military, psychological, emotional, and intellectual. It is carefully phased to unfold over time. The enemy's suspicions and objections have been foreseen and preemptively neutralized. The Trojan Horse ruse is a grand strategy, beautifully conceived, fully worked out, well prepared to be put into execution. Will it work as planned, or will it once again be demonstrated, as the old adage goes, that "No plan survives contact with the enemy"?

Had there been a Trojan Investigative Board of Inquiry, the "After Action Report" would have concluded that Trojan leaders "failed to connect the dots." This would not mean that the Greek plan worked to perfection. There is always some unpredictable, unanticipated, intervening factor.

In this case, it is Laocoön. The more closely you read Virgil's text, the more distinctive, indeed unusual, a character Laocoön seems to be. He is a priest of Apollo, but a renegade priest, fathering a family and making love to his wife as his vows forbade him to do. He seems like a rather outrageous but understandable, admirable rebel. Above all, Laocoön sees and thinks about things clearly. "Of course Ulysses is behind this horse trick, don't you, my fellow Trojans, get it? And let me show you that this is no offering to a divinity. I'll thrust my spear right into it! Listen! Don't you hear men groaning and arms clanking inside it? How stupid can you be not to realize this?"

The Trojans don't act on Laocoön's warning immediately, but neither do they reject him. At that very moment, a major distraction appears—a "defector," brought into the Trojan city—and the people all want to hear what he says. As Sinon tells his phony story, another chance happening is taking place. Laocoön, having been chosen by lot to be a temporary priest of Neptune, is called upon to sacrifice a steer in accordance with that role. So Laocoön happens to be front and center, with the Trojans all watching, when, again by chance, demonic twin serpents race in from the sea to crush Laocoön and his sons in their coils and kill them with their fangs. Why might this be? Because Laocoön—entirely unrelated to the Trojan War—had on an earlier occasion violated his priestly duties to Apollo, who had dispatched these serpents in retribution?

But the circumstances of the moment required another interpretation: Laocoön was being attacked by the snakes because he had thrown his spear at the wooden horse.

Thus a concatenation of happenstance made the Trojan people all the more certain that the invented Greek story must be true. Laocoön had railed against it and had died a hideous death as a result of his refusal to credit the fable.

Are the Trojans to be blamed for not seeing through the Greek plot? Perhaps not; the Greek strategy was ingenious and fully worked out. As with all plans, even brilliant ones, an unexpected event—the emergence of Laocoön—threatened to wreck it. But then another unexpected and misunderstood event—the assault of the serpents—put the Greek plan back on track. The serpents with their tongues of flame so fittingly represented the deceitful Greek scheme that no one could be expected to see through it.

Remember, all this is being told by Aeneas to Dido, and it is not the tale of a hero. Aeneas includes himself ("we," he says) among the Trojans who credited Sinon's phony story. He also says that he joined in opening the walls and pulling the horse inside Troy. But he had not participated when the crowd decided that Laocoön deserved to be killed by the serpents because he had denounced the horse as a trick and speared it. Aeneas seems not to be convinced that all this was divinely ordained. Laocoön the priest had said that the horse had nothing to do with religion. Sinon the infiltrator tells the Trojans that the horse *is* a religious offering. The Trojans fall for the religious explanation. The reader of the *Aeneid* could conclude either that the gods are the enemies of decent, god-fearing people or that the fall of Troy was a matter of human decision making within the course of history and its vicissitudes. The *Aeneid* seems to side with the latter. It was a matter of grand strategy: the Greeks shifted from force to guile, and the gullible Trojans fell for it.

The Trojans usually seem dull-witted about strategy. How many signals did they misread? Laocoön's words of warning. Laocoön's demonstrative act. The attack on Laocoön. The portent of the horse getting stuck repeatedly in the breached wall and the sounds from within it. A warning from Cassandra (the truth-telling seer fated never to be believed). Some of these were warnings, some signs, some evidence; none were read aright.

All through the *Aeneid,* Aeneas in his travels, in his encounter with Dido, in the Underworld and after, is portrayed as rather a dull dog. It will take repeated prophecies and repeated occasions of learning-by-doing before Aeneas really begins to get it. Perhaps we are supposed to conclude that the Greeks are the masters of grand strategy while the Trojans under the slow but steady, relentlessly responsible Aeneas, become the masters of history. The Greek empire will end; the Roman empire will come to seem eternal; which now is the winner?

Something in here centers on the matter of character: individual character, national character. This brings us back to the statue of Laocoön unearthed in 1506. The controversy has many aspects. Is it Greek? Roman? A Roman copy of a Greek original? A forgery produced by Michelangelo and his studio? Above all, the controversy came back again and again to the look, the expression on the face of Laocoön.

Obviously, this was not a classic Greek sculptured head with the face portrayed as some Platonic ideal of beauty. Nor was it carved in the Roman style, which portrayed the real faces, ugly or not, and expressions of actual people. Clearly, Laocoön's expression revealed the pain and agony of the moment. But beyond that, was there something of the Roman stoic in its gaze? Was it a defiance of fate, or recognition of destiny's ultimate power? Did it combine mortal anguish and immortal patience as Byron claimed? Or was it the cry of the revolutionary in resistance, as Shelley saw it? The sculpture was said to be the first discovery of an artistic depiction of the anguished reaction of a body to painful defeat—with the face nonetheless expressing the moral dignity of the hero. When Nathaniel Hawthorne, in Rome, viewed it, he saw "a strange calmness diffused through the strife," the triumph of a great soul in tragic conflict. The look of the individual who might have changed history's course but failed.

The two most famous interpreters of the sculpture seem to agree on one point: that the sculpted face of Laocoön is not crying aloud, that the stricken hero "raises no frightful cries" even though his face represents agony and distress *in extremis*. For one—Winckelmann, the German connoisseur of classical art—this is suffering with dignity. For the other—Lessing, the dramatist and critic of aesthetics—the sculpted face is stoical not because to cry out would reveal an ignoble soul, but because depicting such a cry artistically would distort the expression in a loathsome manner.

I have my interpretation, you have yours. For me it is a look that can be seen across the ages and cultures. It is a look, whether the face is contorted in pain or steady in calm contemplation, of one who can discern the underlying reality of a situation, who can see clearly into the essence of things when other eyes and hearts and minds see only through a glass darkly, fail to feel the beat of their own true feelings, think with minds distracted and crowded by the cloudy thoughts of others. "The Gaze," rightly understood, is a matter of grand strategy.

What does Aeneas look like? We have no sense of this. Virgil makes him faceless and indistinct.[20] Gianlorenzo Bernini could not avoid the challenge when he sculpted the scene of Aeneas carrying his father and leading his son out of burning Troy. It is a great work of art, to be seen in the Villa Borghese, Rome. But it's a nonface. Still, is it meaningless? No.

Aeneas is not an Iliadic warrior arousing himself to fury in battle to gain glory. He is not a Socratic citizen of the Athenian polis debating questions of justice and the good. Aeneas is dedicated to a mission for civilization and world order, and must sacrifice his personal interests— most dramatically his affair with Dido—for that greater good. The price civilization exacts is steep.

All through the *Aeneid,* although we get no sense of what Aeneas looks like, we are repeatedly told what he is looking *at.* When he gazes at the future site of Rome, "Aeneas stares in wonder, sending his ready glances everywhere."

> The Stranger cast around his curious Eyes;
> New Objects viewing still, with new Surprise.
> With greedy Joys enquires of various Things;
> And Acts and Monuments of Ancient Kings.

This is not passivity but an imperial compulsion to take everything in.

Virgil's *Aeneid* most powerfully displays Rome's role as steward of a world-scale international system. Literature's greatest subject is the founding and preservation of a polity. Aeneas stumbles out of the burning ruins of Troy to wander on a mission he does not fully understand until he visits the Underworld—a requirement of every epic hero—where he learns that his fate is to found Rome. T. S. Eliot pronounced Virgil's *Aeneid* a "universal classic," a poem of foundation and preservation of a state and world system, glorious but precarious; gained and maintained only at great cost.

The *Aeneid* is told in the historical present of Aeneas's lifetime, from which he looks back to explain how his story emerges from and elaborates upon the *Iliad* and the *Odyssey.* At the same time, it looks forward, through prophecy and through the invention of lifelike origins of institutions yet to come, to explain how the present of Virgil's lifetime (and Augustus's) came to be what it was. In doing this, the *Aeneid* spans more than a thousand years. Troy fell sometime around 1200 B.C. Aeneas arrives in Italy in 1184. Rome is founded in 753. The Republic is established in 510. The Punic Wars end with the destruction of Carthage in 146. Octavian is victorious at the Battle of Actium in 31 and, as Augustus, is Roman emperor from 27 B.C. to A.D. 14. W. H. Auden put it this way:

> No Virgil, no:
> Not even the first of the Romans can learn

His Roman history in the future tense,
Not even to serve your political turn;
Hindsight as foresight makes no sense.

Auden is rationally right, but poetically wrong. Virgil's use of time creates layers of meaning and feeling in every line. His cross-cutting perspective back and forth across centuries creates an eerie sense that one is actually experiencing the origins of civilization. When Aeneas, in search of allies, goes to the little rustic settlement of old King Evander, who lives in a pastoral setting with cows grazing and birds chirping, we shiver a bit in recognition that he is at the foot of the Palatine Hill in what one day will be Rome, the capital of the world.

The aged King Evander welcomes Aeneas to his humble cottage with the words, "Dare to despise wealth." Doing so would make one worthy of a divine visit such as Hercules had paid Evander. Augustus, Evander's successor in the far future, should dwell simply too, for the same reason. In Evander's hut, Aeneas, the Trojan, will be cured of his luxury-loving "eastern" ways.

Every word and action in the *Aeneid* is loaded with meaning that the reader perceives but Aeneas does not, because this history has not happened yet. The *Aeneid* is a journey toward a historical destiny that is already fulfilled but that has never—until Virgil tells about it—been fully explained or given its portentous significance for the world.

That journey will be accomplished through statecraft. But Aeneas still does not know—or only dimly knows—where he must go, or why. Book 6 is of enormous importance as Aeneas tries to get to the Underworld to meet his dead father, for only in the Underworld can a leader learn of his mission.

Before Aeneas can get to the Underworld, he must bury the body of his comrade Misenus. Misenus must die and be buried so that Aeneas can visit the Underworld and then return to life. Otherwise the body count would not be correct and Aeneas would be trapped down there.

But that's a side issue. The striking scene is when Aeneas and his men plunge into an ancient wood to cut the timber for Misenus's funeral pyre (6: 179–182). In only four lines—in the Latin—Virgil provides a vivid picture, from entering the wood to cutting down the trees, to rolling the felled trunks down the mountain. It is clear that this brief episode stands for more than appears on the surface. This is a project of concentrated, well-directed effort, a microcosm of the power, organization, and focus of the Roman world system to come. In the seventeenth-century translation by John Dryden:

> An ancient Wood, fit for the Work design'd
> (the shady Covert of the Salvage Kind)
> The *Trojans* found: The sounding Axe is ply'd:
> Firs, Pines and Pitch-Trees, and the tow'ring Pride
> Of Forest Ashes, feel the fatal Stroke:
> And piercing Wedges cleave the stubborn Oak
> Huge trunks of Trees, fell'd from the steepy Crown
> Of the bare Mountains, rowl with Ruin down.

An imperial mission is expressed within these lines. The Trojans go far beyond the needs of the job at hand, going farther into the forest, higher on the mountain. They take down huge trees, destroying a savage and ancient land. They do this in retribution for the fall of Troy, which was described in book 2 (line 624) as falling like a giant ash tree (as Dryden puts it in book 6, "the tow'ring Pride of Forest Ashes"). The words *found, oak, crown,* and *wedge* each add to this deeper meaning, *wedge* being a Roman military formation.[21] To act in accordance with nature is Hellenic; to subdue nature in the service of the state is Roman.

That observation leads to the most mysterious and portentous literary image in statecraft: the Golden Bough. No one can descend into the Underworld without plucking from its tree a tough, leafy branch which is both nature's green and metallic gold; it represents nature and man—and destiny too. The Sibyl of Cumae said that when grasped the bough would come away easily if the fates have so determined; if not, no power on earth could tear it off. Aeneas takes hold. It resists. He tears it off.

In the Underworld, Aeneas encounters Dido, Queen of Carthage, whose love he had betrayed. "Deceiver!" she hisses, and turns away. Neither could have carried the affair to marriage, for each was bound by *raison d'état;* she to Carthage, he to the future Rome, something he did not fully grasp until now, in the Underworld. Aeneas also meets the shade of his father, Anchises, who tells Aeneas of his destined mission to found Rome. Above all, Anchises tells Aeneas, the purpose of gaining power is to create and administer an international system that will crown peace with civilization. Other peoples (he means Greeks) will excel in the arts and sciences, but

> Remember Roman, these will be your arts:
> To teach the ways of peace to those you conquer,
> To spare defeated peoples, tame the proud.
> *Romane memento regere populos imperia;*
> *Hae erunt artes tibi: que imponere morem*
> *Pacis, parcere subjectis, et debellare superbos.*

Augustus would erect the great altar Ara Pacis, whose name recalls Virgil's ideal, stated in these Latin lines, for Rome's empire.

While readers have been aware all along that Aeneas was destined to found Rome, Aeneas grasped it only vaguely, making him seem more than a bit dim. Now, hearing the prophecy at last from his departed father, Aeneas gets it. Anchises represents the burden of the past in Troy's fall, which has preoccupied Aeneas throughout his journeys until this moment, when Anchises informs him of the future.

Aeneas leaves the Underworld as he entered it, by giving us a puzzle. Two gates provide exit from the Underworld: the Gate of Horn, through which pass the true, and the Gate of Ivory, which produces false hope. Aeneas's father directs him through the Gate of Ivory. Nothing is obvious in statecraft.

Now begins the second, Iliadic part of the poem, which commentators have found less compelling than the first: warfare is not as interesting in our time as tragic love and scary scenes of Hell. But Virgil must have regarded the second six books as the proper crescendo and climax of his epic. Battle poetry was the highest art form, and the statecraft of empire building the grandest subject matter.

As book 7 opens, Aeneas's ships finally have arrived at the mouth of the Tiber. The sea part of the story is over; the land part begins. Athens was a naval power; Rome will be a land power, and war for land will be the subject from here on.

But Aeneas wants to avoid war. He sends a diplomatic mission to King Latinus, who, predisposed by an oracle, welcomes the Trojans and offers his daughter Lavinia to Aeneas in what classic diplomacy would regard as a dynastic, diplomatic marriage. But war cannot be avoided. Lavinia had been promised to Turnus, who takes the role of Achilles here. If that were not enough, Juno sends the horrifying Fury Allecto to incite the Italians to battle the Trojans.

In complicated diplomatic steps, Aeneas seeks allies. After one effort fails, he concludes a pact with Evander, a tricky business, for Evander is of Greek origin. Associations are starting to form for reasons other than ethnicity or lineage. Accordingly Virgil enlists the greatest Greek hero into the Trojan-Roman cause. Aeneas becomes a second Hercules, and in the far future, Augustus will be a third Hercules, slaying the monstrous Antony and Cleopatra as Hercules slew the monster Cacus. There is a subtext of civilization versus barbarism here. Beheading one's enemies is the ultimate savagery. Marc Antony had the murdered Cicero's head displayed on the rostra. Augustus himself had Brutus's head cut off and displayed. Cacus, a monster who dwelt on the Aventine hill, hung the heads of victims on his gates. Hercules, for one of his twelve labors, slew Cacus on the future site of Rome, an act filled with Virgilian portent. Virgil is here calling upon Augustus, who, like Hercules, would have to defeat the enemies of world order and to preside over an international system with wisdom and justice. In 2001 terrorism was likened to Cerberus, the watchdog of Hades, who in Hercules's twelfth labor sprouted new heads to replace those lopped off.[22]

Now comes the hinge on which the epic swings. Venus goes to the amiable Vulcan and persuades him to forge armor for Aeneas. This recalls the shield forged for Achilles in the *Iliad.* That shield was made to depict a balanced idealized society in which war and peace each had a place. Achilles, however, strapped it on to kill out of bloodlust for personal revenge.

Virgil's shield is something else, the physical embodiment of Anchises' forecasts. Not an idealistic representation, it realistically depicts Roman actions. From the outer rim, the scenes spiral inward, from Romulus and Remus and the Kingship period to a second circle of events during the Republic, to the centerpiece: the triumph of Augustus at Rome to celebrate his victory over Antony and Cleopatra at Actium in 31 B.C. as a world-spanning empire begins. At Actium the Roman civil war turns into a foreign war against Cleopatra's East; the *translatio imperii* is at stake.

Again and again when literary works take up matters of statecraft, images suggest that the foundation stone of world order is located in marriage and the home. When Vulcan starts to forge the shield of Aeneas, he does so "At the hour when a woman awakens the slumbering ashes of her fire." Virgil goes on to depict the household, managed by a wife and mother, as both the basis for statecraft and that which it exists to protect.[23] Across the classics we see marriage, always at the center of the story, grow in political significance, from Helen's marriage betrayed in the *Iliad,* to Penelope's marriage maintained in the *Odyssey,* to marriage and family laws violated in the *Oresteia* and *Oedipus Rex,* to the *Aeneid,* in which marriage has public and political consequences for civilization.[24]

The shield of Achilles depicted a world which cycles in place, in alternation from peace to war and back again. In contrast, the shield of Aeneas spirals forward in time, more history than myth—moving upward toward a culmination in the future. When Aeneas shoulders this shield, he is taking up the burden of the future (in contrast to his shouldering the burden of the past when carrying his father out of Troy). Aeneas is no longer the son of Anchises; he is about to become the father of his country. There is no paradox here as there was with the shield of Achilles: Aeneas willingly takes up this visible representation of the grand strategy that will lead to Imperial Rome. The shield in the *Aeneid,* like the cutting of trees deep in the forest, tells of what can be told only through literature.

Big-power compromises are tried and fail, a cease-fire is set and then broken. Finally Jupiter takes a mediating role, and a grand compromise is struck with Juno. She will give up her efforts to block the Trojan mission to found Rome on condition that the Trojans give up their language, their customs, their national dress, and even the Trojan name itself. They will remain Trojans despite the loss of their state, but they will have to assimilate to their new land and culture.

The final contest pits two world-historical forces. Turnus represents the heroic code of Achilles: life is brief and death inevitable, so extend your fame beyond death by feats of valor. Aeneas represents a new code: the fight is not for yourself but for a civic code, for posterity, and victory is to be followed by magnanimity, generosity, and peaceful reconciliation with your enemy. The *Aeneid* is sprinkled with scenes that show the inadequacy and uselessness of the heroic code; now Aeneas himself will endeavor to leave it behind.

But this is not what happens. The end of the *Aeneid* is shocking, almost incomprehensible. Throughout the poem we have witnessed Aeneas's evolution from Iliadic hero to civic father. Not fury, but piety and duty. At the end, however, Aeneas's slaughter of Turnus is as primordially warrior-like as Achilles at his most furious. One feature of this epic is the number of times that gods intervene. But in the final scene, the most consequential of all, no god steps in. Are they no longer needed?

A giant boulder provides an explanation for why the poem ends as it does, and reveals how life has changed between the time of Homer's *Iliad* and that of Virgil's *Aeneid*. In the *Iliad*, Aeneas the Trojan warrior had lifted a boulder against Achilles, and the Greek fighter Diomedes had thrown one at Aeneas, crushing his hipbone. Here at the end of the *Aeneid*, Turnus hoists a huge boulder to heave it at Aeneas, but

> His knocking Knees are bent beneath the Load:
> And shiv'ring Cold congeals his vital Blood.
> The Stone drops from his Arms; and Falling short,
> For want of Vigor, mocks his vain Effort.

Is it that men are not what they were in Homer's day? Significantly, the boulder in the *Iliad* was a primitive weapon. In the *Aeneid*, however, it is a boundary stone marking the extent of agricultural fields or the jurisdiction of a polity. It represents an agreement in law, a treaty between nations. Turnus has transformed a sign of peace into a weapon of war; he is a breaker of treaties, a violator of the first principle of what will become Roman international order. Turnus's act, had it succeeded, would have reversed the course of civilization. He must fail and pay the ultimate price.

Which means that, at the end of the poem, Aeneas must act like Achilles, the Iliadic warrior-killer. No matter how far humanity may go in seeking to foster the arts of civilization and the ideals of civic peace, there will come times when acts of war are required in order to defend world order and sustain the peace of civilized peoples.

2

CREATIVE DISORDER

There being no universal world government, the "vast external realm" has been regarded as anarchic and ungoverned, yet all regions and times have produced large-scale systems through which polities relate to one another. In 1887, in a low brick room at Tel al-Amarna, a peasant woman stumbled upon an archive of documents relating to the foreign affairs of Akhenaten (Amenhotep IV) revealing intensive diplomatic contacts among the great powers of the time. A mixed language scholars called Amarnaic served as a diplomatic lingua franca among Egypt, Babylonia, the Hittites, the Canaanites, Mittani (Syria), and other states. The international system for the Late Bronze Age was the first of its kind. It permitted statelike polities of different cultures and languages, unequal in power yet accepting common practices, to operate through diplomacy, alliances, and treaties; trade for mutual advantage; keep records and establish precedents; and maintain their independence while using and avoiding war within an understood framework.

Premodern China produced its own versions. The Spring and Autumn Period, 770–476 B.C., displayed a political-economic-military system among the several Han kingdoms of north-central China. Much later, with the rise of dynasties whose reach extended well beyond China proper—the

T'ang, Sung, Yüan, Ming, and Ch'ing—a tribute system with the Imperial Court as the world center regulated international relations.

The range of a Muslim international system was revealed when the Amiriya, a huge madrassa in the town of Rada in southeastern Yemen, was restored from its long-decrepit condition during a 1980s project initiated by the government of the Netherlands. Exuberant architecture marked the structure as "an exotic intrusion" on the Arabian Peninsula. Its arches, ornament, and roof domes were Indian in origin. In the thirteenth century three interlocking trade circuits—Africa and the Muslim Arabian Sea, the Hinduized Indian Ocean and southeast archipelago, and the South China Sea and its coast—made up a vast, far-faring international system. Its geopolitical and demographic foundations were already eroded when the Portuguese moved forcefully into those waters to inherit the system in the fifteenth century.[1] Their gun-ported ships and string of littoral forts centered on the Persian Gulf took charge of the trade routes to impose a new, colonial international system, bringing on the Amiriya's decline.

The modern international system, born in Europe and adopted throughout the world, might be described as a pattern of regular relations among states as the basic units of world politics, operating through designated institutions and generally agreed methods. Commonly dated from the Treaty of Westphalia of 1648, its origins can be found in earlier centuries in Europe's movement from a religious toward a secular view of human affairs, and in the stumbling rise of a sense of distinctive national communities.

When learned monks and scholarly doctors began to gather in Paris in the thirteenth century to try to justify God's ways to Aristotle, the students who came from all over were categorized by their national homelands. Dante apparently went there too. Dante, whose *Divine Comedy,* composed between 1308 and 1321, is the supreme literary treatment of Hell, Purgatory, Heaven, and man's mystical relationship to God, was at the same time, as analyzed by the great critic-philosopher Erich Auerbach, "the poet of the secular world."[2] Dante, despite his God-centered medieval view of the world, was the first great writer to perceive that "in a spiritualist culture, where earthly happening was either disregarded or looked upon as a mere metaphorical existence leading up to man's real and final destiny, man's historical world could be discovered only by way of his final destiny, considered as the goal and meaning of earthly happening. But once the discovery was made in that way, earthly happening could no longer be looked upon with indifference."[3] So it was in the stanzas of Dante's *Divine Comedy* that the novel was prefigured.

Erich Auerbach, in his metahistorical tour de force of literary history, *Mimesis,* declared that the decisive modern moment—antihierarchical and democratic—came in the *Divine Comedy,* the first serious treatment of socially ordinary people as subject matter for literary representation by the greatest writers.

Dante had a foot in both the old and the new. Literature's most famous wood is Dante's, in the opening lines of *Inferno,* set in 1300:

> Midway through the journey of our life I found
> Myself in a dark wood, for I had strayed
> From the straight pathway to this tangled ground.

The scene is linked to Aeneas's descent to the Underworld in the *Aeneid* book 6—important to Dante for its journey to meet the shades of the dead who would reveal the hero's world mission. Dante is a soul alone in a world beset by original sin and bereft of valid political authority, as pope and emperor vie for supreme power. Lost in the wood, he is taken in hand by the shade of Virgil and led into the inferno, where, like Virgil, he may gain understanding of his life's purpose. Both saw reality as basically human, not metaphysical, and from this it was a short step to the political community and the nation-state.

Early modern texts depict the international order deteriorating at the same time that new possibilities are creatively considered. Through the lens of literature, fifteenth- and sixteenth-century statecraft appears inadequate to the disorder and dynamism of the times. The mythohistorical figure of Joan of Arc was used to portray a maelstrom of new forces: nationalism, religious schism, and the very definition of woman. She is one of the few immediately recognizable world figures—Indira Gandhi when a little girl pretended to be Joan—and literary attitudes toward her are an index to the changing role of women in modernity.[4] Shakespeare's early play *Henry VI* shockingly portrays her as the embodiment of Machiavellian deceit. She pulled together the uncertain strands of the early French state and was demonized for it. Later writers return to her repeatedly as representative of both the new patriotism and old, pre-Christian powers of sorcery.

Joan too may have learned of her career purpose in a wood. The improbable emergence of a simple girl from the village of Domrémy who, guided by the voices of saints, brought renewed discipline to French soldiery, led them to break the English siege of Orléans, then was demonized for it and burned alive at the stake in 1431, was impossible for literature to leave alone. Shakespeare, Schiller, Mark Twain, and George Bernard Shaw were all captivated—or nauseated—by Joan of Arc.

Some scholars argue that there was no French nation until the nineteenth century, pointing to nationalism as a modern phenomenon producing such policies as a national education system. True enough, in some political science sense, but "the unique French identity, the consciousness of being *French,* though limited to a narrow elite circle, had existed centuries before it was reinterpreted as *national* identity."[5] The Hundred Years' War, 1337–1453, both disrupted the early stages of national centralization and infused a greater sense of French identity. That was Joan's war.

Shakespeare's *Henry VI,* part I, W. H. Auden wrote, is preoccupied with "the nature of the body politic, what keeps it healthy, what destroys it."[6] Shakespeare depicts it breaking down. If the state in the political philosophy of the Middle Ages is organic, part of nature's order, then Joan, by her conduct reversing the natural order—dressing like a man, commanding troops, heeding no social hierarchy—exemplified the degeneration of the polity. Her words and actions appealed to French patriotism, and Shakespeare in reviling her was caught up in English patriotism and with religion and nationalism intertwined; something like "ideology" is created, and the body politic—English more than French—is coming apart as the English hero Talbot declares:

> Our English troops retire; I cannot stay them;
> A woman clad in armour chaseth them.

By the end of the play, Joan is exposed as a sorceress, a witch, all fraud and shifting stratagems, a "Machiavel" and something unnatural as evidenced in her manly role. As Joan is discredited, the entirely feminine Margaret of Anjou rises, yet she becomes even more dangerous than Joan as she captivates and subverts the kingdom as the bride of Henry VI. The conquest of England has moved from the dark ages to the civilized court, from battlefield to bedroom. Shakespeare's classical references suggest that Margaret is a "Trojan Horse" who will cause the fall of the new Troy, Britain, unless the state can regain its balance between the male and female principles.

Friedrich Schiller's 1802 *Jungfrau von Orléans: eine romantische Tragödie* is one of his dramatizations of great figures from Wallenstein to Mary Stuart to William Tell. *Maid of Orléans* has been called romanticism gone wild amid history rearranged. In fact, it expresses Schiller's theory of government as it reaches the point in history when all earlier forms must be discarded and new transcendent ideals created.

Schiller's Joan is trapped between nature and duty by an uncomprehending society. In Schiller's theory, humans first lived in a state of necessity, dominated by nature, a *Notstaat*. Joan as a girl worried her father by wandering to an old oak tree, where he feared she communed with evil spirits. As a young woman soldier, her natural life is revealed in the play by her sudden infatuation with an English soldier she has captured. Opposed to this is duty, imposed on rational grounds by society, yet rigidly and without insight. This is the *Vernuftstaat* in Schiller's theory.

Joan transcends both nature and duty in her vision of what she must do to save France. She is captured by the English, who chain her to a tree so she cannot lead the French army. She prays to God to turn her chains into spider webs so she can break free. She does so and in Schiller's version is killed on the battlefield, not burned at the stake. She stands for the moment in history—Schiller's own time as the Enlightenment meets Romanticism—when all governance, past and present, must be transcended. Isaiah Berlin found in Schiller's plays "a crucial note in the history of human thought, namely that ideals are not to be discovered at all, they are to be invented; not to be found but to be generated, generated as art is generated."[7] The greatest political problems, Schiller says, can be solved only by aesthetic means.

Schiller's drama follows Rousseau's revolutionary philosophy of history: out of brutish nature humanity created "civilization," which, contrary to common belief, has been stifling and illegitimate. The way ahead must be found by statesmen (and women) who are artists of leadership, who will seek to create new ideals of governance, and who, like Joan, will be destroyed by the societies they would save.

Personal Recollections of Joan of Arc by the Sieur Louis de Conte (S.L.C., that is, or Samuel Langhorne Clemens) was the book prized the most by Mark Twain yet least regarded by his readers. While Joan's century was "the rottenest in history since the darkest ages," the contrast between her and her century was day and night. Twain adored Joan, or the idea of her.

Her character was flawless, unique, perfect. Seeing her country demoralized and in grave distress, "She laid her hand upon this nation, this corpse, and it rose and followed her. . . . And for all regard, the French king whom she had crowned stood supine and indifferent while French priests took the noble child, the most innocent, the most lovely, the most adorable the ages have produced, and burned her alive at the stake."[8] "She was the Genius of Patriotism—she was Patriotism embodied, concreted, made flesh, and palpable to the touch and visible to the eye."[9] We see the reason for the critics' disdain; these are not sentences expected from America's most popular author; not sardonically witty and ironic, but syrupy and overweight.

Twain's adversarial view of Christianity was not left aside when he wrote about Joan. The transcript of Joan's trial reveals an attempt by her interrogators to link her visions and conduct to a tree cult in her native village. Joan would have none of it; to brand her a witch would take more than this. Twain makes a lot out of the story, which almost becomes a spiritual alternative to the expected religious epic of Joan. The *Arbre des Dames* or sometimes *Arbre Fée Bourlémonts* (fairy tree) in Twain's telling has a touch of pre-Christian Europe and the classical Virgilian experiences which shape the hero's future and that of his, or her, nation.[10] An ancient beech tree with far-spreading branches, the home of a fairy population, *Arbre des Dames* is a great attraction for children, who dance around it and, as they grow up, are accompanied by its apparition. A priest, recognizing the tree's power, banishes the fairies. Le Sieur de Conte is devastated and ever thereafter disaffected from the church. In fury, Joan, still a little girl, confronts the priest about this transgression.

In time, word comes to Domrémy about "the wars raging perpetually to the west and north of us." France has been betrayed. The terms of a treaty require the marriage of Catherine of France to Henry of England, the "Butcher of Agincourt." The dauphin has been deprived of his throne. The children talk of going off to fight the English invaders, but laugh at the thought of "little Joan," nicknamed "The Bashful," as a soldier.

Then from behind the fairy tree peers a frightening face. Benoist, the village maniac, has escaped from his cage. The children flee in horror, the girls screaming and crying. Not Joan; she stands her ground, "the maniac gliding stealthily toward her with his axe lifted. The sight was sickening." Joan walks up to him, stands right under his axe and speaks to him. She takes him by the hand and walks him back to the village. She knew him, had in earlier days talked to him, bandaged his wounds, fed him scraps through the bars of his cage.

So here is the source of Joan's stalwart bravery. It comes from within. Joan's femininity is traditional; she regards France as a mother does a child. In fortitude, freshness, humor, and practicality Twain seems to see a new "American" ideal of womanhood.

"Genius," George Bernard Shaw would point out, was a nineteenth-century invention to secularize the idea of divine inspiration. Shaw's *Saint Joan* (1923) is packed with connections between the classical past, the turbulent fifteenth century, and contemporary affairs of state. The play has been scorned for Shaw's blatant attempt to secularize the medieval scene while portraying the very Catholic Joan as a proto-Protestant. At the same time, he has been lauded for conveying the "tone" of Joan's astonishing voice (which Shaw heard in the transcript of her trial published only in the nineteenth century). It is the voice of nationalism at the opening of its self-awareness.

> *Robert* [de Baudricourt, a military captain]. So God says you are to raise the siege of Orléans?
> *Joan.* And to crown the Dauphin in Rheims Cathedral.
> *Robert.* (gasping). Crown the D_____. Gosh!
> *Joan.* And to make the English leave France.
> *Robert.* (sarcastic). Anything else?
> *Joan.* (charming). Not just at present, thank you, squire.
> *Robert.* I suppose you think raising a siege is as easy as chasing a cow out of a meadow. You think soldiering is anybody's job.
> *Joan.* I do not think it can be very difficult if God is on your side, and you are willing to put your life in His hand. But many soldiers are very simple.
> *Robert.* (grimly). Simple! Did you ever see English soldiers fighting?
> *Joan.* They are only men. God made them just like us; but he gave them their own country and their own language; and it is not His will that they should come into our country and try to speak our language.
> *Robert.* Who has been putting such nonsense into your head? Don't you know that soldiers are subject to the feudal lord, and that it is nothing to them or to you whether he is the duke of Burgundy or the king of England or the king of France? What has their language to do with it?

Joan. I do not understand that a bit. We are all subject to the King of Heaven; and He gave us our countries and our languages, and meant us to keep them. If it were not so it would be murder to kill an Englishman in battle; and you, squire, would be in great danger of Hell fire. You must not think about your duty to your feudal lord, but about your duty to God.

In the next scene an English chaplain is speaking to a nobleman. They are discussing the Dauphin:

> *The Chaplain.* He is only a Frenchman, my lord.
> *The Nobleman.* A Frenchman! Where did you pick up that expression? Are these Burgundians and Bretons and Picards and Gascons beginning to call themselves Frenchmen, just as our fellows are beginning to call themselves Englishmen? They actually talk of France and England as their countries. Theirs, if you please! What is to become of me and you if that way of thinking comes into fashion?
> *The Chaplain.* Why, my lord? Can it hurt us?
> *The Nobleman.* Men cannot serve two masters. If this cant of serving their country once takes hold of them, goodbye to the authority of their feudal lords, and goodbye to the authority of the Church. That is, goodbye to you and me.

Some suspected the model for Shaw's Joan was his friend T. E. Lawrence. Shaw was writing *Saint Joan* at the same time Lawrence was working on *Seven Pillars of Wisdom*. Both Joan and Lawrence, in legend, were spiritually driven and untutored military geniuses. Both were nationalists trying to create a unified state and set a monarch upon a throne. Lawrence would do for Feisal and Syria and Transjordan what Joan did for Charles VII and France; both were nuisances to the authorities and both preferred a primitive form of war-fighting and the monastic life of the barracks over love and marriage. Both were mysteries of gender to their contemporaries and to subsequent generations.[11]

The perplexing stirrings of national feeling came in a context of other immense changes: literacy transformed the acquisition of knowledge; commerce caused nature to be seen with fresh eyes; and when world order fractured, diplomacy was disabled by religious schism.

ARCHITECTURE'S EDUCATIONAL ROLE UNDONE

The greatest novel about architecture is Victor Hugo's *Notre-Dame de Paris,* famous in America as *The Hunchback of Notre Dame.* Set in 1482, fifty years after the immolation of Joan, the book depicts the transformation of religion in physical-visual terms. The age of the Gothic cathedral rises from the Île de France to its perfected expressions at Notre Dame, Chartres, and Rheims (where Joan would have her dauphin crowned). The flying buttress made it possible to reduce wall weight and permit the great rose windows, giving the cathedrals a sense of transparency. God was light and light could now fill the interior space. Reason and revelation—light and truth—could be expressed in one structure. The interior space could be discerned from the exterior form, just as God's will could be comprehended from observing this world, as Aquinas would elaborate for all (did he get his inspiration from the architecture?). Aquinas had come north in 1245 to debate the great scholars in what would become universities. Classical Mediterranean civilization would be superseded by Europe's, the *translatio imperii et studii.*

In Victor Hugo's Paris, 250 years after Aquinas, Quasimodo, his one eye a rose window, clambers all over the edifice, hearing it with his eyes, caressing the silent bells and feeling—not hearing—their power when rung. Quasimodo, illiterate, could not read Scripture, and deaf, could not hear doctrine expounded. No need; the edifice was more than enough. The cathedral was an architectural "book" of knowledge constructed for a preliterate people in a preprint era. The building was the Word in visible form. Victor Hugo's novel portrays the last days of that way of knowing. Gutenberg's printed Bibles would make the cathedral as teacher obsolete. Reading a book would supplant experiencing architecture as a text. Hierarchical priesthood would be undermined just as the rigidity of stone would lose meaning. Interpretation would become more democratic and individually determined.

FROM SACRED WOOD TO LUMBER

On December 10, 1513, Niccolò Machiavelli wrote a letter to Francesco Vettori. In this "most celebrated letter in Italian literature," Machiavelli notes that he has just finished *The Prince.* The letter is famous for its description of the writer's work style:

When evening has come, I return to my house and go into my study. At the door, I take off my clothes of the day, covered with mud and mire, and I put on my regal and courtly garments; and decently re-clothed, I enter the ancient courts of ancient me, where, received by them lovingly, I feed on the food that alone is mine and that I was born for.

The bulk of the letter, however, is not ancient but modern, as Ma-chiavelli describes what he was doing earlier in the day. He owns a wood and has been having it cut down for sale. He goes on at length about the commercial bickerings and contentious transactions between himself as seller and his many demanding customers. When the day's wheeling and dealing is done, Machiavelli tells us, as if to make sure that we do not miss the point, he goes off with a copy of Dante under his arm. Dante, fearful for his soul, was lost in his late-Medieval wood. Machiavelli the business-man knows what wood is for: to be chopped and sold. At the end he even credits Dante for inspiring him to "make capital" out of the classic books he reads. Machiavelli has been called the originator of modern politics; here he is on the start of modern business as well.

Modern state-making is the focus of *The Prince,* which opens with the various ways of getting and keeping a state. At the end, Machiavelli returns to Moses as his great model; liberating his people, leading them toward nationhood, ready to order a clarifying act of great violence for the sake of the cause, and sacrificing himself before seeing the result of this leadership: the new polity established. Machiavelli calls for Italian state-building in his own time. The city-states of northern Italy in the Renais-sance will become a seedbed for the modern state and the diplomacy to order relations among them.

DIPLOMACY DISRUPTED: A PICTURE OF THE PROBLEM

Hans Holbein the Younger's dual portrait *The Ambassadors,* 1533, was an enigma for centuries. Two men, apparently a court official and a churchman, stand with a two-tiered shelf between them. One level carries a variety of artifacts: a lute, a globe, and some books or manuals. The other holds some scientific instruments. A tiny crucifix hangs in profile, hardly discernible at the top left of the canvas. A large blur spreads across the floor in front of the two; when viewed from an oblique angle it reveals itself to be a skull: death in contrast to the tiny symbol of life-in-death, the crucifix hanging almost out of sight in a corner of the painting. From now on, reality may best be understood through distortion.

In the late nineteenth century scholarly detective work shed light on the basic meaning of the work. In 1996 thorough cleaning provided more clues.[12] On the left is Jean de Dinteville, the French ambassador to the court of Henry VIII. The other is Georges de Selve, bishop of Lavaur, also in London in 1533. The objects displayed fall into two categories, those associated with the heavens on the top shelf, and those with earthly uses on the lower shelf. Every object is in some way broken or cannot be used for its designed purpose. The lute has a broken string; the astronomical instruments and geographical items are out of line or unworkable; a partly opened arithmetic book shows a page beginning with the word *divide;* and a hymnal is recognizable as a Lutheran version. Every reference tells of a world out of order, with no means available to set it right.[13]

The painting is of a diplomatic dispatch by two envoys of Catholic France who served in London as Henry VIII, whom the pope once called "Defender of the Faith," was breaking with Rome and about to establish the Protestant Church of England. Their ambassadors' message is encrypted. Decoded, it reads, "This is a problem unreachable by diplomacy; the world is theologically fractured and none of our instruments or methods for re-solving the matter will work." The ambassadors report back from their exploratory mission that the situation is beyond repair.[14]

When ideas about the way the world's nations should interact are incompatible, diplomacy is helpless.

A century later, the Westphalian accord would structure a remedy. The state members of the new international system all stipulated that matters of religion would not be allowed on the negotiating table; even bitterly antagonistic religious convictions might coexist in the realm of diplomacy.

If de Dinteville and de Selve had come to the English court under Westphalian rules, they would not have demanded that the English mon-arch submit to their own religious confession. They might then have been able to begin talks about how France and England could stabilize their rela-tionship on mutually beneficial terms, leaving religion out of the picture.

How vainly men themselves amaze
To win the palm, the oak, or bays;
And their incessant labours see
Crown'd from some single herb or tree,
Whose short and narrow verged shade
Does prudently their toils upbraid;
While all flowers and all trees do close
To weave the garlands of repose.

—Marvell

No one was more suited for the garlands of repose, it would seem, than Michel Eyquem de Montaigne, the inventor of the essay, who retired at thirty-seven to his father's estate to spend his days in a tower with a well-stocked library. From there came "his frequent asseverations of his ignorance and irresponsibility in regard to everything related to the outer world"; the only knowledge worth pursuing is self-knowledge.[15] Montaigne had experience in public affairs, however, and had been driven by the violence of the outer world "to rest myself from wars." He would influence affairs of state and through his writing contribute to a new international mentality.

Not long before climbing his tower, Montaigne had gone to Paris to take action in late Renaissance diplomacy. A peace agreement seemed to promise an end to Catholic-Protestant warfare. When negotiations failed, Montaigne retreated to his Perigord estate, a place not as tranquil as its image:

> The district round Montaigne lay in the heart of the tumult. Every pleasure-excursion might end in armed skirmish or death; and always some neighboring chateau—newly built perhaps and without defenses, in the prevailing Italian taste—might redden the night sky with its flames. In the oak and chestnut forests of the Limousin, beyond the sweep of the peaceful Lidoire, lurked war and pitched battle with pillage and private outrage enfranchised, but the portals of the Chateau de Montaigne stood open, with an old porter to do the courtesies of the gate. Amid this adventurous pacifism, in a tower raised above but not removed from men's follies, the *Essays* came to birth.[16]

The *Essais* open with scenes of terror, a catalogue of sieges, mass slaughters and war-fighting—all far from the calmly intricate investigations of his interior being for which Montaigne is famed. These early forays, says Montaigne's biographer, are "little more than strings of anecdotes with a brief conclusion . . . there is little of himself," only false starts by a writer wondering "what shall I write about?"[17] The first essays nonetheless show Montaigne fixated on the warfare all around him, turning over and over in his mind whether peace is more likely to be obtained by a resolute show of courage and readiness to resist or by accommodation, or even by casting oneself on the mercy of the enemy. When besieged, should one go out to negotiate? Montaigne's tower and lands are walled against violent attempts at pillage and worse. Perhaps it will be necessary "to sallie forth to parlie" but it must never be forgotten "that the houre of parlies is dangerous."

Montaigne would be called again into diplomatic service to advise and be dispatched on secret missions by Henri of Navarre, the Huguenot leader whose claim to the throne would be violently opposed by the Catholic League. Out of his experience, Montaigne wrote an essay as though referring to Odysseus in Homer's "Embassy to Achilles." "A Tricke of Certaine Ambassadors," in reporting back to kings, is to have "dissembled the chiefest part" of what had happened. It should be the envoy's duty "truly and exactly to set down things as they were." On the other hand, says Montaigne, it is important to give an ambassador some discretion about *how* best to make the case. So experienced diplomats would "condemne the customs of the kings of Persia, which was to mince the instructions given to their Agents and Lieutenants so small, that in the least accident they might have recourse to their direction and ordinances."

Beyond diplomacy, Montaigne would be called Henri of Navarre's "philosopher" because the essayist—born Catholic—had a tolerant view of religion which may have influenced Henri in his famous declaration that "Paris is worth a Mass." As King Henri IV, he brought peace and order for a time to the French state, yet before long, the greatest religious war of all would break out.

The German novelist Heinrich Mann, elder brother of Thomas, portrayed Montaigne's role as confidential adviser to Henri of Navarre: In 1573, with the Huguenots besieged by Catholic forces of the Duke of Anjou in the seacoast fortress of La Rochelle, a sentry, muffled in a cloak against the sea wind, demands the password. "Saint Bartholomew," the pair call out, naming the massacre of Protestants which had just reignited Catholic-Protestant hatreds and would turn a French civil war into a national struggle.

"What religion is the right one?" asked Henri.

"How do I know?" answered the other.

The words were a self-betrayal and a surrender such as no man would have made had he not recognized a kindred spirit and trusted him without a tremor.

They go to a deserted house, find some wine, then stumble across the shingle to the fortress.

And once more in the turmoil of the storm, Henri said:

"But I am and remain a captive!"

"Nihil est tam populare quam bonitas."

Force is strong but goodness is stronger. Henri never forgot this because he had heard it when it was his sole consolation.[18]

It would result in the Edict of Nantes of 1598, giving legal recognition to minority religious rights, and make Henri IV the most revered king in French history.

Montaigne turns inward yet outward at the same time, investigating "the human condition" as universal, recognizing that as religious differences give rise to widening confrontations, there exists a global dimension in which all might be resolved. Montaigne is one of the first to critique Europe's actions in a global arena. As Emerson recognized, the report of the world that Montaigne gave "was horizontal, not erect."[19] This was no soft-headed one-worldism; Montaigne mocked the idea of one natural law. There is no *consensus gentium.* Contemplation of the diversity of peoples now becoming known to European explorers "will not result in a single conclusion which is inscribed beforehand in the fabric of human nature. The most that will emerge are the various preferences. The ultimate consequences of this point of view could not take effect in an age that was deeply religious. But they emerged more and more with every weakening of the religious tie and every consequent growth of materialist beliefs."[20]

Montaigne observed the French state, the first and most thoroughly administered of all Europe, and compared it to the state of nature as recounted by a native man taken in South America and transported to France. "Of the Cannibales" is an ethnographic essay on what Montaigne saw as an admirably "civilized" way of life even though lived at odds with every practice of European civilization. The "Cannibales" live in long houses "able to containe two or three hundred soules"; they spend the whole day in dancing. Their creed is "First, valour against their enemies, then loving-ness unto their wives," of which the men have many, "and by how much more they are reputed valiant, so much the greater is their number, and "the same jealousie our wives have to keep us from the love and affection of other women, the same have theirs to procure it. . . . They endeavour and apply all their industrie, to have as many rivals as possibly they can, for as much as it is a testimonie to their husbands' vertue."

Montaigne describes with aplomb the way New World people wage war. Every victor brings home the head of his slain enemy and hangs it on his doorpost. Prisoners they keep long and treat well; then, calling an assembly, they kill their captives with swords and roast and eat them in common—not for nourishment but "to represent an extreme revenge." Montaigne declares this preferable to European ways: the natives kill their victims before devouring them while the French eat them alive: "I think there is more barbarism in eating men alive, than to feed upon them be-ing dead; to mangle by tortures and torments a body full of lively sense, to roast him in peeces, to make dogges and swine to gnaw and teare him in mammocks (. . . under pretext of pietie and religion) than to roast and eat him after he is dead." So, Montaigne concludes, "I finde (as farre as I have been informed) there is nothing in that nation, that is either bar-barous or savage, unlesse men call that barbarisme which is not common to them."

Montaigne was one of the great stylists in French literature and his sentences are carefully worked. As Emerson, his successor essayist, said, "cut these words and they would bleed." Puzzling gaps in the logic chain of "Of the Cannibales" thus call for explanation.

Acts of cannibalism—eating parts of the bodies of Huguenots—had taken place after the Saint Bartholomew's Day massacre of 1572. But those bodies were not eaten alive; no one eats living bodies. It becomes clear from the essay that Montaigne really is referring to human corpses thrown to dogs and pigs to eat. So Montaigne's condemnation of Europeans as more barbarous than Amerindians because the French eat people alive is not literal but metaphorical.[21] Montaigne's characterization of the "civilized" French as worse by comparison reflects the array of horrors produced by the religious wars swirling around him. The line dividing primeval from civil society as set out in Aeschylus's *Oresteia* is not only erased in this essay but reversed, with the savage ranked above the civilized. The state may be more barbaric than the state of nature. Yet this condemnation comes along with Montaigne's innovative approaches to self-study, toleration even for radical differences, and recognition that the political "center of gravity" must shift from Europe to the entire world.

Montaigne, the supposedly sequestered philosopher of interiority, ranged across the issues of society, state, and international relations just before the formation of the modern structure for world order. What was to be done about religion's deleterious influence on governance? Can tolerance be based on skepticism alone? Is the achievement of civil society the unalloyed good it has been considered to be? Can civilization be more barbarous than precivilization? Now that the European states have reconnoitered and conquered previously unthought-of peoples, what international architecture could possibly encompass all their unlikeness?

Nothing is more alien to religion than religious wars, Montaigne said; they are not born of faith nor do they make men more pious. For some they are a pretext for ambition, for others an opportunity for enrichment. He points out that saints do not appear in religious wars, causing the reader to reflect on Joan of Arc. Can religion and nationalism be separated? Religious war weakens a nation, making it prey to foreign aggression. The religious division, Protestant versus Catholic, which had dismayed Holbein's *Ambassadors,* left Europe weak against its great foe Islam. Gilbert Keith Chesterton called the Reformation "a Christian mutiny during a Moslem invasion" and turned this image into the battle-song "Lepanto," perhaps the best doggerel poem in the language.

The Ottoman Empire under Sultan Selim II had seized Cyprus and raided Malta, and was threatening the Italian Adriatic. Pope Pius V called for a united defense of Christendom, but Elizabeth I was consolidating the Church of England apart from Rome:

> And the Pope has cast his arms abroad for agony and loss,
> And called the Kings of Christendom for swords about the Cross,
> The cold queen of England [Elizabeth I] is looking in the glass;
> The shadow of the Valois [Henry III] is yawning at the Mass;
> From evening isles fantastical rings faint the Spanish gun
> And the Lord upon the Golden Horn [Selim II] is laughing in the
> sun.

So, unsupported by northern Europe, a "Holy League" was formed: the Papal States, the Venetian republic-empire, Philip II's Spain, and a Christian fleet commanded by Don John of Austria put to sea to fight the Ottoman armada at Lepanto in the Greek Gulf of Patroikos. In the greatest naval engagement since Actium in 31 B.C., the two fleets made battle contact on Sunday, October 7, 1571. Hundreds of galleys and tens of thousands of soldiers clashed all day in what would be the last oar-powered naval conflict—ships grappled together so that "land" warfare could take place across their decks. As one commentator said, "Sultan Selim II would have been adding minarets to the Basilica of Saint Peter in Rome had the Holy League not prevailed at Lepanto." But the victors did not follow up their victory. The Christian fleet had fought "the last battle of the last crusade," but it was no crusade; there was no thought of recovering the Christian Holy Land.

Instead, Philip II, the greatest power of the Holy League, turned his political and military strength to bear on the new Protestant states of northern Europe, where, within five decades, the outbreak of the Thirty Years' War would eventually result in victory for those new states. Empires— Ottoman, Venetian, Spanish—had entered the beginning of their end.

Wounds suffered at Lepanto would cost Cervantes the use of a hand. Chesterson's poem takes no notice of this disability:

Cervantes on his galley sets the sword back in the sheath
(Don John of Austria rides homeward with a wreath.)
And he sees across a weary land a straggling road in Spain,
Up which a lean and foolish knight forever rides in vain,
And he smiles, but not as Sultans smile, and settles back the blade. . . .
(But Don John of Austria rides home from the Crusade.)

The "smile" may be a tribute to Byron, who, in his book-length poem *Don Juan,* wrote that in *Don Quixote,* the first modern novel, Cervantes smiled Spain's chivalry away.

As literature has reflected new forms of world order, a new-forming world produced a new literary form, the novel. The "brutal" rise of the modern state is accompanied by the rise of the novel, a fictional expression of the essential values of classical and Christian civilization with an unrivaled power to formulate and explain problems central to early modern experience.[22]

After surviving Lepanto and other adventures variously vicious and romantic, Cervantes produced *Don Quixote* in two parts—1605 and 1615—just before the start of the Thirty Years' War. The book has two themes, both modern. The first is what a novel is: the instability of the text and uncertainty of authorship. The second is the soul-wrenching yet hilarious struggle of the Don to pursue an inherited cultural narrative of glory, romance, chivalry, and empire while surrounded by the coarse and greedy strivings of an urbanizing commercial state, which pays no attention to the old knight of whom Nabokov wrote, "His blazon is pity, his banner is beauty. He stands for everything that is gentle, forlorn, pure, unselfish and gallant."

Time has passed Don Quixote by. A leftover knight with few worldly goods, he incessantly reads the fanciful tales of a long-gone chivalry, which inspire him to set out into the world to spur his spavined charger against "giants" which are really windmills. He sees "armies" that are vast droves of sheep on the way to city slaughterhouses. The reality of things is so far from romance that it can be explained only by "enchantment."

All across Cervantes's novel are signs of the transformation of society and governance from an old world to a new. Money is appearing, and its meaning is shifting. In part I, a servant boy who asked for back wages is brutally beaten. In part II the Don offers to pay Sancho for each lash he supposedly will give himself to disenchant Dulcinea—and Sancho gets to set the price. The relationship between master and servant is changing from status to contract. Sancho's aspiration, which will be fulfilled, is to become governor of an island; employment as a civil official replaces the dream of knight-errantry.

In part II, Don Quixote's perceptions change after he, in epic fashion, undergoes a visit to the Underworld, where past, present, and future, the intimately personal and the highly political, all come together to reveal his mission and strategy. Don Quixote's descent into the Underworld is a parody of all those revelatory visits stretching across literature from Homer onward. Sigmund Freud plumbed the subconscious in a modern, "scientific" version—"No self-understanding is possible without a trip there"— and won a Nobel Prize in Literature for doing so. The metaphor of a journey to the Underworld is a narrative way to communicate a strategic intuition otherwise difficult to comprehend and accept.[23] Plato's Cave is its philosophic elaboration. At the Cave's depth, one of the prisoners is set free and dragged up the rough, steep way out, so that for the first time he can know the source of all that is right, true, and good.[24] What is the force that sets one free and shows the path to understanding? Plato, the author of the story.

Like Aeneas, the Don must deal with some vatic vegetation at the entrance to "The Cave of Montesinos," which is located in the heart of La Mancha. Instead of a golden bough, the way below is blocked by a thicket of brambles. Quixote slashes his way through them, giving no thought to what may follow. Tied to a long rope held by Sancho, he plunges into the abyss, where he sleeps on a ledge and awakens in a meadow in which stands a crystal castle. There the warden Montesinos shows him the sepulcher of the ancient knight Durandarte, who fell at Roncesvalles, the Pyrenees mountain pass where legend says the hero Roland died fighting the Saracens.

Down in the cave for three days—or perhaps only half an hour—Don Quixote sees three crude peasant girls who Montesinos says are high-born ladies with a spell cast on them. In a bizarre departure from the expected, Dulcinea comes up to ask for a loan of six *reals,* "or more if you have it," and offers a new skirt as security. The Don gives her four *reals,* all he has, and wishes he were a *Fugger*—new merchant bankers of the German cities—so as to be able to come up with more money. Chivalry has met materialistic modernity and come to terms with it. Here the Don realizes what will be his real mission: to disenchant Dulcinea and free her from the spell.

Somewhere in this new adventure lies what Max Weber called "the disenchantment" of the modern world. Instead of enchanters having transformed the glorious beauty, the lady Dulcinea, into a rustic wench, she will become herself and we will understand her as she is, a rustic wench with the potential to change her social position in a secular, modern world. At the end of the novel, Don Quixote, near death, declares that his mind is free of chivalric delusions.

The "Disenchantment of the World," Weber suggested, began at the dawn of history, when the emergence of the state in the first great riverine polities caused magical explanations of all aspects of life to give way to secular explanations. A revival of this transformation comes as Christendom gives way to a secular age.

Cruelty also is changing. *Don Quixote* is a brutish, coarse book, a catalogue of routine violence. Flogging and head-bashing, supposedly hilarious humiliations and hurtful practical jokes abound. Yet as some remnant of courtly love is transposed into a modern respect for women, something from the Don's chivalric code seems to alter the idea of cruelty; by the end of the book it is no longer so funny. There is an incipient sense of what will be thought of as human rights. As Carlos Fuentes has observed, "While [Don Quixote] read, he imitated the epic hero. When he *is* read, the world imitates *him*."[25]

Again, nationalism appears. Thomas Mann, leaving Nazi Germany for America, brings *Don Quixote* to read on the voyage. Mann is struck by the character Ricote, a village shopkeeper, one of the Moriscos—moors of the caliphate of al-Andalus who stayed in Spain after the general expulsion of non-Christians in 1492 and were "converted." Forced into exile in 1609 under the new general decree of Philip III, Ricote makes himself "German." "Then why did he come back?" asks Sancho. "Because," Ricote says, "Wherever we are we weep for Spain," his country of birth, his native land. But, Ricote adds, he also came back "to dig up the treasure I left behind." For Thomas Mann, Don Quixote represents universal humanity yet remains state-bound in national pride and love of country.

Lest the reader accept modern "disenchantment" too readily, as the ocean liner carrying Mann to America enters New York harbor, the novelist notes that the skyscrapers look like "giants."

Troilus and Cressida, one of Shakespeare's last plays, set during the Trojan War, scathingly reworks Homer's "Embassy to Achilles" in the context of a breakdown of early modern political and moral order. For Britons of the time, the epic of Troy's fall was immediately relevant. Britain had been founded, national myth said, by the grandson of Aeneas, a step in the *translatio imperii.* Trojans on the stage would be favored by playgoers and filled with current meaning; Greeks would not get the benefit of the doubt.

The Iliadic Greek warrior Odysseus—"Ulysses" in Shakespeare—declares that the established ways are coming apart. Rank-order and established hierarchy have lost respect. The cosmos itself is in disarray. "The specialty of rule hath been neglected":

> Observe degree, priority, and place,
> Insisture, course, proportion, season, form
> Office and custom, in all line of order. . . .
> But when the planets
> In evil mixture to disorder wander

What plagues and what portents, what mutiny
What raging of the sea, shaking of earth
Commotion in the winds, frights, changes, horrors
Divert and crack, rend and deracinate
The unity and married calm of states.

Theatergoers might assume that Shakespeare was decrying the decay of the traditional structure. It's not that simple. *Troilus and Cressida* is a relentlessly intellectual examination of statecraft, a sour and often cynical work which furthers the demolition of the old courtly, chivalric, and hierarchical system. We may admire the Trojans, who exemplify the brave and noble past, and we may be revolted by the Machiavellian Greeks and their caustic "reason," but this, Shakespeare tells us, is how it's going to be; something new will be needed to replace the collapse of the old order.

Homer's "Embassy to Achilles" repeats itself in Shakespeare as farce. In place of the carefully chosen Iliadic threesome sent to try to negotiate Achilles' return to battle, Shakespeare's Greek commanders are a shapeless group with no apparent diplomatic strategy, in a scene easily played for laughs. Agamemnon, Ulysses, Nestor, Diomedes, and Ajax stand outside Achilles' tent. "Let it be known to him that we are here," Agamemnon says to Patroclus, who ducks in and out of the tent as the go-between. "We saw him at the opening of his tent," Ulysses notes, "He is not sick." Then the delegation begins to quibble among themselves.

Patroclus comes out of the tent:

Achilles bids me say he is much sorry
If anything more than your sport and pleasure
Did move your greatness, and this noble state,
To call upon him; he hopes it is no other
But for your health and your digestion sake,
An after-dinner's breath.

So Achilles portrays the great moment on which the war may turn as an after-dinner stroll by the boys to get a breath of fresh air. He is not disposed to negotiate. The Greeks turn to squabbling over what to do next until Ulysses calls the whole thing off:

There is no tarrying; the hart Achilles
Keeps thicket.

And Agamemnon leads the group back to the Greek camp to hold council.

Achilles and Patroclus pass the time making fun of the Greek commanders. Ulysses scowls to his comrades that Achilles in his tent

> lies mocking our designs, with him Patroclus,
> upon a lazy bed, the livelong day
> breaks scurril jests,
> and with ridiculous and awkward action—
> which, slanderer, his imitation calls—
> his pageants us.

Achilles delights in Patroclus's imitations and asks for more. Achilles

> cries "Excellent!" 'Tis Agamemnon just.
> Now play me Nestor; hem and stroke thy beard;
> as he being dressed to some oration.

So in this fashion, Ulysses complains

> all our abilities, gifts, natures, shapes,
> severals and generals of grace expect,
> achievements, plots, orders, preventions,
> excitements to the field, or speech for truce,
> success or loss, what is or is not, serves
> as stuff for these two to make paradoxes.

Diplomacy having failed to win Achilles' return to the Greek forces, Ulysses contrives a modern ploy—to ignore him while advancing the Machiavellian maxim that reputation matters more than reality. Achilles and Patroclus stand at the entrance to their tent; Agamemnon and Ulysses pretend to ignore them. Achilles:

> What, comes the general to speak with me?
> You know my mind: I'll fight no more 'gainst Troy

They ignore him. Achilles calls out to Ulysses, "What are you reading?" A clever Shakespearean twist: an Iliadic warrior reading a book. Ulysses is perusing a Platonic dialogue which argues:

> That no man is the lord of anything
> Though in and of him that be much consisting,
> Till he communicate his parts to others.

Deeds, Achilles is made to understand, are discounted if no new ones are forthcoming. Achilles having taken himself out of combat, the Greeks will turn to Ajax as their champion. They would have turned to Achilles

> If thou wouldst not entomb thyself alive
> And case they reputation in thy tent.

Achilles gets the message:

> I see my reputation at stake
> My fame is shrewdly gor'd

Thersites, the only commoner in the *Iliad,* ugly, insubordinate, and despised, was pummeled by Odysseus and driven away. Shakespeare's Thersites is all over the play, even enlisted by Achilles as his "ambassador" to the Trojan Hector. Thersites' cameo appearance in the *Iliad* won him a place in political theory as an early populist denouncer of elite rule and precursor of modern equality. In Shakespeare's drama, he no longer speaks truth to power.

In a final, repulsive twist on classic Iliadic virtue, Achilles, when he fights Hector, sets his Myrmidons on the Trojan hero in a swarming disgraceful murder. Achilles then ties the corpse to his horse's tail and drags Hector's remains across the plain. The Greeks are grotesque, self-serving moderns. The Trojans are romantic, chivalrous figures of the past and are crushed. The Trojan voice is courtly, urbane, and elevated; the Greeks are coarse and commercial and they win out.

More than two hundred years earlier, Geoffrey Chaucer, sent as an English diplomat to Italy, read a tale of Boccaccio's which he turned into *Troilus and Criseyde,* called by some the finest long poem in the language. The story turns on a Greek ambassadorial mission sent to the Trojans to negotiate a prisoner exchange in which Troilus's beloved Criseyde would be sent to the Greeks. In Chaucer's handling it is a tragic medieval romance of ruined love. Shakespeare's early modern version is a saga of Cressida's crude, lustful, shameful betrayal of Troilus, causing him to sense that an entire moral order based upon marriage is collapsing and will take affairs of state down with it. The Bard had sensed the times to come.

Parody is as old as time, yet there is something in this literary laughter that seems new: nothing is as sacred now. In a secularizing society, the rising common man comes to the fore with an acid tongue that would scorn and tear down all hierarchies. From this point forward, states may be assessed by the balance they strike between parody and patriotism.

3

SOURCES OF MODERN
WORLD ORDER

"War is the father of all things" the pre-Socratic thinker Heraclitus said. Out of the Thirty Years' War that ravaged Europe from 1618 to 1648 came the elements of the international state system that has shaped world affairs in our time. The war's losses, in proportion to Europe's population, exceeded the fifty million of the Second World War. Such horrors brought internationally significant steps: "laws" to constrain the conduct of war, an understanding that religion should be removed as a cause of conflict, and the idea of the state as the basic entity of international affairs. The concept of balance of power emerged as a matter of expedience over ideology. And the image of "the great statesman," necessarily at times Machiavellian, came to the fore.

War stories, in literature or in history, may be more influential than the truth of what really occurred. Stories told about the Thirty Years' War and the peace treaty that followed it have led a distinctive intellectual life in world affairs.

In 1618, a century after the start of the Protestant Reformation, bitter religious conflict erupted into full-scale war in Prague, Bohemia, a kingdom under the jurisdiction of the Holy Roman Emperor in Vienna. Protestant leaders petitioned for expanded religious freedoms. An assembly was called, then canceled, triggering an angry delegation of Protestants to Hradcany Castle. Two of the king's regents and a secretary were seized and thrown out the upper-story window of the castle.

The famous window is still there on the fourth floor, high above the old city. It can still easily be opened—and widely, as Professor Paul Kennedy learned on a recent Yale alumni trip. Several large ex-Yale football players hoisted him half out of the window for a photograph to commemorate the Defenestration of Prague, the spark that inflamed Europe for thirty years.

As the three frantic, struggling Catholics were shoved out the window, they called to the Blessed Virgin to save them. One of the rebels yelled, "We will see if your Mary will save you!" then, peering down the fifty-foot drop, exclaimed, "By God, his Mary has helped!" All three survived and ran off, the Catholics accounting it a miracle; the Protestants pointing out that they had fallen on one of the castle's immense dung heaps.[1]

Emboldened, the Protestants demanded the kingship itself. At the Battle of White Mountain near Prague in November 1620, the emperor's Catholic army routed the insurgents, and Protestant principalities of Germany and Central Europe suffered successive defeats. In alarm, Protestant rulers in the North mobilized to intervene. Imperial Vienna feared this escalation. The costs in men and money had been huge; a new phase in the war could reverse fortunes drastically.

At this point, Wallenstein of Bohemia, a wealthy Catholic convert, stepped forward to offer the Catholic emperor a huge army, raised, paid for, and commanded by himself. He took to the field and won victory after victory, as well as honors, titles, and increasing political power. By 1628 he had invaded and defeated Denmark for the emperor, who then issued the Edict of Restitution, requiring all lands of the Catholic Church lost to Protestants to be returned—an impossibility that brought even greater escalation as the Protestant King Gustavus Adolphus landed his Swedish army on Germany's Baltic coast.

The grinding warfare across Europe produced the first great German novel, Grimmelshausen's *Adventures of Simplicissimus,* which I first read in Raoul Bergethon's German seminar at Brown a half-century ago. Called a German *Don Quixote, Simplicissimus* is picaresque like Cervantes's novel, and cruel as well, but as a novel of wartime, it takes the brutality far beyond the Spanish book. Being immersed in Grimmelshausen's pages is like finding oneself within the deranged chaos of a painting by Hieronymus Bosch. All is a swirl of lusting, murderous, satanic satire. The hero fights the war as a foot soldier, captain, dragoon, and orderly, captured first by Swedish Protestant forces and next by imperial soldiers.

Simplicissimus, acting as a guide for a group of soldiers, describes an incident typical of the war's brutish character. Armed peasants captured six soldiers who had been reconnoitering for feed. They shot five of them, standing them one behind the other. Since the bullet, having to go through five bodies, had not killed the sixth in line, they forced him to lick their asses, then started to cut off his nose and ears. The captive soldier tried to goad them into killing him, but instead they crammed him into a barrel and buried him alive, saying that since he had tried so hard for death, for reasons of spite they did not want to humor him.

Then, Simplicissimus says, another squad of soldiers captured five peasants, four of whom had humiliated their comrade. One soldier took the fifth peasant aside and promised to let him go if he denied God and all his saints. The peasant answered that he had never given a damn for the saints, didn't know God, and wanted no part of his kingdom. The soldier fired a bullet at his head, "but it ricocheted as if it had hit a steel wall." Then he pulled out his broadsword and shouted, "I promised to let you go to heaven, I am now sending you to Hell!" and split his head apart down to the teeth . . .

> Meanwhile the soldiers tied the other four peasants (the same whom the soldier had to lick) over a fallen tree in such a way as their rumps stuck up. After removing their trousers, they took yards and yards of fuse cord, made knots in it, and neatly ran the knotted cord through the cleft of their behinds until they drew blood. "This is the way to dress their clean backsides," they said. The peasants screamed like pigs, but a lot of good it did them. The soldiers didn't stop until they struck the bone. I was sent back to my hut because the second troop knew the way, so I didn't find out what else they did to the peasants.

The hero, Simplicissimus, is an unspoiled if rascally soul who judges by a set of simple, spiritual values. He finds himself in a torn world ravaged by endless greed, misery, and killing. People feel that they have lost all ability to affect their destinies.

As the adventures roll on, Simplicissimus becomes the world's fool, mocked for guilelessly speaking the truth. Before long, he begins to learn not to say what he thinks. Hypocrisy pays off in comfort, food, and clothing. Being clever becomes far more advantageous than being honest, and he gains some success as an actor, a profession of dissembling. In the Venusberg, all is darkness and bedding. People cohabit without knowing with whom. Simplicissimus reaches rock bottom as a camp follower, a parasite; he no longer can tolerate his own existence. Although his adventures are carnally exciting, he can only react passively. In self-disgust, he withdraws to become a hermit. When an opportunity comes to go back to the world to do good, he refuses, fearing that exposure to his fellow creatures and their debauched society would damage his soul, now dedicated to God.

At the novel's center is "Jupiter," who, in mad harangues, describes a glorious future in which the universal peace, harmony, justice, and order for which Europe yearns will come about. Jupiter will call forth "a great German hero" who will "deprive whole armies of their heads through one stroke through the air, although the men may be behind a mountain and an hour's distance away." He will unite the religions and mold them into one. "Then there will be a constant and everlasting peace among all nations of the world—as in the days of the Emperor Augustus." Wallenstein may have been the inspiration for "Jupiter."

Simplicissimus and Jupiter—polar opposites—offer responses to an incoherent world, both equally futile: impotent realism and impossible idealism.

Purporting to be a military journal by an English gentleman who served with Gustavus Adolphus, Daniel Defoe's *Memoirs of a Cavalier* is an English novel of the Thirty Years' War. Like Defoe's other novels, it is an invented "personal narrative" presented inside a realistic historical structure taken largely from Swedish newspaper accounts of the war. So realistic is the story that Winston Churchill, more than two hundred years later, regarded it as a primary document of war and statecraft. The cavalier describes the situation succinctly: "There had been a long bloody War in the Empire of Germany for twelve years, between the Emperor, the Duke of Bavaria, the King of Spain, and the Popish Princes and Electors on the one side, and the Protestant Princes on the other; and both Sides having been exhausted by the War, and even the Catholicks themselves beginning to dislike the growing power of the House of Austria, 'twas thought all Parties were willing to make Peace."

But no. Gustavus Adolphus enters the war against the empire, turning it, says the cavalier, into "the greatest in Event, filled with the most famous Battles, Sieges, and extraordinary Actions, including its Success and happy Conclusion, of any War ever maintained in the World." The cavalier meets Gustavus in his headquarters and signs on with him, seeing him as a military genius, creative statesman, and moral exemplar. At the Battle of Lutzen in 1632 the imperial forces under "Generalissimo" Wallenstein are routed, but Gustavus is killed at the head of his troops. "The king is dead," laments the cavalier, "So I resolved to quit the Service."

Before the Thirty Years' War there were hundreds of small political units in Europe, overlaid by various degrees of imperial power. A state-making process had been under way for a few hundred years, its key attributes being strong central sovereignty and clearly demarcated borders. Only in Germany, where the Holy Roman Empire blocked the modern state, and in Italy, where small city-states resisted political aggregation, was the state-making process immobilized. The Thirty Years' War would change this, its seemingly endless horrors demanding new ideas and new modes of behavior. Hugo de Groot, called Grotius, published his seminal work *De Jure Belli ac Pacis* (*The Law of War and Peace*) in 1625. He wrote it, he said, "to assuage, as far as I could, that savagery, unworthy of Christians, and even of men, in making and waging war"—the bestial scenes he saw in the early stages of the Thirty Years' War. Grotius, a character recognizable today as an academic turned policy analyst and political appointee, died in 1645, three years before the end of the Thirty Years' War.

His book is "a literary scrap bag, where the author with jubilant abandon accumulates from jurists, historians, poets, dramatists, philosophers, and theologians anything remotely supporting a principle which he wishes to see established."[2] It would be recognized as the first treatise of international law, a work called into being by the profoundly felt need to establish some accepted limits on the use of force in wartime.

Grotius and his book are at the heart of the best modern novel about the Thirty Years' War, *People of the Book,* written in the 1960s by the neglected American novelist David Stacton.

Stacton's Gustavus Adolphus respects Grotius's effort to establish laws of war. But he also knows that in matters of state there are two kinds of morality: personal morality, and the morality that applies to actions that affect an entire people.

It was for such reasons that Gustavus kept a copy of Grotius by him in his tent. That book was wistful as a fairy tale, and as he turned the enchanted pages, he would slightly smile as he read of justice, equity, the law of nations, what Seneca and Cicero had said, and nowhere a word for what Xenophon and Caesar had had to do. Meanwhile, never being one to confuse precedent with experience, he went on revising those sixty pages of *Institutions* which had given him the best-run army in the world, and the most merciful, for so long as he was there to control it.[3]

Grotius himself appears in the novel, having consented, grudgingly, to enter the service of Sweden. He was famous; he would bolster the Swedish cause. The Swedish high command observes of him:

Herr Grotius was a man so breathless after causes that he had never had time to look at any individual face. They were a blur to him. He gave to charity and was put out of countenance by beggars at his gate: they did not queue. He married on principle (also for self-advancement). He had had children on principle. . . . He had no use for anyone who had not principle, and recognized no principles but his own, on principle. Since he acted always in the commonweal, there was no way to get at him. It was all principle. And if his principles were high, so was his nose in the air. For though he realized he was but a man of common clay (humility is popular in these circles), he was also the sacred vessel of a shining principle (International Law). . . . Grotius was famous for having himself smuggled out of the fortress of Loevestein disguised as a box of books. And by God, he *was* a box of books.

On the Law of War and Peace is not a comprehensive treatise but a rambling collection of digressions on religion, ethics, and general legal pedantry. But Grotius does create, or systematize, something new: "Inasmuch as I am convinced," he writes, "that there is a common law between nations which is valid for war and in war, there are many grave reasons why I should undertake to write on the subject. Throughout the Christian world I have seen a lawlessness in warfare that even barbarian races would think shameful. In trifling pretexts, or none at all, men rush to arms, and when once arms are taken up, all respect for the law, whether human or divine is lost, as though by some edict a fury had been let loose to commit every crime."

The Thirty Years' War marked a transition from feudal to modern warfare. New technologies of killing and the devastation of whole civilian populations led Grotius to state principles of "law" to govern operations in international combat. Grotius accepted war as a fact of human existence and assumed that the warring parties would be legitimate states, not governments (governments would change while states remained), each willing to abide by international law as an institution of international society. Not to do so would be "uncivilized."

This was the first expression of the doctrine of the equality of states, a cornerstone of the international state system. The state would provide a stable basis of legitimacy beyond religious allegiance and in a secular public sphere. Grotius made modern an ancient perception—that the diversity of world's peoples are nonetheless a universal society, a "family of nations," or as is said today, "an international community." His concept is in opposition to Machiavelli's and would be a rival to that of Hobbes.

Defoe's cavalier introduces us to France's Cardinal Richelieu as the archetypally amoral international gamesman of balance-of-power politics. "There was no life in any Thing but where the Cardinal was, and he pushed every Thing with extraordinary Conduct, and generally with Success . . . but if Things miscarried it was all laid upon the King." Richelieu had had to negotiate with Grotius when he was in the service of the Swedes, and he loathed him, for he did not much relish bargaining with a mind as good as his own. Both agreed there was one moral standard for princes and another for private persons and that only a great man could be trusted to navigate both. It is "depressing to consider the long, secret talks between the Protestant philosopher of the law of nations and a Catholic cardinal dedicated to the continuation of lawlessness and disorder throughout the empire."[4] The "balance of power," with its built-in threat of war, was an old concept, but Richelieu enshrined it as *the* mechanism for reconciling national interests and international order. Richelieu had no scruple about using violence in the cause of a more stable international order, and indeed considered it a moral imperative.

Richelieu was the grand strategist; Louis XIII simply watched and signed the papers. Stacton describes Richelieu:

His health was bad. He was spindly: He was sometimes spiteful, and often petty. But he was also a personage, ruthless, peremptory. Noble, selfless, always just entering a room but never in it, remote, but truly great, not because of what he was, but because of something he believed in. He believed in France. France to him was not a country, but a principle. When he said we, he did not mean what Louis XIII, his master, meant. He spoke out of the allegory, turning his head. He *was* France. Before his time there had not been such a place. He made it out of nothing but will-power, a weak king wise enough to trust him but a religious maniac, some fractious nobles, and a little land. It was his Host. He transubstantiated it. He had turned it into something sacred.[5]

Richelieu thought his country needed to unify and amass power equal to that of the Holy Roman Empire. Otherwise Bourbon Catholic France would be dominated by its Hapsburg Catholic brethren who ruled in Austria, Spain, and the Spanish Netherlands. First, Richelieu broke the power of the great French nobles and the Protestant Huguenot challengers to consolidate France under the absolute reign of the king; then, by diplomacy, conspiracy, intrigues, and bribes, he began to undermine his rivals in Vienna and Madrid.

The diplomat-artist of the Flemish School, Peter-Paul Rubens, was born in Westphalia, where his father had been exiled for Calvinism, but was educated by Jesuits in the (Spanish Hapsburg) Netherlands. He thus considered himself a Christian universalist under the Holy Roman Empire. In 1622 Rubens was commissioned to execute the great Medici Gallery project in Paris, a series of forty-eight paintings allegorically extolling Marie de Medici as the Mother of France under the protection of the Virgin Mary. Cardinal Richelieu gave his blessing to the plan, as it would make him seem loyal to imperial Catholic Europe. Richelieu was developing his balance-of-power strategy and was not yet ready to show his hand. Protestant forces had been devastated at the Battle of White Mountain, after which no solely German coalition would be able to match the Hapsburgs. Only if Catholic France allied with the northern Protestant states could the European balance be redressed. As yet, France was too weak. The Hapsburg faction remained influential at the French court, and Rubens's project made it seem that Richelieu and France posed no threat. The Medici Gallery was completed on the eve of France's emergence as a great power.[6] Richelieu then threw Catholic France on the side of Protestant Sweden against the Catholic Holy Roman Empire of the Hapsburgs. On May 21, 1635, it was announced in Brussels that His Most Christian Majesty Louis XIII had declared war on His Most Catholic Majesty Philip IV.

At the heart of Richelieu's paradoxical statecraft lies the mystery of his adviser, Père Joseph, a Capuchin monk whose sobriquet, "l'éminence grise," would thereafter attach to any shadowy adviser who had the ear of a prince.[7] Aldous Huxley's 1941 novel *Grey Eminence* depicts Père Joseph as given to evangelizing, preaching, and mystical devotions—and, at the start of the Thirty Years' War, on the side of the Holy Roman Empire against the Protestant rebels. A few years later he switched sides, having come to the belief that Catholic Hapsburgs were an obstacle to France's launch of yet another great crusade against Islam. Père Joseph became Richelieu's right-hand man in allying France to the Protestant north in order to break the Hapsburg ascendancy and make the House of Bourbon the paramount European power. Huxley anguished over Richelieu's and his Grey Eminence's "realism"—that is, their use of balance-of-power statecraft and their disregard for conventional morality, idealism, or peace.

> No episode in history can be entirely irrelevant to any other subsequent episode. But some events are related . . . more significantly than others. We shall find if we look into [this friar's] biography a little closely, [that] his thoughts and feelings and desires were among the significantly determining conditions of the world in which we live today . . . [that they] led to August 1914 and September 1939. In the long chain of crime and madness which binds the present world to its past, one of the most fatally important links was the Thirty Years' War.

Richelieu's balance-of-power strategy, once freed from religious and ideological concerns, became the first tool of statecraft. By using it, Richelieu prolonged the war and its horrors, ruined the Holy Roman Empire, and enabled France's rise to paramount power.

Richelieu's tomb was placed in the Chapel of Sainte Geneviève at the Sorbonne. In 1778 the young abbé Talleyrand visited the chapel "to greet and consult the most dynamic and stimulating of masters: the monumental Cardinal in his tomb." Casually resting his lame foot on the beautiful sculpture, "he opened a dialogue with the dead."[8] Talleyrand would become Richelieu's successor as the most infamous diplomat of his time. Above the tomb today floats Richelieu's red cardinal's hat held by a string fastened to the ceiling. A guide will tell you that when the string finally rots and breaks, and the hat falls, it is the sign that Richelieu has been released from Hell. An attendant will whisper that they regularly check the condition of the string.

At a time of high tension in U.S.-France relations before the 2003 Iraq War, Henry Kissinger said to a State Department official, "The French are treating us as if they are Cardinal Richelieu and we are the Holy Roman Empire"—that is, are taking the side of those who should be a common enemy. "But," Kissinger told me, "the State Department guy had never heard of Cardinal Richelieu."

Richelieu and Père Joseph are a case study for the proposition that most great statesmen possess a certain mad, enigmatic quality. To some, the greatest such personage of the Thirty Years' War was Wallenstein—Albrecht Wenzel Eusebius von Wallenstein, 1583–1634, a commander-manager-statesman of gargantuan ambition, and the originator of an early version of the military-industrial complex.

At the Diet of Ratisbon (1630), Wallenstein met Père Joseph, whom Richelieu had sent ostensibly on good faith negotiations but actually to sow dissension. Wallenstein invited the friar to his quarters for a long confidential talk, the gist of which was sent to Richelieu in Père Joseph's next dispatch. Huxley describes it as a conversation an eavesdropper would have found peculiar, for the men talked about Turkish power, the Holy Land, and joint expeditions—crusades—from the West. Slowly, Père Joseph realized that Wallenstein's interest was driven not by religious fervor but by the desire to extend imperial power, and his own power.

Wallenstein's ambitions led the emperor to replace him as commanding general. But when his replacement was defeated in battle by Gustavus, the emperor had no choice; Wallenstein was recalled to command and given vastly enhanced political powers. He employed his extraordinary organizational abilities and raised a massive military force. At Lützen in 1632, Gustavus Adolphus was killed, but Wallenstein lost the battle. He then proposed a general peace, to which the emperor would not agree. People began to say that Wallenstein was in secret contact with the Swedes to sue for peace, perhaps even to combine with the Swedish army to overthrow the emperor. Wallenstein was soon charged as a traitor by the imperial court, but he continued secretly to negotiate with the Swedes. On February 25, 1634, he was murdered, probably by order of the emperor.

The Wallenstein of Friedrich Schiller's great drama, the greatest work of literature about the Thirty Years' War and "the only drama written after Shakespeare that shows a profound *political* imagination," is far less mundane. Schiller transformed history, it was said, into *eine reinepoetische Fabel,* a fable that would influence history much more than Wallenstein's actual career. Schiller makes "self-concealment, ambiguity, and brooding profundity" the essence of his hero, and this has been the archetype of the statesman ever since.

In November 2005, as the war in Iraq reached a peak of violence, Yale performed the prologue to Schiller's trilogy, "Wallenstein's Camp." Here Wallenstein's secret negotiations with the Swedish Protestants were seen as a great-souled man's doomed attempt to bring about a world of peace, tolerance, and human solidarity above and beyond national or religious animosities.

Schiller's Wallenstein embodies the tensions, paradoxes, and dichotomies of great decisions. Wallenstein's men recount, in an echo of the Defenestration of Prague, that years before his rise to wealth and power he had fallen from a high window without injury. The miracle changed him, causing him to convert to Catholicism and to believe that he had a special, transcendent destiny, exempt from danger. Removed from command, Wallenstein turns to astrology. From this point forward, Catholicism and Protestantism mean nothing to him. Now he will be an instrument of the stars. But astrology is false, so the source of Wallenstein's vision of world peace and tolerance, Schiller indicates, is fatally corrupt.

Wallenstein develops a vision of political community and religious freedom, but at the same time he is a warlord who aspires to rule his land of Bohemia and beyond. A man of action, he hesitates to put his plans into action. "For Wallenstein, the insuperable gap between mind and concrete reality, his progressive emphasis on intention and ideal goal in order to blur the ugliness of deed and the treacherous moral compromise he is drawn to, form the internal drama of his life."[9] His hope for a grand alliance across enemy lines compromises his personal integrity. He is misunderstood; he misunderstands himself. Murdered at last for his failures as well as his lofty aims, he exemplifies the tragic hero brought low by a flaw. In Wallenstein, today's international theories of "idealism" and "realism" live side by side, grand ideals served by immoral acts of statecraft which history may vindicate, but whose failure gains him only remorseless enmity in life and a tormented, violent end.

Schiller, with a poet's genius and dramatic license, saw something in Wallenstein to epitomize the modern world statesman. Wallenstein's rise and fall are fated, yet he is not a classic tragic figure like Sophocles' Oedipus, nor a victim of circumstances that accumulate to crush him eventually.[10] Instead, he is recognizable as a modern individual, a bundle of the drives and aspirations found in many contemporary presidents, prime ministers, and dictators. He is avaricious and easily accumulates wealth, by birth, marriage, or deals. He has immense organizational talent, an eye for detail and delegation, plus a semimagical quality, a charisma that effortlessly wins the allegiance of talented lieutenants and tough henchmen all eager to serve his personal ends and ambition for glory. He enjoys power and thrives on the challenge of hard decisions, yet at the same time he will often ponder and delay, less out of indecisiveness than from some sixth sense which tells him the time is not yet ripe for action. Like all great leaders, he is boundlessly self-absorbed.

These qualities, however representative of statesmen, do not add up to greatness. This comes only when power is joined by some large vision for world-historical transformation. Wallenstein's grand project is a Europe made whole and unified under the concept of religious tolerance. When he cannot lead his own side to accept this cause, he secretly conspires with the enemy to do so. If Wallenstein had asked his army to rebel against the emperor, they would have followed him loyally. But treason was too much for them. Wallenstein's character and ultimate lack of common sense cause his fall. The all-encompassing ideal of universal brotherhood cannot succeed if disengaged from the reality of national and religious particularism.

The definitive biography of Wallenstein, written by Golo Mann, is a massive work of scholarship and a literary work of art. Mann shows Wallenstein as a modern managerial genius: a power-driven, gifted amasser of wealth with no sense of human relationships. At the end of his career, Wallenstein, far from being a grand visionary, is described as sick and delusional, driven by confusion and desperation to do what he did. It seems almost beyond belief, as the historian of the Thirty Years' War C. V. Wedgwood noted, "that in the last six years of his life, he made no attempt to see or speak personally with the Emperor. How could he—how could any man—in such circumstances hope to retain the personal confidence and trust of the man on whom, in the last resort, his position and career depended?"[11]

Wallenstein is transformed by Schiller into a superman who sought the welfare of the German people, world peace and toleration, like Grimmelshausen's Jupiter. In keeping with this interpretation, Schiller's "Ode to Joy," joined to the last movement of Beethoven's Ninth Symphony, would become the anthem of the European Union. But in the character of Wallenstein, Schiller also portrays the crisis of legitimacy of the traditional polity. The once well-ordered system of governance has become confused and crumbling; anonymous new forces are at work and out of control.

Schiller himself is sternly on the side of duty and loyalty and law. Neither the emperor whom Wallenstein serves nor his own troops can understand or accept an alliance with Sweden. Wallenstein falls because he fails to reconcile his absolute, ideal good with the bond of trust that holds society together. He is guilty of not truly standing for the great cause with which he is associated. True only to himself, he betrays himself.

Schiller's *Wallenstein* trilogy warrants more attention by modern statesmen. Schiller touches something that surely was in the real Wallenstein, beyond Golo Mann's conclusion that his conduct near the end was merely a matter of age and ill health. Schiller locates a quality common to many great commanders and statesmen: their motives are mixed, their characters ambiguous, and their drives possibly abnormal. In the end their achievements may be inexplicable. Wallenstein, in Schiller's hands, rivals Goethe's Faust as *the* emblematic figure of the start of the modern era.[12]

After seven years and two sets of negotiations, the Treaty of Westphalia was signed on October 24, 1648, on the thirty-year anniversary of the Defenestration of Prague. For a believer in the Great Dates of History, 1648 marks the founding of the modern world order, the year in which the traditional concept of peace as a universal phenomenon in God's keeping was replaced by the idea of peace as a relationship between states.[13] The key was a change in the idea of war. Religion had been the center of the struggle to manage world affairs and so produced ever bloodier wars of religion until the Thirty Years' War provoked what would be called "The Great Separation" of political and theological thought, institutionalized by the negotiators at Westphalia as the need to keep religion out of international politics. According to the Victorian historian Lecky, it worked: "Wars that were once regarded as simple duties became absolutely impossible. Alliances that were once deemed atrocious sins became habitual and unchallenged. That which had long been the centre around which all other interests revolved, receded and disappeared, and a profound change in the actions of mankind indicated a profound change in their belief."[14] This would largely hold true until the late twentieth century. Adolf Hitler admired Wallenstein's ambition to pursue a statecraft beyond German borders. Hitler would not be a *Grenzpolitiker,* he said, but a *Raumpolitiker:* he would wage war not merely to regain lost German lands but to acquire vast territories beyond. And would, he declared, impose his peace at Münster in Westphalia—to mark the end of the international state system created in 1648.[15]

Günter Grass's novel *The Meeting at Telgte* is set in 1647 in Westphalia. Telgte was a village between Osnabrück, a Protestant town where Holy Roman Empire envoys negotiated with Swedish state representatives, and Münster, thirty miles away, where talks between Catholic Hapsburg and Catholic France were under way. Emissaries rode back and forth between the two towns, a separation necessary because the papacy would not recognize the legitimacy of this new thing, the modern state.

Grass depicts the poets and writers of German literature assembled near this great political event, some under their own names, others lightly disguised. Grass connected the Germany of 1647, savaged by war and split between antagonistic Protestants and Catholics, with Germany in 1947 after Hitler's war, divided between the democratic west and the communist east. Like Grimmelshausen's 1647 group, meeting one hundred years after Martin Luther's translation of the Bible provided a powerful vernacular standard, the writers of 1947's *Gruppe* 47 convene to consider the state of language, which has been abused and distorted by war and social fragmentation.

At the center of the novel is Christoffel Gelnhausen, alias Hans Jakob von Grimmelshausen, author of *Simplicissimus.*[16] Gelnhausen is a composite of the author and his character. Grass identifies himself with both, and with the entire literary company, each one with his local dialect: "Though he had been living and teaching mathematics in Danish Zeeland ever since Wallenstein's invasion of Pomerania, Laurenberg expressed himself in his native Rostock brogue. . . . And into the predominantly Silesian conversation, Moscherosch mixed his Alemmanic, Harsdörfer his peppery Franconian, Büchner and Gerhardt, their Saxon, Grefliner his lower Bavarian gargle, and Dach kneaded and shaped between Memel and Pregel."

They talk of the terror brought by war: children butchered, robbers behind every bush. As the peace talks proceed, the consequences of the conflict are visible all around. "On the outskirts of Telgte, corpses, swollen and putrescent, float down the River Ems, sometimes coupled together in grotesque parody of the love-making of the poets with the maid in the hay loft."

Over the course of the Thirty Years' War, "Everything had been laid waste, words alone kept their luster. And where princes had disgraced themselves, poets had earned respect. They, not the powerful, were assured of immortality."

In a scene reminiscent of *Simplicissimus,* the conference ends in a farcical uproar. The poets have pompously readied a petition to be handed to the negotiating diplomats and captains. Just when a literary man's voice "soared to incorporate the assembled poets into eternity, cutting into his sentence about immortal poesy (during which he lifted up the rolled appeal for peace and likewise dedicated it to immortality)," someone shouts "Fire!" and the tavern goes up in flames. The petition is destroyed, but none of the poets have been harmed. All want only to go home, never to assemble again at Telgte or anywhere else. Grass is saying here that a poet's importance for world affairs comes through literature, not petitions.

Grass's novel links the cause of language and literature to the conduct of high politics, war and peace. In 1947 the polluted language of Nazi Germany still resonated, and the Orwellian newspeak of Stalinism was making civilized discourse impossible. Language renewal was a precondition to the renewal of international comity. The poets' gathering to reconstitute the language in the aftermath of upheaval is a step in the affairs of state as old and as important as "the rectification of names" in Confucius's *Analects.*

Günter Grass drew pictures for the jackets of his books. For *The Meeting at Telgte,* a hand, holding a quill pen, rises out of rubble. The hundred years after 1648 would reveal a struggle to find a language able to comprehend immense international change.

4

WHAT KIND OF STATE?

Thinkers and writers in England in the seventeenth and early eighteenth centuries provided a rich array of substantive concepts for what was taking shape as an international state system: the idea of "the social contract" as the foundation of state governance and a way to tame power, the beginning of the end of the "divine right" to rule, the idea of religious freedom, the importance of "grand strategy," and inquiry into the positive and negative attributes of a variety of kinds of governance within a state.

When Daniel Defoe's fictional cavalier left the German battlefields of the Thirty Years' War in 1632, he returned to England to serve with Royalist forces against the Puritan Revolution, England's version of Europe's religious strife. Parliament demanded popular sovereignty and limitations on the monarchy, whose legitimacy by divine right had long been questioned. Differing visions of England's state religion were contesting as new ideas about tolerance were emerging, weakening the old link between religion and politics. Defoe's cavalier would fight in this English Civil War until his surrender with King Charles's troops in 1645. He was a mercenary in the lineage of Xenophon. On the Continent, he fought against old established order; back in England, he served with the old against the new. Not religion but politics and personal gain guided him and in this, knowingly or not, he was on the side of the future.

The state needed a theory and Thomas Hobbes would provide it. Born in the year of the Spanish Armada, Hobbes called himself a twin brother to fear. Immersed in a world of seemingly perpetual war, Hobbes made his first great project a translation of Thucydides' *Peloponnesian War,* presenting history in literary form. The Thirty Years' War and rising English Civil War affected Hobbes deeply. From his reading of Thucydides, and the war between Athens and Sparta that ravished Greece from 431 to 404 B.C., Hobbes would find answers to questions about the form and purpose of the state which would influence all subsequent international thought under the rubric of *realism,* and become a leading doctrine of modern statecraft.

Hobbes's theory of the state derived less from revelation or reason than from his sense of human psychological drives and passions.[1] To Hobbes, a person's regard for safety and well-being come first, and generate a constant striving for power and rank as protection from a dangerous world. Monarchy imposes order on the human maelstrom. The most chaotic form of polity, and thus the worst, is democracy. Thucydides' narrative makes clear his admiration for Pericles, the leader of democratic Athens.

But Athenian democracy was "direct," designed for swift decisions, not deliberation. In this context, Thucydides invites us to conclude that Pericles' missteps in statecraft, and a plague that suddenly devastates Athens, cause civil order to break down. The consequence is "The Stasis at Corcyra." The story powerfully affected Hobbes, and his translation of "The Stasis" has been called a "persuasion narrative." People rush about, each trying to persuade the others and no one able to do so. Words lose their meaning.

> The received value of names imposed for signification of things was changed into arbitrary. For inconsiderate boldness was counted true-hearted manliness; provident deliberation, a handsome fear; modesty, the cloak of cowardice; to be wise in everything, to be lazy in everything. A furious suddenness was reputed a point of valour. To re-advise for the better security was held for a fair pretext of tergiversation. He that was fierce was always trusty, and he that contraried such a one was suspected. He that did insidiate, if it took, was a wise man; but he that could smell out a trap laid, a more dangerous man

than he. But he that had been so provident as to need to do the one or the other was said to be a dissolver of society and one that stood in fear of his adversary. In brief, he that could outstrip another in the doing of an evil act or that could persuade another thereto that never meant it was commended.[2]

Hobbes's great work of political theory is *Leviathan,* published in 1651, three years after the Treaty of Westphalia concluded the Thirty Years' War. Deeply informed by the stasis at Corcyra, it outlines Hobbes's theory of the social contract, under which citizens confronted by the horrors and chaos of "a war of all against all" voluntarily give up their rights to a sovereign who is then bound to use his monopoly on the use of force to protect the people from violent death.

With religion supposedly excluded from the affairs of state, the doctrine of *cuius regio eius religio* took hold, elaborated upon by Hobbes in *Leviathan;* it was now up to the prince—the ruler of a state—to decide what religion(s) would be recognized within state borders. Religion was thereby recognized and respected, but in diplomatic practice, tamed.

The frontispiece of *Leviathan* is "not merely an accompaniment to the work, but an essential component. . . . It constitutes one of the most profound visual renderings of political theory ever produced."[3] A giant kingly figure looms over a broad landscape of villages and towns scattered among rolling hills. In one hand he holds the sword of state power; in the other hand a bishop's crozier signifying the authority of religion. This is Sovereign Power; above his crowned head is the line "no power on earth can compare." His body is made up of masses of people, the "body politic," who have given their rights to this sovereign, providing him with the power required to keep them safe—safe from each other. The frontispiece has been closely analyzed for visual clues to Hobbes's thinking. One unexplained image is that of a house, a family dwelling, prominently placed in the lower left of the scene, a house with a view over all the land and its sovereign power. Perhaps it is another reference to marriage, home, and family as the foundation for civilization.

Westphalia legitimized the state as the unit of international order. *Leviathan* provided a political theory to justify and explain the necessity of sovereign state authority.[4] But *Leviathan* deals with legitimacy, authority, and governance within the state, not between states, which in Hobbes's

Figure 3. The frontispiece of the first edition of Hobbes's *Leviathan,* "one of the most profound visual renderings of political theory ever produced." Beinecke Rare Book and Manuscript Library, Yale University, reprinted by permission

view remained in a state of nature: "Concerning the offices of one sovereign to another, which are comprehended in that law which is commonly called the law of nations, I need not say anything in this place, because the law of nations and the law of nature is the same thing. And every sovereign hath the same right, in procuring the safety of his people, that any particular man can have, in procuring the safety of his own body."

In other words, it's a jungle out there. Fear is the rule. The only way to save your skin in the international "state of nature" is to grab as much power as you can. Hobbes is the anti-Grotius; there is no "international community." "These are days of shaking . . . and this shaking is universal: the Palatinate, Bohemia, Germany, Catalonia, Portugal, Ireland, England," commented a member of the English House of Parliament, and he might have added to the list Scotland, Holland, Sweden, Italy, France, the Ukraine, Muscovy, and the Ottoman Empire—the whole world seemed beset by violence and of a very new kind, for cannon and artillery had just been successfully employed in the field for the first time.

Contemporaries of Hobbes, the poets Marvell and Milton provided a meta-historical interpretation of world affairs. Like Shakespeare, they located the origins of governing legitimacy in Troy's fall in the East and its transfer westward. As the Thirty Years' War on the Continent shaded into the Puritan English Revolution, Defoe's cavalier reported that in 1642 "we first began to hear of one Oliver Cromwell who like a little Cloud, rose out of the East, and spread first into the North, till it shed down Flood that overwhelmed the three kingdoms. . . . Thus, this Firebrand of War began to blaze, and he soon grew a Terror to the North, for Victory attended him like a Page of Honour, and he was scarce ever known to be beaten, during the whole War." The European War ended in 1648. England's king Charles was beheaded in 1649 by a Puritan Commonwealth under Cromwell as "Lord Protector." As sovereign, Cromwell brought Hobbes's *Leviathan* to life.

Marvell's "An Horatian Ode upon Cromwell's Return from Ireland" was written in 1650. Marvell had a feel for statecraft and served, along with Milton, as an aide in Cromwell's revolutionary regime. The "Horatian Ode" puts a Roman coloration on events: the art of war is prior to the arts of civilization: "Let the forum give way to the camp, leisure to affairs of war, the pen to the sword."[5]

> 'Tis time to leave the Books in dust,
> And oyl th'unused Armour's rust;
> Removing from the Wall
> The Corslet of the Hall.

Marvell surely did not have Wallenstein in mind, but his Cromwell resembles him, rising to power as a result of military organizational skills, fate, and free will. Both an "instrument of fate"[6] and a strong individual, the leader imposes his will on history:

> But through adventurous War
> Urged his active Star.

Horace invented "the poem of state" as future centuries would come to know it.[7] His *Actium Ode* (1: 37) is about the world-transforming battle off the northwest coast of Greece in 31 B.C. in which Rome triumphed over the East, enabling Octavian to become Augustus, emperor of the first world-spanning empire. With the battle over, the call is to drink and dance in the antique Roman style, to celebrate the defeat of the "mad queen" Cleopatra and the end of her attempt to subdue the power of Rome. With her fleet virtually destroyed, her vast ambition becomes deranged fear as her flagship flees the pursuing Octavian.

But the voice of the Roman crowd that at first calls out in triumph and demands vengeance soon sounds drunk and demented. The images of the naval pursuit across the Mediterranean are jumbled in sound and sense. The fleeing Cleopatra is likened to a gentle dove or a startled hare, yet she is also a "monster" to be put in chains. The poetically precise Horace would never mix metaphors without a reason: to depict the swinish behavior of those who are denouncing Cleopatra, the loutish Roman mob. Horace mocks and despises them.

Then the poem's tone shifts, and it is Horace's voice that we hear. The crazed queen panicking in the sea battle and put to flight is now spoken of with respectful awe:

> she looked
> for a nobler death. She did not have a woman's fear
> of the sword, nor did she make
> for secret shores with her swift fleet.

Cleopatra's demeanor is noble and her spirit great-souled, as she grasps the deadly asp, determined to kill herself to deprive Rome of its triumph.

> as though
> she did not wish to cease to be a queen, taken to Rome
> on the galleys of savage Liburnians
> to be a humble woman in a proud triumph.

As Octavian's great victory crushes the wicked, luxurious East, carrying Rome to unparalleled heights of imperial power, the manly victory has dissolved into the brutish, drunken howls of the mob. Suddenly the despised Egyptian queen, faced with disgrace, transforms herself into a paragon of early Roman virtue.[8]

In his own "Horatian" ode, whose subject is meant to rival that of Horace's Battle of Actium, Marvell aims to instruct the statecraft of the ages. Cromwell, like Octavian, is a Caesar whose head is framed in a divine flame ("And Caesar's head at last / Did through his laurels blast") but dedicated to a different outcome. The "ancient rights," the divine right of kings claimed by Charles I, stretched back to the Battle of Actium and the first world imperium it created.

Marvell describes Cromwell modestly cultivating his country house gardens where:

> He lived reserved and austere,
> As if his highest plot
> To plant the bergamot.

"Much to the man is due," says Marvell, because Cromwell valorously rises

> To ruin the great work of Time
> And cast the kingdoms old
> Into another mold.

These wars of the seventeenth century have reversed history's direction; Cromwell has ruined the "great work of Time," the lineage of kingly rule ranging back to Actium. His bloody revolution overturns and replaces it with an entirely different order. Cromwell acted, Marvell suggests, with Machiavellian swiftness to strike a blow of clarifying violence.

> Though Justice against Fate complain,
> And plead the ancient rights in vain,
> [But those do hold or break,
> As men are strong or weak.]

With this bracketed aside to the reader, Marvell marks the end of the *translatio imperii,* the age of empire, which began at Actium, and the beginning of Cromwell's modern republican form of political order.[9]

King Charles then places his head on the executioner's block:

> He nothing common did or mean
> Upon that memorable scene.

Monarchy's death enables the rebirth of the state. Marvell alludes to the bloody head found at the start of the building of Rome:

> A bleeding head, where they begun,
> Did fright the architects to run;
> And yet in that the state,
> Foresaw its happy fate.

With the transference of power to Cromwell's new republic, it is as if decadent imperial Rome had turned back into the virtuous Roman Republic of old.

Marvell composed his Horatian ode at the peak moment of Cromwell's glory. Having signed the death warrant of King Charles in 1649 and taken command of the Roundhead expedition to subdue the Irish, Cromwell's next task was to tame the Scots in the name of liberty of conscience, supposedly freeing them from the tyranny of church hierarchy. Cromwell's most famous line was delivered to Scottish ministers just before the Battle of Dunbar:[10]

> Is it therefore infallibly agreeable to the Word of God all that you say? *I beseech you in the bowels of Christ think it possible that you may be mistaken.*[11]

Cromwell's impassioned plea for honesty rather than deceitful rhetoric comes straight from the Puritan sermon, with its meld of godly authority, politics, and popular entertainment. To Marvell, Cromwell's style was marked by "that powerful language" of preaching. To others, his speech seemed graceless and ambiguous. Cromwell's best biographer noted that

> as an orator, Cromwell ranks amongst those speakers one would like to have heard to have got the full flavor of his style. . . . Certainly his actual words, at times, superbly vivid and direct, are not enough to account for the profound impression he made on his hearers. Force, not to say vehemence, was clearly one paramount quality he possessed from the early days. . . . He also did not lack that form of self-induced emotional drive, the prerogative of some speakers, which it is perhaps not too fanciful to link with his inherited Welsh blood. The Venetian ambassador, trying to sum up this particular rolling fervour dispassionately, described him more like a preacher than a statesman. At times, this produced tears in his own eyes, at times in the eyes of his enthusiastic audience: and at times it produced the snarl of "hypocrite" on the lips of his enemies.[12]

Many of his hearers thought him rambling, obscure, ambiguous, and needlessly complex. In an otherwise powerful and effective orator, this is often a deliberate tactic of statecraft, observable in speeches from Queen Elizabeth I to President Dwight D. Eisenhower.

Cromwell made England a great power. His Puritan sense of election, of predestined greatness, helped to form the modern British state.[13] Cromwell wholly believed in the cause of liberty of conscience, and it is in America that his legacy seems most fully influential.

Cromwell had America on his mind. In a late speech reflecting on the causes of the war, he said:

> Religion was not the first thing contested for, but God brought it to that issue at last; and gave it unto us by war of redundancy; and at last it proved that which was most dear to us. And wherein consisted this more than in obtaining that liberty from the tyranny of the bishops to all species of Protestants to worship God according to their own light and consciences, for want of which many of our brethren forsook their native countries to seek their bread from strangers and to live in howling wildernesses.[14]

Cromwell had at one point considered joining the Puritan settlements in the American "howling wilderness" himself. Cromwell's commonwealth wrought great change, but did not survive his death. Monarchy was restored in 1660 in the person of King Charles II.

Some years ago at Yale, I wandered through a nearly deserted building that once had been the "tomb" of the secret society called Wolf's Head. A marvelous New Amsterdam Dutch-gabled stone structure, it had been given up by the society in favor of larger quarters. On the dust-covered top floor, in what surely had been the chapter room, I found, face down, the old engraving by Houbraken of Oliver Cromwell, showing him in profile, "warts and all." At the bottom was a sketched depiction of Cromwell's refusal, like Caesar's, of the crown of kingship. The three judges—Whalley, Goffe, and Dixwell—who had sentenced Charles I to death had to flee for their lives to New England, where they hid for a time in a cave on West Rock at New Haven. They are remembered in the names of three streets, Whalley, Goffe, and Dixwell, that meet next to Yale's Payne Whitney Gymnasium—and by a motel near West Rock called The Three Judges. Here, again, is the mark of the *translatio imperii,* as world power moves from east to west, from the Mediterranean to Europe to Britain to America . . .

John Milton also had to flee, but not overseas. His books were burned but he survived.[15] Milton wrote an ode to Cromwell praising him as "our chief of men." Cromwell's personal motto was *Pax Quaeritur Bello,* let peace be sought through war. Milton's ode contained the to-be-famous line:

> Peace hath her victories
> No less renown'd than war.

Milton's *Ode,* unlike Marvell's exaltation of Cromwell's transforming role in world history, is more like an action memo or petition. Like Marvell, Milton knew how statecraft was practiced. He had been made Cromwell's "Secretary for Foreign Tongues," engaged to draft messages of state from the new English republic to the governments of Europe—a foreign policy job, in other words, through which Milton had a bird's-eye view of the workings of Cromwell's republic. From this perch he would develop quite a feel for "Grand Strategy." His poetic lines "abound with courtiers, generals, diplomats, dictators, counselors, and kings, all engaged in debate, negotiation, ceremony, conquest, and the play of political power, mirroring the actions of figures he encountered, either through correspondence, or within council chambers, during his decade of service."[16]

Milton urges Cromwell to permit nonorthodox religious teaching, at a time when Puritan ministers seemed poised to suppress religious freedom just as their own religious freedom had been suppressed:

> new foes arise
> Threatening to bind our souls with secular chains:
> To help us to save free conscience from the paw
> Of hireling wolves, whose gospel is their maw.

The poem builds upon the Westphalian conclusion: keep religion out of affairs of state. In *Paradise Lost,* Milton may even be saying that God, once His plan is achieved, will abdicate as Cromwell gives up the kingship, as there will be no more need for hierarchical authority:

> Then thou thy regal scepter shalt lay by,
> For regal scepter then no more shall need,
> God shall be all in all.

Satan, in *Paradise Lost,* describes Cromwell as a revolutionary against divine rule and the founder of parliamentary government. In Satan some see Charles I. But far beyond the politics of the day *Paradise Lost* is Milton's comprehensive commentary on modern warfare, revolution, founding a polity; on strategy, leadership, intelligence, individual choice under conditions of modern statecraft; and on the justification of God's ways to men. Milton survived Cromwell's fall and, under general amnesty, was able to live quietly for the rest of his life, and write, largely through dictation in his growing blindness.

Epic poems often begin *in medias res,* in the middle of things, and *Paradise Lost* is no exception. The *Iliad* begins in the tenth year of the Trojan War. Accordingly we too may begin not with Milton's book 1 but with book 5, because that is where the story really starts, with God.

God summons the angels to hear his decree that his "begotten" Son will henceforth be elevated to be the head of the entire angelic population: "to him shall bow / All knees in Heav'n, and shall confess him Lord." Milton does not tell us why God does this, not directly.

God, as many have noted, is depicted by Milton in language that is flat, blunt, and with little emotion other than testiness and ire. He is omnipotent and omniscient—pure power. (William Empson said that Milton's God reminded him of Stalin.) God is also invisible. There is no nuance, no self-reflection in this God. We may suppose that God begets and elevates the

Son in order to have a visible expression of himself and to create a dimension of passion, love, and feeling that God himself lacks. Perhaps the Son can help the Father learn what it is *not* to be omnipotent, *not* to be omniscient. God's creation of this "other" is thus a monumental act of consciousness.

Satan will not accept this. He is jealous; he feels demoted; his pride will not stand for this insult. He gathers an angelic band under the pretext of consulting about how to receive their new leader, and proceeds to rouse them to rebellion. Satan displays what Hobbes sees, in *Leviathan,* to be the core of brute human nature: "perpetual and restless desire of power after power." What God has done, Satan suggests, is to violate a principle of Heaven itself, a transgression as overarching as flouting the doctrine of the equality of states under international law.

Though the residents of Heaven are not equal in power to God, Satan says, they nonetheless possess a form of sovereign equality (again, the equality of states doctrine), and God has violated this fundamental right. Moreover, Satan declaims, we angels begat ourselves; our power is our own. Do we remember God making us? No! "We know no time when we were not as now." With its single-syllable drumbeat of self-regard, it is an amazing sentence. Satan's rhetoric persuades one-third of the Heavenly Host to follow him in launching a rebellion in Heaven.

The foundations of two opposing grand strategies now seem to be in place: God's expansiveness, aimed at self-reflection, assessment, and rectification; Satan's antagonistic defiance and self-regard. One aims at tempering power, the other at regaining, accumulating, and aggrandizing power.

THE WAR IN HEAVEN

War, of course, is the great and essential subject for an epic poem, as in the *Iliad* and the *Aeneid.* In Milton's epic, war is the subject of book 6, placed exactly at the center of the text, but Milton's view of war is not that of his Greek and Roman predecessors. Early in book 6 we learn that God has ordered his defense force of "armed Saints" to be equal in number to Satan's rebel army; that is, one-third versus one-third, a fair fight. The remaining third of the Heavenly Host will not be called to do battle. Satan has mounted the strongest force possible, but God has made a policy decision to fight a limited war. "Limited war" is a concept well known in our time, and widely disparaged.

Why have limited wars been fought in our time? Three reasons: 1) because one side is too powerful, so to employ that power in full would be immorally devastating (thus, for example, the eschewal of nuclear weapons); 2) because the use of full power might escalate the war by drawing other parties into the conflict; and 3) because an "excessive" use of force might cause a loss of political support on one's own side.

God's reasons for choosing to fight a limited war against Satan in *Paradise Lost* can only be guessed at. Let us speculate that to use his full power would prevent him from making the point he wanted to make. So what *is* that point? Evidently, God is not dedicated to omnipotence in the Hobbesian sense.

Carl von Clausewitz addressed the question of limited and absolute war in *On War.* The limited war, he said, is a war of "observation," and the absolute war is a war of "decision," to eliminate your opponent's independence. Although Clausewitz argues that it takes two to fight a limited war (if your opponent goes all-out, you must be prepared to escalate), this is not the case with Milton's war in Heaven. Satan exerts his forces to the utmost, but God does not—and need not—because in the end Satan could never prevail. This raises the question of God's motives. The poem suggests that God has it in mind to create a new race of beings apart from the angels— beings with free will. Only when Satan's rebellion depopulates Heaven does God decide to use the new race to replace the fallen angels. Thus God does not want to do away with Satan and his rebel horde, for they are useful to him. They will provide the human race with a choice between good and evil. True virtue is that which is tested and withstands temptation.

The first day of the battle is fought in Iliadic epic style. The angel Abdiel smites Satan on his "proud crest." The archangel Michael, captain of the righteous army, engages Satan in single combat and wounds him grievously. Satan's comrades-in-arms carry him off the battlefield on their shields. Gabriel then contends with Moloch, and Abdiel takes on three of Satan's warrior-angels. God's forces win the day, but not the war, and a truce is called for the night. In the *Iliad,* battles always end at nightfall.

The second day is anything but Iliadic. Modern warfare arrives. Satan becomes a mining engineer, a metallurgical scientist, and an arms manufacturer. The earth is ripped apart to produce weapons of mass destruction. Satan's artillery barrages devastate the forces of God. Mechanization takes command.[17] The righteous angels flee to the mountains, where they tear up great hills of earth and fling them back at the Satanic troops. Fighting by throwing mountains was a recognized tactic in Greek mythology. Here, classic warfare does battle with modern warfare. "And now all Heav'n/Had gone to wrack, with ruin overspread."

For the third day, God places his son in command of the loyal angels. Here, certainly, is God's point in having limited the war thus far. The Son puts on not the armor of the classical warrior but the whole armor of God.[18]

> And into terror change
> His count'nance, too severe to be beheld
> And full of wrath bent on his enemies.

Christ is the fighting commander of an armored tank column—his fierce chariot rolls through the ranks of the enemy. He carries no ordinary weapons but

> Full soon
> Among them he arrived, in his right hand
> Grasping ten thousand thunders

fired like rockets or missiles. Satan's army is routed.

Yet here, too, the Son fights a limited war.

> Yet half his strength he put not forth, but checked
> His thunder in mid-volley, for he meant
> Not to destroy, but root them out of Heav'n.

The devils are pursued right to the wall of Heaven, which opens up, and they fall. "Nine days they fell. . . . Hell at last / Yawning received them whole, and on them closed."

God's strategy has worked—so far. How should we sum it up?

Omnipotent God somehow recognizes that the possession and exercise of total power brings with it a certain incomprehension about the reality of existence. An omnipotent being cannot understand the lives of those lacking such power. He therefore begets a Son who will come to experience real life. God decrees that the Son will be head above all the angels, but the Son will not exercise total power in that role. Nonetheless, the decree ignites a rebellion against God. In putting down this uprising, God limits his reactions. The result is inconclusive at first. Then the enemy, desperate to avoid defeat, ingeniously invents hideous new forms of destruction.

For God to intervene in a plenipotentiary way would be to abandon his original insight and plan. Instead he employs his Son, again in a limited way, to achieve a victory but not to annihilate his adversary.

But God's Heavenly Kingdom is left in a severely depleted condition. One-third of his commonwealth has been cast into exile. A new dimension and direction for God's strategy are necessary.

SATAN REGROUPS HIS FALLEN HORDE

Here we come to the point where Milton starts his *Paradise Lost*—*in medias res.* Having been "Hurled headlong flaming from the ethereal sky," Satan, "with his horrid crew / Lay vanquished, rolling in the fiery gulf." By his side, next to him in power and next in crime, is Beelzebub (the Lord of the Flies). Satan says he was deceived. "Who knew?" he says, "who knew / The force of these dire arms?" Somehow, when he was in Heaven, Satan lacked the perception, or an intelligence service that might have informed him, of just how strong God and his Son were. Had he been so informed, he would not have attempted to wage a revolutionary war against God's forces. So Satan realizes that he must reconsider his strategy. The question is whether "to wage by force or guile eternal war." (One might recall the debate which supposedly took place between Achilles and Odysseus at Troy over whether to try to take the city by force or by guile.)

Milton then describes Satan in unforgettable terms. He is gigantic, floating in the sea of flames. He is as huge as the sea-beast Leviathan, of such monstrous size that sailors might anchor at his side, mistakenly thinking they had come to a safe port for the night. Surely Milton here is referring to Hobbes's *Leviathan.* Those who follow Hobbes's advice to yield their rights to an all-powerful sovereign may awake to find themselves oppressed by a tyrannous regime of immense proportions.

As Satan calls his legions together, Milton describes him in an image that mingles classical and biblical references as well as modern science, which probably comes from Milton's experience of looking through telescopes during a visit to Galileo years earlier.[19] Satan carries an immense and ponderous shield, reminiscent of those of Achilles and Aeneas. But Satan carries his shield on his back, behind him, where it hangs "on his shoulders like the moon, whose orb / Through optic glass the Tuscan artist [Galileo] views." In other words, the shield is either gigantic or, as seen through a telescope, as small as the nail on your little finger. Similarly, Satan's spear is as tall as the mainmast of an admiral's flagship, or as small as a slender "wand."

When we first see Satan's legions, Milton describes them—in an image that can be traced from Homer to Virgil to Dante—as leaves. Here they lay "thick as autumnal leaves that strow the brooks / In Vallombrosa," a wooded region south of Florence that Milton saw on his Italian journey. Suddenly, they are no longer leaves but the corpses of Pharoah's army floating amid the wreckage of their chariots, crushed when the waters of the Red Sea, which had parted for the exodus of the Israelites, closed upon them.[20]

What does this mean?

That those who follow the ways of war as hailed in ancient epics are doomed. That from our modern perspective, what is great or small is a product of one's mind: "The mind is its own place, and in itself / Can make a Heav'n of Hell, a Hell of Heav'n."

And that the search for freedom, like the wanderings of the Chosen People on the way to the Promised Land, is the way of the righteous.

Now Satan reveals that he and his horde *are* those who followed the ways of war as hailed in ancient epics. At the end of book 1, in the manner of the great catalogue of names in Homer, we get roll calls of the leaders of the band of fallen angels now clustered around their potentate. The references make it clear that in the history of the world yet to come, these—under new names—will become the pagan gods of antiquity. Here in Hell, they are a disciplined fighting force in the style of the warriors of ancient myth and epic:

> and now
> Advanced in view that stand . . . in guise
> Of warriors old, with ordered spear and shield
> Awaiting what command their mighty Chief
> Had to impose.

Satan is a classic war leader of the epic kind. He holds court from his royal throne. He is rhetorically eloquent. He rallies and inspires his men at times when all seems lost. He embodies the heroic ideal: finding meaningful life by fighting for glory and pride. "War, then war" is the cause they adopt. Pandemonium is built. An opulent orientalized structure, it is part temple and part palace—an architectural combination of church and state. The two, if not separated, will be an abomination, the seat of an odious dictatorship. The structure includes a hall of parliamentary assembly (though no true parliament could exist under such tyrannous conditions).

At the end of book 1, the legions of the fallen angels are described as a swarm of angry bees. They have been reduced in size in order that they may fit into the council chamber. Here, "After short silence then / And summons read, the great consult began."

THE SPEECHES IN PANDEMONIUM

In this monstrous building, both parliament and palace, "high on a throne of royal state," Satan presides over the great debate on what policy to adopt. "By what best way," Satan says, "Whether of open war or covert guile, / We now debate: who can advise, may speak."

First to speak is Moloch, the strongest and the fiercest spirit who straightforwardly calls for open war against God:

> We feel
> Our power sufficient to disturb his heav'n
> And with perpetual inroads to alarm,
> Though inaccessible, his fatal throne:
> Which if not victory is yet revenge.

Next comes Belial, who represents the power of rhetoric. Even before he speaks, he charms by his appearance.

> Up rose
> Belial, in act more graceful and humane;
> A fairer person lost not heav'n; he seem'd
> For dignity compos'd and high exploit:
> But all was false and hollow; though his Tongue
> Dropt Manna, and could make the worse appear
> The better reason, to perplex and dash
> Maturest counsels: for his thoughts were low . . .
> 　　　　　yet he pleas'd the ear.
> And with persuasive accent thus began.

Avoid open war, he says, and cause no more offense. Make the best of our situation and over time God may relent. Thus, says Milton,

Belial with words cloth'd in reason's garb
Counsell'd ignoble ease and peaceful sloth.

Mammon then rises to address the assembly. He offers a proactive version of Belial's proposed option: adapt to the conditions of Hell; seek to prosper, improve, grow in strength until our realm can become a rival to God's. To thrive under evil is perfectly possible. Mammon's proposal meets with a burst of applause; the chamber seems about to endorse Mammon's position.

At this point, Henry Kissinger's remarks on "The Option C Memorandum" phenomenon seem pertinent. Option A: launch a destructive but hopeless war. Option B: do nothing. Option C: work to improve the situation.

Beelzebub, Satan's right-hand man, intervenes. He must speak quickly, for Mammon is about to win the debate. Beelzebub has the look of a great statesman. His listeners are awed. He has "command presence":

> With grave
> Aspect he rose, and in his rising assumed
> A pillar of state; deep on his front engraven
> Deliberation sat and public care;
> And princely counsel in his face yet shone,
> Majestic though in ruin: sage he stood
> With Atlantean shoulders fit to bear
> The weight of mightiest monarchies; his look
> Drew audience and attention still as night
> Or summer's noontide air, while thus he spake.

There is another way, Beelzebub says, an easier way. Another world exists, peopled by a new race called Man, just now being created. God has done this to produce creatures qualified to repopulate heaven, so depleted by the fall of Satan and his forces. Let us then, Beelzebub says, study who these people are and learn how best to subvert them, and

> If not drive,
> Seduce them to our party, that their God
> May prove their foe, and with repenting hand
> Abolish his own works.

The assembly, delighted by this plan to ruin God's plan, votes its full approval.

Beelzebub, of course, has merely elaborated upon the plan obliquely put forth earlier by Satan (1: 650–656). On Satan's part the debate in Pandemonium is a sham. Satan already has received an intelligence report that God was planning this new world scheme but has held this information back, waiting to see what emerges from his counselors' statements. Only when Mammon's words are about to sway the assembly in the undesired direction does Satan direct Beelzebub to release the news.

God's grand strategy is now becoming clear. Being omniscient and prescient, God had known Satan's rebellion was coming, and that one of every three angels among the Heavenly Host would defect.[21] He therefore formed his counterplan, which now has been put into action. A man and a woman have been created: Adam and Eve. They dwell in a newly created world, a paradise, the Garden of Eden. They will be fruitful and multiply, and their offspring, across the generations, will provide the masses of saints needed by God to repopulate his depleted realm.

Satan has a large objective: to defeat God's grand strategy by seducing and subverting this new race of mankind. He also has contrived the means of doing so: sin and death. What Satan lacks at this point is a way to relate the means to the end. In order to design this relationship he will first have to send a reconnaissance patrol to spy out this newly created world. Heroically, he himself will carry out this mission. When Satan volunteers for this hazardous duty, he is, in fact, an actor taking his cue from Beelzebub in a scenario that Satan has written for himself. I will go alone, he says, and

> Through all the coasts of dark destruction seek
> Deliverance for us all: this enterprise
> None shall partake with me.

So saying, he makes his dramatic departure. He has realized that when he was in Heaven, his intelligence capabilities were inadequate ("Who knew?"). This time he will gather more data before he commits his forces.

While Satan is out on his mission, his devilish followers engage in games modeled on those staged by Achilles and Aeneas in the *Iliad* and the *Aeneid:* funeral games in honor of the dead. Here they honor not merely the dead but "Death" itself. Death is the key to Satan's grand strategy. Here Milton takes us into allegory, the only way in which concepts that are ultimately beyond human comprehension can be represented to the common mind.

Satan

> Puts on swift wings, and towards the gates of Hell
> Explores his solitary flight; sometimes
> He scours the right hand coast, sometimes the left,
> Now shaves with level wing the deep, then soars
> Up to the fiery concave tow'ring high.

Finally he comes to the gates of Hell, before which sit "on either side a formidable shape." One appears as a woman to the waist; below that "a serpent armed with a mortal sting." This is Sin. The other is of no distinguishable shape: "What seemed his head / The likeness of a kingly crown had on." This is Death, whose crown symbolizes his rule over us all.

Satan's lust for power by way of rebellion impregnates Sin, who gives birth to Death. Satan offers Sin and Death a use for their energies; they can prey on the new race of humanity. If only Satan can devise a strategy to make the new pair fall into sin, then the wages of sin will be death, and God's strategy will be defeated.

THE TEMPTATION

Satan at last reaches the edge of the newly created world at the point of the *Primum Mobile,* in a scene that recalls Dante's depiction of the shape and velocity of the universe. Satan sees Jacob's ladder (3: 503–540), with angels going up and down. He encounters the angel Uriel and asks about man. Uriel does not recognize Satan, and thinking him a good, loyal angel, gives him the directions to Paradise. Satan glides down to earth (to the mountain where later he will tempt Christ).

He arrives at Eden. We first see the tree from Satan's point of view. It is "right use" that makes this tree into a "pledge of immortality." Absolute knowledge would preclude virtue. God's prohibition against tasting the fruit of the tree of the knowledge of good and evil makes virtue possible, because only free choice can result in virtue. God, having absolute knowledge, cannot be virtuous; he has made Adam and Eve to instruct him in virtue. "God creates man with the gift of reason to be his own chooser," wrote Milton in his pamphlet *Areopagitica.*

Eden is a pastoral paradise, a Heaven on earth. Spying on Adam and Eve, Satan overhears them speaking of the prohibition against eating from the tree in the midst of the garden on penalty of death. "Whatever death is," says Adam. This is the missing piece of intelligence Satan has been searching for; this will provide the relationship between his means and his end. Satan's task now will be "to excite their minds/With more desire to know" so that they will "taste and die." At this point the key question of whether Satan's strategy should be conducted by force or guile is resolved in favor of guile. Instead of marshaling his hordes for a frontal assault on God's forces, Satan will carry on the war alone, by stealth.

At this point, the pastoral mood of book 4 is replaced by the suspense and tension of a military raid. Satan is no longer the commanding general of a regular army; he is a spy who has penetrated the camp of the enemy. To spy on Eden he has disguised himself, variously, as a cormorant, a lion, and a tiger.

Now, as Satan reconnoiters the garden, Uriel arrives to warn Gabriel, the captain of the angelic guard posted by God to provide security for Eden, that one of the evil angels cast out of Heaven has escaped from Hell and may have slipped through the perimeter. Gabriel posts a guard to watch over the bower of Adam and Eve. There they discover Satan as a toad, whispering in the ear of the sleeping Eve. They touch the toad lightly with their spear, and instantly Satan appears as himself. He has gone from rebel to general to hero to spy to guerrilla to what today we would call "an unlawful combatant." (He is not in uniform; he is not carrying arms openly; he refuses to answer questions; and he lies about his intentions.) God, observing all this, weighs the situation. Should Gabriel and Satan engage in combat or not? The answer is no, and Satan is allowed to flee the scene. The decision is not to finish Satan off.

The temptation resumes in book 9. Satan, now in the form of the serpent, sees that his grand strategic moment of opportunity has arrived; here is his chance to divide and conquer.

God rules Heaven as a monarch. Satan proceeds to establish a rival monarchy in Hell. Adam and Eve both exercise free choice: Eve is beguiled into choosing to disobey God; Adam does so in full knowledge of the consequences. They will have to establish another kind of polity. Satan's grand strategy seems at first to have been successful. God's strategy is thwarted when Eve makes her choice and Adam follows. But Satan does not emerge victorious, because Adam and Eve leave Eden with knowledge of good and evil and with their free will intact.

They leave in the possession of something else—something that, as Milton presents it, passes the understanding even of God: their marriage. The physical and spiritual bond between Adam and Eve is one of the most powerful themes in the poem.

Marriage is the fundamental, prepolitical unit, as Aristotle explained to us. The private bond is the basis of the public good. The marriage of Adam and Eve will be the foundation stone of the republic.

At the end of the poem, Milton looks back at the Israelites on their journey in the wilderness—their exodus to freedom. Israel is the model republic of biblical times. With the English republic gone, the Puritans would conduct their own exodus, their passage to the promised land of New England to lay the foundations for a new republic. At this time the political reality of all Europe, including Britain, was being transformed by the rise of centralized political authority, just as Hobbes would have it. It was just then that the republican American polity took root in New England as a system not of centralized sovereign power but of separation of powers, a republic such as Milton had envisioned.[22]

Milton wrote *Paradise Lost* at a time when overseas exploration and the planting of colonies were in the very air he breathed—enterprises that were wrapped up in religion. English Puritans had embarked upon their "errand into the wilderness." *Paradise Lost* "breathes an Atlantic air" and "plays out in mythic form some of the deepest and most disturbing contradictions in England's experience of the New World."[23]

The link between *Paradise Lost* and America has endlessly intrigued critics: if America had not been discovered, *Paradise Lost* would not have been written. America, the very idea of it, is transgressive, an upsetting, ongoing challenge to the way the Old World understood God's plan. The "logic chain" starts with Dante's *Inferno,* canto 26, when Ulysses sails out beyond the Pillars of Hercules, the limits of the known world, and for his effrontery, perishes with his entire crew. Columbus's voyages conveyed the idea of an earthly paradise; perhaps Saint Augustine was wrong and Joachim of Fiore's "Third Age" of heaven on earth was correct. Montaigne's cannibals and Shakespeare's Calibans present a dark and primitive dimension but perhaps a more authentic one. The discovery of America was disrupting God's plan, so Milton had to begin afresh to "justify the ways of God to Men." All through the poem are references to "this new world," "this rumored creation." Satan, like Ulysses, voyages out beyond God's known creation in order to subvert this new race and ensure that God cannot carry out his strategy to incorporate it. And he succeeds. In *Paradise Lost* the options were A) to refrain from seeking knowledge and obey God, or B) to disobey and go for the fruit of the tree of knowledge. Somewhere in this European sense of what the New World meant to the human condition may be the source of what by now has emerged as centuries of anti-Americanism.[24] But for Milton it may be that the objective of his grand strategy is realized in the United States of America, which is a new Eden, a new man and woman, and a paradise lost—all set in an idea of history as "going someplace."[25]

The peace settlement put forward at Westphalia in 1648 challenged "Empire" as the preeminent form of governance. Increasingly, the state would be recognized as the basic component of what would become the international system of states, eventually adopted in every part of the world. But what *kind* of a state? A state is a form or structure for governance; what would fill the form could vary widely. Jonathan Swift's *Gulliver's Travels,* "one of the longest-range books ever written," involves varieties of state experience.[26]

The "terrible greatness" of *Gulliver's Travels* can be analyzed from almost every intellectual, literary, and psychological angle.[27] Written at a time when the substance that would fill the state form was an open question, Swift's novel reviews the options. This time of opportunity was grasped by the greatest statesman of the post-Westphalian period, Louis XIV, "by far the ablest man born in modern times on the steps of a throne," according to Lord Acton.[28] Louis XIV commandeered the state form and filled it with exaggerated displays of pomp and power associated with the most elaborate imperial imaginings. The Sun King produced a "theatre state" for the purposes of empire.[29]

Jonathan Swift gained a keen sense of statecraft from his patron, Sir William Temple, a great diplomat and the first, Samuel Johnson said, "to give cadence to English prose."[30] Temple had negotiated the triple alliance of England, Sweden, and the Netherlands to check the military and political advances of Louis XIV. After brokering the strategic marriage of William of Orange and Mary of England, Sir William retired to Moor Park, where Swift served as his secretary in the late 1690s and early 1700s.

Travels into Several Remote Nations of the World, by Lemuel Gulliver, starts with the empire of Lilliput. The depiction of Gulliver, a giant in the land of tiny human beings, tied down by a hundred little ropes, has thrived ever after as an image of a big power rendered helpless by a supposedly lesser people. When taken to the capital, Gulliver finds himself a captive in an absolute monarchy, suggesting Louis XIV's court at Versailles. The emperor, like Louis, is protected and coddled within concentric rings of courtiers. Intrigue is rampant in every endeavor. Trivial differences become the basis for ideologically rigid and intolerant factions, such as those who favor opening boiled eggs at the big ends as against the "little-enders." The most elaborate formal procedures fail to guarantee protection against the arbitrary whims of the ruler. Lilliput has a standing army—a sure indication of tyranny in Swift's view—and, like Louis, the emperor of Lilliput has imperial ambitions. Gulliver puts his powers at the service of the monarch, and having captured the fleet of the rival empire Blefuscu, realizes that it is to become a province of Lilliput.

Gulliver soon finds himself enmeshed in court intrigue. The lord high treasurer tells the emperor that Gulliver, in his command of the naval operation against Blefuscu, has nearly bankrupted the realm and should be dismissed. The real reason for this smear is "the Malice of some evil Tongues," who had informed the lord high treasurer that his wife had "a violent Affection" for Gulliver, "and a Court-Scandal ran for some time that she came privately to my Lodging." This Gulliver vehemently denies, defying his accusers "to prove that any Person ever came to me *incognito.*"

But on the next page Gulliver reports that a highly placed person at court "came to my House very privately at Night in a close Chair, and without sending his Name, desired Admittance" to tell Gulliver of another aspect of the cabal against him. So Swift draws our attention to Gulliver's contradiction of his earlier claim. But then we note that he did not, on the first occasion, deny that anyone ever came privately to his quarters; he defied anyone to prove it. We are here in the familiar territory of diplomatic sophistry.

Gulliver's naval victory over Blefuscu has aroused the jealous wrath of the high admiral, who has conspired with the lord high treasurer to destroy Gulliver through gossip and scandal-mongering. Articles of impeachment, treason, and other capital crimes are brought, and Gulliver must flee the jurisdiction. The story, like many in Washington and other world capitals, reveals how seemingly trivial personal indiscretions can destroy careers and shape great events.

Swift depicts the Lilliputians as diminutive humans: petty, trivial, and cruel, grasping and contemptible. By comparison Gulliver, really a dolt, seems quite an admirable fellow. Here, then, is a court like Louis XIV's, a revolting despotism. At the *real* court of Louis XIV, the greatest—certainly the most prolific—memoirist in all literature, the duc de Saint-Simon, recorded the intrigues and strategies of the Sun King. Saint-Simon was akin to Don Quixote, a figure from the chivalric past confronted by a modernizing present. He describes in silken, scathing prose a ruthless new state in the making, yet disguised by the Sun King as an exquisitely sophisticated empire of yore. Louis XIV was hijacking the modern state for the purposes of the divine-right-claiming monarch and his very modern ambitions. As Gulliver perceived, this was not the model for others to follow.

Gulliver's second voyage, to Brobdingnag, is a study of a different governmental form and style. Gulliver's observations of each newly encountered society follow a similar pattern. He studies the ways of each people almost as an anthropologist. Instead of commenting on premodern island tribes, however, Gulliver reports on civilized, sophisticated, and developed polities.

This time, Gulliver is the diminutive one. The Brobdingnagians are towering figures—ten times human size—an indication of their political and social superiority. Unlike the powerful, commercial, empire-seeking kingdom of Lilliput, Brobdingnag is something of a Burkean (before the fact) ideal of an organically rooted commonwealth. A secluded land with an agricultural economy and a Ciceronian mixed constitution (monarchy-aristocracy-democracy all in one), Brobdingnag is guided by a philosopher-king, who may well have been modeled on Swift's patron-preceptor, Sir William Temple.[31]

The philosopher-king, a large part of whose reputation comes from his role in "the quarrel between the ancients and the modern," here presides over a polity that seems based on a veneration for the great works of the past, and which stands in wary opposition to the "modern" ways of thought which Gulliver considers superior. Here the reader begins to realize that Swift is not to be identified with Gulliver and, indeed, that Gulliver's approbation of the politics and governmental structure of a place may be a sign that Swift disapproves of it. Gulliver holds Brobdingnag in disdain, even contempt, so it probably is a society worthy of our admiration.

In Brobdingnag, learning is simple and practical; no theories, abstractions, or conceptualizing goes on. There is a "well-regulated militia" rather than a standing army. The architecture of the capital is quite unlike the Versailles-like palace of Lilliput. It is a homely pile of buildings that has emerged over time from the very roots of the culture of the land. Politics are faction free. The legal system is clear, plain, and functional, not a tool to be manipulated by lawyers. There is a structure of governance, but it is diffused with a moral dimension. The "Sir William" of the land is a member of a genteel, probably hereditary landed gentry. Far from being a "Sun King" of unquestioned perfection, he learns and adjusts as he goes along. The idea of acquiring gunpowder as a weapon for the state fills him with horror, and Europe, as described by Gulliver, he regards as repulsive. This prince is the antithesis to Machiavelli's ideal prince.

Finally, in Brobdingnag we begin to see that Gulliver does not seem able to learn from experience. Those who value the ancients and the great books are learned, admirable, and educated in ways that can elegantly be adapted to the vicissitudes of life. Gulliver, though, as a "modern," is intellectually constricted and unable to learn because he is not in touch with the ancient texts.

Brobdingnag is no utopia. Swift portrays it as above all human, with the flaws and shortcomings that attend the human condition. But it is a good society, one that "muddles through" in the admirable English way when England is governed well.

Apart from the size of its inhabitants, Lilliput and Brobdingnag are plausible alternatives for the governance of a state. Gulliver's next voyage, however, is an encounter with a utopian conception of the ideal modern polity.

Laputa is the thoroughly "modern" creation of Enlightenment science and reason. Citizens of this flying island, up in the clouds far above mundane reality, are lost in abstract concepts of mathematical complexity. Prophetically, this abstract state will, through the use of reason, turn itself into a police state. When every issue is subjected to rational analysis, with no foundational check available because religion and tradition have been suspended, every form of behavior will become codified and regulated. This is a realm of political scientists, experts who ignore the reality of politics in search of "scientific" answers to some trivial or obvious aspect of a problem. The Laputans are caught up with the kind of knowledge that Gulliver tried to force on the Brobdingnagians; abstractions, numbers, reason without either revelation or imagination.

The flying island exercises colonial rule over its estates below, down on earthbound Lagado. In contrast to the "moderns" (here is Sir William Temple's "Battle of the Books" controversy again), Lagado is the home of Lord Minodi, an "ancient" now living in disgrace, who remains a paragon of virtue and good sense. Minodi is a gentleman of ancient virtues who manages his estate as Horace managed his Sabine farm. With Laputa and Lagado, Swift is depicting Enlightenment England with its colonial possessions, the rural squirearchical Ireland—Swift's own land—but the significance for statecraft ranges far beyond such identifications.

In Gulliver's fourth and final voyage, we are immersed in what may be the most famous ancient text of all, Plato's *Republic,* and Gulliver is wholly captivated by it. He visits the most utopian of all polities, the fully reasoned-out commonwealth of justice, the land of the Houyhnhnms (probably pronounced, as the population is equine, "whin-ims," with a neigh). Here, as in the *Republic,* we are presented with an entirely new start to mankind's primary task of figuring out how to establish and manage a political community. Socrates, after the Peloponnesian War leaves the Athenian polis in ruins, leads a dialogue of how to construct, out of nothing, the just society. In *Gulliver's Travels,* we see the animal world having achieved, in a wholly new start, a wholly different political system from the one we actually dwell in.

The Houyhnhnms are horses, and they have achieved the only true republic in Swift's book. They are wholly rational, and their principles of government are clear, simple, and incontrovertible. In stark contrast, in Houyhnhnm-Land also dwell the Yahoos, primitive, bestial brutes. At first Gulliver does not recognize the Yahoos as human beings, but that is what they are. They might be some primitive, brutish tribe such as those encountered by explorers in Swift's time on their voyages. But these Yahoos are Europeans, a people whose bestiality is undisguised in this new setting. So the human beings are the disgusting creatures, and the horses are the superior beings. What we think of as "animals" has been turned upside down. The horses regard Gulliver as somewhere between the disgusting Yahoos and their own perfect beings. In Hobbesian terms, the Yahoos are in the state of nature, their lives "solitary, poor, nasty, brutish, and short," while the Houyhnhnms have not only attained civil society but carried it to its finest and final point.

Figure 4. Gulliver taking leave of the Houyhnhnms, by Sawrey Gilpin (1733–1807).
Yale Center for British Art, used by permission

Horses are commonly regarded as admirable, even noble, creatures, and an Irishman like Swift would be especially likely to regard them so, Ireland being a horse-infatuated island. The reader too may be led toward infatuation with this horse republic. But something is not quite right about all this, for we are in a realm in which the obviously excessive *rationality* of the Laputans is transcended by the exquisite *reason* of the Houyhnhnms— yet reason in that degree has alarming qualities. The Houyhnhnms debate (4: 9) whether the Yahoos should be exterminated, a quite rational idea and, as Claude Rawson has shown, an echo of Genesis 6:7, where God speaks of destroying man. If so, Gulliver would be a Noah, selected to survive the genocide.[32]

Gulliver is completely captivated by his horse tutors and determines to adopt their intellectual and moral conclusions. But here again, he is un-educable. He cannot comprehend this text, just as he could not read Plato's *Republic* correctly, for Gulliver is a modern, not an ancient. He adopts this ideal republic, and in doing so loses his humanity through intellectual ar-rogance. He is self-deceived as to his own character and dangerously enam-ored of the efficacy and morality of reason. Similarly, most readers across the centuries have taken Plato's *Republic* seriously, rather than ironically, as it was intended. Socrates' arguments for the *Kallipolis* are delivered with tongue firmly in cheek, as one set of arguments after another leads his circle to fanatical results, such as the abolition of the family, women being held in common by men, and the eradication—Khmer Rouge style—of everyone over the age of ten. Swift's Houyhnhnms-Land is Plato's *Republic,* which Gulliver misreads as the typical modern misreads Plato. Gulliver represents the modern temptation and gives in to it, and what is truly human is over-looked, neglected, or rejected. When the ideal state through reason alone provides all the answers, nothing is left for the soul to do.

This misreading of the essence of the human condition is displayed in Gulliver's homecoming, in which his arrogant, demanding, nasty nature— all products of his adherence to the utopian ideals of the Horse Republic— are an unsettling contrast to the decent Portuguese sea captain who rescues him, a courteous Japanese pirate, and the honest loyalty of the wife who welcomes him back.

Gulliver's Travels is an epic of statecraft and so it must include, as epics do, a descent by the hero to the Underworld. There, as in the voyages of Odysseus and Aeneas to the nether regions, Gulliver directly encounters notable figures from the past. But unlike the classic—and modern—heroes who glimpse the meaning of life and their mission in it by conversing with the shades of the departed, Gulliver does not learn, even here, because "moderns" reject the great ancient texts and Gulliver is a modern man.

When Gulliver, on the island of Glubdubdrib, is escorted to the Underworld (by "two gentlemen": Odysseus and Aeneas?), he learns how history has been distorted. The captain of one of Octavian's ships at the Battle of Actium is there. Contrary to the version accepted by Horace, Shakespeare, and Marvell—that Cleopatra suddenly fled with her ships and Antony followed her to Egypt—the captain tells Gulliver that by sheer luck he happened to break through Antony's naval line of battle, sink three of Antony's ships and capture a fourth, "which was the sole cause of Antony's flight." Instead of being promoted, however, the captain is charged with dereliction of duty so that he may be passed over for promotion, and command of a greater ship is given instead to a favorite of one of Octavian's mistresses.

So for Swift, the history of the world since Actium is neither "the great work of time," the *translatio imperii,* nor the admirable "ruin" of empire after the English Revolution that created the modern republic praised by Marvell. Instead, it is the same old story of favoritism and rotten politics. Before Actium, Swift implies, Rome was a fundamentally well-governed polity. After that battle, the Augustan Age brought empire, vanity, and decadence. Swift, living in the Augustan Age of Britain, revealed through his satire of Gulliver the great flaws in the system.

In the Underworld, Gulliver meets the great heroes and thinkers of the past. Like other epic figures who visit the nether realm, Gulliver "discovered the true Causes of many great Events that have surprised the World: how a Whore can govern the Back-stairs, the Back-stairs a Council, and the Council a Senate." He did not need to go below to gain this knowledge. The scandal that brought his impeachment in Lilliput sent him there.

From Machiavelli's northern Italy to Henri IV's France and Cromwell's Commonwealth, the rise of the modern state with its delineated borders and sovereign powers is reflected in, and illuminated by, the literature of its time. A stumbling process of fits and false starts begins, over time, to fill the vessel of the state with political theory that favors governance legitimated by the consent of the governed. The Enlightenment will strengthen this movement yet at the same time give birth to a potent ideological foe: revolution.

5

ENLIGHTENMENT: CRITIQUE OF DIPLOMACY, STATE, AND SYSTEM

The Enlightenment drew a line across history. From then on, everything would be "modern." This would require rethinking and rewriting the Westphalian system. If the international state system was born at Westphalia in 1648, a second transition came at the end of the eighteenth century with the Age of the Enlightenment in response to religion-driven conflicts like the Thirty Years' War. Philosophy, rational inquiry, scientific standards of progress, toleration, and secular politics were to displace "superstition," the primary cause of mankind's self-imposed immaturity, as Kant put it. With this came "critique"—reason contesting against reason to challenge the foundations of Western civilization, making it the only civilization in history whose major artists and intellects have radically questioned or rejected its core values.[1]

The Enlightenment challenged three matters of significance:

Diplomacy: Would diplomacy be taken seriously as the legitimate mechanism for managing international disputes?
War and Peace: Is peace the overarching goal which the international system approaches, however imperfectly?

Religion: What, if anything, would be the role of religion in the international state system?

Jean-Jacques Rousseau, who declared the international realm beyond his comprehension, did more than any thinker to shape it: by legitimating the authoritarian state; by inciting revolution against established order; and by mocking diplomacy as a problem-solving method. Rousseau was at once the most consequential political force of modernity and a clever rascal who seemed to laugh at the institutions he played with even as his innovative thought influenced them in unforeseen ways.

The Empire of Venice, stretching across the eastern Mediterranean, had been a commercial, naval, and diplomatic power. The Republic of Venice played an important part in Imperial Hapsburg diplomacy. With its imperial power in decline, challenged by Islam, Venetian statecraft sought to define the social, economic, and political boundaries of the state and to strengthen those boundaries against outsiders. Ultimately, Venice failed to become a modern state because of its inability to define and defend the first principle of sovereign statehood: clear borders.[2] By the eighteenth century, Venice's power was long gone and its glory had given way to decadence. Nonetheless, Venice remained a place of diplomatic significance, not least owing to its strategic position between central Europe and Italy, and between western Europe and the Middle East.

The decline of Venetian influence left a power vacuum in northern Italy in which major outside powers—Austria, Spain, and France—made high-handed use of Italy for their diplomatic intrigues and military maneuvers, without ever dealing an adversary a mortal blow. It became an endless, fluctuating game in the balance of power. This was the political backdrop for Rousseau's *Confessions* (1782).

Rousseau, rather improbably, was employed as a secretary to the French embassy in Venice. As he tells us in his *Confessions,* his days and nights at the Venetian embassy were filled with petty strivings for the recognition of rank: his titles, his dinner invitations, the incessant squabbles and insults between him and his incompetent ambassador, the comte de Montaigu. Rousseau portrays diplomacy as a farcical game. His prose is light and frothy, corresponding to his critical aim of delegitimizing the state, the international system, and the civilization they serve.

There is a great, silent tradition of statecraft behind Rousseau's tale of his Venetian embassy. Venice, first as an outpost of Byzantium, from which the art of "Byzantine" diplomacy is learned, then as an empire and great power in its own right, set a pattern of diplomacy other governments would studiously emulate. Venice produced the first systematized diplomatic service in history, and its style of conducting international relations spread through all of Europe. Venetian diplomats were highly trained, professionally fixated on the interests of the state, bound to collect and register every detail of international transactions, and held to the strictest rules of personal conduct and discipline, to the point of austerity. During his tour of duty a Venetian envoy was not permitted a single day's absence from his post. In Venice diplomacy was staged as a grand spectacle, "impressing all foreign envoys and their retinue with its dignity, munificence, and decorum."[3]

Rousseau does not take diplomacy seriously; for him it is a playground for dolts and debauchers. A diplomatic bagatelle might affect the course of war or peace, but if it did, it was only because clever Jean-Jacques happened to be on the spot. Without him, anything might have happened.

Rousseau describes Ambassador Montaigu doing what many weak diplomats do: reporting his task to be well in hand when in fact it was not. Rousseau writes that his ambassador's only important duty was to persuade the Venetians to maintain their neutrality in the War of the Austrian Succession. The Venetians, well aware of this, never failed to protest their fidelity to neutrality, while openly supplying the Austrian troops with munitions and recruits.

Montaigu dealt with this by insisting, over Rousseau's protestations, that his secretary "state in all his dispatches Venice would never violate her neutrality." Rousseau notes: "In such a position as I then filled, the slightest of mistakes are not without their consequences. I devoted my whole attention, therefore, to avoiding errors that might have been detrimental to my services. I was till the last most orderly and most punctilious in every detail of my essential duties." Rousseau's self-serving tale comes as the War of the Austrian Succession is spreading into northern Italy and Austrian Prince Lobkowitz plans to march on the Bourbon kingdom of Naples. As the crisis is building, Rousseau is working diligently, he says, to see that embassy business is conducted despite the flaws and lapses of Ambassador Montaigu. One Saturday, the day that, as diplomats say, "the bag closes," when couriers leave with the dispatches, Rousseau is alone at his desk in the embassy, the ambassador as usual having gone on some inconsequential errand.

An important note arrives from the French chargé d'affaires in Vienna, M. Vincent, with an intelligence report that "a man whose signature M. Vincent enclosed, was leaving Vienna and was to pass by way of Venice on a secret journey into the Abruzzi for the purpose of promoting a popular uprising" in support of the approaching Austrians.

Ambassador Montaigu being absent, Rousseau decides to take action himself. He sends the intelligence report to the French ambassador in Naples, the Marquis de l'Hôpital, "and so timely was it that it is perhaps thanks to the much abused Jean-Jacques that the Bourbons owe the preservation of the Kingdom of Naples."[4] For his decisiveness, Rousseau is "mentioned in dispatches." When l'Hôpital sends a message of appreciation to Montaigu, noting the service of his secretary Rousseau, Montaigu takes it in ill humor.

This episode, Rousseau claims, was disparaged and discredited ever since the publication of his *Confessions.* Rousseau's forwarding of the intelligence report would have been virtually meaningless, it was said, because many such rumors would have been available in Naples. Others pointed to discrepancies in the diplomatic documentary record.[5]

The placement and handling of this episode in *The Confessions* indicate its importance to Rousseau. The record does show that Montaigu was sorely vexed by l'Hôpital's notice of Rousseau's services, and this perhaps led Montaigu to destroy some documents and decide to replace Rousseau as his secretary. The warning Rousseau forwarded may well have been the first intelligence Naples had of Austrian efforts to foment an uprising in the Abruzzi.

Who cares about the War of the Austrian Succession? Very few. But out of the war, Prussia emerged as a great power, and Austria turned eastward thereafter in seeking allies. Seeds of the First World War may have been sown then. Rousseau seems intuitively to have perceived that he had been close to a potentially great event, and may have tried to elaborate the importance of his part. But his approach to diplomacy was above all frivolous, a mark of his larger political philosophy.

Rousseau's days at the Venice embassy were only partly spent carping at his ambassador and delivering such "brilliant" strokes as saving the kingdom of Naples. Jean-Jacques reveled in the society, the theater, the music, and the ladies of the decadent city-state, for Venetian courtesans had a recognized diplomatic liaison role in the city's foreign relations.[6] In high spirits, Jean-Jacques loved to combine diplomatic business with personal pleasure:

> It was carnival time. I took a domino and a mask, and set off for the Palazzo Giustiniani. Everyone who saw my gondola arrive with the ambassador's livery was impressed: Venice had never witnessed such a thing. I entered and had myself announced as *una siora maschera.* But once inside, I took off my mask and gave my name. The senator turned pale, and stood dumbfounded. "Sir," I said to him in the Venetian dialect, "I am sorry to trouble your Excellency by my visit; but you have in your Teatro di San Luce a man called Veronese, who is now under contract to the King. He has been claimed from you, but without success. I have come to ask for him in His Majesty's name." My short speech was effective.

Thus did Rousseau settle yet another international dispute. He relished his official duties as a kind of grand joke.

He did not remain long as a diplomat in Venice, and returned to his own city-state of Geneva, but his experience there may have had larger unforeseen consequences. Within a few years, Rousseau entered the essay contests set by the Academy of Dijon and wrote the "Discourses" in the same insouciant spirit. In his "Discourse on the Origins of Inequality," Rousseau declares that there never has been, nor is there now, a legitimate government. Nor will there ever be a legitimate polity on earth until Rousseau's guidelines are followed. Rousseau elaborates on these in his *Social Contract.* Each must "give all to all." Only then will "The People" be created (before this there were "people," but not "The People"). And The People's attribute would be The General Will, which would be all-determinative, although initially it would need to be guided by an exceptional genius—The Legislator, that is —someone as brilliant and unconstrained as Jean-Jacques Rousseau.

Here were the foundations for the idea, later developed not in witty insouciance but all grim earnestness, that all of Western civilization is an oppressive fraud and that some "Maximum Leader" or "Great Helmsman" will be needed to steer The People toward utopia on earth. And those who disagree? Well, as Rousseau writes in his *Social Contract,* they "will be forced to be free." Humanity has been plagued by this version of the grand strategy idea ever since Jean-Jacques Rousseau wrote it down, in all his charmingly lighthearted, smiling, and cynical self-satisfaction.[7]

Like Defoe's Cavalier, the Scotsman Richard Cant fought with the army of Gustavus Adolphus in the Thirty Years' War. His great-grandson, Immanuel Kant of Königsberg in East Prussia, adored Rousseau and was thrilled by the French Revolution, yet ultimately gave the international system the substantive project for peace that it had lacked. The system posited the state as the basic component of international life, and added elements like diplomacy to facilitate state-to-state interaction. Beyond that it did not go. The state was a vessel into which any manner of governance might be poured. If governance produced a toxic, dangerous state, then other states could only try to shift "the balance of power" against the noxious party.

Kant's brief essay "What Is Enlightenment?" explained that through Enlightenment, mankind would leave its "self-imposed immaturity"; that is, give up any and all "foundations"—religion, tradition, and the like—that previously gave moral and intellectual guidance. With the mind liberated in this way, old problems could be thought through anew. Observation and reason would suffice to work out every issue from the ground up, *ab initio*. Kant's famous part in this effort was his "categorical imperative," a thinking-through of what might qualify as rightful human action without reference to outside authority.

Kant, admirably, took up the challenge of doing the same for international life. Political philosophers had previously devoted themselves to the quest for justice and good governance *inside* the borders of the political entity—polis, city-state, nation. The space beyond the borders of sovereign states was ungoverned and unphilosophized about; Grotius's vision was as yet unrealized. The vast external realm was anarchic and could be survived only through the accumulation and wielding of power.

Hobbes regarded the international arena as ruled by the "law of nature"—nasty and brutish—and like Rousseau, he declared that his philosophy could not extend so far. Hobbes and Rousseau provided links in what Peter Gay called the great chain of treatises in political theory that began with Plato's *Republic*.[8] All were attempts to provide a modern basis for governance within the boundaries of a political community; international affairs were beyond them.

What Hobbes and Rousseau turned away from, Kant met head-on, and did so as Enlightenment precepts dictated: from the ground up, without reference to past authorities or intellectual foundations. In *Perpetual Peace,* Kant thinks through the questions of international order without any reference to the Treaty of Westphalia or any other supposedly foundational principle supplied by the past, concluding by reasoning alone that yes, the state is the basic unit of the international system. He then adds a new element as structurally essential: government by consent of the governed. The argument is presented through an imaginative story. Outside a Dutch tavern a sign is creaking in the wind. *Zum Ewigen Frieden* is the name on the sign: "At the sign of Perpetual Peace." It's a joke; the picture on the sign is a graveyard. Kant looked back on a time of seemingly perpetual war: the Thirty Years' War (1618–1648), the wars of Louis XIV, the War of the Spanish Succession (1702–1714), the English-Dutch wars, Russia's destruction of Poland's independence, the wars with the Turks, and the Seven Years' War (1756–1763), the first truly global war.

Kant's writing is convoluted and difficult. *Perpetual Peace* also has a misleading structure. The first part, called "Preliminary Articles," contains specific requirements such as "no secret treaties." Next comes "Definitive Articles," which call for republican government and a federation of free republics. Then come two "Supplements," which deal with questions raised in the first two parts. If read straight through from start to finish, Kant's arguments are hard to grasp and unpersuasive. But when we read them backward, or almost backward, a coherent line of thought emerges.[9] The argument actually starts in the first Supplement, with reindeer.[10] "It is in itself wonderful that moss can still grow in the cold wastes around the Arctic Ocean; the reindeer can scrape it out from beneath the snow, and can thus itself serve as nourishment or as a draft animal for the Ostiaks or Samoyeds."[11] Nature, and animals such as the reindeer, thus make it possible for human beings to live in extremely inhospitable parts of the world. War is a basic part of the human condition, and wars have driven people into every part of the world. The differences of resources, climate, and other conditions vary greatly, so that many different products result, and this leads to trade relations among peoples. While trade is conducive to peaceful relations, wars continue, because war "is grafted onto human nature."

Kant, the archetypal Enlightenment thinker, is here presenting an Enlightenment argument. He is not turning to any established, foundational source of authority, whether religious, moral, metaphysical, traditional, or otherwise, but is instead thinking through the problem of war and peace from the ground up, unaided by anything but his observation and his reason.

In his second Supplement, Kant observes that wars have forced people to form themselves into different states, entities of governance, each for its particular part of the world. Ideally, it would seem that one universal, cosmopolitan government should arise for all the world, but politically that wouldn't work, because peoples and their lands vary so widely. There is no realistic possibility of global governance.

But the idealistic and the realistic, and the moral and the political, factors can yield an agreement on something. All human beings desire justice. For people to obtain justice, Kant says, there needs to be "publicity." Today it is called "transparency." The governed need to know what the government is doing. This means that the best form of government is a republic: a state in which sovereignty belongs to the people and which is administered by officials who in some real way are representative of, and answerable to, the people.

Then we turn to Kant's arguments in his "Definitive Articles," in which the points made in the Supplements are translated into political recommendations. A republic is the best form of government not only because it is best able to ensure justice for its citizens but also because it will act against inclinations to go to war. A king, Kant says, can simply order his army to march against a rival kingdom. But a republic's citizens will have a say in any such decision. And because it is they who will provide the soldiers, they will have a braking effect on the implementation of war plans.

If this is so, then the more republics, the better. An association of republics would be better still, because then the trend would be stronger for peace than for war.

States also will be connected by mutual self-interest. Kant makes a utilitarian argument: "The spirit of commerce sooner or later takes hold of every people, and it cannot exist side by side with war. . . . Thus states find themselves compelled to promote the noble cause of peace, though not exactly from motives of morality."[12] Put this together with the peaceful propensities of the individual republics and the world might be pointed toward the goal of "perpetual peace."

Kant's concepts amount to a form of grand strategy for an international system seeking world order, peace, justice, and progress. When placed alongside the international state system brought into being with the 1648 Treaty of Westphalia, this "Kantian Project" became the way the world's nations have come to work with each other. International law, universal human rights, and the United Nations and other established international organizations all are in some way colored by the arguments set out by Kant in *Perpetual Peace.*

The United Nations is not, it is important to note, Kant's federation of republics. Whatever merits it may have, the UN has sought to admit all states no matter what their form of government. Kant's concept would include NATO and the European Union, because these associations require a republican form of government as a condition for membership. From a Kantian point of view, the international state system will make progress toward peace to the extent that it increases the number of republics—democracies—within it.

Edward Gibbon's *The Decline and Fall of the Roman Empire,* 1776–1788, a work as much about the Enlightenment as about the vicissitudes of imperial Rome, was in significant ways an anti-Christian manifesto. The Westphalian system was designed for differing religions to flourish without serving as sources of conflict. Could that system withstand the rejection of its own foundational faith?[13]

When I was a schoolboy, I was obviously nearsighted, so I was sent to the school optometrist for an eye examination and was issued glasses. After a few regular eye checkups, I realized that every eye chart used the same text for that top line of minuscule print. So I memorized that line, which was the first sentence of *Decline and Fall:*

> In the second century of the Christian era, the empire of Rome comprehended the fairest part of the earth and the most civilized portion of mankind.

Gibbon goes on to praise Rome for "the gentle but powerful influence of laws and manners. . . . The image of a free constitution was preserved with decent reverence. . . . The Roman Senate appeared to possess the sovereign authority, and devolved on the emperors all the executive powers of government." The fall of Rome, which brought an end to such good governance, Gibbon wrote, was an immense catastrophe that "will ever be remembered, and still felt by the nations of the earth."

Why did Rome fall? What were the crucial factors? Overextension of military commitments? The centralization of decision making? Luxury and corruption? The replacement of the antique virtues of manliness, sacrifice, frugality, civility, patriotism, and loyalty with meliorism, sentimentality, a yearning for peace and fellow feeling? All these factors can be found in Gibbon's pages.

Gibbon's paragraphs, chapters, and volumes demonstrate his ability to master vast amounts of material over great expanses of space and time. As one astute reader noted of Gibbon, "However far his eye may range, the clue is always firmly in his fingers, and the conclusion of the third volume was in draft before the first volume was written."[14] This is the mark of an epic. An epic, it has been said, is a work of high seriousness, amplitude (that's a Gibbonian word), and inclusiveness, an exercise of willpower over material, and an expression of the sense of an entire period or culture. If Virgil is the epic of Rome, if Dante is the epic of Christendom, if Milton is the epic of the Renaissance and Reformation, Gibbon is the epic of the Enlightenment.[15] His work is universal, secular, skeptical, rational, and ironic—and eager to reveal the errors, misdeeds, failures, and deceptions of the past.

Gibbon's most distinctive quality is irony. He does not mention Christians until he has described the conversion of Constantine in 312. Then the two chapters—15 and 16—hit like a thunderclap. The Christians are described in an ironic tone that cannot mask Gibbon's genuinely devastating views on their errors, corruption, and self-satisfaction. He sees them smitten by pride and seduced by a love of power that, under artful disguises, insinuates itself into even the hearts of saints.

Chapter 15 is a rhetorical masterpiece, with every example of early Christianity marshaled to discredit believers. In it, Sir Leslie Stephen said, Gibbon struck Christianity "by far the heaviest blow which it had yet received from any single hand."[16] Gibbon proceeds "to relate the progress, the persecutions, the establishment, the divisions, the final triumph, and the gradual corruption, of Christianity." He delays, until chapter 37, his treatment of the monastic life: the wait has only heightened Gibbon's delight in his own exquisite irony:

The Ascetics, who obeyed and abused the rigid precepts of the gospel, were inspired by the savage enthusiasm which represents man as a criminal, and God as a tyrant. They seriously renounced the business, and the pleasures of the age; abjured the use of wine, of flesh, and of marriage; chastised their body, mortified their affections, and embraced a life of misery, as the price of eternal happiness. . . . They soon acquired the respect of the world, which they despised; and the loudest applause was bestowed on this DIVINE PHILOSOPHY, which surpassed, without the aid of science or reason, the laborious virtues of the Grecian schools.

Decline and Fall is an answer to *City of God,* Saint Augustine's attempt to refute charges in his time that Christianity, with its soft virtues of faith, hope, and charity, had so undermined the antique, manly Roman virtues that the city was rendered helpless in the face of the assault by Alaric's Goths in 410, and that the pagan gods had taken their revenge on a Christian Rome that suppressed pagan sacrifices.

Augustine retells and reinterprets stories of ancient Rome. He transforms the story of Regulus, the Roman held hostage by Carthage and then sent on oath to Rome to negotiate. It is no longer a story about the old Roman virtue of upholding one's oath; now Regulus is a worshiper of pagan gods who failed to preserve him. The story of Lucretia, who killed herself for Roman honor, becomes a way for Augustine to assert that a Christian woman would have been chaste in the sight of God, caring nothing for the opinions of this world and taking comfort in the prospect of her reception into the next.

For Gibbon, Christianity's perversion of ancient Roman virtues led to the collapse of the empire. Antique paganism, for Gibbon, was eclectic, tolerant, flexible, moderate, and practical. Christianity erupted as an alien, corrosive force, intolerant, dogmatic, zealous, contemptuous of the world around it. The Christian church grew rapidly as a result of the inflexible zeal that Christians derived from Judaism, the doctrine of a future life, the miraculous powers ascribed to the Christian faith, the pure and austere morals of the Christians, and Christian unity and discipline, which formed an independent state in the heart of the Roman Empire. Each of these points corroded the core of the antique Roman character: instead of flexibility, intolerance; instead of practicality, otherworldliness; instead of reason, belief in miracles; instead of manly virtue, pious rectitude; and instead of the City of Man, the City of God.

And once in power, Gibbon says, Christianity's bigotry turned inward, splintering the Christian world into irreconcilable antagonistic sects. For Gibbon, society, nature, and humanity, the love of pleasure and of action, tempered by reason and moderation, are the sources of happiness and virtue. But it was not in *this* world that the Christians wanted to make themselves useful or agreeable. Gibbon professed, ironically, to be surprised when his chapters on Christianity caused an uproar. He had thought, he declared, "that an age of light and liberty would receive, without scandal, an inquiry into the human causes of the process and establishment of Christianity."

Gibbon sought to bequeath a book for the guidance of statesmen. *The Decline and Fall* is a warning. Here in the desolation of a thousand years of history lies proof of the destiny of states that depart from the maxims of the Roman republic.[17]

Cicero gave Gibbon a glimpse of what politics should strive to create: a republic. When he read Cicero, "I breathed the spirit of freedom, and I imbibed from his precepts and examples the public and private sense of a man." There is a parallel between Gibbon's portrait of the perfection of human nature and the standard set forth in Cicero's *De Officiis* (On Duties). Cicero sets out an ideal of excellence and insists that the ideal can be realized through a self-imposed discipline in which the passions are subjected to the control of reason. At one extreme is the oppression of tyranny; at the other is the anarchy of perfect equality. The best lies in the balance of freedom and justice in conditions of order.[18] So Gibbon arrived at the same conclusion as Kant, but from a different angle: a republic is the best form of government for a state.

Following Cicero, Gibbon believed that the essence of civilization consists in the control of passions and instincts by the law of nature and nations which reason has inscribed: "the different characteristics which distinguish the civilized nations of the globe may be ascribed to the use and abuse of reason," and reason, he insists, can function only under conditions of liberty. The vices of the corrupted Romans of the empire, unworthy successors of the republic, constituted a betrayal of the rule of right reason inscribed on the virtuous mind—and thus a betrayal of civilization.

The narrative carries the story to Rome's subjection by barbarians in the fifth century, then from Justinian's Constantinople to the final split between the eastern and western empires in 800, and on to the Turkish conquest of Constantinople in 1453. The larger, underlying theme is the migration of the empire from Rome to Constantinople, to the East, leaving "the ghosts of the deceased Roman Empire sitting crowned upon the grave thereof." This is, of course, going the wrong way. The *translatio imperii,* the transfer of imperial power, is supposed to go from east to west. For Gibbon, the conversion to Christianity of the Emperor Constantine in 312 pulled the cultural and political center of gravity of Rome eastward toward the luxurious civilizations of Asia.

Christianity was an oriental religion in the process of becoming an oriental monarchy. "The simplicity of Roman manners was insensibly corrupted by the stately affectation of the courts of Asia." Byzantium was an oriental despotism at the other end of the political spectrum from the mixed constitution of Republican Rome. The empire sickens and shrinks until, at the end, the Byzantine empire has contracted to the limits of one city—Constantinople, threatened by the armies of Islam.

Enlightenment *philosophes* expressed their anticlericalism by presenting the Prophet Muhammad as a great legislator (recall Rousseau's Social Contract) whose objectives had been liberty, tolerance, social justice, and enlightened statecraft.[19] Gibbon's chapter 50, on the life of Muhammad,[20] is written in such elegant and inspiring prose that it might itself serve as a sacred text of the faith. His praise for the character of Islam and the Prophet serves as an oblique attack on Christian belief and practice, although much of this praise would not be accepted by Muslims.[21]

If any religion can be admired by an Enlightenment savant, Gibbon seems to say, it is Islam, which is rooted in reason:

> The creed of Mahomet is free from suspicion or ambiguity; and the Koran is a glorious testimony to the unity of God. The prophet of Mecca rejected the worship of idols and men, of stars and planets, on the rational principle that whatever rises must set, that whatever is born must die, that whatever is corruptible must decay and perish. In the Author of the universe his rational enthusiasm confessed and adored an infinite and eternal being, without form or place, without issue or similitude, present to our most secret thoughts, existing by the necessity of his own nature, and deriving from himself all moral and intellectual perfection. These sublime truths, thus announced in the language of the prophet, are firmly held by his disciples, and

defined with metaphysical precision by the interpreters of the Koran. A philosophic theist might subscribe to the popular creed of
the Mohammedans: a creed too sublime perhaps for our present
faculties.[22]

Islam is the admirable counterexample to Gibbon's indictment of
Christianity, and he uses "Mahomet" to represent the Muslim state. Here
was a religion with a human founder, without monks or priests, that demanded simplicity and resisted complication, organizationally loose, so that
human progress would not be obstructed as the Christian church had done.
Islam was to Gibbon "a model of that judicious blend between rationally
demonstrable verity and socially useful prejudice which is the best that can
be hoped for in a religion."

Gibbon's appreciation of Muhammad and Islam is praiseworthy at a
time when Catholics and Protestants were vying to demonize Christianity's
nearest alternative faith. But Gibbon's exalted prose masks his use of Islam
merely as a foil in his anti-Christian polemic. He certainly had great success in debunking Christianity in the Europe of today, but his picture of a
non-"priest-ridden" Islam is no longer recognizable in the Imam-, Mullah-,
and Ayatollah-ruled Muslim world. Something in the practices of that world
has turned out to "obstruct human progress" more effectively than Gibbon
ever accused Christianity of doing.

Like Thucydides, Gibbon considers his epic "a possession for all
time." To Gibbon, his project is greater because it takes on the two great
Western intellectual traditions: classical and biblical. Gibbon tries to outstrip his classical model by engaging the empire greatest in power and
extent—Rome—and to supersede his foremost religious model, Milton's
Paradise Lost. If the First Fall was that of Lucifer and the Second that of
Adam and Eve, Gibbon is writing of the Third Fall. The Fall of Rome, yes,
but the Fall of Christianity as well.

The cause of both biblical falls was pride. Gibbon makes it clear that
the fall of the Roman Empire was likewise caused by pride—Christian
pride. Religion left society unable to defend itself, weakening the empire
and allowing barbarism to triumph. As Gibbon put it, "the clergy successfully preached the doctrine of patience and pusillanimity; the active
virtues of society were discouraged; and the last remains of military spirit
were buried in the cloister."

A literary wave following Gibbon's admiration for Muhammad would transform the West's view of Islam. As Gibbon praised its rationality, Goethe romanticized it in his 1819 collection of lyric poems *West-östlicher Diwan*.[23] Thomas Carlyle, in his *Heroes, Hero-Worship, and the Heroic in History* of 1841, lectured on "The Hero as Prophet-Mahomet," a lecture described as the definitive reversal of the medieval world's picture of Islam as the great enemy.[24]

Washington Irving, attached to the American legation in Madrid, became fascinated by the life of the Prophet. Irving was the first American to win an international literary reputation ("Rip van Winkle," "The Legend of Sleepy Hollow," and *Knickerbocker's History of New York*). In 1832 Irving published what would become his most internationally famous book, *Tales of the Alhambra*, romantic sketches of the long-departed Arab caliphate and its fairy-tale palace on a rocky spur above Granada.

In 1842 Irving was appointed American minister to Spain (the United States at the time refused to name ambassadors as a means of keeping the international state system at arm's length). There he read Europe's first serious and sympathetic study of the Prophet, by the German scholar Gustav Weil.[25] Irving then began work on the book project he claimed to have had on his mind for decades. His two-volume *Mahomet and His Successors* was published in 1849 and sold well for years.[26] Irving wanted to depict Muhammad as both a God-inspired prophet and a world-historical figure, consciously rejecting the antipathy of the pre-Enlightenment West. He turned the record over and over, examining each disparaging accusation and refuting each in turn as if he were Muhammad's lawyer. As a good Christian, Irving concludes that Muhammad was an inspired genius, but a *literary*—although illiterate—rather than a religious genius: "All the parts of the Koran supposed to have been promulgated by him at this time, incoherently as they have come down to us, and marred as their pristine beauty must be in passing through various hands, are of a pure and elevated character, and breathe poetical, if not religious, inspiration."

A signal change took place, Irving writes, after Muhammad's flight to Medina, when he finds himself revered as the Prophet: "From this time worldly passions and worldly schemes too often give the impulse to his actions, instead of that visionary enthusiasm which, even if mistaken, threw a glow of piety on his earlier deeds." Here were the seeds, Irving found, of Islam's swift transformation of the world, but also the sources of its downfall, when the Arab empire pressed too far and, counterattacked, the Caliphate of Cordoba was lost in 1031. Little territory was left in Muslim hands except Granada, which fell to the Catholic *Reconquista* in 1492.

At the end of his book, however, Irving's admiration for Muhammad seems even greater, not from vainglory over the Prophet's victories or admiration of the mere wealth that poured in as spoils of war, but because Muhammad never altered his simplicity of manner and appearance but used his wealth to promote the faith and to relieve the poor. Throughout it all, "Prayer, that vital duty of Islamism and that infallible purifier of the soul, was his constant practice."[27]

Irving depicts the launch of a rising and seemingly irresistible universal, monotheist system of world order within the caliphate under the leadership of the Prophet, then its overreaching, recession, and decline. Irving singles out Jesus, not the Prophet, as *the* divinely inspired figure in his biography, yet regards Muhammad as worthy of praise. Pledged as an American diplomat to the separation of church and state, Irving nevertheless fully appreciated the power of religion, and Islam, in world affairs.

The End of History, Francis Fukuyama's influential work of political theory based on Hegel's idea of the state and human freedom, depicts the end of the Cold War as the clarifying moment in history when the great question of the human condition, "What form of governance is best?" had been answered definitively. No alternative to liberal democracy could be found. The title brought the author scorn; every time trouble erupted anywhere in the world, Fukuyama's critics would gleefully point out that history had not come to an end. In reply, Fukuyama quite correctly said: "To refute my thesis it is not enough to suggest that the future holds in store momentous events. One has to show that these events were driven by a *systematic idea* of political and social justice that claimed to supersede liberalism."[28] Communism had been just such a systematic idea, and it had been defeated. Now Islamism was coming forward as a systemic alternative, something glimpsed in the years of the European and American Enlightenment by Edward Gibbon and Washington Irving.

6

AMERICA:
A NEW IDEA

The discovery and settlement of the New World forced changes to some key assumptions about world order and relations among states. The European encounter with other peoples raised an idea of universal human nature, and the encounter with nature forced hierarchy to give way to equality. The struggle to control new lands had to take some account of the global balance of power and international state system, producing fresh thought about liberty and democracy. The New World invited a major rethinking of the enterprise of "founding," of the form that a polity should take, and the political substance that should fill it.

America defined and redefined itself as both within the classical tradition and uniquely different from it. The founding accomplished by the revolutionary generation was reworked to confront slaveholding and to carry democracy to a universal level. Religion was addressed again and again in the process of working out America's distinctive compatibility between religiosity and church-state separation.

Did American "exceptionalism" require that the nation keep its distance from the international state system? The geographic extension and growing economic and military strength of the United States forced the choice of whether to be in or out, or to try to have it both ways. The Civil

War brought these tensions to a high point through the founding of another state, the Confederacy, the dire need to preserve the Union, and recognition of the importance of relations with major foreign powers.

One of history's great rhetorical events took place in 1550 in Valladolid, Spain: the debate between Bartolomé de las Casas and Juan Ginés de Sepúlveda on whether American Indians were natural slaves of the Spanish. Las Casas prevailed. His view, based on Francisco de Vitoria's treatise "On the Indies" and ratified by the University of Salamanca, determined that Native Americans had souls and were fellow humans, and that conquest of the New World was unjustified on its merits. The Conquistadors, as Las Casas portrayed them, were no better than cannibals. "I love the University of Salamanca," said Johnson with great emotion to Boswell, "for when the Spaniards were in doubt as to the lawfulness of their conquering America the University of Salamanca gave it as their opinion that it was not lawful."[1]

Sepúlveda had argued that war against the Indians was justified in order to convert them. Las Casas responded:

> For the Creator of every being has not so despised these peoples of the New World that he willed them to lack reason and made them like brute animals, to that they should be called barbarians, savages, wild men, and brutes, as they [the Sepulvedistas] think or imagine. On the contrary, they are of such gentleness and decency that they are, more than the other nations of the entire world, supremely fitted and prepared to abandon the worship of idols and to accept, province by province and people by people, the word of God and the preaching of the truth.[2]

It was a moral argument based on natural law in the field of international relations, produced by the most momentous event in world history—the fifteenth and sixteenth centuries' global reconnaissance and exploration, particularly bringing widespread awareness of the New World of the Western Hemisphere. This imposed upon the world's peoples the reality of the planet's vast cultural, social, and religious diversity. From this came a growing realization that only *procedural* arrangements for international interaction could accommodate such a plethora of peoples, polities, and beliefs. From this point forward, nations would design an international system based on a minimum number of procedural requirements: to be a state, to accept international law and organizations and universal human rights (this coming from the debate at Valladolid), and to use professional military and diplomatic services. As a procedural system it could encompass widely divergent political and social ideas, but it would have to defend itself against substantive ideologies which would arise to oppose and try to replace it.

Sir Walter Ralegh was a favored courtier until he took up with a lady-in-waiting, causing Queen Elizabeth to clap him into the Tower of London. Ralegh was the exemplar of the Renaissance man: a successful administrator of mines, an explorer and sea captain in battle, and a literary man. A friend of the great poet Edmund Spenser, he wrote some of the finest Elizabethan verse, and his vast prose work, modestly titled *The History of the World,* was unique in compiling and intercalating the biblical story with the classical Hellenic saga. His adventures would break the papacy's hegemony over the Western Hemisphere, making way for private as well as state-sponsored exploration.

Ralegh's most mysterious, intriguing poem is the sprawling, passion-ridden "The Ocean to Cynthia," which escapes all efforts to explicate. "Cynthia" is the moon and Queen Elizabeth, it seems. The ocean is Ralegh. The lines go on forever in a global reconnaissance of longing and energy that enmeshes the swashbuckling poet in the destiny of empire. In one of its clearer passages Ralegh writes:

> To seeke new worlds, for golde, for prayse, for glory,
> to try to desire, to try love severed farr
> When I was gonn shee sent her memory
> more strange than weare ten thousand shipps of war
> to call mee back, to leve great honors thought,
> to leve my friends, my fortune, my attempte
> to leve the purpose I so longe had sought
> and holde bothe cares, and comforts in contempt.

The courtier's infatuation with his queen, the mingled excitement, estrangement, and melancholy of the adventurer, and the opening of the New World sent Ralegh to the colonies. He would be a key actor in the huge ongoing shift from a later medieval to a modern conception of world order.

In 1585 Ralegh conceived, organized, and dispatched the English colonizing expedition that would end in death at Roanoke Island, which lay in territory considered by the Spanish Empire, since the discovery of the New World in the late 1400s, to be its exclusive territorial right. The English landed and proceeded to build "The Citie of Ralegh." A supply voyage that arrived in 1591 found that the expedition had tragically disappeared, leaving behind only mysterious clues ("Croatan" carved on a tree) as to what might have befallen "the Lost Colony." Bitter diplomatic protests by Spain to the English Crown followed.

The papacy was a recognized authority in international affairs in the fifteenth century, particularly as arbiter of international disputes and the Christianization of the New World. Portugal in 1455 asked the pope to confirm its title to lands that its seafarers had discovered in Africa and beyond. Spain did the same in 1493 regarding the discoveries of Columbus. In 1494, in the Spanish town of Tordesillas, Portugal and Spain signed a treaty that divided the entire non-Christian world between them. In a papal bull, Pope Alexander VI drew a line passing through the North and South poles down what was thought to be the mid-Atlantic Ocean which handed almost the entire New World to Spain, Africa and India to Portugal. This line, recorded in the Treaty of Tordesillas, ran through the eastern part of South America, thus giving Brazil to Portugal. This was how the world would order itself under the then-accepted international system.[3]

Ralegh, held in the Tower under Elizabeth's sentence of death, was released in 1617 on the strength of his proposal to find "El Dorado," the gold fields said to be located near the Orinoco River in Guinea. He had won approval for this scheme through a narrative of his earlier explorations, *The Discovery of the Large, Rich and Beautiful Empire of Guinea,* a notable example of Elizabethan prose (some of Ralegh's exotic names and Edenic descriptions influenced Milton's *Paradise Lost*).

Spain protested Ralegh's expedition, and after his return to England in 1618, having found no gold, the Spanish ambassador to the Court of Saint James's demanded that action be taken against him. King James ordered Ralegh put to death under the sentence placed upon him years before.

Shakespeare's *The Tempest,* the first great work of literature identified with the New World, is a play about books, a plethora of near-direct quotations and submarine allusions to classical, biblical, medieval, and Elizabethan literature, most notably Virgil's *Aeneid,* Montaigne's "Of the Cannibales," and Ovid's retelling of Jason and the Argonauts. Prospero, the ducal magus who presides over the play, is another Aeneas as founder of a new polity. Prospero's power comes from the books brought with him as cargo when he put out to sea on his journey of exile. *The Tempest* itself is a book that Prospero is writing even as the drama acts it out, texts within layers of interconnected books across time and space, all making an international literary system. Caliban, the supposedly base indigenous man—man in the State of Nature—actually displays Montaigne's rejection of savagery and civilization as antithetical. At the end of the play Prospero says of Caliban,

> This thing of darkness I
> acknowledge mine.

Slave? Perhaps, but also "mine" as a fellow human, an acknowledgment of universal kinship that increasingly would characterize internationalism.

The Tempest is a work of imagination, but it was inspired by a real event and it is keenly aware of the settling of a new world. In 1609 the *Sea-Adventure,* a ship carrying colonists led by Sir Thomas Gates to join John Smith's Virginia colony, was driven by a storm onto rocks at Bermuda. All passengers made it safely to shore and were able to return to the shipwreck to salvage some of its stores and cargo. News of the survival of the passengers after the shipwreck reached England before the end of 1609, and Shakespeare heard of it.

The Tempest, first performed in 1611, opens with disaster looming. On a ship at sea in the New World, "a tempestuous noise of thunder and lightning" is heard. Conflict breaks out between the boatswain, who commands the ship in the storm and the high-born good-for-nothings who can only scream denunciations in their anxiety to maintain their privileged standing.[4] Then the disaster arrives. The cry comes, as the scene ends, "We split, we split, we split!" The ship of state crashes on the rocky shore and the old order is left behind. A new one will have to be built in a new land, under very different conditions.

The changing status of individuals would be accompanied by changes in the political order. By this time, colonizing activities of the English, Dutch, and French had poked holes in the Treaty of Tordesillas. The old paradigm of world order would collapse definitively when, under the Treaty of Westphalia, the Hapsburgs gave up Spanish-occupied Netherlands and recognized it as an independent sovereign state. The treaty gave specific legitimacy to the trade and navigation of the Dutch in both the Eastern and the Western hemispheres. A new international state system now challenged the Catholic Church's monopoly on universalism.

The New World opening of the *Tempest,* however, is rebuffed by its ending when Prospero returns to the old world of the European state, leaving the audience with a more restrictive sense of human freedom than Americans would proceed to acquire.[5]

America's story is an elaboration of the classic proposition described by Cicero: "In no realm has human excellence approached so closely the paths of the gods as it does in the founding of new and preservation of already founded communities."

At about the same time Daniel Defoe was working on his *Memoirs of a Cavalier,* he was writing *Robinson Crusoe* (1719) in which, as the legal historian Frederic William Maitland said, "for the first time, the Absolute State confronted the Absolute Individual."[6] *Robinson Crusoe* has been read as a children's story, an adventure story, a brief for man's return to a state of nature, a document of capitalism, a spiritual autobiography, a myth of modern individualism, and more. It is none and all of these spun into a novel whose theme is the founding of a state in the New World, showing the relevance of Aristotle's *Politics* to the enterprise.

Published in 1719, the book is the story of the years, from 1659 to 1686, in which its hero was stranded on a desert island. These were the years of the Restoration in England, the return of the monarchy under Charles II to replace the Puritan Commonwealth of the "Great Protector," Oliver Cromwell. Robinson Crusoe is cast away the year before the king returns and comes back to England the year after William and Mary are crowned. Defoe supported the Puritan revolution and opposed the Restoration as the return of "the divine right of kings" and the possible return of Catholicism to England. Robinson Crusoe thus has been seen as Defoe's "government-in-exile," an alternative polity to the regime at home.[7]

In a sense, *Robinson Crusoe* is a tract of political theory about the modern state as a component of the international system of states. Defoe today would be called a political "realist," who saw world affairs as a vast, essentially anarchic realm in which each state must look first to its own defense and sovereign integrity, with survival as its first priority.[8]

Jean-Jacques Rousseau, in his novel *Emile,* has the tutor give his pupil a copy of *Robinson Crusoe* as a depiction of man in a state of nature before civil society replaces the original human condition. But Robinson Crusoe is not in a state of nature at all; he is a civilized man who uses immense ingenuity to preserve himself when cut off from the civilized world. Shipwrecked and cast ashore, Crusoe swims back to the wreck again and again to salvage essential tools and stores. He starts his island life not with nothing but with the basics, much like the colonists of the New World. The fascination of the narrative is that he must do everything himself, learning to employ tools in ways he never imagined. He is not starting the world anew but starting it again, a rebirth of the idea of a polity. Both the material and metaphysical achievements of the past must be preserved and drawn upon if civilization is to prevail.

Robinson Crusoe's first priority is defense. He constructs a small, fortified place, his "castle," with three loaded muskets as his cannon. He locates himself where he can see the ocean but where he cannot be seen unless he chooses to be.

Economy is his constant preoccupation and provides much of the fascination of the book. Crusoe's island is the antithesis of Adam Smith's prescription for the division of labor. Crusoe follows a Marxian approach tracking the labor theory of value—a thing is valued by how much time it takes to work it up, not by its market value, inasmuch as there is no market on a desert island. He is delighted to find that "I can hunt in the morning, fish in the afternoon, breed cattle in the evening, and critique after dinner, just as I like." The island is in some respects a utopia.[9]

The state did not easily gain its place as the basic unit of the international system. Other forms of governance—empires, city-states, the league of Hanseatic ports—were rival forms. The state won out because of two characteristics: clearly defined borders and sovereignty.[10] Not until about ten months have passed does Crusoe begin to survey the island. Will the island itself provide the borders of his state? Although he perceives that he had been "reduced to a meer State of Nature," he is constructing a civil society, even though it is a society of one person. Not until the sixth year of his reign, or captivity, does he build a boat and attempt to circumnavigate the island to determine its extent.

According to Aristotle, "First among the materials required by the statesman is population." All that Crusoe's state lacks is a population. This changes in one of the most memorable passages in all literature.

It happen'd one Day about Noon going towards my Boat. I was exceedingly surpriz'd with the Print of a Man's naked Foot on the Shore, which was very plain to be seen in the Sand; I stood like one Thunderstruck, or if I had seen an Apparition; I listen'd, I look'd round me. I could hear nothing, nor see any Thing; I went up to a rising Ground to look farther; I went up the Shore and down the Shore, but it was all one. I could see no other Impression but that one, I went to it again to see if there were any more, and to observe if it might not be my Fancy; but there was no Room for that, for there was exactly the very Print of a Foot, Toes, Heel, and every part of a Foot; how it came thither, I knew not, nor could in the least imagine.

Having made a dramatic escape from cannibals, whose practice is to come to the island to perform their savage rites, "Friday" is given refuge by Crusoe. Friday, who truly *is* in a state of nature, takes instruction from Crusoe and is converted to Christianity and brought into the civil society of his state.

Eventually another cannibal party comes ashore, leading to the rescue of Friday's father and a Spaniard.

My island was now peopled, and I thought myself very rich in Subjects; and it was a merry Reflection, which I frequently made, how like a King I looked. First of all, the whole Country was my own meer Property, so that I had an undoubted Right of Dominion. Secondly, my people were perfectly subjected. I was absolute Lord and Lawgiver; they all owed their Lives to me, and were ready to lay down their Lives, if there had been Occasion of it, for me. It was remarkable, too, we had but three Subjects, and they were of three different Religions. My Man Friday was a Protestant, his father was a Pagan and a cannibal, and the Spaniard was a Papist. However, I allow'd liberty of Conscience throughout my Dominions.

Having new Society enough, and our Number being sufficient to put us out of Fear of the Savages, if they had come, unless their Number had been very great, we went freely all over the Island, wherever we found Occasion.

Crusoe's island now has achieved the population, borders, sovereignty, and governance needed to qualify as a state. Next will come the test of its place within the international system. Friday alerts Crusoe, who "saw a Boat at about a league and a half's Distance, standing in for the Shore, with a Shoulder of Mutton Sail, as they call it; and the Wind blowing pretty fair to bring them in."

Mutineers in command of the ship put the captain, the mate, and a passenger ashore to perish. Crusoe surreptitiously approaches the captain, who understandably is alarmed at his appearance: "Am I talking to God, or Man! Is it a real Man, or an Angel!" Crusoe replies, "If God had sent an Angel to relieve you, he would have come better Cloath'd and Arm'd after another manner than you see me in; pray lay aside your Fears. I am a Man, an Englishman, and dispos'd to assist you."

Crusoe then commits his state to the international order. He sides with the recognized authority of the captain against unlawful mutineer-pirates, and under the laws of war, "I immediately advanc'd with my whole Army, which was now eight men, viz. My self Generalissimo, Friday my lieutenant-general, the captain and his two men, and the three Prisoners of War, who we had trusted with Arms."

Crusoe has founded a state, made it sovereign and qualified for recognition internationally. In this final crisis he leads his forces to war against those who set themselves against the international order. Then the sovereign of the island returns to England, his native country. The State of Crusoeland seemed viable when it was inhabited by Robinson Crusoe alone; with its expanded population it might prove far less so.

Hobbes's social contract led to the obvious next step: what if the sovereign broke the contract and deserved to be deposed? What if some rights are inalienable and not transferable to the sovereign? America provided answers.

John Locke, in his *Second Treatise of Government* (1690), announced that "in the beginning all the world was *America*." This was a concept something like biology's "ontogeny recapitulates phylogeny": that the changes to be seen in the New World, from life in the state of nature through a social contract that created civil society, equivalent to all that mankind had achieved across eons of prehistorical and historical time, could be achieved in a mere generation.

In this treatise, Locke set forth the elements for a polity to "begin the world anew," to replace the old order that Shakespeare's *Tempest* swept away with the wreck of the ship of state. Among these were the right to own property and to increase it through the free market; the individual's ownership of property in himself; the corollary that slavery is impermissible; the establishment of government by consent of the governed; and—in contrast to Hobbes's Anglo-European social contract—the inalienability of the rights of life, liberty, property, and freedom from absolute, arbitrary power.

Locke ends his treatise with another literary depiction of the ship of state, in a case study in strategic decision making. There may come a time, Locke says, when the right of rebellion against arbitrary government comes to the fore. If you are a passenger on a ship bound for say, America, but observe that a "long train of actions" indicates that the captain may be deceptively steering a different course, what do you do?

> How can man any more hinder himself from being persuaded in his own mind, which way things are going; or from casting about how to save himself, than he could from believing the captain of the ship he was in, was carrying him, and the rest of the company, to *Algiers* [that is, into slavery], when he found him always steering that course, though cross winds, leaks in his ship and want of men and provisions did often force him to turn his course another way for some time, which he steadily returned to again, as soon as the wind, weather, and other circumstances would let him?

Locke, by this literary anecdote, made the case for the American Revolution. His tale is, as well, a remarkable prevision of the rebellion on board the Spanish slave ship *Amistad* in 1839.[11] In a New Haven courthouse the slave ship's Africans were the subject of a debate on universality, property, law, and liberty—all ideas given an American twist—and adjudged free. Locke's literary anecdote made the case for the American Revolution and then for the Emancipation Proclamation.

The crux of the modern era may be located in the thought and differences among Hobbes, Kant, and Locke.

For Hobbes, power makes the law; there is nothing else to which to appeal. For Kant, utility will make peace; those in commerce with each other won't want to spoil their trade by war. Both are Enlightenment thinkers, and their political writings are "post-metaphysical." But opposed to these two and their ideas, the political effects of which are obvious, is a more strongly metaphysical current of thought. A decade before becoming Pope Benedict XVI, Joseph Cardinal Ratzinger wrote: "I am thinking of the three fundamental rights laid down by John Locke in his *Second Treatise of Government* (1690): life, freedom, property. The background to this is the *Magna Carta,* the *Bill of Rights,* and ultimately the natural law tradition. Here is a quite explicit claim that the rights of the person precede the state's enactments of law. Locke's way of expressing the rights of man doctrine is clearly directed at the state. It is of revolutionary significance."[12]

The astonishing fact about America is that the state would be designed to protect the individual's "metaphysical" rights of life, freedom, and property.

Locke's political philosophy provides a basis for American exceptionalism and a theme that will reappear across American diplomacy from colonial times to the present: that America at once is, and is not, a part of the international state system. Private property is at the heart of Locke's theory, as indispensable for freedom as it is for material accumulation. In *America* (Locke always italicizes the name), property is not finite but infinitely available. This breaks the Old World link between property and the bounded territory of a state. "America," Locke wrote, "is made both continuous and discontinuous with already extant nation-states by relegating the business of making new landed property, and the state-making associated with that possession, to a place outside the system of nations." This will make the United States' recognition of, and relationship to, "the international" an ambiguous matter.

The Declaration of Independence was a message from the United States to the world community of sovereign states, all of equal status. By speaking like a state, the Declaration sought to bring the United States into being as a state. As it did, it marked the birth of a new genre of political writing. Its argument and literary form have been models for the founding of other states that reject empires ever since. The United States' role in the international system would be like that of no other polity in history.[13]

The early pages of *The Federalist Papers*—Hamilton, Madison, and Jay writing as "Publius" to instruct newspaper readers on the importance and meaning of the new Constitution—show the American Founders to be close readers of the great books of political thought. They joined the literary-historical conversation of great texts about strategy, statecraft, and power across centuries. Publius reveals the Constitution as meant to avoid the flaws of democracy as revealed in classic texts.

The first paragraph of *Federalist* no. 1 takes up Rousseau's charge that no government in existence now or at any time in history has been legitimate. Rousseau was perhaps the first major thinker of the West to declare that civilization as we know it had been from the start, back in the far mists of time past, an abominable mistake. All began to go wrong, Rousseau said, when someone said, "This is mine"; the idea of property ushered in millennia of injustice and greed-driven violence. So, says Publius, "it seems to have been reserved to the people of this country, by their conduct and example, to decide the important question, whether societies of men are really capable or not of establishing good government from reflection and choice, or whether they are forever destined to depend for their political constitutions on accident and force." If we could not see and meet this challenge, or choose wrongly, our failure would "deserve to be considered as the general misfortune of mankind."

The first requirement, wrote Hamilton in no. 1, is union, to be one united people. The people correctly perceive that "a cordial Union, under an efficient national government, affords them the best security that can be devised against hostilities from abroad." In Jay's no. 4 we hear a reference to the Peloponnesian War that devastated ancient Greece from 431 to 404 B.C. As described by Thucydides and later by Plutarch, Athens's rising power alarmed the Spartans so much that they concluded they must go to war at once against the Athenians; delay would only allow Athenian power to grow too dominant for Sparta to do anything other than submit to Athens's will. "It is easy to see," writes Jay, "that jealousies and uneasiness may gradually slide into the minds and cabinets of other nations, and that we are not to expect that they should regard our advancement in union, in power and consequence by land and by sea, with an eye of indifference and composure." But: "If they see that our national government is efficient and well administered, our trade prudently regulated, our militia properly organized and disciplined, our resources and finances discreetly managed, our credit re-established, our people free, contented and united, they will be much more disposed to cultivate our friendship than provoke our resentment."

In other words, the new United States should not act like the Athens of old.

Hamilton elaborates on this in no. 6, in his characterization of the Athenian leader Pericles, whom history generally considers one of the most admirable statesmen and orators of all time. "The celebrated Pericles," says Hamilton, and we can hear the contempt in his tone,

> stimulated by private pique against the Megaranesians, another nation of Greece, or to avoid a prosecution with which he was threatened as an accomplice in a supposed theft of the statuary of Phidias, or to get rid of accusations prepared to be brought against him for dissipating the funds of the state in the purchase of popularity, or for a combination of all of these causes, was the primitive author of that famous and fatal war, distinguished in the Grecian annals by the name of the Peloponnesian War; which, after various vicissitudes, intermissions, and renewals, terminated in the ruin of the Athenian commonwealth.

Hamilton seems to conclude that at times of testing, the great Pericles showed some serious flaws as a statesman—and that Athenian democracy itself was flawed.

Hamilton refers to the blockade imposed by Athens to halt trade between Megara and Sparta. Sparta was willing to call off the war if Athens would only lift its embargo. Pericles, speaking publicly, rejected this proposal. Megara might seem a minor matter, he said, but should Athens show a lack of resolve in small things, its credibility in large issues could be undermined. The terrible costs of the war to come, as Hamilton saw it, make Pericles' position seem a matter more of pride than of statesmanship.

Pericles misstepped again with the "statuary of Phidias" in the Parthenon. Pericles had the gold vestments on Athena's statue designed in sheaths so that each section could be removed and its exact weight recorded should it become necessary to refute charges of corruption in its construction. Pericles, in his speech to the Athenians on the eve of war, pointed out that should the war be prolonged and costly, the gold could be removed and melted down to pay for war material. This seemed impious, undermining the morale of the people even as Pericles was calling upon them to wage war for their city under the protection of their patroness Athena.

As citizens of a "direct democracy," not a republic of checks and balances, Athenians could be called to assembly repeatedly and swayed by a leader of oratorical skill. War could be launched at once, preempting any effort at careful deliberation. So vivid was Thucydides' description of the Athenian mobs during the Peloponnesian War, in what was considered the definitive history of Athens, that even many friends of democracy in America avoided using the word. Like the advocates of mixed government, they used the word *republic* and emphasized the stability fostered by representation.[14]

The *Federalist* writers aimed to design a free society to avoid Athens's susceptibility to internal discord, but they held no illusions about peace in the external realm. Hamilton in no. 6 refers to "perpetual peace," and in his fiercely distinctive style he rejects the argument put forward by Rousseau and later elaborated by Kant that republics, or democracies, would be less inclined than other forms of government to wage war. Nor does he accept the corollary that international trade would help very much to keep the peace.

> Have republics in practice been less addicted to war than monarchies? Are not the former administered by *men* as well as the latter? Are there not aversions, predilections, rivalships and desires of unjust acquisitions that affect nations as well as kings? Are not popular assemblies frequently subject to the impulses of rage, resentment, jealousy, avarice, and of other irregular and violent propensities? . . . Has commerce hitherto done any thing more than change the objects of war? . . . Have there not been as many wars founded upon commercial motives since that has become the prevailing system of nations, as were before occasioned by the cupidity of territory or dominion?

Hamilton's no. 9 and Madison's no. 10 describe the unprecedented, even bizarre political-economic machinery by which the United States would run itself. America was not to be Athens. It would be a unique polity that would need "The Enlargement of the Orbit"; that is, it would need to grow to embrace the continent, and to embrace factionalism rather than seek to suppress or contain it like other political systems. The more contending factions the better, and the more wealth, class, and property discrepancies, the better. Diversity would permit America to avoid the catastrophe that direct democracy had inflicted on Athens in the Peloponnesian War.

The United States, its Founders insisted, would define itself as a state unlike any other. They had read carefully statecraft's classic texts, filled with accounts of mistakes the new United States would be designed to avoid.

Washington's Farewell Address, in large part "ghostwritten" by a trio of statesmen yet nonetheless authentically Washington's testament, represented his wisdom and concerns gathered during his service in war and peace. Modern American presidents have made their speeches in the same way: speechwriters produce the drafts—usually many drafts—but the product truly represents the thought and emotions of the principal. If it doesn't, the people will quickly know it, and the president quickly be embarrassed by it. Washington wrote a first draft which bears out his own assessment that he "had little confidence in his literary gifts."[15]

Washington enlisted Alexander Hamilton to work on the speech and turn it to its best advantage. Hamilton had done much drafting for Washington and could be counted on to greatly improve both its style and its substance. Yet Hamilton knew Washington's steely character and self-regard well. He would never accept a text that did not fully express his own thought and mood about the material covered.

Washington wanted the address to incorporate an earlier draft that James Madison had written for him as a valedictory in 1792. By this time, the late 1790s, Hamilton and Madison were intellectual rivals, leaders of the two political parties, the Federalists and the Republicans. The record seems to show Washington maneuvering between the two—getting Madison's approval to incorporate his early draft, and persuading Hamilton not to fight it—almost as a way of consolidating American policy by assigning them this common task. Hamilton's own contribution closely tracks his writing in *The Federalist,* so much so that scholars are almost certain that he drew on it for the text.[16]

Within the immensely rich text of the Farewell Address can be found, or felt, virtually every major concept expressed in the literature of statecraft. First, the fear, well expressed by Thucydides, that popular (that is, direct) democracy is liable to break down into bitter factionalism: "The baneful effects of the spirit of party . . . exist under different shapes in all governments, more or less stifled, controlled, or repressed, but in those of the popular form, it is seen in its greatest rankness and is truly their worst enemy." Second, unchecked popular democracy's tendency swiftly and heedlessly to propel the country into war without good cause. There is a healthy Hamiltonian suspicion of Kant's faith in the peacefulness of republics.

Hobbes's "realism" also lurks here. Every state on the international scene may be expected to strive ceaselessly to increase its power in order to advance its particular interests. Madison and Hamilton, in *Federalist Papers* 9, 10, and 51, had devised a system to operate *within* the United States to provide security, order, justice, and energy. (Would it work? Washington's address answers: experience will tell us.) Outside the nation's borders however, a power struggle will go on. "There can be no greater error than to expect or calculate upon real favors from nation to nation," Washington says, and "against the insidious wiles of foreign influence (I conjure you to believe me, fellow-citizens) the jealousy of a free people ought to be constantly awake."

Yet realism is paired with idealism. Washington considers religion the mainstay of morality. The two together are "indispensable supports" for prosperity, for "where is the security for property, for reputation, for life, if the sense of religious obligation desert the oaths which are the instruments of investigation in courts of justice? Add to these the general diffusion of knowledge and sound fiscal management, and the nation will be prepared to "observe good faith and justice towards all nations; cultivate peace and harmony with all."

This leads to Washington's conception of America as exceptional. Americans should exult in "the name of America," which transcends all other sectional or functional allegiances. America is a new and geographically different place that stands apart from and does not naturally belong to the European (Westphalian) system. So, says Washington, "Why forgo the advantages of so peculiar a situation? Why quit on our own to stand upon foreign ground? Why, by interweaving our destiny with that of any part of Europe, entangle our peace and prosperity in the toils of European ambition, rivalship, interest, humor, or caprice?"

In this founding text of American Idealism, Washington concludes that America "will be worthy of a free, enlightened, and at no distant period, a great nation, to give to mankind the magnanimous and too novel example of a people always guided by an exalted justice and benevolence."

The speech goes beyond *The Federalist.* Washington knew that the American polity would have to depend upon more than its political institutions, no matter how brilliant their design. The future would depend upon private virtues, on the habits and dispositions of the people, on the formation of an American national character capable of preserving the constitution and conducting self-government. Nearly two centuries later, Martin Luther King, Jr., would stress "the content of their character," the importance of virtue for the success of a free society.[17]

Every major shift and dimension of American foreign policy—the ambiguity, the tension between withdrawal and engagement, the contradictions of raw power politics and "exalted justice and benevolence"—are all here in Washington, Hamilton, and Madison's rhetorical masterpiece.

The epic of founding is followed, and matched, by sharp efforts to redefine, and monumental sacrifices to preserve, the still-new American polity. Ralph Waldo Emerson, "the American Shakespeare," exalted self-reliance—not self-indulgence but self-disciplined democratic individualism—as the only true way to honor human dignity and civil rights.[18] But the chasm between ideal and real led a sour Henry David Thoreau to go into the woods to design and practice the founding of the republic all over again, to try to get it right this time. *Walden* has been read every year since as one of the texts of American holy scripture, exhorting us to recall what we should do even though we know we can't.

Henry David Thoreau went to Walden Pond and built a simple house there. He began to occupy his house on the Fourth of July, 1845, the anniversary of The Declaration of Independence that was sparked by a skirmish a short distance away, in the village of Concord.[19] The book that Thoreau would write there, *Walden,* describes his thoughts about revisiting the original July 4 so as to restart the whole process of state-building. *Walden* makes clear that Thoreau opposed every major aspect of the American republic that had emerged in the decades since Independence. Commerce, industry, technology, politics, culture, architecture, and progress itself—all had to be rethought and re-created from the ground up. The United States had not turned out the way Thoreau would have wanted it.

Walden is an American rewriting of the most influential treatise on the origin, legitimacy, and meaning of governance ever written: Aristotle's *Politics.* Like Aristotle, Thoreau explores the fundamentals of human nature and human needs so as to ground and explain how a polity comes into being.

Aristotle's starting point is the "natural" subsistence economy of the household, the smallest and most necessary community. His treatise repels the modern reader by dwelling on slavery, depicting it as "natural." It becomes clear that slavery must be faced and explained in the process of polity-building since it is a universal phenomenon. Some people are naturally servile, others natural managers and masters. Slaves are property, Aristotle says, and the management of property belongs to the household. Other relationships are similar: the soul rules over the body; the farmer rules over the oxen. The slave is to the master as the part is to the whole; to harm the part is to harm the whole.

From here Aristotle describes the process that leads to the polis, the city-state. The village is an extended household, and the polis is the goal of the household and the village. The polis is natural too, because a thing's nature is what it is when it has reached its goal, as the oak is the outcome of the acorn's nature. Think of it as movement from natural to Natural with a capital *N*. The slave's Natural destination is freedom.

Politics is thus about transformation. It is natural for a household with a subsistence farm to grow a crop and consume it all. But trading for money in the village is also natural, for living well together is the intention of nature. The polis, in this sense, is "prior to" the household. All are attained through politics, the supreme discipline. Human beings, unlike other animals, do not possess an innate social structure; thus "man is the *political* animal": our nature is to be political.

So, says Aristotle, the subsistence household arises from natural needs, and groups of households can form a village. But the subsistence household and the village are too narrow for humans to fulfill their nature. The polis then is the natural entity for human fulfillment. The vital functions of ruling, educating, protecting, and increasing all require a polis—the only place where politics can fully function—in order for these functions to be carried out as nature intended through a natural division of labor.

Walden takes a "from the ground up" approach, as does Aristotle's *Politics,* but Thoreau turns the transformative process in the opposite direction. Like Aristotle, he starts with the economy of the household; "Economy" is the longest section of *Walden.* The direction runs from the polis back to the household, in this case a household of one. The most natural starting point for Thoreau is not the household of man and woman, parents and children, master and slave, farmer and farm animals, but of the solitary person: "In most books, the *I,* or first person, is omitted; in this it will be retained; that, in respect to egotism, is the main difference. We commonly do not remember that it is, after all, always the first person that is speaking. I should not talk so much about myself if there was anybody else whom I knew as well." Thoreau here is carrying the American inclination to individualism to its farthest edge, the "absolute necessity for every Person to act singly . . . as if there was not another human creature upon earth."[20] On the other hand, Thoreau's rural household is utterly at odds with the American Farmer described by Crèvecoeur, or the agricultural yeoman who serves as the foundation stone of Thomas Jefferson's thought.

Like Aristotle, Thoreau takes up the issue of slavery right from the start. Thoreau was an abolitionist, deeply opposed to the practice of slave-holding in America. At the start of *Walden,* he carries this view to the subsistence household itself. Farming in all its dimensions—the ownership or lease of land and buildings, the keeping of herds or draft animals, the need for credit, the search for markets, the toil and the account-keeping— all this is another form of slavery. He sees young men "whose misfortune it is to have inherited farms, houses, barns, cattle, and farming-tools: for these are more easily acquired than got rid of. . . . Who made them serfs of the soil?" The attention given to "Negro Slavery" may even seem frivolous when "there are so many keen and subtle masters that enslave both North and South": "It is hard to have a southern overseer; it is worse to have a northern one; but worst of all when you are the slave-driver yourself."

Thoreau turns the Aristotelian progression around. The necessities of life are food, clothing, shelter, and fuel. In the village or city, the complexity of arrangements surrounding each has created a distorted nature, and only by simplifying each category can the truly natural be achieved. Take fuel, for example: "Some, not wise, go to the other side of the globe, to barbarous and unhealthy regions, and devote themselves to trade for ten or twenty years, in order that they may live—that is, keep comfortably warm—and die in New England at last."

At the heart of this is the question of one's labor. Thoreau rejects John Locke's view of America and the matter of increase through trade.

> Not long since, a strolling Indian went to sell baskets at the house of a well-known lawyer in my neighborhood. "Do you wish to buy any baskets?" he asked. "No, we do not want any," was the reply. "What!" exclaimed the Indian as he went out the gate, "do you mean to starve us?" Having seen his industrious white neighbors so well off—that

the lawyer had only to weave arguments, and by some magic wealth and standing followed, he had said to himself: I will go into business; I will weave baskets; it is a thing which I can do. Thinking that when he had made the baskets he would have done his part, and then it would be the white man's to buy them.

Here Aristotle, Locke, and Adam Smith are turned on their heads. The "natural" native American has been drawn by stages from subsistence, or necessary, labor through "the labor theory of value" and into the village world of market value; each step taking him farther away from human nature. "My thoughts are murder to the State," Thoreau wrote in his journal. *Walden*, in its search for the economically simplified life of the Indian, is a meditation on savagism, albeit transcendental savagism. Thoreau "had Indians on the brain" and, as Hawthorne said, seemed "inclined to lead a sort of Indian life among civilized men." His friendships were with fish, birds, and animals, he could predict the weather, handle his boat with only one paddle, and strangest of all, find arrowheads and relics as if the red men's "spirits willed him to be the inheritor of their simple wealth."[21]

Thoreau does not reject civilization, he uses and exploits it. He is a land surveyor, measuring the metes and bounds of his jurisdiction, eager to plumb the unknown bottom of his pond (but only the loon, with "demonic laughter," can dive to such a depth; nature eludes civilization's skills). Thoreau accepts the advantages which the invention and industry of mankind offer, to use its materials in a wiser way. As Robinson Crusoe makes use of the tools salvaged from the shipwreck, so Thoreau borrows an axe, for "it is difficult to begin without borrowing." He then buys the shanty of an Irish railway worker in order to take it to pieces for its boards and shingles and nails, which he will use in constructing his cabin at Walden Pond. As he carts the building materials away, he imagines "this seemingly insignificant event one with the removal of the gods of Troy" when Aeneas left the ruined city to set out on a journey to found a new polity.

I long ago lost a hound, a bay horse, and a turtle-dove, and am still on their trail.

Any attempt to interpret this famous vatic line from *Walden* would be an offense against literature; its meaning is just what it says. Nonetheless, as Aristotle takes note of the different economic cultures across time—the hunting (hound), the farming (horse) ways—so something in this line suggests that those ways are gone, and Thoreau seeks another as he listens for "the voice of the turtle," which Bunyan's *Pilgrim's Progress* hears in Beulah, land of spiritual contentment, and God's new Israel. Thoreau, like the nation, can be born again after baptism in Walden Pond's waters.

As he carefully erects his cabin and keeps his famously minute accounts, Thoreau never factors in his own labor as a cost; there is no labor or market theory of value here. He has scrounged what he needs from the polis and is engaged in transforming its imperfect nature into a perfected new life. And of course, he will get his laundry and mending done by others, and take many meals at the house of his neighbor, Ralph Waldo Emerson. Thoreau has made civilization *his* servant.

All this is set out in *Walden*'s long first chapter. From this revisionist-Aristotelian foundation, Thoreau explains "where I lived, and what I lived for." Then from three chapters about his private self—"Reading," "Sounds," and "Solitude"—he turns to the public dimension in "Visitors" and "The Bean-Field," after which he goes into "The Village," as if to test whether his philosophy is borne out. Is the village, for Aristotle a stage *more* natural than the household, less so for Thoreau? Yes, he is vindicated in his expectations: "The vitals of the village were the grocery, the bar-room, the post-office and the bank. . . . Signs were hung out on all sides to allure him; some to catch him by the appetite, as the tavern and victualling cellar; some by the fancy, as the dry goods store and the jeweller's; and others by the hair or the feet or the skirts, as the barber, the shoemaker, or the tailor."

Here in the village, Thoreau is seized and jailed because "I did not pay tax to, or recognize the authority of, the state which buys and sells men, women and children, like cattle at the door of its senate-house." Thoreau's fantasy of restarting the United States was summarized by his one political act in this belief: the night he spent in the town jail in 1846 for refusing to pay his poll tax, a protest against the Mexican War. ("Henry! What are you doing in there?" "Waldo, what are you doing *out* there?") Released the next day, he returned to the woods, to his alternative polity of one.

Thoreau found the American state that began on July 4, 1776, unworthy of his allegiance, and he set out to redo it, to start all over again. What he achieved was an impossibility as a polity, but for Americans ever after, it would remain a compelling dream which would have great impact upon our political life.

In 1859 Thoreau found his hero: John Brown, whose raid on Harper's Ferry had failed, and who was under sentence of death for treason. In Brown's defiant act and death, Thoreau glimpsed a potential new American beginning. He was emboldened to call a town meeting, remarkable for him, to try to convince the citizens of Concord that Brown's cause was of momentous significance for America. "As Brown acted, so we must act now. . . . The selectmen would not have the town bell ring, so Thoreau rang it himself."[22]

Thoreau's "Plea for Captain John Brown" is an essay in the line of his other essays. It has been called as well a lecture, as Emerson would give it on the lecture circuit. Above all it is a speech, and the reader today easily can hear Thoreau's flat, often sardonic tone and familiar cadence. His plea creates John Brown as a literary figure.

Thoreau portrays Brown as a paragon, an old-fashioned patriot, a man "of great common sense" and admirably Spartan habits. Thoreau met Brown when he visited Concord and had been taken with his manner and substance of speech. "He did not overstate any thing, but spoke within bounds. I remember, particularly, how, in his speech here, he referred to what his family had suffered in Kansas, without ever giving the least vent to his pent-up fire. It was a volcano with an ordinary chimney-flue. . . . He was not in the least a rhetorician. . . . It was like the speeches of Cromwell."

In truth, Brown was a ne'er-do-well and troublemaker who had failed in every undertaking and left behind a trail of lawsuits and bitterness as he bounced from one moneymaking scheme to another. In Kansas, undoubtedly, he was a terrorist.[23] At Pottawatomie, the weapons used on unarmed men had been short broadswords, hollow and loaded with quicksilver. "When held upright, the quicksilver dropped to the hold, but slid upward to the point in striking motion so as to increase the force of the blow. . . . Fierce, heavy blows sliced through upraised arms, and the awful blades split their skulls almost to the neck."[24] If Thoreau knew about Brown's actions in Kansas—and he probably didn't know much—he chose not to credit the tales.

Thoreau's significant insight lay in his interpretation of Harper's Ferry. Brown had established a secret network of supporters, many well-to-do and influential, stretching from New England as far west as Iowa. When the raid took place, "very few even of the most dedicated friends of John Brown expected the act of war he launched against the United States arsenal at Harper's Ferry." Apparently they thought he was planning a different action—to attack a slaveholding state, liberate as many slaves as possible, and retreat to a free state. The Harper's Ferry raid shocked and immobilized Brown's backers.[25]

Not Thoreau. He sensed that Brown and his raid were uniquely symbolic. Thoreau's "Plea" sets out the case for a new America, arguing from Brown's epic struggle. Throughout his oration, Thoreau refers to John Brown in the past tense, as though he already had been hanged. He was therefore pleading not for Brown's life but for a recognition that his act and his death to redeem a new republic.

Thoreau begins by asserting that John Brown was better than those embattled farmers who fired "the shot heard 'round the world." Brown, Thoreau said, was "firmer and higher-principled than any that I have chanced to hear of as there"—a stunning thing to say to a Concord audience.

Why was Brown a better man? Because he did not go to Harvard, and so "was not fed on the pap that is there furnished." Instead, he went to the great university of the West, where he studied liberty and practiced humanity—such were *his humanities.* Brown is of Puritan heritage, Thoreau says, the re-creation of Cromwell, in whose time he must have fought and died, "but he reappeared here. Why should he not? Some of the Puritan stock are said to have come over and settled in New England." Here is Thoreau at his scathing best, telling this Massachusetts meeting that *you,* my hearers, are not the men your forebears were, but *he* is, because he knew himself "the equal of any and all governments. In that sense he was the most American of us all."

The citizens of the United States in 1859, Thoreau says, are tainted by a slavery in which all are complicit but Brown, then turns to an image right out of John Locke's "Ship to Algiers": "The slave-ship is on her way, crowded with its dying victims; new cargoes are being added in mid-ocean; a small crew of slave holders, countenanced by a large body of passengers, is smothering four millions under the hatches, and yet the politician asserts that the only proper way by which deliverance is to be obtained, is by 'the quiet diffusion of the sentiments of humanity.' . . . What is that I hear cast overboard? The bodies of the dead that have found deliverance."

The ship of state is a slave ship. The effect of Brown's raid on Harper's Ferry was to cause words to lose their meaning. People in the North, Thoreau says, "saw that what was called order was confusion, what was called justice, injustice, and that the best was deemed the worst."

Brown was fond of repeating Hebrews 9:22: "Without the shedding of blood is no remission" of sins. As he made his way to the scaffold he handed a note to a jailer. "I, John Brown, am now quite certain that the crime of this guilty land will never be purged away but with blood." Thoreau senses or foresees this at the end of his "Plea" as he compares John Brown to Christ: "Some eighteen hundred years ago Christ was crucified; this morning, perchance, Captain Brown was hung."

At the end of his oration, Thoreau, who admits that Brown was no rhetorician, returns to the "sweet and noble strain" of his words, quoting five passages from Brown's statements to his captors. Thoreau strives for transcendence of his own, almost in an attempt to surpass Brown's act: "I foresee the time when the painter will paint that scene, no longer going to Rome for a subject; the poet will sing it; the historian record it; and with the landing of the Pilgrims and Declaration of Independence, it will be the ornament of some future national gallery, when at least the present form of slavery shall be no more here. We shall then be at liberty to weep for Captain Brown. Then, and not till then, we will take our revenge."

Thoreau tries here too to surpass Emerson, whose "The American Scholar" was taken as our declaration of literary independence. Thoreau here says our literature and art cannot be independent until we produce our authentic epic, and that will be when Brown's act is finally understood and exalted. Just as Thoreau's refounding at Walden went awry as to the laws of economics, Brown went wrong at Pottawatomie by transgressing the moral bar on terrorism. American literary notables, led by Thoreau and Emerson, undertook the nearly impossible task of portraying Brown, widely considered a dangerous lunatic, as a noble, sanctified hero. "It was a moment when literature and history collided and literature re-wrote history."[26]

But John Brown, that loser, crank, monomaniac, and terrorist, through his doomed raid on the arsenal at Harper's Ferry, got the last laugh, for his myth as trumpeted by Henry Thoreau did start the country over again—in the great Civil War that brought forth the mystic vision of Abraham Lincoln.

In November 1856 Thoreau was taken to meet Walt Whitman in his Brooklyn cottage. An eyewitness described them as two wary animals, uncompromising rivals "in smelling out 'all nature.'" Thoreau later praised *Leaves of Grass* as "a great primitive poem—an alarum or trumpet-note ringing through the American camp."[27]

Whitman's purpose was to declaim the American dream as an eschatological event that would provide humanity with its ultimate significance. Alexis de Tocqueville explained Whitman's poetry before it was written. In his 1835 *Democracy in America*—"the best book on democracy and the best book on America"—Tocqueville notes that in aristocracies, a leading class will prescribe rules that may not be broken.[28] The literature produced will place the highest value on works of refinement and delicacy. "The slightest work will be polished in every detail." Style and form will be as important as substance and thought. And to distinguish themselves from the vulgar, the aristocrats will produce a vocabulary of their own.

By contrast, a democracy will mingle classes, stimulate mobility, scatter knowledge widely, and chip away at traditions and settled habits. And so "it is from the heterogeneous, stirring crowd that authors spring, and from it they must win profit and renown. . . . By and large the literature of a democracy will never exhibit the order, regularity, skill and art characteristic of aristocratic literature. . . . The style will often be strange, incorrect, overburdened, and loose, and almost always strong and bold. . . . There will be rude and untutored vigor of thought with great variety and singular fecundity."

But poetry, Tocqueville says, is "the fairest flower of language," and democracies do not have the taste for it that aristocracies do. In democratic societies, poets can never take a particular man as the subject of their poetry because "each man, as he looks at himself, sees all his fellows at the same time." So the spread of democracy around the world dries up the old springs of poetry. "I gladly agree," Tocqueville says, "that there are no American poets."

Here Tocqueville, as with so many subjects, becomes eerily prescient. Other "springs of poetry" are out there waiting to be tapped. Tocqueville intuits why the tradition of epic poetry that began with Homer ran out with Milton: "When skepticism had depopulated heaven, and equality had cut each man to a smaller and better known size, the poets, wondering what to substitute for the great themes lost with the aristocracy, first turned their eyes to inanimate nature. Gods and heroes gone, they began by painting rivers and mountains." He then starts to speculate about what as yet unexplored sources of poetry might exist within democracy. If democracy shuts the past to poetry, it opens the future: "Here then are wide vistas."

Although there is nothing more "antipoetic" than the petty, insipid, paltry daily life of an American, there is at the same time one great thought that is full of poetic potential: "the picture of one vast democracy in which a nation counts as a single citizen. Thus, for the first time all mankind can be seen together in broad daylight." In a democratic age, "Human destiny . . . will for these peoples be the chief and almost sole object of poetry. One can already be sure that this will be so if one considers the greatest poets that have appeared in the world since it turned toward democracy."

Tocqueville could not have known that Whitman was then at work; and Whitman did not read *Democracy in America*. But Tocqueville's sense of an epic democratic poetry to come describes Whitman exactly: "There is no need to traverse earth and sky to find a wondrous object full of contrasts of infinite greatness and littleness, of deep gloom and amazing brightness, capable at the same time of arousing piety, wonder, scorn and terror. I have only to contemplate myself."

Tocqueville declared democracy to be a force of history, inexorably moving across the centuries to undermine hierarchical political systems in its widening drive for ever more equality. We recall that the Founders of the United States were vividly aware that direct democracy had destroyed ancient Athens. Madison's *Federalist* no. 10 devised an unprecedentedly complex system to check democracy's excesses, defend the liberty of the individual in all his merit or eccentricity, and thus hold back the drive toward a leveling kind of equality.

Whitman would take up the democratic challenge of equality that preoccupied Tocqueville. With the instincts of a statesman, Whitman would create a new form of epic poetry, but Whitman's democracy would be starkly at odds with that of Publius, an all-inclusive collectivity rather than a concatenation of individual strivers. The tension between them would drive American politics.

Whitman announces his epic intentions in the first (1855) edition of *Leaves of Grass* with a line that calls up the two greatest ancient poets. Virgil begins the *Aeneid,* "I sing of arms and the man." "Arms" refers to Homer's *Iliad,* the epic of the Trojan War and power. "Man" refers to the *Odyssey,* Homer's epic of homecoming through intelligent guile. Whitman's first line mocks them both: "I celebrate myself." In case we didn't get it, Whitman rewrites it in a later edition:

> One's-self I sing, a simple separate *person*
> Yet *utter* the *word* Democratic, the *word* for En-Masse

Leaves of Grass is an anti-epic, aimed at making obsolete the classic, traditional epic of great mythological or historic wars and adventures. Whitman reexamines and recasts democracy. He makes it universally available. Correspondingly, *Leaves of Grass* is translated and absorbed into cultures all around the world. "Even the peasants in Denmark know him," Ezra Pound would say. Grass, the universal plant, the regenerative masses, is his symbol.

The 1855 first edition opens with an outrageous declarative preface: a great poetry is coming that will equal the significance of the United States itself. The self, the individual, is at one with the democratic whole. But this is not a leveling equality that erases differences. The self remains at the forefront. The particular and the universal are in phase.

The poem merges national and international. Whitman "celebrated with equal fervor his native country, his 'nation,' as well as 'all nations, colors, barbarisms, civilizations, languages, / all identities that have existed or may exist on this globe, or / any globe.' "[29] Concomitantly Whitman speaks strongly for immigration. The United States is "the modern composite Nation, formed from all, with room for all, welcoming all immigrants."[30]

Whitman's epic has a powerfully intentional political thrust. The self participates in nature's regeneration like the "leaves of grass" that cover the earth. The democratic principle is regeneration, both in nature and in the story of the nation's founding.[31] To Whitman, literature in the classic, perfected sense of Virgil's *Aeneid* is an enemy to be overcome. America is open, boundless, ever-changing. It will be a civilization capable of overcoming state structures that have stifled poets since Rome. Says one scholar, Whitman "worked all his life, it seems, to accomplish the death of Virgil."[32]

To Whitman, the United States is a poem. America is synonymous with democracy. It embodies democracy as a force of history, and as such it is the first truly global nation because born from an idea. In this way, standing on the shoulders of John Locke, Thomas Jefferson, and Madison, Hamilton, and Jay of the *Federalist Papers,* Whitman made America into a political theory. Seen from one angle, his bombastic patriotism might seem a theory of overbearing imperialism, for he welcomed territorial expansion via the annexation of Canada, Cuba, Mexico, and beyond. From another angle, however, Whitman's epic linked self, nation, state, and world to the dynamic principles of liberation and equality. This would be seen in Woodrow Wilson's "making the world safe for democracy," in the democratization of Japan and Germany in the post–World War II occupation period, and in American leadership of the free world in the Cold War. It is also manifest in the national security strategy of 2002, which dared in an age of relativism to declare a set of principles that all people share, including "the right to choose your own government."[33]

In 1857 Whitman called for a "Redeemer President" to come out of "the real West, the log hut, the clearing, the woods, the prairie, the hillside." He wanted to see some "heroic, shrewd, fully-informed, healthy-bodied, middle-aged, beard-faced American blacksmith or boatman come from the West and walk into the presidency." This sounds much like Thoreau's paean to John Brown, who studied liberty and practiced humanity to prepare himself to transform America in the American heartland.

In 1858 Whitman appealed for "a revolution in American oratory" and "a great leading representative man, with perfect power, perfect confidence in his power . . . who will make free the American soul." Whitman the poet was summoning Lincoln the orator statesman. The poetry in Lincoln is what has made him an enigmatically stirring American president. It is probably what elevated his statecraft to its great achievement.[34]

The ties between Whitman's poetry and Lincoln's oratory have been convincingly sketched by Daniel Mark Epstein. Lincoln's law partner Billy Herndon, a passionate book collector, bought in Chicago a copy of the second, 1856, edition of *Leaves of Grass,* and Lincoln, who would sprawl out in their Springfield, Illinois, law office for a time every day just to read, voraciously if slowly, and out loud, picked up the volume. As Herndon pointed out, Lincoln did not read many books, but those he did read he absorbed completely. Lincoln kept at *Leaves of Grass,* seemingly oblivious to the furor it was causing in the country and among the young men who were reading law for the bar in the Lincoln-Herndon office.

Describing Lincoln's reading, Epstein notes that his favorite author was Euclid, for the logic and clarity of his propositions. Lincoln was searching for more, however.

"The Greek formed Lincoln's style of debate. Now Lincoln was searching for a still center of the turning world of human nature, a diamond-hard pivot on which he might set his compass to draw the circle of American civilization."[35] Everything in Whitman's poetry appealed to Lincoln's character, ambition, and vision.

Lincoln's writing and speaking before and after he read *Leaves of*

Grass were markedly different. His solid, logical, but unexceptional early prose style is transformed in the late 1850s into the vivid imagery, rooted in the work and words of the people, for which he was ever after famous.

In 1857 Lincoln's speech responding to Stephen A. Douglas's defense of the Dred Scott decision was dramatically unlike anything he had done before. The hourlong argument contained "more poetic tropes than any speech Lincoln had ever given . . . a poetry of surprises, challenges, and brazen disregard for propriety and convention. It is Whitmanesque. Lincoln appears to be under the poet's spell."[36]

On April 6, 1858, Lincoln delivered a lecture on "Discoveries and Inventions," a seemingly dry and uninspiring topic but one that he had been interested in from his earliest days as a public figure. This "lecture" is anything but; it is more like a Homeric hymn, if such a hymn had been sung by Whitman:

> All creation is a mine, and every man, a miner.
> The whole earth, and all *within* it, *upon* it, and *round about* it,
> including *himself* in his physical, moral, and intellectual
> nature, and his susceptibilities, are the infinitely
> various "leads" from which, man, from the first, was to
> dig out his destiny.
> In the beginning, the mine was unopened, and the miner stood
> *naked,* and *knowledgeless,* upon it.

Whitman's poem "A Song for Occupations" is filled with a catalogue of the same discoveries and inventions that Lincoln celebrates. Epstein does not conclude that Lincoln composed any speech with *Leaves of Grass* open before him, but "the poet's fingerprints are all over the Lecture on Discoveries and Inventions."

Lincoln's "House Divided" oration, the speech that probably made him president, wed his own pre-Whitman images—from the King James Bible, and the line that government cannot endure "half slave and half free"—with Whitmanesque cadences and diction. Whitman made an entire poem a single great metaphor for America; Lincoln's "House Divided" did so as well: the American nation as a single-family house, the "balloon frame" invention of prairie folk. The timbers joined together to make the frame. All the tenons and mortices exactly fitting, and all the lengths and proportions of the different pieces exactly adapted to their respective places, and not a piece too many or too few—not even omitting scaffolding—or if a piece be lacking, "we can see the place in the frame exactly fitted and prepared to yet bring such a piece in." We can know that the framers "all understood one another from the beginning, and all worked upon a common plan or draft drawn up before the first lick was struck." So Lincoln described the democratic family home as the way to understand the history and future of the nation.[37] Deeply moved by Whitman, Lincoln first imitated him, then—Whitman having unlocked some barrier in him—proceeded to become himself the statesman-poet counterpart to Whitman's poet-statesman.

The Civil War, as Lincoln led the Union through it, was a global event. America was rebooted as a powerful federal state (not at all what Thoreau had in mind) during the same period in which Germany and Japan gained centralized modern power. Just as or more important, the moral effect of mass emancipation (of which Thoreau dreamed) was enormous. "Across the British Empire, early colonial nationalists were distantly but powerfully affected by the outcome of the Civil War."[38]

The 1648 Westphalian settlement understood religion to be a "cause of quarrel" that had propelled Europe into a series of horrendous wars. Afterward, states might be predominantly of one or another religion, but they would be expected to accept religious minorities within their jurisdictions and, most important, to keep religion off the negotiating table in international diplomacy. Except for Christendom's lingering wars with the Turk, the Westphalian effort to take religion out of world political affairs succeeded remarkably well.

American history is suffused with religion, from the founding of Massachusetts Bay Colony to the Founding Fathers. Tocqueville saw that religion had a key role in America: religion sees political freedom as "a sphere intended by the Creator for the free play of intelligence." Freedom sees religion "as the companion of its struggles and triumphs, the cradle of its infancy, and the divine source of its rights." This fine balance, Tocqueville claimed, was maintained by the clergy's inclination to avoid direct political activity.

Lincoln and Whitman were vastly different when it came to religion. The Emancipation Proclamation exemplified the American nation as the fulfillment of divine promise. Lincoln calls the Divine to his service and in his rhetoric invokes the Eternal at a specific moment in history in order to carry out God's plan.[39]

For Whitman, there was no God, no heaven, no need for religion. The sum of things was found in the earthly here and now. Man, the self, "myself," is the only divinity. In "Crossing Brooklyn Ferry" Whitman notices once again the halo around his own head, like the flame around heroes from Aeneas to Cromwell:

> I too many and many a time cross'd the river of old . . .
> Look'd at the fine centrifugal spokes of light around the
> shape of my head in the sunlit water. . . .

This is "an aureole available to anyone." It is "The American Religion."[40] If religion was to be removed from national and international affairs, its certainties and consolations could henceforth be embodied in the democratically liberated individual, for the glory of the self: ego-theism.[41]

Whitman had announced this right from the start of his poetic career, in the preface to his first edition of *Leaves of Grass:*

> There soon will be no more priests. Their work is done. They may wait awhile . . . perhaps a generation or two . . . dropping off by degrees.
>
> A superior breed shall take their place . . . the gangs of kosmos and prophets en mass shall take their place . . . through the divinity of themselves shall the kosmos and the new breed of poets be interpreters of men and women and of all events and things. They shall find their inspiration in real objects today, symptoms of the past and future.

Kenneth Rexroth noted that Whitman is the only major modern artist who did *not* follow Rousseau's lead to reject Western and civilizational values. This is what uniquely made Whitman the statesman-in-the-poet, who identified with Abraham Lincoln and with natural right and individual freedom. In his great threnody on Lincoln's death, Whitman stepped forward to fill the absence left by the Great Emancipator. In doing so, Whitman would aim to lift poetry above policy, to situate poetry where other instruments of mind find impossibility. Where Lincoln saw right and wrong, Whitman saw undifferentiated inclusion, democracy without limitations, a democracy of world-spanning appeal, but also a democracy of impossibility.[42] As the American Founders recognized, those who love democracy without limits doom it.

✶ ✶ ✶

Whitman (1819–1892) was a nearly exact contemporary of Oliver Wendell Holmes (1809–1894)—America's most popular poet, far more so than Whitman. The two poets could not be more unlike: Walt, "one of the roughs" and Holmes, proper Boston's "Autocrat of the Breakfast Table," yet they shared the belief that America's original Puritan ethic was no more. Whitman vatically addressed his invisible listeners of the future;[43] Holmes merrily depicted the collapse of the entire intellectual tradition in his "The Wonderful One-Hoss-Shay," a poem recited by generations of Yankee schoolchildren. The buggy was the Deacon's masterpiece, built so it *couldn't* break down. For, said the Deacon, "'tis mighty plain that the weakest place must stand the strain." The way to do that, the Deacon maintained,

> Is only jest
> T' make that place uz strong uz the rest
> So the Deacon inquired of the village folk
> Where he could find the strongest oak
> That couldn't be split nor bent nor broke,—
> That was for spokes and floors and sills;
> He sent for lancewood to make the thills;
> The crossbars were ash, from the straightest trees;
> The panels of white-wood, that cuts like cheese
> But lasts like iron for things like these.

And so it lasted for a hundred years:

> Little of all we value here
> Wakes on the morn of its hundredth year . . .
> Now, small boys, get out of the way!
> Here comes the wonderful one-horse-shay.

But:

> All at once the horse stood still
> Close by the meeting-house on the hill.

And the whole contraption shuddered and collapsed in a heap.

> It went to pieces all at once,—
> All at once, and nothing first,—
> Just as bubbles do when they burst.

Oliver Wendell Holmes's one-horse shay represented New England Puritanism, which dominated the religious and intellectual American scene—until it didn't. Was this the end of Western civilization's Christian belief, as Whitman prophesied? Yes and no. The American view of the world would retain something of the Puritans' "Right makes Might" even after the peace of Westphalia relegated religion to the sidelines of the international state system. The Enlightenment exalted reason over "superstition," that is, faith. Then Darwin undermined the idea of man as created in the image of God. By the late twentieth century, most statesmen and strategists of the West not only saw no place for religion in their policy calculations but were so discomfited as to avoid the subject whenever raised. But at critical international moments, American presidents might speak in the tones of the Deacon's Puritanism about a national mission to seek order and redemption in a fallen world.

The young United States of America would never have been able to achieve its independence were it not for diplomacy, especially that of Benjamin Franklin with France. But in the first half of the nineteenth century, the nation's energies were largely confined to the North American continent. The United States stayed aloof from the international diplomatic scene, taking to heart Washington's advice to "avoid foreign entanglements."

The Civil War changed that. Great Britain's attitude toward the war was of desperate concern to the Union. Britons regarded American democracy as abhorrent and chaotic, a reason in itself for the rise of the Confederacy. Political commentators in England created an antinorthern public sentiment. That the Union might have to fight a two-front war, one with the South and a second with Britain, was a serious possibility. That would have meant the end of the American republic.

A vivid, bitter conflict arose between British and American writers. In England, Thomas Carlyle deplored American hypocrisy in drawing a distinction between Negro slavery in the South and industry's exploitation of workers in the North. (One "hires servants for life"; the other hires servants "by the month or the day.") Charles Dickens excoriated American politics and culture as crass and debased. Alfred Lord Tennyson, Britain's poet laureate, declared southern secession constitutional by America's standards. The British cultural arbiter and eminent poet Matthew Arnold endorsed the Confederacy.

American writers reacted in disbelief and anger. Oliver Wendell Holmes's son (later Supreme Court Justice) Oliver Wendell Holmes, Jr., fought for the North, as did Henry Wadsworth Longfellow's son; both were wounded. Their writer-fathers were baffled by their British counterparts' defense of slavery and indifference to the cause of freedom. Most outspoken of American literary figures was Ralph Waldo Emerson, who declared that Britain's "joy was great at seeing our nation broken, and her interest in the success of the rebellion was undisguised."[44]

The secession of southern states created an international conundrum. To the new Confederacy, it all seemed clear and simple at first. Secession was legal, they said, even anticipated and provided for in United States founding documents. The federal government would never go so far as to try to reverse a secession militarily, for the American Revolution itself formed the precedent.[45] If the thirteen colonies could break free of Great Britain, why couldn't the South break free of the North? Tocqueville, in *Democracy in America,* had pointed out the South's social and cultural un-likeness to the North. There was slavery, of course, but much more besides; the bustling, industrializing, commercial North had little in common with "a feudal plantation economy below the Ohio, veneered with chivalry and living in an outworn dream." The northern mind was about progress and striving. The South was anything but; it embraced limits and opposed all that might destroy "the poetic-religious myths and create the mass-state."[46]

The Confederate States of America adopted a constitution scarcely distinguishable from that of the United States and designed a flag resembling an early version of the Stars and Stripes. The Confederacy would be an American polity that would return to first principles. President Jefferson Davis's inaugural address sounded much like the inaugural rhetoric of President Abraham Lincoln. The Confederacy stood ready to take its rightful place among the nations of the earth. Southern statecraft had gathered the ideas, set the policies, and taken the actions needed to create its own nation; the primary task thereafter would be in diplomacy, to gain international legitimacy from the great nations of Britain and France.

Great Britain could claim the moral high ground, having taken the lead internationally in banning the Atlantic slave trade. Britons noted that Lincoln's war was being fought less to free the slaves than to preserve the Union. The mills of Manchester depended on southern cotton. If the United States broke up it would be Great Britain's gain.

The brilliant diplomacy of Franklin and Jefferson's time had passed. The Civil War would redefine American statecraft. Henry Adams participated and reflected on this change in *The Education of Henry Adams*, which one survey named the "number one" book of the American twentieth century. Adams and his father were products of the American literary circles that were appalled by England's stance toward the war. *The Education* took as its centerpiece the little-known, but vastly consequential, engagement of American diplomacy with the world, not an easy thing for a people who had come to the new land to get away from the fancy yet dangerous diplomacy of the old world. The Adamses' diplomatic perplexities would foreshadow the split personality of American diplomacy toward the external world ever since.

George Kennan considered the American diplomatic memoir a unique genre of literature. Its importance lies in its authors' reporting what was known at the time decisions had to be taken—not writing as historians with retrospective knowledge. Adams's book stands at the crossroads of statecraft and literature. He re-creates the reality that diplomatic decisions must be taken before all the facts can be known. He later tries to comprehend what happened and admits that he cannot. From this comes awareness that some "sixth sense"—a literary sense—is needed in statecraft. Adams knows that his father had it and he did not.

Taking Adams's diplomatic chapters at face value, the literary arbiter Edmund Wilson rendered an unsurprisingly scathing verdict. Henry's brother "had acted in the Unionist drama; whereas Henry was quite outside it: he had been working with his father in the Embassy in London while the fighting was going on, and he had hardly been touched by the Lincolnian vision. . . . One feels that the effect of the war had been simply to make him feel uncomfortable."[47] The young Henry Adams depicted in *The Education* is callow, shallow, vain, pretentious, self-absorbed, self-pitying, and quite unattractive in most regards.

The diplomatic chapters provide the reader with frustrations, perplexities, inconsistencies, and annoyances. It seems impossible to say with certainty what they add up to. Yet in these chapters we can see Adams presenting diplomacy both as an *education* and as one of the humanities.

The parts on diplomacy in *The Education* reveal Adams's famous fixation on his family's past greatness. Although far from uncritical about his forebears, Adams saw that their lives were intertwined with the fate of nations. Here the Civil War epic is connected to the world at large, with insights about the passing of the republic and the coming rise of empire. Diplomacy is presented as a way of getting a grasp on the complexity, within unity, of the human condition. Adams regards its practice as crucial to his "education," and he writes it as a three-act play.

The first act, opening in 1861, describes the anomalous condition of American diplomacy and the atmosphere of anti-Americanism in London. The second is a meditation on ethics and politics. The final act points to the significance of his father's diplomacy to the fate of the American nation yet also to the impossibility of truly understanding what has happened. What is clear is that the United States cannot remain aloof from world affairs.

Edmund Wilson mistakenly wrote of the "Embassy in London." Charles Francis Adams was not an ambassador, only a minister, and his mission was exercised through a legation, not an embassy. The United States was determined not to acquiesce either in traditional European balance-of-power politics or in the pomp and circumstance of diplomatic protocol and hierarchy. Benjamin Franklin appeared in Paris in homespun and a beaver cap. As a result, the United States suffered a chronic diplomatic disrespect, with its representatives always seated below the salt and at the tail end of every official list. Minister Adams was often ignored or treated as negligible.

Compounding this was the vituperative anti-Americanism in Britain that Henry Adams records throughout his work. Lincoln was a crude brute, and Seward, the American secretary of state, a demon—or the other way around. Adams's reports sound familiar in the twenty-first century. "The limits and defects of the American mind," he wrote, "were one of the favorite topics of the European. From the old-world point of view, the American had no mind. . . . The American mind exasperated the European as a buzz-saw might exasperate a pine-forest. . . . The American mind was not a thought at all; it was a convention, superficial, narrow, and ignorant: a mere cutting instrument, practical, economical, sharp, and direct."

Henry's family had answered the call to diplomatic service at earlier times of national danger. His father, grandfather, and great-grandfather (John Quincy Adams in 1809, John Adams in 1778) had all held the diplomatic post of American chief of mission to the Court of St. James's. But this situation seems to overwhelm young Henry.

As the Adamses disembarked at Liverpool, Britain had just declared neutrality and conferred "belligerent" status on the Confederacy, enabling

Britain to deal equally with North and South—tantamount to diplomatic recognition of the South as an independent state in the international system.[48] This shocking fait accompli at the moment of their arrival, says Henry, tore up the roots of his Harvard and German education. Britain wanted the South to be an independent nation and to lock this in before his father could act. The blow "was likely to be fatal. . . . No other shock so violent and sudden could possibly recur. . . . The outlook was desperate, beyond retrieving or contesting." To young Henry, it felt as if they were "a family of early Christian martyrs about to be flung into an arena of lions."

Two months later, in July 1861, came the Union defeat at Bull Run. This, Adams says, was a worse diplomatic than military defeat. All Europe was waiting to see the U.S. legation pack up and go home. In November 1861 came the famous *Trent* affair, in which the Confederate envoys Mason and Slidell were seized when the *USS San Jacinto* stopped the mail steamer *Trent* bound for Britain. The captain of the *San Jacinto* would be the guest of honor at Emerson and Holmes's literary club. But seizure of the *Trent* was an immensely dangerous act, making war with Britain a real possibility. As the American historian-diplomat John Lothrop Motley has written, this confrontation would have to be swiftly resolved or Great Britain would come into the war "with the largest fleet which the world has ever seen as champions and allies of the Southern Confederacy," spelling the end of the United States.[49] This moment, Adams says, was *the* crisis of his father's diplomatic career. The *Trent* affair had been met with "a typhoon of fury" in Britain and raucous celebration in the United States. If a transatlantic cable had existed to carry the news, the public mood would have ignited a British-American war.

Tennyson, in the dedication to his most ambitious poem, *Idylls of the King,* says "imminent war" was prevented when Queen Victoria and Prince Albert rewrote a diplomatic dispatch, which may have been British Foreign Secretary Russell's demand for the release of Mason and Slidell. The draft was sent to Victoria at Windsor Castle for urgent approval, as the packet-boat would sail the next day. Victoria discussed it with Albert, then in his dying days. Albert sent back a memorandum saying that the queen "should have liked to have seen the expression of a hope that the American captain did not act under instructions. . . . HMG are unwilling to believe that the USG intended wantonly to put an insult upon this country." The dispatch was redrafted accordingly. The United States took the opening, disavowed the captain's decision, and released Mason and Slidell. War was averted.[50] Secretary of State Seward then turned the argument back on the British, noting that they now had come around to the long-held American policy against the halting of neutral ships on the high seas.

Throughout its few decades of existence, the new American republic feared, and undertook to prevent, entanglement with or takeover by a European power or powers. Now the United States had fractured, and European ambitions were reawakened. In Britain's case, substantial national interests were on the line. Lincoln's blockade of southern ports would, in time, stop shipments of cotton to Lancashire mills, causing unemployment and labor unrest in Britain. Eighty percent of the cotton used in Britain's textile factories came from the American South. The economic rise of the United States was also a cause for British and European concern; two lesser republics would be easier to deal with than one powerful nation. Separation would also offer new angles for renewed European penetration of the Western Hemisphere. Napoleon III of France was scheming to put a puppet emperor, Maximilian, on the Mexican throne. The danger to the republic was real, unless American diplomacy could somehow keep British and European powers from giving recognition, support, and almost certain victory to the South.

In August 1862 came the second Union defeat at Bull Run. Henry Adams was "exasperated, furious, bitter, and choking with tears." Every morning's London *Times* blared "Another Disastrous Federal Defeat." English society's hatred for Lincoln and Seward "seemed demented," and Lord Palmerston seemed bent on provoking a quarrel with the American minister of legation. Palmerston was believed to "lay traps."

In the first act, the stakes are gigantic. The situation faced by Minister Adams could scarcely have been more unfavorable. The second act features Henry Adams himself and his search for "education."

His formal college education had been "torn up by the roots." Wars happen all the time. Empires rise and fall. Diplomats outlast them all. That, he said, "was his whole diplomatic education." He had sought to be helpful to his father but found that he could not be. He had thought to deal usefully with the press but had violated the diplomat's first principle: "Above all, beware of zeal!"[51] And the *Trent* affair, he felt, made all individual effort insignificant. By the end of 1862 what he had acquired, if anything, in the way of education he would gladly have forgotten.

In the second act, entitled "Political Morality (1862)," the movement, symphonically speaking, is slower, as Henry settles in to ponder the question, Can politicians be trusted? "To settle this point became the main object of the diplomatic education so laboriously pursued." There followed, he writes, "one of the most perfect educational courses in politics and diplomacy" that a young man could ever pursue. To the end of his life he would labor over the lessons he was taught in London. Take those who are considered the most honorable, powerful, and respected leaders of Her Majesty's government. If one found that one could not trust them, then one could trust no one, and truth in politics could be ignored as a delusion. In this effort, Henry seemed to be defining himself against his father. Minister Adams viewed the nature of diplomacy differently. One's official counterpart might or might not have the intention to lie, deceive, or do harm to you or your interests. One the whole, Charles Francis Adams would acquit the British ministers of the charge of seeking the worst for the United States. He recognized that he had to be indifferent to the moral question that so preoccupied his son.

Somewhere in the midst of his rather tedious and immature approach, Henry Adams seems to stumble on more significant aspects of diplomacy, education, human nature, and life in general. This is when his story focuses on warships being built in British shipyards; on the three formidable British statesmen Palmerston, Russell, and Gladstone; and on the question of what one knows when, and what must be done before one knows all the facts.

In the third act, Adams begins to tell his readers that his search for certainty was impossible, because at the time diplomatic decisions had to be taken, no one could fully know the facts of the situation. It would be decades before documents could be released and memoirs published providing Adams with something like a coherent picture of the main events.

The ups and downs of the Union's military fortunes in the field provide the shifting context for the decisions of the three British leaders whom Minister Adams, and Henry, were attempting to influence. Second Bull Run and Lee's foray into Maryland made it possible that Washington might fall. Not until 1889 would Henry Adams learn that this prospect led Palmerston to suggest that Britain take steps to arrange the "separation" of the Union into two national entities and that Russell favored recognizing the Confederacy as an independent state. Henry Adams's reading of these leaders at the time, he says, "had been altogether wrong."

Then came the southern defeat at Antietam and Lee's retreat. The Emancipation Proclamation undercut any moral stance the British could claim. Lincoln's proclamation was an act of grand strategy. He adopted it when it became clear that the Confederacy could not be overcome unless its social and economic system—slavery—was attacked directly. Lincoln decided on the Emancipation Proclamation in July 1862 but did not issue it until the North had gained a clear victory. He needed the military victory so that the Proclamation would not be seen as an act of desperation. Once it had been made, there was no turning back. After Antietam and the issuance of the proclamation it would be impossible to end the war with a compromise. No course remained but Union victory.

Henry concluded that "all the world had been at cross-purposes, had misunderstood themselves and the situation, had followed wrong paths, drawn wrong conclusions, and had known none of the facts." One could find no firm foundation for diplomacy.

Henry Adams conveys the monumental importance, for the fate of the United States, of the diplomatic front. In retrospect, it appears, if anything, even more important than Adams portrays it to be. If Britain had decided to repeat the War of 1812 in the United States in 1862, the Union would have broken up, the Confederacy would have gained recognition as an independent nation, and slavery would have continued.

The poet James Russell Lowell, later head of the London legation himself, said: "None of our generals in the field, nor Grant himself, did us better or more trying service than [Charles Francis Adams] in his forlorn outpost of London."[52] The diplomatic historian Thomas A. Bailey said of Minister Adams, "no other diplomatic representative of the United States has ever had to endure, at least for so protracted a period, such critical official responsibility combined with a tense excitement and a hostile atmosphere. And his foot did not slip once."[53] So Henry Adams had been involved with a great national challenge worthy of his ancestors. He fully understood the Adams family's role in the nation's destiny. He understood that in London he was offered an opportunity to play a similar role. And he understood that the stakes—the survival of the Union—were as great as any faced by his Adams predecessors.

Henry Adams concluded that "he would never again find education to compare with the life and death alternatives of this two and a half year struggle in London. . . . The English campaign seemed to him as creditable to the State Department as the Vicksburg campaign to the War Department, and more decisive." He found diplomacy "a pointless puzzle," because he could locate no foundational principles on which it could be based. The Enlightenment had done its work. "One would have done better to draw no conclusions at all. One's diplomatic education was a long mistake."[54] Throughout, Adams portrays himself as inadequate to the task—because of his temperament and education, his immaturity, and a kind of obtuseness. Young Henry displayed nearly every fault a diplomat in his position could have: he displayed too much zeal; he gave way to despair; he psychologized; he put his own interests above the nation's interests; he exaggerated; he lost credibility. These chapters of *The Education* offer an education in statecraft. Adams has shown us how *not* to do it.

In later life, Henry Adams had to admit that he had misunderstood the entire matter. He did not comprehend the full story until after the documents were published decades after the event. These documents "upset from top to bottom the results of the private secretary's diplomatic education forty years after he had supposed it to be complete. They made a picture different from anything he had conceived and rendered worthless his whole painful diplomatic experience."

Only long after the war had ended, Adams tells us, did he conclude that the British leaders were not complex. They deceived by their simplicity. Gladstone was the sum of contradictions. In his memoir of 1896 Gladstone declared that his support for the South as a nation was really intended as an act of friendliness to all America. His opinion, Gladstone confessed, was "founded on a false estimate of the facts." So, "Long and patiently . . . did the private secretary, forty years afterwards in the twilight of a life of study read and re-read and reflect upon [Gladstone's] confession. Then, it seemed, he had seen nothing correctly at the time."

Minister Adams's success was founded on his recognition (the recognition that proved so difficult for his son) that decisions in diplomacy must be taken before all the facts are in, when all the implications cannot be known. With this as one's foundation, what do you do? That's where diplomacy must be practiced as one of the humanities and informed by all of humanistic learning.

Walden, Leaves of Grass, and Adams's *Education* are examples of what the poet Wallace Stevens called the American search for "a supreme fiction." Thoreau wanted to remake the United States all over again, a drive for perpetual renewal that would continue to revivify the polity. Whitman did something similar, turning the Founders' worries about democracy into a brazen celebration of it as the universal force of history that Tocqueville sensed it was. Henry Adams, alarmed by the dangers exuberance, fragmentation, and exceptionalism could pose for the survival of the American state, tried to explain how his father engaged the United States with the international state system in order to preserve it. America's ambiguous relation to the international world prefigured by John Locke became lodged in the very name "The United States of America." Adams's diplomatic saga was a step toward resolving that ambiguity by finding a way for the country to play in the game of nations.

The Civil War ended with the nation made whole, but what of the state of its soul? Eugene O'Neill's 1931 *Mourning Becomes Electra* is a retelling of the *Oresteia* and a refutation of Tocqueville's depiction of the American woman as the foundation for marriage, family, and the state.

The trilogy—*Homecoming, The Hunted, The Haunted*—is remarkably faithful to Aeschylus's tone yet rejects the hopeful ending of the classic prototype. Ezra Mannon (Agamemnon), a general, returns home at the end of the Civil War to his wife Christine (Clytemnestra), who has been conducting an affair with Captain Brant (Aegisthus). The lovers murder the general when Christine causes his heart trouble to flare up and then gives him as "medicine" a poison provided by the captain.

In O'Neill's American version it is Electra rather than Orestes who takes the lead in avenging her father's death. Lavinia induces Orin to kill Captain Brant, an act which causes Christine to kill herself. Unlike the *Oresteia,* the play does not end with an act of public justice that bids to put an end to the fated cycle of family revenge-taking. The "Furies" do not accept a new and positive societal-governmental role but instead bore into the psyches of brother and sister. Orin commits suicide, and Lavinia, having destroyed her chance for happiness in marriage, becomes a recluse inside the boarded-up mansion. In the aftermath of the Trojan War, the Greeks went on to greatness. O'Neill locates in the aftermath of the American Civil War the seeds of disaster should the family revert to its grim past rather than fulfill the promise given it by Tocqueville.

The line that Aeschylus depicted being crossed from blood-feuds of clans to the law-ordered civilization of the state was recrossed by O'Neill.

Backwoods feuding by American clans would be comically treated by Mark Twain in *Huckleberry Finn,* but the theme of civilization as a degenerating, doomed construction would haunt the predominantly positive Age of Enlightenment. From Gibbon and Rousseau to Nietzsche and Heidegger, and into the American 1960s, a generation which changed the American direction, O'Neill's ponderous trilogy was on to something.

7

DISORDER AND WAR

The Enlightenment opened the Age of Revolution. To Rousseau, war is revolution's first step because aggressors will never cede power peacefully. Oppression is itself a form of war; revolutionary war to defeat it is therefore the only path to peace. Revolutionary ideologies reject state borders and sovereignty and are universal in scope. In this sense, every major war of the modern age may be seen as an effort to destroy the established international system and replace it with an alternative world order based on an alternative ideology.

The international state system was massively threatened by revolutionary ideology. The French Revolution ideologically legitimized terror. Late imperial warfare gave an opening for the Paris Commune as an international symbol. Communism—in European, Russian, and Asian forms— aimed to overthrow and replace established world order. Terrorism and revolutionary fervor in London, Moscow, and Shanghai added layers of meaning to a worldwide enemy of the Westphalian idea. As this external enemy gathered force, the international system moved toward what would be "the first world war," fought within its own international context.

Among diplomats, a favorite anecdote is Henry A. Kissinger's question to Chinese Premier Chou En-lai: "Was the French Revolution a good thing?" Chou's reply, "It's too soon to tell." But few go on to explain the underlying meaning of this exchange. It supposedly took place at the time of the "opening" in 1972 between the United States of America as "leader of the Free World"—that is, the international state system—and the most radically revolutionary power set against that system, the People's Republic of China. These two statesmen did not need to elaborate: the question was whether the French Revolution of 1789 had made a contribution to human "liberty, fraternity, and equality," beneficial to East and West alike, or whether it had launched an ideological movement that would overwhelm the international state system and replace it with a world order shaped by socialism and communism.

The first principle of grand strategy is that one must understand what is going on in the world. The question "What's happening?" is more than a cheerful greeting. Policies and decisions will follow from such an assessment, and confrontations may emerge from differing views about what is taking place and why. Yet those who are living through great historical events can rarely even glimpse the significance of what is going on all around them.

When the Indian Mutiny broke out, Charles Dickens was writing *A Tale of Two Cities*. Seething, inexplicable menace and mass terror connected the 1789 revolution in France, in Dickens's mind, with the Sepoy Rebellion of 1857. The uprising in Delhi was atavistic: Indian troops, fearing Christianization, revolted against the issuance of cartridges said to be greased with fat from cows (taboo to Hindus) and pigs (taboo to Muslims). The upheaval in Paris, by contrast, was driven by an Age of Reason ideology. These twin outbreaks, in France and India, seemed somehow of world-historical consequence. *A Tale of Two Cities* conveys the pairing and its contradictions in its famous first paragraph:

> It was the best of times, it was the worst of times,
> it was the age of wisdom, it was the age of foolishness,
> it was the epoch of belief, it was the epoch of incredulity,
> it was the season of light, it was the season of darkness,
> it was the spring of hope, it was the winter of despair,
> we had everything before us, we had nothing before us.

"Fighting stories" contend to answer such questions as "Was the French Revolution a good thing?" and many new versions challenge the established narrative. *A Tale of Two Cities* has been a winner in the contest to characterize the French Revolution. Dickens drew from Thomas Carlyle's *The French Revolution,* but the novel, the most accessible of all Dickens's books, and one that was put before young people for generations, has far outstripped the history book that lies behind it.

The French Revolution erupted from an ideology determined to confront and replace the international state system. The Westphalian concept was procedural—adhere to the form, and your ideology was your own affair. But not if that ideology was a system itself, and not if by inventing "The People" it could declare some people to be "enemies of the People," justifying the use of terror against them. This was the message Margaret Thatcher, never subtle, conveyed when on the bicentennial of the French Revolution she presented the president of France with a copy of *A Tale of Two Cities.*

The turbulence in which Dickens's characters are immersed permits them only a hazy sense of what is happening. They are in the midst of a "revolution," but its meaning is not clear. None of the major real-life figures of the revolution—Marat or Robespierre—figures in this story; only the central events of the fall of the Bastille and the rise of the Terror frame the *Tale.* But Dickens leads the reader through stages of increasing clarity about its meaning. The *Tale* begins four years before the storming of the Bastille, in a Paris and London both of whose arrogant, heedless aristocracies oppress and wreak injustice on the common people: "There were a king with a large jaw and a queen with a plain face on the throne of England; there were a king with a large jaw and a queen with a plain face on the throne of France. In both countries is was clearer than crystal to the lords of the state preserves of loaves and fishes, that things in general were settled for ever."

The Peace of Westphalia had invested state power in autocracies. France entertained herself "with such humane achievements as sentencing a youth to have his hands cut off, his tongue torn out with pincers, and his body burned alive, because he had not kneeled down in the rain to do honour to a dirty procession of monks which passed within his view, at a distance of some fifty or sixty yards."

From the first pages, Dickens tells us that such oppression has planted the seeds of upheaval. Wheeled vehicles, coaches, carts, and wagons recur throughout the novel as symbols of the inexorable motion of history: "It is likely enough that in the rough outhouses of some tillers of the heavy lands adjacent to Paris, there were sheltered from the weather that very day, rude carts, bespattered with rustic mire, snuffed about by pigs, and roosted in by poultry, which the farmer, Death, had already set apart to be his tumbrels of the Revolution." In England, violent crime was rife, in a vicious circle caused by hierarchical oppression. The downtrodden poor steal and are brutally punished; they, or their like, turn to worse misadventures, which are met with even greater social and economic repression until the hangman "was in constant requisition."[1]

Dickens pairs the monarchical England with France by likening the British bank Tellson's—and its branch in the Saint Germain quarter of Paris—to the Bastille. If the Bastille could fall, so could Tellson's, and England. The title, *A Tale of Two Cities,* is an after-the-fact commentary on Edmund Burke's *Reflections on the Revolution in France,* by which is meant not "The French Revolution," but "The Revolution," a universal force of history, which erupted first in France and could spread to England and beyond.

The course of the story runs otherwise. What at first seems an understandable, even justified cause soon begins to loom as a monstrous, uncontrollable evil. A large cask of wine for the wine shop of Monsieur and Madame Defarge is dropped and broken in getting it out of a cart. "All the people within reach had suspended their business, or their idleness, to run to the spot and drink the wine." The red wine soon stains the hands and faces and feet of everyone, and those who had been most greedy "had acquired a tigerish smear about the mouth." One so besmirched "scrawled upon a wall with his finger dipped in muddy wine—BLOOD."

From this prophetic moment on, Dickens slowly ratchets up the violence and the horror until

> The new era began; the King was tried, doomed, and beheaded; the Republic of Liberty, Equality, Fraternity, or Death declared for victory or death against the world in arms; the black flag waved night and day from the great towers of Notre-Dame; three hundred thousand men, summoned to rise against the tyrants of the earth, rose from all the varying soils of France, as if the dragon's teeth had been sown broadcast. . . . What private solicitude could rear itself against the deluge of the Year One of Liberty—the deluge rising from below, not falling from above, and with the windows of Heaven shut, not opened!

This grand awakening soon turns on itself. The people suspect, denounce, condemn, and swiftly execute the supposed enemies of the people—not just aristocrats but others too, until "along the Paris streets, the death carts rumble, hollow and harsh. Six tumbrels carry the day's wine to La Guillotine. All the devouring and insatiable Monsters imagined since imagination could record itself, are fused in one realization, Guillotine." Madame Defarge, the calm center of the revolution, sits knitting, the most famous image in *A Tale*.

The two cities now grow unlike. Dickens counterpoises England and the virtues of the English to the fury of the French. Tellson's bank branch becomes a refuge for Parisians fleeing execution. The French Revolution threatens to engulf world order; English common sense upholds the civilized system. England is a haven for sanity. Private life can exist in London; in Paris everything is acted out in front of the People, who become a mob.

History records of the French Revolution that the Terror had become a system, the arm of the revolutionary regime. In the spring of 1794 came the Law of 22 Prairial (June 10), which permitted charges to be brought against "counterrevolutionaries" merely on the basis of denunciations. Robespierre presided over the session of 22 Prairial. The number of arrests between 1793 and 1794 reached a half million. Some 16,600 were executed after summary sentencing by a revolutionary court; others were put in prison without trial. The Terror—death by guillotine, or firing squad—continued until March 1794.

A Tale of Two Cities presents a full array of the characteristics of revolution and terrorism in the nineteenth, twentieth, and twenty-first centuries. Spying and surveillance turn families, friends, and communities against their own. History is abolished or declared to begin again; all past governance, as Rousseau said, has been illegitimate—only the revolution is authentic. Violence purifies. As in medieval times, it bears proof of rectitude, or sin. Hobbes is contradicted in his analysis of human nature, as is his proof of the origins of the state, for death is eagerly sought. The present must be sacrificed by "martyrs" for the sake of the future. Beheading takes on a special meaning. The seat of reason is struck down by revolutionary reason, and civilization itself is rejected and destroyed. Religion is banned and condemned. "Sainte Guillotine" replaces the Christian Cross as the focus of veneration.[2] The "original sin" of Christian doctrine is replaced by the original sin of membership in a counterrevolutionary class, a secular sin for which no salvation is available. Above all, the individual is enveloped and erased by the collective. The married love of a man and a woman becomes the symbol of all that the revolution abhors as Charles Darnay and Lucie stand before the slaughter machine.

Dickens anticipates the later debate over whether the Modern Age is "legitimate" or whether Marxism and other "progressive" movements since the Enlightenment have merely been religion substitutes. Karl Marx, writing at about the same time as Charles Dickens, would assess the French Revolution and declare it wanting, a mere political revolution. The goals of liberty, fraternity, and equality were not enough, Marx said; true revolution would transform human nature itself. *A Tale of Two Cities* makes it clear that if the French Revolution fell short in Marx's eyes, it nonetheless contained the seeds of the most radical ideological movements that followed it.

The French Revolution and the Terror have been called a crisis of rhetoric—of valiant words calling for an end to oppression, as well as of language abused to justify a new dictatorship. In *A Tale,* the killing mounts, carrying the revolution forward, and at the end, Carton famously takes Darnay's place on the scaffold. In Thucydides, speeches propel the war; in *A Tale,* the speeches of Robespierre propel the Terror. There are no great men in *A Tale;* the revolution is made by small men. Robespierre was one of them, an early example of "the banality of evil."

Robespierre made his debut as an orator on July 20, 1789, in a speech praising the taking of the Bastille. Then came the question of what to do with Louis XVI. Speaking on December 3, 1792, Robespierre declared that although he generally opposed the death penalty, here he supported execution. Furthermore, he argued, no trial was necessary, for resort to the law has never been required to depose and dispose of a tyrant.

Robespierre was a lawyer, but beyond that he was a literary intellectual. His rigorous logic drew from Descartes; he emulated Rousseau's style by turning expected, conventional arguments on their heads, sweeping his audience along by sheer daring, and incorporating Rousseau's confessional style to his political oratory.[3] He considered himself to embody Kant's "What is Enlightenment?"—calling upon mankind to stride forth from its self-imposed immaturity—and also saw himself as the great "legislator" of Rousseau's *On the Social Contract.* Appropriately, he won the epithet "the Incorruptible."

As an ordinary attorney from Arras, Robespierre resembled Cromwell, an ordinary country squire, and he seems to have known it; both were unremarkable individuals suddenly thrust to the forefront in revolutionary times. Robespierre, who only vaguely understood Cromwell, loathed him for being ambitious and avaricious, and for turning the English Revolution into republican governance; to Robespierre, a true revolution went far beyond that, as indeed it did, when he called for the Terror and it was accepted by the people as legitimate.

Cromwell had led a revolution in the cause of religion; Robespierre feared the Revolution might "de-Christianize" France and thus alienate the religious peasantry. This then might fuel counterrevolution by shifting support to the nobility. To avoid this, Robespierre, inspired by Rousseau, proposed a deistic new civic religion, a cult of "The Supreme Being," in a clever move to co-opt religion's mystery and charisma for the Revolution.[4]

Robespierre immediately grasped the first principle of revolutionary oratory: be always ready to speak anywhere, at any time. In the Constituent Assembly alone he spoke 68 times in 1789, 125 times in 1790, and 328 times in 1791. He addressed the Jacobin Club innumerable times, demonstrating great persistence and zeal.[5] The secret of his legitimacy and influence lay in his improbable presence at the podium. He was not a rabble-rouser; he did not harangue his hearers. As described in 1794: "When he mounts the rostrum, it is not with a studied indifference or exaggerated gravity, nor does he rush at it like Marat; but he is calm, as though he wished to show from the outset that this is the place which, without challenge, is his by right."[6]

"He spoke with a marked regional accent. His voice, too high-pitched to be naturally pleasant, also lacked volume and tonal variation. His physical stature was unimpressive. He was short and slight, with a large head. His weak eyes required glasses, which he often pushed up on his forehead while speaking, so he could rub his eyes. His gestures at the podium were small, fussy, and cramped. These deficiencies were accentuated by his habit of reading his speeches from a pile of manuscripts, with his head buried in the text."[7] Such an old-fashioned figure was all the more credible in the radical actions he justified to the people.

Robespierre had literary ambitions. As a "man of letters," he used erudite allusions to span the fields of politics and literature, lacing his orations with quotations from such great figures as Leibniz, Montesquieu, and

Rousseau, as well as classic references—all to create a rhetoric of the revolution. "Robespierre perfected ideological discourse in the highest degree because he was himself ideology incarnate."[8]

Speaking on behalf of the Committee of Public Safety on 17 Pluviôse, Year II (February 5, 1794), Robespierre gave a speech revealingly entitled "On the Principles of Moral Policy That Ought to Guide the National Convention in the Internal Administration of the Republic." "In order to lay the foundations of democracy and to consolidate it," he says,

> in order to arrive at the peaceful reign of constitutional law, we must finish the war of liberty against tyranny and safely cross through the storms of the revolution. . . . Now, what is the fundamental principle of popular or democratic government, that is to say, the essential mainspring which sustains it and makes it move? It is virtue. I speak of public virtue which worked so many wonders in Greece and Rome and which ought to produce even more astonishing things in republican France—that virtue which is nothing other than the love of the nation and its laws.

Robespierre declares the French to be "the first people of the world who have established real democracy." The soul of their creation is virtue. Then comes the clang of logic being turned upside down.

> If the mainspring of popular government in peacetime is virtue, amid revolution it is at the same time both virtue and *terror*. Virtue, without which terror is fatal; terror, without which virtue is impotent. Terror is nothing but prompt, severe, inflexible justice; it is therefore an emanation of justice. . . . Subdue liberty's enemies by terror, and you will be right, as Founders of the Republic. The government of the revolution is the despotism of liberty against tyranny. Is force made only to protect crime? And is it not to strike the heads of the proud that lightning is destined?

Robespierre makes every error Thucydides said had occurred in Athens: direct democracy (which Robespierre never ceased to defend); disordered upheavals so great that "words lose their meaning" and *terror* is held to mean virtue. His oratory foreshadows the brutal ideologies of the twentieth century: the interminable speeches; allegations of conspiracy that foment a pernicious atmosphere of mistrust; demagogues claiming to be the "guardians of the people's rights"; and most telling of all, advocacy of "the Terror." In what would become part of a veritable Revolution Handbook, Robespierre did not order the liquidation of the enemies of the people; he would halt just at the moment when, suspicion having been sown, the outcome was a certainty. As he said to the Jacobin Club: "It is not up to me to indicate these measures, not I who am consumed by a slow fever and above all by the fever of patriotism. I have said that at this moment I have no further duties."[9]

In response to a speech that promised even more terror, a coalition arose in the convention to arrest Robespierre on July 27, 1794. His jaw shattered by a pistol shot, he was unable to deploy his rhetoric in his own defense. He was guillotined the next morning.

The Revolution, the Terror, Bonapartism, and the Napoleonic wars had torn Europe apart. Talleyrand, at the Congress of Vienna, restored the continent to its prerevolutionary status under his encompassing principle of "legitimacy." It would be reactionary, undemocratic, and imperial but also civilized and dynamic. Talleyrand did it with convoluted compromises and renovated the Westphalian system. A French novel set in the last years of the Second Empire, the 1860s, portrays a village family scene:

> "Well," says Father, "since you aren't thinking about anything you can tell me the date of the signing of the Peace of Westphalia."
>
> Antoine neither moved nor answered. His father remonstrated in a shrill voice. . . . "You hear that everyone? He doesn't know the date of the Peace of Westphalia! He ought to be ashamed of himself!"
>
> The carriage was filled with a shocked silence. For her brother's benefit Lucienne mentally recited a prayer recommended by the Desmoiselles Hermeline as an aid to recalling the Great Dates of History. Frédéric drew the figures in the air with his finger, and Mme Haudouin tried to catch her son's eye in order to comfort him with an affectionate smile. But Antoine, staring down at his boots, refused to see anything. . . .
>
> And finally, Antoine's breast heaved with a sob. . . . He gulped and muttered in a stifled voice: "1648."[10]

In this Talleyrand-designed age, new states clustered around, or were inhabited by, old dynasties and monarchies. The Franco-Prussian War of 1870–1871 brought them all into conflict for power within the international state system. From this brew emerged a new force—communism—that wished to destroy the system altogether.

The Franco-Prussian War was a nexus of international change. Germany, which paradoxically did not emerge from the Thirty Years' War and the Peace of Westphalia as a state, finally achieved statehood under the brilliant diplomatic and military leadership of Bismarck. This transformation raised hopes, and fears, of the revival of the Holy Roman Empire under the banner of the Second Reich. France, regarded since Napoleon's time as the epitome of military valor and power, was humiliated on the battlefield, beginning its new reputation as the butt of jokes about ineptitude in warfare. With the Prussian siege of Paris and the flight of the French government from Paris to Versailles, there arose in 1871 the Paris Commune, whose sordid, criminal, and terrorist reality would be shaped by later narratives into an ideal of pure communist ideology by revolutionaries from Karl Marx to Mao Zedong.

The question of who would succeed to the Spanish throne offered a priceless opportunity for international intrigue. The old Holy Roman Empire had been, since long before the Thirty Years' War, the possession of the Catholic Hapsburg dynasty that spanned Europe from Madrid to Vienna. The late Spanish monarch had been a Hapsburg. Now in June 1870 Bismarck would contrive to propose Prince Leopold of Hohenzollern-Sigmaringen, a relative of King Wilhelm of Prussia, as the next king of Spain.

With this we are suddenly back in the Thirty Years' War era: Catholic Bourbons versus the Hapsburg Holy Roman Empire versus northern European Protestants. The French were alarmed in 1871 over Bismarck's diplomatic game-playing with the succession to the Spanish throne. Could his goal be to reconstitute the Holy Roman Empire under northern European *Protestant* power? A Hohenzollern in Madrid would surely be the creature of Bismarck's Prussia.[11] In July 1870 the Prussian War Council met in Berlin to consider the all-important question: What if France makes the Hohenzollern candidacy for the Spanish throne a cause for war? The answer: do not take partial measures. General von Moltke had assured Bismarck that the Prussian army would defeat the French.[12]

Bismarck's imaginative creation of the Franco-Prussian War was a dramatic masterpiece in both real life and literature. In July 1870 King Wilhelm of Prussia was taking the waters at the spa at Ems. The French had strongly protested the Hohenzollern candidacy for the Spanish throne. To accommodate the French, Wilhelm had used his influence to get Leopold to withdraw.

Bismarck in his memoirs would declare that this news of the Hohenzollern withdrawal came as a shock. The French demands asserting that it would be a casus belli made it seem a humiliating Prussian concession. Bismarck writes that he saw only two choices before him: resign, or wipe out this dishonor by going to war against France. If it was war, then France must be tricked into provoking it.

At a dinner in Berlin on July 13, 1870, word came to Bismarck that the French ambassador had requested a meeting with Wilhelm in Ems to ask for assurances that the Hohenzollern candidacy had been permanently canceled. This was too much; what else would the French demand from Prussia?

A few minutes later a telegram arrived from Ems. The French ambassador had accosted Wilhelm on the public promenade to ask him urgently to promise never again to support a Hohenzollern for the Spanish throne. Wilhelm had refused the request, but later sent an aide to the ambassador to confirm that the Hohenzollern candidacy had been withdrawn. In his memoirs, Bismarck claimed that the dinner party in Berlin was shocked at the effrontery of the French ambassador. But he must have been delighted at the possibilities it offered for portraying France as having goaded Prussia into war.

Then came one of the most famous moments in diplomatic history, a *literary* moment. Bismarck knew the power of words and, as Thucydides wrote, knew that states go to war from either fear, honor, or interest. For the French, it would be honor. To draw them into war, Bismarck *edited* the telegram from Ems. It had reported that Wilhelm had refused the French ambassador's request for Prussia's assurances that the Hohenzollern candidacy would never be revived. Bismarck changed it to state that: "His Majesty the King thereupon decided not to receive the French ambassador again, and sent an aide-de-camp on duty to tell him that His Majesty had nothing further to communicate." Now, said von Moltke, it has a different ring: before a *schmade* (parley); now a *fanfare* (flourish).

Whereas the original dispatch reported that Wilhelm put off meeting with the French ambassador because it had been confirmed that Leopold had withdrawn his candidacy, Bismarck's rewritten version portrayed the king as rudely canceling the audience without explanation. Bismarck immediately "leaked" his changed text so that newspapers would trumpet the "insult" to France on their front pages. The peoples of both nations would regard it as a matter of foreign aggression. And by tricking France into declaring war first, Bismarck ensured that international opinion would lean against the French. A decade earlier, Victoria and Albert reworded a dispatch to prevent a war; Bismarck did it to incite one.

Almost all of this episode seems to have been a product of the literary imagination. Nietzsche called Bismarck the only poet left in Germany. Bismarck knew that Prussia had eclipsed France as the leading military power; he wanted war in order to seal his unification of Germany as a state and elevate it to the status of an empire—*Reich*—under Wilhelm, not as king but as *Kaiser*. Bismarck would arrange to have Wilhelm declared Kaiser in the Hall of Mirrors at Versailles in 1871 as the capstone of Prussia's victory.[13]

The Franco-Prussian War began the breakup of the old European entity. The old dynasties transcended nations; now the nation-state would begin to supplant both dynasties and empires. Bismarck seems to have sensed this in the way he used the Ems telegram to turn a dynastic insult into a national one. Through the siege of Paris, the war also gave rise, momentously, to the Paris Commune; this would ever after be regarded as the pure moment and model of revolution, the first time that workers took state power into their own hands. The anthem of the international communist movement, "The Internationale," was written in 1871 to celebrate the Commune:

Arise ye workers from your slumbers
Arise ye prisoners of want
For reason in revolt now thunders . . .

Here are the signs of Marxism as a religion, a substitute Christianity, with biblical and evangelical formulas transposed into the revolutionary vernacular. The Soviet dissident poet Andrei Sinyavsky pointed out that in the biblical Apocalypse the time will come when in a single instant, the entire human social order will be overturned and "the last shall be the first."[14] As sung in the Internationale:

No more tradition's chains shall bind us,
Arise, ye slaves, no more in thrall!

The earth shall rise on new foundations,
We have been naught, we shall be all!

Karl Marx moved swiftly to endow the March-to-May 1871 Commune—for which he had not wished—with a "Marxist" meaning. His article "The Civil War in France" interpreted the uprising as the antithesis of the dynastic empires and as the beginning of the complete destruction of the state and the international state system, as yet only partly adumbrated by the French Revolution.[15]

In the Franco-Prussian War, French and German leaders, fixated on imperial visions of a lost past, blundered into a conflict that brought the army of Otto von Bismarck to lay siege to Paris. This, in turn, immiserated the city to the point where an uprising of radical Communards seized control of the capital in the spring of 1871.

Three great figures of modern literature were present.

Friedrich Nietzsche was serving in Bismarck's army as a medic or orderly at the Battle of Metz. The eruption of the Paris Commune impressed him greatly. "What use is an intellectual faced with such a cultural earthquake?" he wrote. Invalided out of the army with diphtheria, Nietzsche completed *The Birth of Tragedy* while convalescing.

The Enlightenment, Nietzsche said, is a fraud. It has not emancipated mankind as Kant claimed but is just another chapter of a Western civilization enfeebled by Christianity. "God is dead"—and we have killed him. We must go farther back, back before Western civilization was perverted by rationalism and religion, to recover the spirit of the unsullied pre-Socratic age of Greece.

Also on hand in 1871 was Arthur Rimbaud, the perfect image of the bohemian, avant-garde, rebellious adolescent poet. Rimbaud walked from his home in Charleville to the stews of Paris and the barricades of the Commune, observing a deranged modernity amid the heaped paving stones, toppled columns, and meals of rats for the starving. When he emerged, it was to write poems in praise of the flames of revolution, and then to produce works of staggering ambiguity and fragmentation. *Une Saison en Enfer* (A season in hell) and *Le Bateau ivre* (The drunken boat) inaugurated modern literature's breaking of forms and demolition of foundations. In a letter of May 15, 1871, Rimbaud created a new relation between the writer and the state:

The first study of the man who wishes to be a Poet is knowledge of himself, wholly. . . . I say that one must be a visionary, make oneself a VISIONARY. The poet must make himself a *visionary* by a long, immense and reasoned *derangement* of all the *senses.* He seeks in himself every kind of love, of suffering, of madness, he exhausts all the poisons in himself in order to keep only their quintessence. Unspeakable torment in which he has need of all faith, all superhuman power, in which he becomes among all the Great Invalid, the Great Criminal, the Great Damned—the Supreme Scholar!—for he comes to the *unknown.* For the Poet is truly the thief of fire, charged with the government of humanity, the animals even; and he must make his discoveries felt, touched, heard. If the things he has dredged from down there have form, he gives them form; if they are formless, he gives them formlessness.

In Rimbaud's poetry can be located all the attributes of modern thought: the search for primitive, precivilizational sources of energy; the juxtaposition of mismatched, inconsistent fragments of ideas and objects; and the use of techniques in ways and in combinations for which they never were intended. In sum, doing violence to and transgressing all established boundaries, in the cause of revolution.

Fyodor Dostoevsky was also in Germany in 1871, watching the Paris Commune closely. "Take a look at Paris, at the Commune," he wrote in a letter of May 30, 1871, which he sent to a friend in Russia. "Throughout the whole of the nineteenth century this movement has either been dreaming of paradise on earth, or, as soon as it begins to act, it demonstrates a humiliating inability to say anything remotely positive. . . . They chop off heads, but why? Solely because this is easier than anything else. . . . The burning of Paris is a monstrosity." The flaming towers of fires set in the Paris Commune stimulated Dostoevsky to put a major act of arson at the center of *Demons,* or *The Possessed.* For Dostoevsky, the demons are ideas. The end of faith brought by atheistic communism enabled the rise of a philosophy of revolutionary terror conceived as a moral imperative.

Dostoevsky scorned "the novel" as a genre. To him, it was Western, romantic, decadent: he did not, he insisted, write novels. *Demons* is an anti-novel. As the literary scholar Michael Holquist put it, in the "orchestra of nations" Russia was not first violin but a primitive balalaika. In geographical space, Russia was out on the far edge; in time, it was off the clock, following a different calendar from western Europe. Dostoevsky is dead set against the Enlightenment as having committed the great sin of world affairs—aspiring to utopia on earth. In *Demons,* he portrays the Enlightenment-inspired revolutionaries who aim to carry out this earthly project. Like the Gadarene swine, in the biblical parable which informs the book, their number is legion and they are all possessed. With the return of the true spirit of faith, they will all rush over a cliff and fall to their doom.

Demons draws upon the case of one Nechaev, a young member of international revolutionary circles who has fled Russia to exile in Geneva with leaders of the anarchist movement. "There Nechaev generated a torrent of proclamations, written in vengeful spirit and millenarian tone" and sent them by post back to Russia. Returning to Moscow in 1869, Nechaev organizes student circles under the banner of a Committee of the People's Revenge and becomes notorious when he leads and carries out the murder, in a grotto in a remote part of the grounds of the Moscow Agricultural Academy, of a student named Ivanov. Nechaev claims that Ivanov intended to betray the secret cell; he is lured to the grotto by a request to help recover a printing press buried there for later use by the revolutionaries. Beaten by members of the group, Ivanov is then shot in the head, and his body, weighted by bricks, is thrown into a pond. Nechaev's hand is badly bitten during the killing, and he carelessly leaves his hat at the scene. It is believed that he arranged the murder primarily to bind the members of the group together through their common participation in the crime.

Dostoevsky adapted a real murder case for the plot of his novel. What then makes *Demons* anything more than a fictionalized real-life crime story? A great deal.

There is a logic chain located here. Through it, Dostoevsky pulls together the main elements of what he regards as the wrongful course taken since the opening of the modern era, examines it, explains it, and then offers a better, transcendent alternative.

The first element is the liberal intelligentsia's call for universality to supersede nationality. "It is," he says in his letter of May 1871, "all the same old Rousseau dream of changing the world on the basis of reason." Rousseau declared that no government has ever been legitimate; no government is legitimate; and none ever can be legitimate—none, that is, until Man is perfected, when "The People" take power and establish a utopian order. This is the messianic and eschatological theology of Joachim of Fiore, the twelfth-century Calabrian monk who interpreted the Book of Revelation as foretelling a new age of Heaven on Earth. Rousseau updated it in secular form. It is Blake's call to "build Jerusalem in England's green and pleasant land."

In terms of Russia, the argument runs like this: first, the misery of the Russian peasants is a national crime for which the privileged Russian elite is responsible. Indeed, the Russia system—tsarist theocratic autocracy—is the root cause of the injustice. The system generates violence and therefore must be destroyed by violence. The radical revolutionary ideology emerging from the Enlightenment, the French Revolution, and the Paris Commune would destroy Russia's tsarism and create a perfected society.

Second, the loss of nationality will be the loss of God and the coming of a new god: equality. Dostoevsky says, in a letter of October 1870, that he who loses his nationality loses his tradition, loses his culture, and loses God. "This is precisely the theme of my novel," he says. It is also precisely the theme of the Enlightenment: universality superseding nationality, reason supplanting God. Atheism, internationalism, and materialism were to preside over a progressive and ever more perfected earthly paradise. The mechanism to bring this about would be equality, achieved by "each giving all to all," as Rousseau said. But as Dostoevsky contemptuously put it in his May 1871 letter, "The Paris Commune and Western Socialism do not desire better men (that would mean a new aristocracy, an aristocracy of talent and merit but evermore more equality). They would cut off the heads of Shakespeare and Raphael."

Third, if there is no God, then men are as gods and everything is permitted. If the old system must be overthrown by violence, then there are no limits on the kind and extent of violence that will be necessary and justified. Pyotr Stepanovich Verkhovensky says, "We believe our program is correct; that is why we have decided on blood."

Fourth is the novel itself, a description of how, in Russia, that which the evangelist Luke described came to pass. "You see, it's exactly like our Russia," Stepan Trofimovich says, "these demons who came out of a sick man and enter into swine. . . . And we will rush, insane and raging, from the cliff down into the sea, and all be drowned and good riddance to us. . . . But the sick man will be healed and seated at the feet of Jesus."

"Exactly the same thing has happened in Russia," Dostoevsky says. "Russia has puked up the filth she has been fed."

The enigmatic central figure of *Demons* is Stavrogin, who will become an archetypal generator of terrorism. Stavrogin is the one around whom others orbit, even when he is not present. Others project their yearnings onto him as he imperceptibly shapes them to his will.

Before Stavrogin's arrival his existence is conveyed through rumor and hearsay. Surrounded by ambiguity, by uncertainty, his personality is like a shadow cast by the expectations of others. He does not appear until one-third of the way through the book, but very early in the novel, he is foreshadowed in Stepan Trofimovich's prose poem: "Suddenly a youth of indescribable beauty rides in on a black horse, followed by a terrible multitude of all the nations. The youth represents death, and all the nations yearn for it." The gods are overthrown, and Man becomes God.

The actual Stavrogin is passive, intangible, yet exerts an immense gravitational pull as the elusive center of the work. He hardly speaks or acts, and yet his charismatic influence over others is all-powerful.

Pyotr Stepanovich Verkhovensky: I invented you [Stavrogin] when I looked at you. . . .

You are my leader, my sun, and I am your worm. [We can hear the masses singing "The East is Red" to Chairman Mao.]

Kirillov: Remember what you've meant in my life, Stavrogin! [We can be assured that Stavrogin will not remember.]

Shatov: I can't tear you out of my heart, Nikolai Stavrogin! [But Stavrogin directs Shatov on a path that leads to violent death.]

Stavrogin is like the great Legislator of Rousseau's *Social Contract.* He has no official role or responsibility. He is nowhere and everywhere. He is Stalin, Mao, and Osama bin Laden. All are drawn to him, only to be turned to destructive and ultimately self-destructive purposes. The void of his personality is filled not by his own design but by the hopes and fears that others project onto him. He dominates, yet does nothing beyond suggesting, mocking, and conveying fear. He is, Thomas Mann wrote, "that icy and contemptible, masterful person before whom weaker creatures grovel in the dust, probably one of the most vividly attractive characters in world literature." He is the spirit of negation, the vacuum left by free will when the people have become exhausted of using it.

Stavrogin initiates the core plot of the revolutionary cell. Laughing as he does so, he tells Pyotr Stepanovich what forces make up such a circle:

"Get four members of a circle to bump off a fifth on the pretense of his being an informer, and with this shed blood you'll immediately tie them together in a single knot. They'll become your slaves, they won't dare rebel or call you to account. Ha, ha, ha!"

The revolutionary cell gets the message, both strategically and tactically. "What I propose is . . . earthly paradise," Shigalyov says. "Instead of paradise," Lyamshin shouts, "I'd take these nine-tenths of mankind, since there's really nothing to do about them, and blow them sky-high." Soon the talk turns to "radically lopping off" a hundred million heads. As Lenin would later say, "It does not matter if three-fourths of mankind is destroyed; all that counts is that the last quarter become Communist."

And Pyotr Stepanovich understands: "A new religion is on its way to replace the old one. Stavrogin has already inspired or created the instrumentalities of the movement. Kirillov lusts to kill himself, for by doing so, he dethrones God, taking God's powers over life and death. Kirillov is consumed by a quest to reverse the death of Christ; to eliminate God and a world beyond this from human consciousness. Doing so, he will create the Man-God.

Stavrogin's other mission is Shatov, who is consumed with Russian Orthodoxy. For Shatov, reason cannot determine good and evil; only religion and faith can do that via the messianic idea of Russia as a God-fearing people. Dostoevsky opposes the revolutionary for his atheism; he opposes the Slavophile as well.

So the plot is readied. Pyotr Stepanovich will have the cell murder Shatov in order to create revolutionary solidarity. The conspirators will be protected by the suicide of Kirillov, who will leave a note saying he killed Shatov.

Stavrogin's face, we are told more than once, is a mask. Only one person is able to see through the mask: the lame, feebleminded Marya Timofeevna Lebyadina, whom Stavrogin married "on a bet, after a drunken dinner." She expresses authentic Russian culture springing from the people's faith.

Only at the end, in a letter, does Stavrogin reveal himself as a pure nihilist: "I've tested my powers everywhere. . . . But what to apply those powers to . . . only negation has flowed from them, without magnanimity and without force. Not even negation." If Christ is God as Son, Stavrogin is man as God.

The name Stavrogin contains a meaning of "the cross." In the writings of Saint Augustine there is the image of the *Muscipula Diaboli* (The Devil's mousetrap). After the Fall of Adam and Eve, mankind was in the grip of Satan. The cross was a mousetrap set to catch Satan, a trap baited with the blood of Christ. Satan took the bait, and mankind was liberated. In Dostoevsky, however, mankind is turning away from God. The cross is a mousetrap set by Stavrogin, the Antichrist. He himself is the bait, and when the bait is taken and the trap is sprung, it is the blood of mankind that is shed.

The novel does not, however, belong to Stavrogin; it begins and ends with Stepan Trofimovich Verkhovensky. We see him as a figure to be satirized: weak, dependent, affected, pathetic, passé.

Stepan Trofimovich, a liberal of the past generation, is the progenitor both of Pyotr Stepanovich, his biological son, and of Nikolai Vsevolodovich Stavrogin, his ideological son, in whom liberalism becomes nihilism and ultimately despotism. At the same time, Stepan Trofimovich is "the little boy" (despite his advanced age) of Varvara Stavrogina, Stavrogin's biological mother. This makes him, in a sense, the brother of Stavrogin. Stepan Trofimovich in some sense encompasses everyone, and everyone in some way touches him.

In a world increasingly materialistic, grasping, brutal, and murderous, Stepan Trofimovich possesses an antique sense of gallantry. His banner is beauty, as Nabokov says of Don Quixote. "Boots are inferior to Pushkin," he declares, in opposition to the revolutionaries' rejection of aesthetic values. Stepan Trofimovich's great speech at the fête is about beauty, and it is a speech to "decide his fate," we are told loftily, or "something like that"—which reminds us that he remains a ridiculous figure whose grand illusions usually deflate on contact with reality.

So he seems to be something like a Don Quixote. At the end, he sets out on a quest for salvation—to the village Spasov, a name suggesting "savior"—with an umbrella. He meets real peasants, not the revolutionaries' imaginary ones, who give him a ride on their cart, and Sophia Mateevna, a seller of gospels, to whom he becomes devoted. Her simplicity and clarity of vision sharply contrast with all others in the story. He who once adopted the citizenship of Uri, a canton in Switzerland, a nation without nationality, returns to the Russian countryside and finds reconciliation. In the rain, he drops to his knees, a baptism by the land.

He is also an endless traveler who never arrives. He fails to board the ferry to Spasov for the ridiculous Quixote-like reasons of a stomachache and a misread timetable. Like other epic visionaries, he dies without ever reaching the Promised Land.

Dostoevsky is an Augustinian: the City of Man and the City of God are not the same. Those who would build a paradise on earth can do so only by abolishing freedom and beauty, and by terrorist dictatorship.

Joseph Conrad followed Dostoevsky in depicting terror as a plaything for intellectuals. Conrad's *The Secret Agent,* set in 1886 but published in 1907, read today, seems filled with prescient insights. It even, in a sense, predicts the war on terror—that is, terrorism's war on, and in, the international state system. In the aftermath of the attacks on the United States on September 11, 2001, *The Secret Agent* was referred to countless times in the media, and Conrad was called "a literary Nostradamus."[16]

The modern reader of the novel encounters an array of reminders of twenty-first-century terrorism: a radical ideology that would destroy the state and the international system; the label and concept of *terrorist;* a commitment to and infatuation with unspeakable acts and mass murder; a suicide bomber with his fingers always on the detonating device in his clothing that will blow him and everyone around him to bloody bits; the quiet, "nice," ordinary lives lived by those involved in terror; the blundering, arrogant officials who are both the killers' targets and their pursuers; the elite who fawn over terrorists who would obliterate them; the press, which creates and imposes a reality of its own, reporting on events while taking a starring role in them; and above all, the vulnerability of civilization, along with its production of civilized savages bent on exploiting its flaws.

Verloc is the ordinary man in a quiet life, a London shopkeeper who deals in pornography. His decent, quiet wife, Winnie, has a feebleminded brother Stevie, who lives with the couple and is watched over by Winnie with maternal vigilance. Stevie, fair, slight, and innocent, spends hours drawing "cosmic" circles at the kitchen table. Stevie reveres Verloc: "You could do anything with that boy," Winnie said to her husband. "He would go through fire for you." But Verloc "extended as much recognition as a man not particularly fond of animals may give to his wife's beloved cat."

Verloc is a "revolutionary," active in radical societies. He poses as an anarchist but is really an agent-provocateur in the pay of the Russian embassy in London. Called one morning, most unusually, to the chancery, Verloc is berated by Vladimir, the first secretary of the embassy. Verloc has failed to produce the act of incomprehensible violence on British life that would cause the authorities to crack down on real anarchists and, at the same time, pass repressive legislation that would undermine the British people's faith and confidence in the legal system and legality itself.

The rhetoric of Vladimir's orders to Verloc reveals a theme of the novel as a whole: the ease with which the deadly enemies of civilized world order can use its values against itself. Vladimir uses the language of capitalism to pressure Verloc to act against the capitalist system: "I tell you plainly that you will have to earn your money. . . . No work, no pay. . . . When you cease to be useful you shall cease to be employed."[17]

Similarly, the cultivated, liberal elite of society can be counted on to rhapsodize and subsidize the very revolutionaries who aim to eradicate them. And the police, the keepers of order and justice, are often so smug and obtuse that their efforts at counterterrorism only make the situation worse. In this sense, *The Secret Agent* can be read as a satire on civilized society. In the final pages, however, it shows us the unspeakable, unfathomable delusions of a death cultist, and his lust for obliterating himself and as many others as possible. Only then can the reader see the horrifying seriousness beneath the satire.

Vladimir analyzes for the dumbstruck Verloc exactly the kind of brilliant stroke that is needed. He presents "the philosophy of bomb throwing," the goal being "to make a clean sweep of the social creation." Assassinations are no longer sensational; a murderous assault on a theater is a used-up idea; a bomb in the National Gallery would not be serious enough. What is needed is "an act of destructive ferocity so absurd as to be incomprehensible, inexplicable. . . . The attack must have all the shocking senselessness of gratuitous blasphemy." The target, Vladimir says, should be the Greenwich Observatory, a monument to science, to world civilization, the marker of the first meridian, the standard for universal time, an icon of which the whole civilized world has heard.

Verloc obtains a bomb from "the Professor," the most radically committed member of a revolutionary underworld rife with plots to destroy Western civilization. His employment by the Russian embassy at stake, Verloc persuades Stevie to undertake what the boy believes is a humanitarian mission. Carrying the bomb to Greenwich, Stevie stumbles over a tree root and is obliterated by the explosion: "Blown to small bits: limbs, gravel, clothing, bones, splinters—all mixed up together. I tell you they had to fetch a shovel to gather him up with."

For all its chilling hideousness, Conrad's portrayal of the anarchist–agent provocateur world is close to a cartoon. Each individual in the lowlife scene is given an epithet that Conrad repeats again and again: "Robust" Comrad Ossipon, known as "the Doctor"; Michaelis "the ticket-of-leave [out on probation] apostle"; Karl Yundt "the terrorist"; and Verloc himself, described repeatedly as a delegate of the Central Red Committee. With each such labeling, the characters seem less substantial, more preposterous. The novel begins to suggest that terrorism is a farce, something that society just has to—and can—live with. Only the retarded Stevie possesses the ability to carry out the kind of attack the revolutionaries fantasize about.

When Conrad shifts to the investigative authorities, the language—narrative and direct dialogue—changes significantly. A kind of high-tea English fills the page, with fragments of Sherlock Holmes, Edward Gibbon, and Oxbridge dons. Satire flows, exposing the flaws and failings of civilization itself at its root, "the irony of great plans having trivial results and of the weightiest results being effected by trivial means."[18]

Chief Inspector Heat finds a scrap of cloth from Stevie's coat on which Winnie had inked his address, as a mother would for a small boy. This leads the inspector to Verloc. Verloc has been a useful informant for Heat in the past, so Heat is inclined to look at Michaelis as the instigator of the bomb attempt at Greenwich.

At this point the assistant commissioner enters the investigation. He does not want to see Michaelis as the terrorist because his wife is closely connected to "the lady patroness of Michaelis," a society grand dame who practices radical chic and has even entertained the terrorist at the spa at Marienbad. Her drawing room had been a place an assistant commissioner of police could rub shoulders with a convict on probation in society. As a suspect, Michaelis would be instantly reincarcerated.

The assistant commissioner takes over the inquiry. He obtains authorization from Sir Ethelred (the Unready?) to offer Verloc protection in return for turning state's evidence against the Russian embassy.

The description of the assistant commissioner's interview with Sir Ethelred might come out of a Sherlock Holmes story. The assistant commissioner found himself with the great personage in a large room. . . . The great man put his arms akimbo, the backs of his big hands resting on his hips.

"Very well. Go on. Only no details, pray. Spare me the details."

"You shall not be troubled with them, Sir Ethelred," the Assistant Commissioner began, with a calm and untroubled assurance. While he was speaking the hands on the face of the clock behind the great man's back—a heavy, glistening affair of massive scrolls in the same dark marble as the mantelpiece, and even with a ghostly, evanescent tick—had moved through the space of seven minutes. He spoke with a studious fidelity to a parenthetical manner into which every fact— that is, every detail—fitted with delightful ease. Not a murmur nor even a movement hinted at interruption. The great Personage might have been the statue of one of his own princely ancestors stripped of a Crusader's war harness and put into an ill-fitting frock coat.

The assistant commissioner is arranging a legal way out for Verloc when Verloc is killed by Winnie, crazed by the knowledge that her husband has sent Stevie out to murder him. Then, after dallying with the robust Comrade Ossipon on a plan to escape to the Continent, Winnie is abandoned by Ossipon and kills herself: "Suicide of a Lady from a Cross Channel Boat."

Conrad brilliantly blurs the terrorists with the establishment they seek to destroy. Verloc and Winnie and Stevie were a dysfunctional family in which Winnie cares for her retarded boy and Verloc rejects his paternal role.

The Secret Agent is a guidebook of warnings to civilization. At first, Conrad portrays terrorism as hardly a threat at all. It is state authority that is pompous, ridiculous, bogus, even deserving of the fate that the terrorists have in store. And if the terrorists succeed? Well, the authorities would have brought it on themselves, wouldn't they? Conrad's irony almost creates a satire on terrorism. But by the end of the novel, "the irony is drained of humor and becomes an austere and terrible truth-teller."[19]

The Secret Agent is packed with mentions of newspapers and can be read as sounding an alarm about the power of the press. Terrorism is theater. The plan to blow up the Greenwich Observatory was ideally modern in being "senseless," but the plot was bungled and the press took no notice. Conrad's book of 1907 is our contemporary over a century later. He was groping to understand a newly perplexing problem: how to understand the media's conquest of knowledge by information.[20]

Most ominously, there is "the Professor," the one who keeps his hand constantly on the detonator of his body-bomb. Trained in chemistry at a technical institute, the Professor looms up at the very end of the novel; he alone is "incorruptible." *The Secret Agent* ends with what amounts to a poem about the Professor, the archetypal terrorist:

> He had no future. He disdained it.
> He was a force. His thoughts caressed
> The images of ruin and destruction.
> He walked frail, insignificant, shabby, miserable—
> And terrible in the simplicity of his idea
> Calling madness and despair to
> The regeneration of the world. Nobody
> Looked at him. He passed on unsuspected
> And deadly, like a pest in the street
> Full of men.

These final words recall the subtitle to the novel: "A Simple Tale." The "simplicity of his idea—mass death and destruction, followed by 'the regeneration of the world'" on his terms. Perfectly simple.

Most prescient of all is the Professor's foreshadowing of the twenty-first-century Islamist declaration, "You love life; we love death." Early in *The Secret Agent,* the Professor explains to Ossipon that civilized Britain is "inferior":

> Their character is built upon
> Conventional morality. It leans
> On the social order. Mine stands
> Free from everything artificial
> They are bound in all sorts of conventions
> *They depend on life* . . . a complex, organized
> Fact open to attach at every point; whereas
> I depend on death, which knows no restraint
> And cannot be attached. My superiority
> Is evident.[21]

The question, Conrad implies, is whether civilization is capable of defending itself against pure evil in the form of terrorism when it is so immersed in its own weaknesses, delusions, and contradictions. For Hobbes, fear of violent death underlay the social contract and called political community into being to grant the individual basic security. Hobbes's social contract became the theoretical foundation stone of modern society. In Conrad, the terrorist's infatuation with death overturns this foundation of civilization.

Through most of the twentieth century, the revolutionary ideology of Marxist-Leninist communism posed the largest, most openly declared assault on the international state system. Henry Kissinger described the challenge it posed to world order:

> Nothing remotely resembling the Soviet Union had appeared on the horizon of European diplomacy since the French Revolution. For the first time in over a century, a country had dedicated itself officially to overthrowing the established order. The French revolutionaries had striven to change the character of the state; the Bolsheviks, going a step further, proposed to abolish the state altogether. Once the state had withered away, in Lenin's phrase, there would be no need for diplomacy or foreign policy. . . .
>
> Since after a few months or years the state was expected to disappear altogether, the principal task of early Soviet foreign policy was believed to be the encouragement of world revolution, not the management of relations among states.[22]

In the decades-long Cold War, a war waged by the Communist International against the international state system, no event gained more intellectual and artistic attention than the publication in the West of Boris Pasternak's novel *Doctor Zhivago.*

The Russian Revolution, propelled by Marxist-Leninist ideology, aimed to overthrow the old order and proceed to build an entirely different, "socialist" system which would produce the "new man." The French Revolution, Marx declared, had not been a real revolution, only a political transformation; true revolution would transform every aspect of life so that each person would be wholly devoted to "The People." In *Doctor Zhivago,* the love between Lara and Yury therefore posed a fundamental threat to the revolutionary cause. Love, marriage, and family formed the basis not of society but of its enemy, as *The Communist Manifesto,* Marx's literary masterpiece, made clear.

Pasternak, a Russian poet born in Moscow in 1890 to a painter father and pianist mother, had studied music with Scriabin and philosophy at Germany's University of Marburg. His poetry, autobiographical writings, and personal magnetism had made him a noted figure in the Soviet Union. There was an aura about him; some even thought that Pasternak "had inspired Stalin with some mysterious fear." For all this, Pasternak was scarcely known, even in intellectual circles, outside the USSR.

In 1957 the Italian publisher Feltrinelli brought out *Doctor Zhivago.* It was an immediate international sensation. The manuscript had been rejected by Soviet publishers and condemned by communist authorities for "its spirit of non-acceptance of the Socialist Revolution." Nothing promoted the swift growth of interest in *Doctor Zhivago* more than these clumsy attempts to prevent publication.[23] An English translation was rushed to completion and published in the United States in 1958. Within the year it was awarded the Nobel Prize for Literature. The uproar of interest goaded Soviet officials into ever-greater denunciations. Pasternak feared that he would be deported, a fate he viewed as artistic death because it would deprive him of his subject, Russia itself. Were he allowed to go to Stockholm to accept the prize, he would not be allowed to return to Moscow. Pasternak declined the honor: "In view of the meaning given to this honor in the community to which I belong, I should abstain from the undeserved prize that has been awarded to me. Do not meet my voluntary refusal with ill will."[24] Pasternak was permitted to continue writing and to keep his dacha at the intellectual-artist retreat of Peredelkino.[25]

The novel's story line spans the revolutionary years from 1903 to 1929 and is centered on the violent transformation of tsarist Russia into the Union of Soviet Socialist Republics. The plot seems rambling, disjointed, and at best tangentially connected to great historical events. There are two central relationships: between Yury and Lara and between Yury and Pasha. The book opens at the funeral of Yury's mother and, elsewhere, with Lara's seduction by a wealthy lecher. They grow up in separate spheres, although their paths cross. Yury is an observer, not an activist. He sees something of the 1905 Revolution. When Yury and Lara finally become acquainted, each has married: Yury to Tanya and Lara to Pasha. Yury is sent to the front in the First World War as a doctor. Lara is there too, as a nurse searching for her husband. When they meet, the revolution has broken out in Saint Petersburg. Yury falls in love with Lara, but their lives remain separate.

With the Bolshevik seizure of power in 1917, Yury is advised to seek refuge in the far countryside, at Tanya's family estate in Siberia. The long train journey across Russia brings Yury into contact with Pasha, Lara's missing husband, who has transformed himself into "Strelnikov," a revolutionary paragon. Separately, Yury by coincidence meets Lara. They now truly begin their love affair, only to be torn apart when Yury is kidnapped by Bolshevik partisans who, waging civil war for power over Russia, demand his services as a doctor. After more than a year with the Red fighters, Yury escapes and finds Lara again, still in Siberia. Yury's wife, Tanya, and their child have fled. To avoid the new Bolshevik regime, Yury and Lara find brief Edenic respite in a rural retreat. Lara is lured away to the Far East. Yury meets Strelnikov again, shortly before Strelnikov kills himself. He then treks back across Russia to Moscow. There he writes, scrapes by, and takes a common-law wife, Marina. Just as his creativity seems to regenerate, he is stricken by a heart attack and dies. Lara appears too late to see him alive. Yury's death takes place in 1929; at the end of the book it is suddenly 1943, the middle of the Second World War. We see Tanya, a laundry girl, the daughter of Yury and Lara. Five or ten years later, old friends of Yury's read his books and contemplate the future of the Revolution and Russia.

A more pointless and boring sequence of aimless coincidence-ridden happenings is hard to imagine. How could this thin, pathetic collection of nonsequential encounters become the most sensational literary work of the Cold War era? As the poet Andrei Sinyavksy astutely recognized, *Zhivago,* written in the guise of a historical novel, really was about the future.

Superficially, the novel contains only a very few direct criticisms of the Soviet regime. The collectivization of agriculture is called a disaster. Stalin's polices are derided, and the prison camp archipelago is condemned. As sporadic as these criticisms are, they go far beyond the limited criticisms leveled against Stalin's policies in Khrushchev's 'secret speech' of 1956 one year before the publication of *Doctor Zhivago* in Italy.

At a deeper, almost subconscious level, the text undermines the scientific and philosophical foundations of the communist ideology. The idea that Marxism is scientifically true is scoffed at. Revolution itself, and even political thought and action, are made to appear beneath the attention of anyone who would take life seriously. Taken together, these attitudes "constitute a downright blasphemy against Soviet doctrine."[26]

These points, and Pasternak's personal standing, would be more than enough to explain official Soviet outrage over the novel. But a more profound dimension exists, and it is this that accounts for praise given the work by serious commentators in the West. "A militantly counter-revolutionary work would have been far less objectionable than *Doctor Zhivago*, [for the authorities] would have known where they were with that."[27]

The genius, the brilliance of Pasternak's conception was to reverse thoroughly this approach. Astrophysicists determine the presence of a black hole by what it blocks out. This was Pasternak's method. *Doctor Zhivago*'s "principal aim is to convey its creator's conception of all that is most positive and worthwhile in human existence."[28] Marx, in his early writings, denounced the French Revolution as not a real revolution; it revolutionized *political* life but left the rest of life still determined by private choice and association.[29] The true revolution, Marx said, must be total: no aspect of human life could remain unaffected—least of all the individual, who under revolutionary education must sacrifice himself for a communist future in which human nature, as Rousseau had declared, would be "perfected."

Doctor Zhivago portrays those things in human life and relations that the revolution could not reach; what was left of a person whose life is threatened by erasure, and is then erased. The novel's focus on nature, the family, religion, art, and the love of man and woman implicitly refutes the transformation of these things by the Marxist regime that had been so stridently alleged. Thus an otherwise conventional love story between realistic human beings touched off a literary sensation in Soviet Russia. Recognizing this fact, with great human empathy, the rest of the world responded like the Russians.

For the communist, nature as depicted by Pasternak is a challenge to be subdued and mastered, by railroads, hydroelectric dams, and vast new productive complexes such as Magnetogorsk, the Soviet steel mill city constructed from the ground up and which cost more lives than the Battle of the Marne: Enlightenment reason carried to maniacal extremes. *The Communist Manifesto* also declared, "Abolish the family!" The bourgeois family, said Marx, is based on capital, on private gain, and would vanish as a matter of course when capital vanished after the revolution. Religion was a mere symptom of the alienation of people under capitalism, a dreamworld to substitute for the emotional comforts denied by bourgeois society. "Religion is the sigh of the oppressed creature, the heart of a heartless world, as it is the spirit of spiritless conditions. It is the *opium* of the people." Religion would be abolished as people's illusory happiness when communism provided them with real happiness.[30] Poetry and the arts, too, were mere manifestations of capitalism's need to distract and to amuse the oppressed. They would reemerge under communism in healthier form as "socialist realism."

Above all, *Doctor Zhivago* was a love story, of Yury and Lara. This was the ultimate defiance of the proclaimed Soviet transformation of humanity. Yury and Lara are the antithesis of the "new Soviet man" and "new Soviet woman." They are just man and woman, whose love remains in a private place, inaccessible to totalitarian reconstruction. They are ineluctably individual. The oppression of the regime makes them grow ever closer; their love ever deeper. "Their low-voiced talk, however unimportant, was as full of meanings as the Dialogue of Plato."

Doctor Zhivago brought front and center—not through denunciation, but by implication—the Soviet regime's drive to abolish precommunist civilization through power, terror, and deadening rhetoric. Pasternak, and Zhivago, were exhilarated by the Revolution at its birth. But contrary to Marx and Lenin, the state had not been "smashed," nor had it "withered away." Instead, it took on grotesque, gargantuan form under Stalin. *Doctor Zhivago* condemns the Soviet state as a degeneration from the Revolution that had been a moment of liberation, of assertion of the forces of life. Zhivago represents the revolution of the human spirit against the total state.

Unable to destroy the basic attributes of civilized life and replace them with the collective, the Soviet regime turns to the use of terror to intimidate and compel compliance. Lara says, "The whole human way of life has been destroyed and ruined. All that's left is the naked human soul stripped to the last shred. . . . You and I are like Adam and Eve, the first two people on earth who at the beginning of the world had nothing to cover themselves with—and now at the end of it we are just as naked and homeless."

At the end, Zhivago dead, Lara disappears into the Soviet terror system: "One day Lara Feodorovna went out and did not come back. She must have been arrested in the street at that time. She vanished without a trace and probably died somewhere, forgotten as a nameless number on a list that afterwards got mislaid, in one of the innumerable mixed or women's concentration camps in the north."

Charles Dickens's *A Tale of Two Cities* was never far from Pasternak's desk as he wrote *Doctor Zhivago*. In their portrayal of revolutionary terror, both Dickens and Pasternak distill the essence of the revolution's impact in their main characters. Each brilliantly grasps the dehumanization of utopian, all-encompassing ideologies.

Pasternak's *Zhivago,* like many epic works, perhaps most vividly Thucydides' *Peloponnesian War,* locates the source of what goes wrong in the dehumanization of a society, in particular when language becomes debased, at those moments of unhinged crisis "when words lose their meaning." Lara says, "The main misfortune, the root of all evil to come was the loss of confidence in the value of one's own opinion. People imagined that it was out of date to follow their own moral sense." Falsity in language is a clue to something deeper, to a rot in the heart of the regime. Yury is unnerved and incapacitated by the verbiage spewed out by the regime, the gargantuan rhetoric made with an eye to obliterating the individual in all his uniqueness, to mold people into a type of being eager to bow down before clichés such as "sacrifice for the future" or "to build for tomorrow."[31]

The size and sweep of *Doctor Zhivago* led many commentators to compare it, unfavorably, to Tolstoy's *War and Peace,* but apart from their mutual fixation on the matter of Russia, the two works have little in common. Comparison with two other epic works can be more revealing.

Pasternak's novel clearly follows and reflects Virgil's *Aeneid.* Yury, like Aeneas, has a series of three wives: Tanya (Creusa), who stands for the old order; Lara, his true, doomed love (Dido); and Marina (Lavinia), a spouse who represents the new order. Early in the epic Lara realizes "the purpose of her life. She was on earth to grasp the meaning of its wild enchantment and to call each thing by its right name." Later, midway in the text, Yury is transformed, in proper epic fashion, by a death-and-rebirth experience gained by seizing the branches of a rowan tree, Pasternak's version of Virgil's golden bough. His purpose is revealed: to find and love Lara and to be a poet. Yet in the end Yury emerges like Aeneas in manner: a bit passive and uncertain, submissive to the world-historical establishment of a new universal order. Aeneas is supposed to celebrate the coming of the Augustan world order, but his poem conveys a dark and troubled dimension. Virgil's *Aeneid* and Pasternak's *Zhivago* are, above all, about the conflict between the personal and the public, between love and duty. In each epic, the personal is transcendentally important, but the public wins out in the end: the cause of Roman Empire and of communist ideology. Such a vast transformative project can succeed only at a huge cost to humanity. Like the *Aeneid, Zhivago* leaves the reader feeling that the national epic may depict a grand endeavor gone wrong.

Then there is the antiepic Whitman. A visitor to Pasternak's Peredelkino dacha in 1957 found that the poet knew little of American literature. No knowledge of Melville or *Moby-Dick*. The name Henry James was barely familiar. No awareness of Faulkner.[32] But Whitman, the first American poet to win international recognition, somehow got through. And as for Russia, "It would be difficult to overestimate the importance of Walt Whitman in the history of twentieth-century Russian letters. His audience, reputation, and influence have been enormous."[33] A record exists of Pasternak's warm expression of thanks to Kornei Chukovsky for the gift of Chukovsky's translation of *Leaves of Grass*. After Zhivago's death, a note is found among his papers referring to Whitman: "The seemingly incongruous and arbitrary jumble of things and ideas . . . is not a stylistic caprice. This is a new order of impressions, taken directly from life."

To counter the dark Virgilian tone of the novel, Pasternak ends *Doctor Zhivago* uniquely, with a poem cycle. This is not an appendix but the last chapter of the book, an ending that raises the question whether this is indeed a novel or a hybrid prose-poem composition. Pasternak certainly does not emulate Whitman's poetic style, although his "jumble of things and ideas" at times seems Whitmanesque.

Pasternak and Whitman converge in the idea of regeneration. Nature and history, as Italo Calvino pointed out, are in *Doctor Zhivago* not two different orders but a continuum in which human lives find themselves immersed.[34] For Whitman life is endless regeneration and self-renewal, like grass. For Pasternak, regeneration is the resurrection as depicted in the Gospels. The end of *Doctor Zhivago* is suffused in Christianity, a flat rejection of atheistic communism, and it was undoubtedly this that most galled Soviet officialdom. For Pasternak, Christ was the giver of liberty and human choice. "Pasternak repeats Hegel's account of the historical role of Christianity in creating the modern man, who need no longer be either master or slave."[35]

Pasternak's fellow writer Andrei Sinyavsky wrote: "As if to refute Soviet literature, which for so long has so doggedly denigrated the intelligentsia, Pasternak depicted the purest intellectual, his sad fate in the new society, and his feat: the feat of not killing, of refusing on moral grounds to obey the laws of the class struggle, where people annihilate each other for ideological or political reasons and require that everyone do the same."[36]

"The locomotive of history," the Communist Party, is derailed by Pasternak's novel. *Doctor Zhivago* stood for irreducible humanity against a Marxism that had sought to eradicate and replace humanity with its own false and final answer to the meaning of life and the purpose of history. The railway train, an icon of modern Russia, recurs in the book—crossing the vast Eurasian heartland or, a bold red star emblazoned on its boiler, leading a revolution. But trains in *Doctor Zhivago* go wrong, they break down. In the end Yury dies, almost farcically, on a streetcar.

In the same year that Woodrow Wilson drafted his Fourteen Points, 1918, Vladimir Ilyich Lenin was desperate to finish *The State and Revolution* before "they do me in"; it would be his ultimate commentary on the world.

The state was at the center. Every state, Lenin said, exists to serve the ruling class as "an instrument for the exploitation of the oppressed class." The ruling class monopolizes the use of violence to maintain the existing order, and would never cede this power without armed struggle. Therefore the state must be overthrown, "smashed" by violent revolution for "the dictatorship of the proletariat." The purpose of the state is oppression; under communism there would be no need for the state. It would "wither away," Lenin reasoned. What would replace the state? Lenin pointed to Marx's admiration for the Paris Commune of 1871. Mass participation in the joys of communism was enough; the collectivity would produce, each according to his abilities, and consume, each according to his needs, without need for administration.

This would require "The Eradication of Parliamentarianism." In other words, the elimination of representative democracy. Here is Lenin in his own prose style:

> To decide once every few years which member of the ruling class is to repress and crush the people in parliament: this is the real essence of bourgeois parliamentarianism not only in parliamentary-constitutional monarchies but also in the most democratic republics.
>
> But if we pose the question of the state and if we examine parliamentarianism as one of the state's institutions, from the view-point of the tasks of the proletariat in *this* field, what is the way out of parliamentarianism? How can we do without it? . . .
>
> "Not a parliamentary but a working" institution: this strikes right

between the eyes of the present-day parliamentarians and parliamentary lap dogs of social democracy! . . .

The commune replaces the venal and rotten parliamentarianism of bourgeois society.[37]

The rhetoric returns again and again to the same formula: there are "isms" to be wiped out. Rhetorical questions lock in their own answers. Labels ("bourgeois") are repeated endlessly and turn venomous with exclamation points: "Lap dogs!" This is a tract not for "the proletariat" but for those who require indoctrination in the grand strategy of Marxism-Leninism.

From its outset, the Soviet Union, as Sinyavsky recognized, sought to eliminate the very vocabulary connected with the concept of "the state." A linguistic revolution would be required to effectuate the political revolution. The title of "Minister" was replaced by "People's Commissar." "Government" became "The Dictatorship of the Proletariat." Governance itself was conducted by slogans: "all power to the Soviets!" except that the Soviets did not exercise power. "The Soviet people unanimously support the resolutions of the Twenty-Fifth Party Congress!" when no one had any idea what had been resolved, if anything, at the party congress.[38] All this is captured in George Orwell's *Animal Farm* (1945), a satiric fable of the Soviet Union in which pigs and horses and other creatures in the barnyard revolt against a human farmer and are enslaved when their language is systematically distorted until: "All animals are equal, but some animals are more equal than others."

As revolutionary ideology challenged international order from without, the twentieth century generated wars within the system itself: civil wars within civilization. Thomas Mann's *The Magic Mountain,* one of the few truly great novels of modern world literature, depicts Europe's intellectual and moral spiral downward toward the great wars that would shatter the established world order.[39]

Allegory—in which characters personify big ideas, concepts, or institutions—is associated with medieval, not modern, literature. Mann adopts the device in *The Magic Mountain* (Melville's *Moby-Dick* is another example) by creating characters who are realistic in everyday detail even as the reader comes to sense that they also stand for vast intellectual and historical concepts. Allegory was clearly present in *Paradise Lost* when Sin and Death suddenly appeared. Before the Fall, words and things were one and the same. "Are not the relationships that join art and war together completely allegorical?" wrote Mann, in a wartime essay that compared novel writing with the work of a military strategist.[40]

The setting is Davos, Switzerland, where the Berghof, a sanatorium high in the Alps, is a community of the sick, those dying of consumption— tuberculosis—and those who have been convinced, by themselves or others, that they are afflicted. The magic mountain allegorically depicts the fallen state of humanity. The patients come from all across the continent, enabled by the wealth of the modern bourgeois industrial economy to prolong their "cure" for years, in a grail quest for cultural health.

The title, taken by Mann from Friedrich Nietzsche's *The Birth of Tragedy* (1872), refers to the Olympian heights where "the gods justify the life of men by living it themselves."[41] Nietzsche depicts early Greek drama as balanced between the rationality of Apollo and the sensuality of Dionysius. For him, German culture had lost that balance; on Mann's allegorical magic mountain, the two sides will debate what this loss of balance means to the fate of humanity.

Like Xenophon's soldiers, those signed into the Berghof clinic make up a polis, a polity. The Berghof describes itself as international, each member with his or her own nationality; together they represent all of European civilization. The sanatorium is high on a mountain, but in a way familiar to nearly every literary epic, it is the underworld, the nether world of shades, the living dead. The novel's protagonist, Hans Castorp, visits them there. Like Odysseus or Aeneas in the underworld, he is not touched by death. He assumes he will return to the land of the living. And he has come there, as did the classical figures, to learn something about the meaning of life and his mission within it.

Hans is an engineer, preparing to take up his profession by reading a book he brings with him, *Ocean Steamships.* From Hamburg, he represents an industrializing new Germany, looking outward over the seas to gain wealth and power on a world scale. The naval rivalry between Germany and Britain is not stated but is felt by the history-attuned reader. Hans soon will accept the suggestion that he too has been touched by the disease, may have "a moist spot on the lung"; he will remain on *Der Zauberberg* from 1907 to 1914, the seven years before the Great War.[42]

Hans, like Germany at the time, will be in the middle, geographically and ideologically, between two competing world views.

Early in Hans's stay at the Berghof he is regaled by Herr Settembrini, an Italian and a man of the Enlightenment's Age of Reason. His clothes are mismatched, his mannerisms effusive, his enthusiasms those of a somewhat scatterbrained idealist. Settembrini is active in the "International League for the Organization of Progress." He advocates peace and democracy, the sole purpose of which "is to provide an individualistic corrective to the absolutism of the state."

Settembrini thinks in terms of dualisms: force or justice, tyranny or freedom, reason or emotion, the modern Enlightenment versus the premodern Medieval mind. His aim is to reconcile liberalism with the state, to transform the international system of states into one world federation of republics.

The listening Hans Castorp lightheartedly laughs that he himself pays no attention to politics:

> "don't understand a thing about it. I've never once glanced at a newspaper since I've been here." . . .
>
> Settembrini found this reprehensible; he at once proved to be very well informed about major current events—and approved of what was happening, since things were taking a course favorable to civilization. The general European atmosphere was imbued with ideas of peace and plans for disarmament. Democratic ideals were on the march. He claimed to have confidential information that the Young Turks had just completed preparations for their revolutionary uprising. Turkey as a constitutional nation-state—what a triumph for humanity!

Walking along with them is a newcomer, Naphta. Small, skinny, clean-shaven, and corrosively ugly. "Somehow everything about him was caustic: the aquiline nose dominating the face; the small pursed mouth; the pale gray eyes behind thick lenses in the light frames of his glasses . . . he was very well dressed: his suit was dark blue flannel with white pinstripes, its cut elegant, understated, stylish."

Naphta is everything Settembrini is not. Born into an orthodox Jewish family in Poland, his father a *schochet* (ritual slaughterer) who had been murdered by crucifixion in a pogrom, Naphta is a Jesuit, and the adversary of every Enlightenment principle. He is a reactionary, a romantic, a rejectionist of the idea of "the individual." To Naphta, Settembrini, the man of progress, is a nihilist. His liberalism and pacifism are formless nothings;

as a rationalist he is a denier of God. As a Jesuit, Naphta regards statecraft as his domain; his favored world system seems to be a theocratic form of communism.

Naphta sneers at Settembrini's optimism about the Young Turk movement. "The liberalism of Islam," Naphta scoffed. "Excellent. Enlightened fanaticism—how fine," and proceeds to describe catastrophic international consequences.

Settembrini's "enlightened" approach to world affairs is to take the Westphalian state system, properly liberalized, to the next higher—highest—step: a world republic. To Naphta, this is a Rousseauian fantasy, "a rationalist bastardization of the Church's doctrine of man's original sinless, stateless condition, of his primal direct relationship to God, as a child of God, to which condition he shall return." In this, Naphta is making the charge that the modern age is illegitimate: not "modern" at all, just an atheistic version of Christianity.[43] And as for democracy and idealism, they "are nothing but the last, feeble twitches of what little instinct for self preservation a doomed international system still has."

Here, in the years leading up to the First World War, both Left (Settembrini) and Right (Naphta) are intellectually bent on eliminating the international state system, bitterly quarreling over which utopian, oppressive, or imagined alternative world system would be preferable to what exists—which they neglect and disparage as a matter of course. Settembrini seeks the apotheosis of the principle of the state in a unified world government. Naphta abhors the state; its origin is in the will of the people rather than divine decree, and therefore it is a manifestation of evil.[44]

What our age needs, Naphta says, is terror, terror to overcome the pluralism of modernity and to enforce a medieval-like wholeness or unity in the world. Paradoxically, Settembrini's Enlightenment of reason, unchecked by faith, also will move inexorably toward the acceptance of terror as required to eliminate those who reject rational outcomes. His International League for the Organization of Progress has taken up research in eugenics, for the improvement of the racial stock.

As the increasingly bitter debate between the two goes on, their positions seem to overlap, to interpenetrate, until their deadly antagonism moves toward a common doom. They continue to harangue each other, but Hans Castorp has ceased to listen.

Hans has become engrossed in Clawdia Chauchat, the sinuous silken female presence who lurks, or slinks, somewhere near the core of the novel's meaning, and who embodies a multiplicity of meanings in herself. She is erotic, decadent, transnational, a traveler who comes and goes from the magic mountain. She too has been touched by the disease; Hans possesses—and obsesses over—a pocket-size X-ray, a glamour photo for her fans. At the same time, she is somewhat coarse and crude; her nails are bitten, she unfailingly slams every door she passes through. Clearly, she is a threat to the progressive spirit of the times as advocated by Settembrini, who cannot stand her.

Clawdia also embodies one of those evanescent references to the international political scene that dot the landscape of Mann's novel. Her husband is French (she is Russian), assigned as an administrator for Russia in Daghestan, in the Caucasus. Interpretive researches in the military-economic situation of the time—joined by the several references in the novel to oils (of the skin, of painting)—have led to the thought that Clawdia's husband has been sent there as part of the newly intense need for petroleum, oil, and lubricants for industrial and military uses called for in prewar planning. Hans and Clawdia's flirtation—Hans is given an hour of intimate pleasure with her—may be straining for a metaphor at a time when the Royal Navy is planning the balance-of-power-shifting Dreadnought class of battleship, to be fueled not by coal but by oil. Hans's profession of engineer and career in ocean shipping take on more significance in this context. The British-German naval arms race will be a major cause of the war to come.[45] Significant as well is Clawdia's orientalized appearance (Kirghiz eyes) and the many references to Turkey and the Middle East. There, too, oil is being produced in unprecedented quantities, and Germany, with its plans for a Berlin-to-Baghdad railway, aims to be at the grand strategic forefront.

These background hints of the modern military-industrial complex are accompanied by equally suggestive references to the ancient temptation of the West by the orientalized East: Hans Castorp's Aeneas to Clawdia Chauchat's Dido.

Hans is filled with anticipation when the sanatorium director announces, in his distinctive fashion, that Clawdia will soon return from her most recent travels: "Well, Castorp, old boy, it pays to be perseverant. Our little pussycat will come slinking home evening after next."

But Hans is not at all prepared for Clawdia's arrival from the Davos

Dorf train station with Mynheer Peeperkorn in the same sleigh, nor for the pair to proceed to the restaurant to dine together.

Peeperkorn is aged and grizzled, a man from another era. He has the powerful hands and weather-creased face of the sea captain he once was. His beard, wide stance, strangely cut clothes, and incoherent guttural pronouncements make him a figure like Ahab in *Moby-Dick*. Immensely wealthy, gin-sodden, and afflicted with tropical fever, he is nonetheless a huge personality, broad and manly. Once a coffee trader from the Dutch East Indies colonies, he, as Hans says, "puts us all in his pocket." At the same time, he is on the edge of decrepitude. The novel's descriptions portray him as a phallus, struggling against the coming impotence of age, attempting to stand erect but no longer able to do so. Nonetheless, Clawdia is in thrall to him. Peeperkorn represents the adventurous vitality of a greater European age. Just as Germany now seeks to rise to greater wealth and world power, Peeperkorn has arrived as if to declare that its modern men are not up to the task; the age of European dominance is over.

And Peeperkorn knows his time is over as well. He has designed an ingenious device of gold, steel, and ivory—a mechanical replica of a cobra's fangs. He uses it to kill himself with a deadly venom. His Malay manservant dons traditional dress to guard the corpse.

In the midst of these intrigues, Thomas Mann turns literary tradition on its head. Hans Castorp's visit to the "underworld" of the Berghof is punctuated by a counterexperience in the "overworld." Though athletics are forbidden by the sanatorium, Hans acquires a pair of skis, "good solid ash," long and pliant. On a long, solitary run into inhospitable, "deadly" high elevations, he is engulfed in a massive, disorienting snowstorm, "a hell of a state of affairs." As he takes shelter under the eaves of an abandoned hut, his mind drifts into a pastoral vision of delight paralleled by a hellish scene of cannibalism. Two ancient witches crouch before a brazier, dismembering a child, cracking its bones in their jaws, their lips dripping blood. In an instant the snow stops and the sun comes out. He has glimpsed something of the nature of man: more noble than death is freedom of the mind; more noble than life is freedom of the heart. Now with a sense of mission, he returns to the world of the living dead.

"The Great Petulance" infects the sanatorium. "What was in the air? A love of quarrels. Acute petulance. Nameless impatience. A universal penchant for nasty verbal exchanges and outbursts of rage, even for fisticuffs. Every day fierce arguments, out-of-control shouting matches would erupt between individuals and among entire groups; but the distinguishing mark was that bystanders, instead of being disgusted by those caught up in it or trying to intervene, found their sympathies aroused and abandoned themselves emotionally to the frenzy." In this, the Berghof is all Europe in microcosm; the Great War would be a man-made catastrophe created by a series of deliberate political acts. And instead of being appalled, the peoples of Europe enthusiastically join in.

Settembrini and Naphta, representing their rival ideologies which have come to resemble each other more than their advocates know, carry the new era of quarrel to the end. What once would have been light intellectual banter becomes deadly. A little joke about Virgil is compounded into an affair of "honor." The two agree to fight a duel with pistols. The elevated discourse of world betterment and divine purpose is suddenly shattered. Civil society collapses in a return to the state of nature, a war of all against all.

Settembrini is to fire first. As a man of liberal progress, he cannot bring himself to kill his adversary. He fires in the air. Naphta, enraged, kills himself with a bullet to the head. Settembrini is doomed by the emotions of his heart. Naphta destroys the realm of his intellect.

Then comes Sarajevo, "The Thunderbolt." Hans Castorp has left the mountain to join a volunteer regiment. He and his generation welcomed the war as a clarifying relief from civilization's modern complexities and the suffocating neurasthenia of the sanatorium that was Europe. On a Western Front battlefield, a shell lands. It's over.

The novel concludes with a question: "Out of this universal feast of death . . . may it be that love one day shall mount?"

Mann's *The Magic Mountain* was a work in progress at the same time as Oswald Spengler's *The Decline of the West* (*Der Untergang des Abendlandes*), "the most powerful statement of anti-Enlightenment historical thought yet produced."[46] Mann scorned Spengler as a "hyena of history" and "the clever ape of Nietzsche," yet read *The Decline of the West* as a great "intellectual novel." In a strange adversarial identification with Spengler, Mann seems to have written his own great novel as his own Nietzschean assessment of the destiny of the modern West.[47] The turning point comes when Clawdia, representing the East, returns to Davos with Peeperkorn, the ghost of past Western global power. The pistol duel between Settembrini and Naphta prefigures the gunshot in Sarajevo that would begin the Great War that ended "the West" as it had been known. Mann has rewritten Spengler ironically. When a civilization's tone becomes predominantly ironic, has it lost its confidence? Or does some sly hope remain?

In 1870 Bismarck's Prussian forces invaded France, so swiftly overwhelming the French Army that Napoleon III surrendered unconditionally. The day after France capitulated, Dr. Adrien Proust married Jeanne Weil in Paris, and Marcel Proust was born on July 10, 1872. During the pregnancy, the French Second Empire had fallen, Bismarck had stage-managed, in the Hall of Mirrors at Versailles, the elevation of King Wilhelm II to Kaiser Wilhelm of the Second Reich of Germany, and the Paris Commune had risen and collapsed. Jeanne had suffered from poor nutrition and fear throughout her nine months, and Adrien had nearly been shot dead by a communist sniper. Marcel, weak and sickly, would grow up fixated on the experience of war.[48] When the Great War of 1914–1918 came, he would follow its vicissitudes closely.

The final volume of Proust's vast novel *In Search of Lost Time* (or *Remembrance of Things Past*) has been treated rather like one of Beethoven's last quartets: somewhat scrambled and hard to comprehend, but touched by genius. In fact, volume 6, *Time Regained,* has the coherence of an epic in its own right, an *Iliad* "appropriate to the squalor and dishonorable carnage of modern warfare and an Odyssey tailor-made for a bourgeois wanderer in aristocratic salons. . . . Homer, together with Virgil, Dante, and Hugo, is an inexorable phantom within it."[49]

Marcel has emerged from the sanatorium where his asthma was treated. He is reading in the *Goncourt Journal* some episodes from the past of which he has had personal experiences, and finds that the Goncourt version is far different from what he knows to have taken place. The question of what is, or has, happened is the primary consideration. We as readers are immersed in a novel that is not—not yet—the novel Marcel will later decide to write in order to search for and regain time.

Up to this point, Proust's literary work bears "the indelible imprint" of the forty-three years of international peace that France experienced from the end of the Franco-Prussian War in 1871 to the start of the Great War in 1914, an age of calm and social stability in which the slightest disturbances were registered in the public mind with the sensitivity of a seismograph.[50]

Paris in wartime is a very different city from that which Marcel knew before. The opening third of *Time Regained* depicts a dark, degenerate scene. Marcel is now interested only in the war. So too is Robert de Saint-Loup, who studies the "etymology of battles" and the tactics of lateral envelopment. "No doubt like his friends, Saint-Loup had formed the habit of inwardly cultivating, as the truest part of himself, the search for and the elaboration of the best possible maneuvers which would lead to the greatest strategic and tactical successes." In a 1916 letter to Marcel, Robert wrote that since 1914 the war really has been a series of wars, the lessons of each one influencing the conduct of the one that followed. "War," he wrote, "does not escape the laws of our old friend Hegel. It is in a state of perpetual becoming." It would be a short war, said Saint-Loup, quoting von Moltke in 1913 on the need for only a few reserve troops.

At the outset, Paris has taken to war as to an intriguing, even charming, new adventure. Fashions were "very war," with ladies wearing gaiters like the boys at the front, and jewelry which suggested the army, with rings and bracelets made from exploded 75mm artillery shells. "One of the happiest consequences of this sad war," a newspaper noted, "will be that we have achieved some charming results in the realm of fashion."

"One of the ideas most in vogue was that pre-war days were separated from the war by something as profound, something apparently of as long a duration, as a geological period." The experience could be droll. Mme. Verdurin began to refer to "GHQ" as she used to drop the nicknames of princes ("Grigri") to show that she was in the know. At teatime, in the still light sky, "one saw, far off, little brown dots, which one might have taken, in the blue evening, for midges or birds," but each of which was "an aeroplane with a crew of men keeping guard over Paris."

But it also could be ominous. The restaurants were full. A wretched soldier on leave from fear and death and about to return to the trenches stopped to gaze at the illuminated windows to see "the shirkers jostling one another in their efforts to secure a table."

And at the front, the war was grinding ever deeper into lives and land. A letter comes from Gilberte:

> You have no idea what this war is like, my dear friend, or of the importance that a road, a bridge, a height can assume. How often have I thought of you, of those walks of ours together which you made so delightful, through all this now ravaged countryside, where vast

battles are fought to gain possession of some path, some slope which you once loved and which we so often explored together! . . . The battle of Méséglise lasted for more than eight months; the Germans lost in it more than six hundred thousand men, they destroyed Méséglise, but they did not capture it. As for the short cut up the hill which you were so fond of and which we used to call the hawthorn path, where you claim that as a small child you fell in love with me (whereas I assure you in all truthfulness it was I who was in love with you), I cannot tell you how important it has become. The huge field of corn upon which it emerges is the famous Hill 307, which you must have seen mentioned again and again in the bulletins.

To Marcel, the idea of a war and the idea of a book begin to merge. Like Clausewitz on the concept of "friction" generated in battle, Marcel finds that "a general is like a writer who sets out to write a certain play, a certain book, and then the book itself . . . makes him deviate to an enormous degree from his preconceived plan."

The Parisian aristocracy assaulted by the Revolution in Dickens's *A Tale of Two Cities* has returned in Proust's novel. Indeed, at first it seems that nations at war are simply larger versions of the intrigues and antagonisms of high society salons; they exhibit the same kind of desires, indignations, and theatrical gestures. Social rivalries can be described in terms of military operations, and military operations in terms of social rivalries:

The body Germany and the body France, and the allied and enemy bodies, were behaving to some extent like individuals, and the blows which they were exchanging were governed by the innumerable rules of that art of boxing which Saint-Loup had expounded to me; but since, even if one chose to consider them as individuals, they were at the same time giant assemblages of individuals, the quarrel took on immense and magnificent forms, like the surge of a million-waved ocean which tries to shatter an age-old line of cliffs.

The Guermantes way and clique are like Germany; the Verdurin salon equate to France. Marcel's small social world is disappearing; but the great world appears to resemble it more each day, as the war drags on indefinitely.

More significant are the indicators that the established system that had seemed to provide those forty-three years of international peace is breaking down. The idea of an aristocratic class that spanned nations to make up a pan-European allegiance is ending. Charlus, who belongs no more to France than to Germany, nonetheless turns out to be pro-German. And Saint-Loup is of the aristocracy that puts France above all else. Patriotism has to be asserted constantly. A professor might write a remarkable book on Schiller, "but the reviewer would have to say that the author had been at the Marne or had sons killed before his book could be praised. Schiller could be called 'great' but not 'that great German,' that great Boche."

Saint-Loup perceives that the balance-of-power concept, once thought to be the best guarantor of stability, was a cause of the war, and that the international conference system that maintained the balance of power was defunct. "The age of the Congress of Vienna is dead and gone; the old secret diplomacy must be replaced by concrete diplomacy."

The rise of an alternative international system was felt. Charlus delivers a long soliloquy declaring that "any day now I expect to see myself placed at table beneath a Russian revolutionary," apparently in the belief that the greatest danger presented by the Bolsheviks lies in the protocol of being seated at table. "So turns the wheel of the world," he concludes.

Time Regained shows how "the abstract" triumphs in private, professional, national, and international life. The First World War, "far from being the last of the national conflicts, is the first of the great abstract conflicts of the twentieth century."[51]

Out of the sanatorium and back in Paris in 1916, Marcel finds that invitations still come to him. He enters the house of the prince de Guermantes as into the house of the dead. Charlus is there, now looking aged and crazed, a King Lear figure. The roll of the dead is called, each name followed by the booming declaration: "dead!"

Boson de Talleyrand, dead!

Marcel, like Aeneas, has entered the Underworld, where he encounters the dead and the living dead. Everyone in the room appears to have put on a disguise: "A young woman whom I had known long ago, white-haired now, and compressed into a little old witch."

And, like the heroes of classical epic poetry, Marcel in this netherworld glimpses his true mission. He trips on an uneven paving stone; a servant knocks a spoon against a plate. "And just as on the day when I had dipped the madeleine in the hot tea . . . today at this moment [in] the library of the Prince de Guermantes . . . a sensation . . . which was common both to my actual surroundings and to another place . . . the sensation common to past and present had sought to re-create the former scene around itself, while the actual scene which had taken the former one's place opposed with all the resistance of material inertia this incursion into a house in Paris of a Normandy beach or a railway embankment."

Out of a great war an international system was produced, and national societies shaped themselves within that system. But societies also create wars, and a war of great magnitude can bring the international system to the edge of collapse and do away with the societies that depended upon the system. *Time Regained* shows how war changed everything. The international system which undergirded the Parisian social scene was crumbling, and society would pass away as a result. "Thus in the Fauberg Saint-Germain their apparently impregnable positions, of the Duc and Duchesse de Guermantes and the Baron Charlus, had lost their inviolability, changing, as all things change in this world, under the action of an inherent principle, which at first had attracted nobody's attention."

For Proust, only literary art can provide a stay against change. A life can be realized within the confines of a book. Like Dante at the end of *Paradiso,* Proust sees the ultimate answer, the divine, in the form of a book. In this vision the war and society mean nothing in comparison with the literary achievement of time regained. "This notion of time embodied, of years past but not separated from us, it was now my intention to emphasize as strongly as possible in my work." Greatness comes from bearing the burden of time, and regaining it through creating a book. The past never dies but remains with us, accessible through the exploitation of involuntary memory—the madeleine—and by the recollection and re-creation of the past moment through literature.

Proust will now proceed to write the book we have been reading—which at the same time will be entirely new, the way Borges saw *Don Quixote* "rewritten." Proust's book will try "to transcribe a universe which had to be totally redrawn." The world of Combray is gone and cannot in reality be regained or re-created. The question that remains is whether the war also has destroyed the modern international system, or whether it can be renewed.

Marcel Proust sensed the old world of Europe at its end. So, too, did statesmen of the time. The protracted, hideous violence of the Great War demanded an answer to the question "What went wrong?" What flaws in the old order allowed this to happen? The answers would be provided by Woodrow Wilson in an attempt to call into being new ideas and institutions for the future.

Wilson knew that words make things happen. As a presidential candidate in 1912, he had begun a search for a new rhetoric that would persuade the nation to adopt a new politics.[52] As the United States entered World War I, Wilson sent his closest adviser, Colonel Edward House, to Europe to urge the Allies to make a joint statement of war aims, but House was rebuffed by both the British and the French. So work was begun, largely by Walter Lippmann and Colonel House, to draft an American statement to which the international community as a whole could subscribe.

On January 8, 1918, without previous notice, a courier arrived on Capitol Hill to convey the president's intention to appear that day before both houses of Congress to deliver an important message. This was "The Fourteen Points," the most influential document in American diplomatic history. It was Wilson's analysis of the fundamental causes of modern war in general and European war in particular. And it listed specific changes necessary for peace, with a sweeping elaboration of principles for the government of relations among nations.[53]

To the average reader today, the Fourteen Points are tedious and obscure. But the document bears close study as a rhetorical masterwork, in that its most specifically detailed provisions silently represented large principles. The memorandum of recommendations sent to Wilson states: "Every act of Germany towards Alsace-Lorraine for half a century has proclaimed that these provinces are foreign territory, and no genuine part of the German Empire. Germany cannot be permitted to escape the stern logic of her own conduct. The wrong done in 1871 must be undone."

In other words, the Germans had acknowledged that Alsace-Lorraine is French. Wilson transformed this recommendation into Point VIII: "The wrong done by Prussia in 1871 in the matter of Alsace-Lorraine which has unsettled the peace of the world for nearly fifty years, should be righted in order that peace may once more be made secure in the interest of all." A particular territorial dispute was redrafted as a matter affecting world peace, and seeds were sown for the growth of the general principle of "no acquisition of territory by force." And note the crafty change from "German Empire" to "Prussia."

The Fourteen Points emerge as a very Kantian document, not only in their prescription for an end to secret treaties and a commitment to international trade, but in their far-reaching reconstitution of the international state system. Richelieu's seventeenth-century balance-of-power concept had become the guide for great power diplomacy from the Congress of Vienna's settlement of the Napoleonic Wars in 1814 to outbreak of war in 1914. But the concept accepted, even required, war as the way to redress the balance, again and again. To replace, or reconceptualize, balance of power, the idea of "collective security" was proposed.

This called forth the need for a world forum, the lack of which before 1914 was seen as permitting a sudden leap from peace to war with no buffering time or venue for international talks. The League of Nations, a Wilsonian invention (Point XIV), offered an alternative to conventional interpretations of international order. The League was supposed to embody a world-spanning commitment, undergirded by world public opinion, that would deter and resist aggression wherever it appeared. Security would now be maintained collectively, by a new kind of international community.

The conflict that broke out in 1914 was regarded in retrospect as virtually inevitable because of an "arms race" among rival regimes—most prominently Germany and Great Britain—fueled by arms merchants and corporate makers of munitions. There would have to be serious international efforts at "arms control" (Point IV).

A fundamental source of the confrontations that led to the Great War, indeed the proximate cause, was thought to be the suppression of self-determination. The restive south Slavic peoples, chafing under the Austro-Hungarian Empire, sparked the war when a Serbian nationalist assassin struck down the Archduke Ferdinand in August 1914. Only an acceptance of self-determination, that is, *the acceptance of new states into legitimate membership in the international state system,* could hope to contain this source of war (Points V and X).

These points made up the postwar agenda of the 1920s and 1930s. All failed. The United States Senate rejected American participation in the League of Nations, and Japan's seizure of Manchuria in 1931 revealed the collective security pledge to be hollow. There was no international blocking of Mussolini's invasion of Abyssinia or Hitler's move into the Rhineland. Arms control efforts at the Washington Conference—specifically the limitations on the Japanese, American, and British battleships—and the Kellogg-

Briand Pact of 1928, which renounced war as a legitimate instrument of national policy, both proved to be ludicrously idealistic.

The grand promise of self-determination and statehood for subject peoples was ignored, betrayed, or undermined from the start, even at the Versailles Peace Conference itself. Ho Chi Minh was there, but Vietnam remained a French colony. Japan's control of China's Shantung Province was accepted. Germany would thwart the hopes of many central European peoples for the creation of newly independent states. The story of Wilson's inability to carry through on his grand rhetoric of "idealism" is one of the tragic epics in the history of world affairs. His failing health has been blamed. Some scholars recently have claimed to find the failure's source in the contradictions within Wilson's own personal and political philosophy, perhaps another example of America's ambiguous relation to the international system.

The 1930s would bring a near collapse of international order. Japan and Germany each withdrew from the League of Nations. The United States, not a member, nonetheless through the Herculean efforts of Secretary of State Henry Stimson sought desperately to preserve the structure of international affairs. "The Stimson Doctrine" could not summon a collective military response to Japanese or German aggression, but it did provide a focus for world public opinion and an international commitment that the depredations of Imperial Japan and the Third Reich would never be accepted as legally valid.

A further condition for world order seemed to have failed. The World Economic Conference held in Geneva in 1927 had concluded that international peace depended on cooperative economic progress. The idea of a "business civilization" for the world was taking hold. But the Great Depression fractured the foundations of that idea. By the time President Herbert Hoover left office in March 1933, the international state system seemed on the verge of collapse.[54]

T. S. Eliot's *The Waste Land,* from its publication in 1922 to the present, has been the most persistent point of reference in modern literature. I had never heard of it when I arrived at Brown University as a freshman, yet it had been an intellectual fixation for decades. On that first day, as I leaned out of Grier Horner's first-floor window in South Littlefield, watching Bill Littell toss a football with some dormitory mates, I heard Paul Oppenheim, just below the window, talking about *The Waste Land.*

Soon several of us had formed our own reading group to wrestle with it, fascinated above all by the footnotes Eliot had appended to his own poem. Forty years on, when I began to teach in Yale University's Directed Studies literature course for freshmen, I found *The Waste Land* assigned at the very end of the yearlong syllabus, not least because its bewildering array of references to the world's cultures seemed a vehicle for recapitulating the year's reading of great books and contemplating what had become of civilization.

The title is itself a compendium of fragments from the past. Eliot, in his notes appended to the poem—notes certainly intended to perplex more than enlighten the reader—says that the title was suggested by Jessie L. Weston's *From Ritual to Romance*. Eliot, in college, owned a copy of William Morris's co-translation of *Volsunga Saga,* which refers in the prologue to a "waste land." Augustine mentions the term in his *Confessions*. The Red Crosse Knight in Spenser's *The Faerie Queene* goes out in a waste land of evil to slay dragons, fight false knights, find the Grail, and thereby restore the land to health. A poem "Waste Land" was published in *Poetry* magazine in 1913. The phrase appears in the Apocrypha of the King James Bible. Jane Austen's *Northanger Abbey* uses it. Conrad uses it in *Lord Jim* and again in *Nostromo*. One likely source is not mentioned by Eliot or the commentators: Tennyson's *Idylls of the King.*

Any cultural-intellectual shift as immense as modernism, which originates in the arts (or even in science) and spreads to other disciplines, eventually will find a correlation in statecraft and the international system. *The Waste Land* has established itself as the all-purpose text for the modern crack-up. Beginning with a trivial incident that somehow leads to the Great War, it might be compared to Herodotus's story of how a Phoenician merchant ship beached in an Argive cove led to the Trojan War, or Thucydides' description of the minor scuffle at Epidamnus as the proximate cause of the Peloponnesian War. The poem is about everything, a race through the museum of the West, the Grail legend, Frazer's *The Golden Bough,* and the world-ranging story of the king who must die. At the same time, its references reach into the great non-Western cultures of the world. For contemporary statecraft it suggests that civilization may be abandoning its linear sense of time—of history unfolding in a progressive direction. The poem opens a window on the way in which cultural fragmentation and fascination with primitive sources of energy have made their way into today's structures of international relations.

Religions suffuse the poem. The Christian references are barren, cli-chéd, debased. But the idea of rebirth, of resurrection, is itself renewed by setting it in a culture-spanning, eons-deep collection of references to pre-Christian vegetation rites. Eliot notes his indebtedness to Frazer's *The Golden Bough* for "vegetation ceremonies." The quest for the Grail is a central theme in the sense of finding the way to heal the sovereign and restore a sick society. Eliot pulls bits and pieces of many religions into some juxtaposition, to try to rehabilitate the idea of religion. Its accumulation of fragments, its collage of ideas, phrases, and scavenged scenes is in the high modernist style, and each element refers to contemporary world affairs and to changes in the international system.[55]

Eliot first critiques representation. Traditional and once-obvious ways of depiction or description are distorted or disarranged. Here is Eliot's por-trait of London's "unreal city," the financial district. The crowd that flows over London Bridge is not a real crowd moving from one location to another on a real day. Instead, the scene evokes Dante's *Inferno* (3: 55–57):

> so many,
> I had not thought death had undone so many.
> Sighs, short and infrequent, were exhaled,
> And each man fixed his eyes before his feet.

Eliot steps into the unreal scene and arranges time and place as well.

> There I saw one I knew, and stopped him, crying: "Stetson!
> You who were with me in the ships at Mylae!"[56]

Modernism's critique of representation also comments upon diplo-macy's core function, to "represent" one's country to the government and people of the state to which he is accredited. Benjamin Franklin, in his dress and demeanor, represented to the court of Louis XVI and the French people not only American foreign policy but an image of the new, demo-cratic America nation building on the edge of a continental wilderness.

Today's diplomatic representation is fragmented and evanescent. Nearly every agency of government sends its representatives abroad. There are also nongovernmental organizations, tourists, athletic teams, celebrities, corporations, films, and every form of art and entertainment. The diplomat does not represent so much as vie for attention. One reason ambassadors are increasingly chosen from among the president's personal friends is that they have a better chance of being regarded as representative of the country's chief executive officer.

A second marker of modernism is a fascination for the primitive, the primeval as a source of energy and authenticity. Eliot probes and pokes into various ancient, hieratic forms; in a search for this reference point he touches the Hebrew Bible, Anglo-Saxon ballads, tarot cards, Arthurian legends, back and farther back until the poet reaches the sources of the Indo-European linguistic family, Sanskrit scriptures from a time before recorded time, the famous *Datta, Dayadvam, Damyatta, Shantih, Shantih, Shantih.*[57] Here Eliot draws together the propensity in modern Western civilization, from Emerson to Nietzsche to Heidegger to the counterculture of the 1960s and after, to believe that civilization is fundamentally flawed, and that authenticity can be found only by reaching back before civilization (to, for example, Nietzsche's pre-Socratic thinkers).

Third in modernism's canon are innovations and experiments with technical means. This is the modern poem itself, self-liberated from established conventions of meter, rhyme, line length, category (sonnet or villanelle), or even formality of language, genre, or tone. Eliot gives us a character, not introduced, narrating her previous conversation with another, along with the voice of the pubkeeper announcing that the bar is about to close:

> When Lil's husband got demobbed, I said—
> I didn't mince my words, I said to her myself,
> HURRY UP PLEASE IT'S TIME
> Now Albert's coming back, make yourself a bit smart.
> He'll want to know what you done with that money he gave you
> To get yourself some teeth. He did, I was there.
> You have them all out, Lil, and get a nice set,
> He said, I swear, I can't bear to look at you.

Fourth is the juxtaposition of elements traditionally considered irreconcilable. The section of the poem called "The Fire Sermon" juxtaposes the Buddha, a Puritan poet, a medieval knight, an ancient Greek seer, Shakespeare, Queen Elizabeth, Dante, and Saint Augustine, just to mention the most prominent figures.

Modernism's fragmentation and rearrangement of traditional forms are also apparent in the newly arranged international system set out in Wilson's Fourteen Points, which disassembled important sectors of the old system and poured new content into a redesigned international order.[58] A critique of representation now took place that had been lacking in its creation and reworking before the Great War. The League of Nations would be a kind of parliament of parliaments. Beyond the representation of a people by a state authority, states would now be members of a world organization to represent a metaorder to symbolize peace and the outlawing, or prevention, of aggression by one state against another.

Admiration for the primitive and for authenticity came in the post–World War I recognition of the rights of self-determination of nations that had not before achieved statehood. "Nationalism" was seen as a force that represented land, blood, culture, language, and religion and which, bundled together in a people, must not, and could not, long be denied.

Innovative experimentation was attempted with the technical mechanisms of statecraft. A naval treaty set a 5:5:3 ratio for the battleship fleets of Britain, the United States, and Japan. The Kellogg-Briand Pact to "outlaw war" was a noble if preposterous experiment. Formerly irreconcilable elements were juxtaposed in a variety of places and ways. All-sovereign states, unified, indivisible, integral, and defined by defended borders, gave way in places to hybrids: the Palestine Mandate, the Free City of Danzig, plebiscitary government for the Saarland, trust territories, and other camelopards. Typically of modernism, and under its explicit influence, between the First and Second World Wars the international state system disassembled and reassembled itself in innumerable ways.

The Waste Land had a powerful and unexpected impact on leading writers of the non-Western world, who saw in it a tool for liberation from European cultural supremacy. The literary West took in raw cultural materials from the rest of the world and by doing so set Eastern and Western texts in dialogue with each other, giving the Eastern quotation the capacity to be heard.[59] So literary modernism helped to transpose the Westphalian system into a worldwide structure for international relations.

Franz Kafka's last major work, *Das Schloss* (*The Castle*), presents eerie resemblances to Chairman Mao's favorite novel, the book he declared to be China's gift to the world, *The Dream of the Red Chamber.* Kafka's novel is a dream, or nightmare, of a familiar sort—the inability to get to where you must go, a dream of approaching the dark castle yet never reaching it. Primordial psychology matches the modern predicament in the "Kafkaesque."

In the Chinese novel, a family household—the family as a microcosm of the state—is in dissolution, its hero Jia Bao-yu surrounded by swirls of women of high-standing romantic decadence. Mao, his doctor said, replicated the Jia family scene in his compound, the Garden of Abundant Beneficence, where he dallied sordidly with girls in attendance.

Kafka's "hero" K also is at the center of amorous females, present and former mistresses of the castle's overseer, barmaids, the landlady, and others of low taste, significant in view of Kafka's personal conviction that marriage and family—something he never experienced—represent the utmost human achievement. Written almost contemporaneously with T. S. Eliot's *The Waste Land* and also set in central Europe just before the Great War, *The Castle* depicts Western civilization in distress.

Of all writers, Kafka is the greatest expert on power. Hradcany Castle, looming over Prague, would be sufficient for a writer "seeking in it forms of power, magical forces, mystical, even apparitional associations, emblems of history and memory, and all the rest Kafka infused it with."[60] A better model, however, had come to him in 1911 when on a countryside trip he observed in Friedland a castle that had belonged to Wallenstein. Kafka took away a picture postcard showing the castle's drawbridge and environs.[61] The opening passage of *The Castle:*

> It was late in the evening when K arrived. The village lay deep in snow. The castle hill was hidden in darkness and fog, and not even the merest glimmer of light indicated the presence of a castle. K stood for a long time on the wooden bridge leading from the main road into the village, gazing at the seeming emptiness above him.

Like Thomas Mann's Hans Castorp in the snow, K has come, Virgil-like, to the netherworld, where he will learn his purpose in life. But this time, for the first time in literature, the hero cannot gain access to the place and so never understands his mission. The lord of the castle, the suggestively named Count Westwest, is unreachable.

K is a land surveyor, come to provide his services to the castle. An empire, however, is incompatible with land surveyors. Empires have clear sovereignty but unclear borders and they like it that way. States, and the international state system, require clearly demarcated and recognized borders. So the land surveyor is always turned away. The state supposedly replaced the empire as the main form of governance, but Kafka's castle is a modern empire, a bureaucratic one: the telephone is an instrument which works well for it as K is placed, as we say today, "on hold." Negotiations here are not done by diplomacy but are the one-sided dealings of officials with the public. In Mao's dream novel, the family is disintegrating in frivolity, and the fall of the greater political and moral order is the silent context. In Kafka's dream novel, the collapse—or near-collapse—is already upon us in the absence of love, marriage, and family, and is accompanied by scenes of random couplings that might come from Grimmelshausen's novel of the Thirty Years' War.

K and Don Quixote both carry out epic attempts to make the disorder of modern reality conform to an ideal order of the good. Don Quixote goes forth in the service of an epic order that no longer corresponds to reality, an order which has been replaced by forces whose underlying design cannot easily be grasped. The Don defends his epic certainties even as they are scorned or erased; he seeks to restore normative order to a crazy world and is himself pronounced crazy. K is a twentieth-century Don Quixote. Like the Don, K is trying to reaffirm a kind of universal library of virtuous works. But K's task is more difficult "when literary models are scattered, nuanced, confused, and attenuated, when new values are not so much opposed to the old as they are scrambled, lost in infinity, or, on the contrary, become highly specialized . . . come to mirror each other's confusion and fragility."[62] The Don and K share a common purpose: to apply the fictional truth of books to an uncomprehending and brutal reality. Both fail, but each lives on in the imaginative awareness of reader-citizens that a noble vision of virtue is needed.

If Dante's "Ulysses" Canto (*Inferno* 26) begins a logic chain about the emergence of the idea of the New World in world order, Tennyson's 1833 poem "Ulysses" may mark the start of the old European world's recessional. The poem seems to be a hearty tribute of praise for bold, forward-leaning adventure:

> Come, my friends.
> 'Tis not too late to seek a newer world.
> Push off, and sitting well in order smite
> The sounding Furrows: for my purpose holds
> To sail beyond the sunset, and the baths
> Of all the western stars, until I die. . . .
> It may be we shall touch the Happy Isles,

And see the great Achilles, whom we knew. . . .
To strive, to see, to find, and not to yield.

Tennyson said that "Ulysses was written soon after Arthur Hallam's death, and gave my feeling about the need of going forward, and braving the struggle of life perhaps more simply than anything in *In Memoriam.*"[63] But Tennyson completed the poem before his friend died, and read at a different angle, it portrays a querulous and heedless adventurer, not someone the poet would take as a model. Ulysses' ways were not congenial to Tennyson's; the hero overreached and perished for his presumption.[64] So much for the vaunted "New World."

Another ancient story retold as a modern strategic message—the old world's disenchantment with the new, or indeed with the world at large—is *The Unquiet Grave: A Word Cycle by Palinurus,* a text compiled during the Second World War by Cyril Connolly and intended to be a masterpiece, or at least "a classic." Connolly's claim to status may not have been far off the mark; the text increasingly represents Europe's self-determined destiny.

Like *The Waste Land, The Unquiet Grave* amasses fragments picked up from across the centuries of Western civilization and juxtaposes them at a ruinous time. The author is admittedly obsessed with pleasure at a time when pleasures were forbidden. Writing "as a European," the author evokes the French seaside "to be reminded that beaches did not exist for mines and pill-boxes and barbed wire but for us to bathe from and that, one day, we would enjoy them again."[65]

The soft pleasures of an achieved civilization were now being lost. Had the harsh and heavy costs of building that civilization been worth the effort? What about the rough work of rebuilding world order? Here Connolly turns to Palinurus. "Who was Palinurus?" he asks in his epilogue. He is the pilot-steersman of Aeneas's ship, who has seen the hero's betrayal of Dido and witnessed the other difficult duties endured in the service of the world-historical Trojan mission.

Venus begs Neptune to inflict no more sea storms upon Aeneas at Juno's behest. Neptune agrees, but one life must be sacrificed for saving so many others. Palinurus falls asleep and falls overboard, taking the tiller and a piece of the stern with him. He washes up on shore, where he is killed by robbers who leave his body unburied. His death is paralleled by that of

Misenus the bugler and Caieta the nurse—three technical specialists—all just before Aeneas's visit to the Underworld. This, says Connolly, "may suggest that there was an 'old guard' who had had enough of it, who unconsciously did not wish to enter the promised land or go through with the fighting necessary to possess it. The Palinurus passages, Connolly says, are so charged with haunting images and golden cadences as to suggest that Virgil identified himself with his pilot; that Palinurus was to Aeneas as Virgil was to the object of his supposedly epic tribute to Augustus; neither the pilot nor the poet was "on board" with the great imperial mission.

So as a myth, Palinurus "stands for a certain will-to-failure or repugnance-to-success, a desire to give up at the last minute, an urge toward loneliness, isolation, and obscurity." Palinurus deserts his post in the moment of victory and opts for the unknown shore. "With the sea—age old symbol of the unconscious—his relations were always close and harmonious, and not until he reaches land is he miserably done to death." Like many who resign from the struggle because they found something vulgar in success, he feels remorse at his abdication and wishes he had remained where he was: "Doing is overrated, and success undesirable, but the bitterness of failure even more so."[66]

The Unquiet Grave, written to be a classic in Europe's midcentury wartime, increasingly looks even more relevant to Europe at the start of the twenty-first century, as its civilization celebrates its pleasures while another civilization encroaches upon it.

8

THE IMPORTED STATE

As soon as the Minister's Cadillac arrived at the head of a long motorcade the hunters dashed this way and that and let off their last shots, throwing their guns about with frightening freedom. The dancers capered and stamped, filling the dry-season air with dust. . . . The Minister stepped out wearing damask and gold chains and acknowledging cheers with his ever-present fan of animal skin which they said fanned away all evil designs and shafts of malevolence thrown at him by the wicked.

This scene occurs in Chinua Achebe's *A Man of the People.* As he concludes his most effective speech, the minister explains that he would have preferred not to speak to his own kinsmen in English, which is after all a foreign language, but he has learned from experience that speeches made in the vernacular are liable to be distorted and misquoted in the press.

Later on in the Proprietor's Lodge, I said to the Minister: "You must have spent a fortune today." He smiled at the glass of cold beer in his hand and said: "You call this spend? You never see some thing, my brother. I no keep anini for myself, na so so troway. If some person come to you and say 'I wan' make you Minister' make you run like blazes comot. Na true word I tell you. To God who made me." He showed the tip of his tongue to the sky to confirm the oath. "Minister de sweet for eye but too much katakata de for inside. Believe me yours sincerely." "Big man, big palaver," said the one-eyed man standing by.

The state as a governance form won out over rival forms in early modern Europe because it most effectively served the interests of security, efficiency, and prosperity. Many non-Western polities observed this and, when entering modernity, sought statehood within the established international system. Those who resisted could be compelled to accept statehood. But the complex of symbols, methods, and institutions of European origin had few analogues in traditional non-Western societies. The "social contract" as understood in the West from Lucretius to Hobbes proved difficult to carry out elsewhere; people might theoretically cede their rights to the sovereign, but the state might prove unable or unwilling to provide security and opportunity in return. In Asia a great culture of governance collapsed under the pressure of an intrusive modern world. Christianity, communism, and capitalism—all alien to traditional China—successively imposed themselves on the society, which still struggles to find a state expression of its own. In the Middle East, Arab and Jewish peoples struggled for or against statehood under terms imposed by the world at large. In South Asia the end of the British Raj created problems for national and personal identity that remain contested. Viewed together, these struggles have produced the three primary challenges to international relations today: the shift of power from West to East (or perhaps just the continuation of the *translatio imperii*); the Islamist-terrorist threat to world order; and a new model of governance which attempts to weld economic freedom to political authoritarianism.

Kafka read deeply in classical Chinese literature. "The Great Wall of China," written not long after the 1911 revolution brought down the Ch'ing Dynasty, is a political theory prose poem on the conundrum of modern Chinese statecraft: the tension between foreign influence and domestic integrity. The wall is a symbol of the Chinese state. The writer, a student, questions the claim that it was built to defend China from barbarian invasion because it was constructed piece by piece, a method unsuited for national security. Instead, it was a vast communal project of nation-building, phased so as to spur the energy and pride of one locality after another across the years. Beyond this, one scholar claimed, it would create "for the first time in the history of mankind, a strong architectural foundation for a new Tower of Babel." But no, says the student, how could a wall provide the foundation for a tower? Actually, the wall as an achievement was "scarcely inferior to the building of the Tower of Babel" and represents "as far as divine approval goes, . . . at least by human reckoning, the very opposite of that structure."[1]

Of all the obscure institutions of China, the tale continues, one is unquestionably the empire itself. To grasp it, one must turn to the common people since they, after all, are where the empire has its final support. But the land is vast and "Pekin is only a dot, and the imperial palace less than a dot." A parable expresses the relationship: if the emperor "sent a message expressly for you, his solitary wretch of a subject," the message would never arrive, or it would come too late. Thirty years after it was dispatched, the student, then ten years old, was standing with his father on the river bank when a boatman came to say that "a great wall is going to be built to protect the emperor" from foreign tribes with demons among them."[2]

China was once a great naval power but gave it up to defend its inner frontiers. Foreign intrusion, when it came, was from the sea, led by the British. The story could be said to start in Singapore.

On January 29, 1819, Sir Thomas Stamford Raffles, aboard the merchant ship *Indiana,* landed on an island at the site of a small "bamboo village" called Singapore. There he arranged with the local Malay prince for an enclave to be established by the East India Company, it being feared that the Dutch, the colonial power in the East Indies, otherwise would take control of the Strait of Malacca and block British trade between India and Canton, China.

Raffles's biographer found him to be "more than a statesman intent on providing his country with a strong post for extending its commerce. He is a thinker who senses the approach of an Asiatic revolution, greater than the French Revolution, one that will transform all those countries, including the high civilizations of China and Japan, and cause them to imbibe not only what was most useful but, he hopes, the best in Western thought and practice. Alone of his contemporaries, he has a glimpse of the end of old Asia, its metamorphosis, a commingling of East and West."[3]

Three years later Raffles returned to Singapore and was delighted with what he saw. "Here all is life and activity," he said. "It would be difficult to name a place on the face of the globe with brighter prospects or more present satisfaction. In little more than three years it has risen from an insignificant fishing village to a large and prosperous town of over 10,000 inhabitants, actively engaged in commercial pursuits."⁴ There was a sudden large influx of immigrant labor, mainly from China and south India. Within ten years of the founding of the settlement, the Chinese had become the largest ethnic group.

At the very time that Raffles was securing the sea route from India to the China coast for the East India Company, intellectual changes propelled by the Enlightenment led Britain to take the lead in trying to break down China's imperial worldview and force that country into the Westphalian state system. By the early nineteenth century the reconnaissance of the world by an expanding West brought two different systems of world order into conflict. Imperial China regarded itself as the center of its own world order, whose outlying realms were tribute-bearing satellites. In stark contrast, the European-centered international system was based upon states with some degree of juridical equality. The conflict would focus on trade. For China, trade was tribute, heavily regulated and assumed to benefit China one-sidedly. So long as the West embraced the doctrine of mercantilism, the two civilizations' economic views had a certain similarity. But when Adam Smith's ideas about free trade grew influential, confrontations arose.

Britain's East India Company established a post at Canton as early as 1699. The English bought tea and paid for it in silver. China did not buy English goods, so the Chinese saw the inflow under this "Canton System" as entirely right and proper.

Aggressive free traders began to move in. The East India Company, which controlled opium, sold the drug to private "country traders" who resold it along the China coast. Demand soared and buyers paid in silver. Quickly the balance of trade was reversed. The "tribute-trade" mentality of China was frontally challenged. And the opium trade proved unregulatable by the Imperial Court. Soon the British pressed for other ports on the China coast.

An "Opium War" broke out in 1839. Alarmed at the draining of China's silver coffers, the court ordered Commissioner Lin Tse-hsu to stop the opium traffic. The resulting clashes began what has been called the "Twenty-one Years' War," one of the pivotal conflicts in world history, the conflict of two fundamentally opposed concepts of how the world should be ordered.

Opium War clashes caused Britain to escalate the crisis, seizing ports up the coast as far as Shanghai by 1842. Lord Palmerston secretly instructed the queen's representative in Canton, Captain Charles Elliott, "to place Britain's relationship with China on a proper footing." The meaning was unmistakable: force China into the international state system. The result was a series of what would become known as the "unequal treaties," beginning in 1842 with the Treaty of Nanking, in which China ceded five "treaty ports," including Shanghai, to Britain under terms which granted "extraterritoriality," meaning that British law, not Chinese, would apply there. Hong Kong was handed over to Britain.

In 1850 the huge Taiping Rebellion swept across south central China. For millennia there had been peasant revolts and rebellions in the empire, sometimes resulting in the imperial court's loss of the "Mandate of Heaven." This rebellion was different. It was propelled by a misreading of the faith then being spread by foreign Christian missionaries. Hung Hsiu-Ch'üan, a failed mandarin examination candidate, raised a vast army, declared himself to be the second son of God, and moved north and east against imperial provincial capitals. This was not another attempt to replace one dynasty with another, but an entirely new, foreign-inspired utopian vision of governance. The Taiping Rebellion was the largest-scale war of the century, with millions killed and millions more devastated. It dealt a terminal blow to traditional China.

In 1856 a perceived Chinese insult to the British Union Jack sparked the *Arrow* War. Britain used the crisis to send Lord Elgin (he of the marbles) to Peking to insist on a treaty that would permit Western diplomats to reside there permanently. The Imperial Court resisted: the treaty violated the Chinese view of world order—the tributary system—by putting China and the state sending such diplomats on a basis of state-to-state equality. To overcome this opposition, Lord Elgin returned in 1860 with a fighting force, causing the emperor to flee the capital. The invading troops burned the Imperial Summer Palace.[5]

China's foreign relations were thereby entirely reordered. The Sinocentric worldview and the tribute system were destroyed. In 1861 China established a new institution, the Tsungli Yamen or "Office for General Management of Affairs with the Various Nations," a kind of incipient ministry of foreign affairs. Within a few years, China sent its first diplomatic missions overseas, and by 1879 it had established some permanent embassies abroad.

China was hauled into the international state system on terms that made an appearance of equal treatment but which in fact left a culturally devastated China in a condition of inferiority and disarray. Although the British had dragged China into the system, China was not of it. The Boxer Rebellion of 1900 was anti-Christian and antiforeign. The Imperial Court, expecting the rebels to succeed, supported their assault on the diplomatic quarter of Peking. The dynasty itself declared war on the foreign missions, a rejection of the international system it had been forced to accept through unequal treaties. This brought the Boxer Relief Expedition to Peking in the international system's first act of "collective security," with British, American, French, German, Belgian, Austro-Hungarian, Italian, Indian, and Japanese troops all involved.

CHINA'S STORM-TOSSED SHIP OF STATE

The Travels of Lao Ts'an, written between 1904 and 1907, describes China in the throes of a gigantic struggle between the traditional and the modern. The haughty, dreamy certainties and fancies of the imperial Central Kingdom are splintered a thousand ways by the clash and clatter of intrusive Westernization. The author, Liu T'ieh-yün, also called Liu E, was born in the year of the Taiping Rebellion, experienced the vicissitudes of China's imperial collapse in the late decades of the nineteenth century, saw the Boxer Rebellion, and wrote the *Travels* just before his death as China spun down toward the Revolution of 1911.

Liu's story displays China's predicament. To serve his country's needs he studied river conservancy. Casting off his scholar's gown, he strode among the coolies working to repair the dike after the Yellow River burst out in 1888. His flood-control theories could have made him a formidable disputant in the nineteenth-century rivalry between Eads and the Corps of Engineers over how to tame the Mississippi. Yet Liu was also a practitioner of traditional medicine, peddling his herbs and elixirs from village to village. From these travels came the hauntingly evocative scenes in his novel: the calligrapher warming his ink stone over an inn's brazier; the witty lady in her patterned jacket and tight-fitting trousers which revealed her "gold lotuses"—slippered bound feet; the crack of ice on the river at night.[6]

In 1894 Liu was summoned to take the examination for the new Tsungli Yamen, the "foreign office" that China had to create in order to deal with the international system of which it was unwillingly a part. After the Boxer Rebellion was suppressed, Liu came up with a project to bring food relief to the devastated city of Peking and negotiated an agreement to gain the withdrawal of the international Boxer Relief Expeditionary Force. So Liu knew China's miseries from every angle. He could write about the failure of statecraft; explaining how to recover China's national strength and prestige was far more difficult.[7]

The *Travels* opens with Lao Ts'an's story of what is soon recognizable as China's "ship of state." As in act I, scene 1 of Shakespeare's *The Tempest,* the vision sets out a stark strategic crisis. Lao Ts'an and two friends go, in the fashion of ancient Chinese poets, to drink wine all night and watch the sun rise from the P'englai Pavilion, on the north shore of the Shantung Peninsula. Through spyglasses they see a great ship in distress out at sea. A storm threatens to shake it apart and sink it. The captain sits on the poop deck, officers attend to the masts, but the sailors are robbing passengers of food and clothing. It is quickly evident that this is the Chinese ship of state. The captain is the emperor, those at the masts are the heads of the boards of government, and the sailors are bureaucrats and petty officials who prey on the people. The ship is gashed on its sides by the depredations of China's territories Manchuria and Shantung. One mast with a worn sail is the Tsungli Yamen, a symbol of the empire's forced need to deal with foreigners on international terms rather than as the sole civilization among tributaries.

Lao Ts'an and his friends take a nearby fishing boat to try to help the giant ship. The reason the ship is in trouble, Lao Ts'an says, is that it was not prepared for the storm and doesn't know where it is going. So the three will take modern navigational equipment to the captain (in other words, the answer to China's national distress lies in the adoption of modern Western technology).

When they reach the ship, one passenger is calling upon the others to take action. He collects money from them and tells them they must organize themselves. The outcome is that he gets the money while they shed their blood (this, the allegory tells us, is the way of revolution). When Lao Ts'an's boat comes alongside the great ship to deliver the navigational equipment, the would-be rescuers are denounced by the passengers because the equipment is foreign. The passengers begin to tear their own ship apart in order to throw planks at Lao Ts'an's small boat to sink it.

With this allegory of China's ship of state heading for disaster, Lao Ts'an sets out on his travels.

To a Western reader the tales then told are pointless, tedious, and virtually incomprehensible. Liu T'ieh-yün had been educated in the classics of Chinese philosophy, poetry, and music, and the book is packed with allusions beyond the comprehension of anyone but a specialist. But staying with the text gains the reader flashes of spare beauty on the dirt roads of north China and, more rewarding, a sense of a mentality and sensibility utterly unlike that of the modern West. The immense shock of this culture in its attempt to comprehend and survive the coming of the international state system is revealed here in all aspects.

In a small room set in a cave in the mountains, surrounded by books and listening to music of the Chinese zither and lute, the companions try to make sense of China's current predicament through the only intellectual framework available to them: traditional wisdom. They try to figure out what is happening in the world, and what strategy China should follow.

Yellow Dragon said, They will be just as I have said: Boxers in the North, revolution in the South. Preparations for the Boxer outbreak in the North began in *Wu-Tzu* [1888] and were already mature by *Chia-Wu* [1894]. In *Keng-Tzu* [1900] *Tzu* [rat] and *Wu* [horse] will clash with a great explosion. Their rise will be sudden, their fall will be equally abrupt. They are "the political force in the north." Those who believe in them will range from dwellers in the palace to generals and ministers. Their policy will be to suppress the Chinese.

Scholars of the text have pointed out that in this paragraph alone are references to the ancient Chinese zodiac, the "Doctrine of Mean" in the Chinese classics, the Empress Dowager, and the Manchu bannermen.

These Boxers are like a man's fist. He strikes, and if he succeeds, he succeeds; if he doesn't succeed, he stops, and nothing serious happens. . . . That blow of the northern Boxers will go near to smashing the country and will be very terrifying. Yet, since it will be only a single blow the country will get over it easily. Then there is the revolution [*ke*]. The character *ke* means a hide, like a horse's hide or ox hide. It covers the body from head to foot. However, don't think that what we are talking about is merely a mild disease of the skin, for you must know that if eruptions appear all over the body, they can be fatal. The one good thing about it is that such a disease proceeds slowly and if you take pains to cure it, it doesn't cause serious harm. Now this character *ke* can be traced back to one of the hexagrams of the Book of Changes, and therefore must not be neglected. Fear and avoid revolution, both of you! If you get drawn into that party, later you will rot away with them and lose your life!

The *Travels of Lao Ts'an* opens with the sentence: "When a baby is born, he weeps *wa-wa;* and when a man is old and dying, his family form a circle around him and wail, *hao-t'ao.*" This is a book that anticipates much weeping and wailing. It is an elegy for the old China that can be no more. In the end Lao Ts'an adopts the old ways, the Taoist doctrine of *wu-wei,* no resistance. The *Travels* ends as an antipolitics book. Political action will be useless. The message is that Chinese cultural values are under attack, yet the only hope lies in the survival and triumph of those same values, somehow transmogrified. The disputants in the snowbound North China cave predict it: "The introduction of a new culture from Europe will revivify our ancient culture of the Three Rulers and Five Emperors, and very rapidly we shall achieve a universal culture. But these things are still far off."

The revolution warned against in *The Travels of Lao Ts'an* would come, with devastating consequences. There began decades of cultural disintegration and political upheaval. The Revolution of 1911 deposed the emperor and established the Republic of China. Officially, this seemed to install China as a member of the international system. But China was a state in name only. Traditional China was collapsing; modern China was not functional. Many leading intellectuals, as though emulating Lao Ts'an, withdrew from politics, among them the brilliant scholar-statesman Hu Shih, who had written an introduction to the novel's first publication.

In the aftermath of World War I, fired by promises of self-determination from the great powers, students and reformers in China were obsessed with state-building. "Values, institutions, ideas—the whole content of culture— must be judged in terms of one criterion: will it preserve and strengthen the nation-state?" These hopes were overwhelmed by warlordism in north China and by civil war. The concept of the state did not take hold. The

Nationalist Kuomintang corrupted the state and the Communists rejected the idea of the state and the international system altogether.

The name Shanghai carries a unique modern meaning: oriental intrigue, colonial greed, the meeting of East and West in a place like no other: sex, money, power, opium, gangsters, and revolutionaries. Shanghai's location as a port city—just off the mouth of the Yangtze River (*Shanghai* means "above the sea")—facilitated its rise to commercial and political power. More significantly, it was a city outside the regular governance of both China and the West. The Ch'ing Empire had been compelled after the Opium War of 1839–1842 to cede Shanghai as one of the "treaty ports" on the China coast open to Western (mainly British) merchants, so the writ of the imperial court did not run inside the city boundaries. For the British and the French, the Japanese, Russians, Americans, and others who came to the port, Shanghai was not a colony but a city to be managed and exploited.

I came to my fascination with Shanghai, like many other American boys, through the comic strip *Terry and the Pirates,* featuring the exotic Dragon Lady and the exploits of intrepid American adventurers on the shores of the South China Sea in the 1930s. A worldwide audience of young people saw Shanghai depicted at one of its most romantic and dangerous moments in one of the adventures of Tintin by Herge, the Belgian master cartoonist: *The Blue Lotus,* set in 1931, when imperial Japanese forces staged the "Manchurian Incident" and occupied Shanghai as well. Then there was the spellbinding novel by Vicki Baum, *Shanghai 1937,* dealing with the rise to power of a Chinese boy from the lowest, most despised level of society and his contest with the city's Western elite. And there were the movies: *Shanghai Express, The Shanghai Gesture, The Lady from Shanghai.*

To get a feel for Shanghai at one of its most important turning points, we read André Malraux's novel *Man's Fate* (also titled *The Human Condition*), set in the fateful year of 1927 as the Nationalist Chinese, struggling to adapt the imported state system, confront Chinese communism's determination to itself become the international system.[8] Malraux's novel is about the Shanghai Uprising of 1927, but it is not titled *Uprising in Shanghai;* it is about a larger human confrontation and the origins of terrorism. China's destiny will be determined by the civil war being waged between the Nationalists— the Kuomintang or KMT—and the Communists, who are committed to party discipline as expounded by advisers from the Soviet Union.

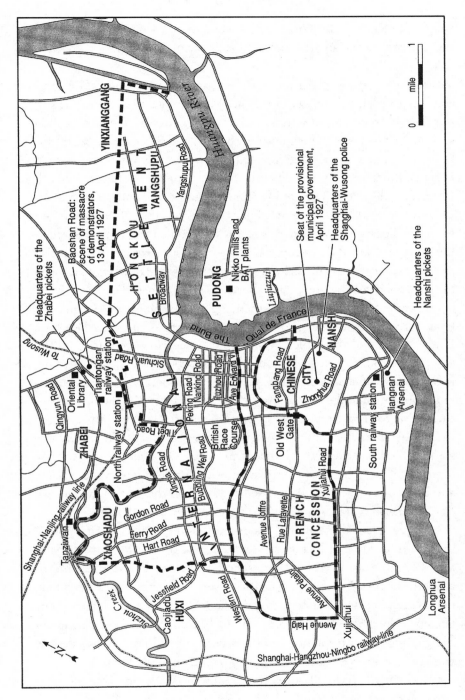

Figure 5. Shanghai in 1927. Hanchao Lu, *Beyond the Neon Lights: Everyday Shanghai in the Early Twentieth Century* (Berkeley: University of California Press, 1999), reprinted by permission

The Communists are based underground in Shanghai. According to the Marxist-Leninist ideology, only the proletariat, urban factory workers, have the correct consciousness to make the revolution. The KMT, led by General Chiang Kai-shek, is also ideologically based on a variation on Lenin's democratic centralism. But the KMT is a nationalist, authoritarian movement, while the Chinese Communist Party is internationalist, committed to the solidarity of the "workers of the world." In 1923, pressured by the Comintern in Moscow and with the approval of Stalin, the CCP formed an alliance with the KMT, a tactic often adopted by Moscow as a way of buying time to consolidate Communist strength in preparation for an eventual takeover. Now, in the winter of 1927, Chiang has turned his army toward Shanghai. He halts his forces just outside the city as the Communists launch a coup to seize power. Chiang will move in to take the city and destroy the CCP and all its members.

Katov is the Communist cadre and ideologist. The revolution, under the direction of the Comintern in Moscow, requires the individual to be subordinated to the needs of the party, for only the party can recognize and align itself with the scientific direction of history as recognized through Marxism-Leninism. Katov knows that CCP members must sacrifice themselves for the revolution. To maintain the CCP-KMT alliance on the larger scene, the Shanghai party members must do nothing when the KMT comes to destroy them.

Kyo is a Communist also but feels a metaphysical tension between fate, as defined by the party, and man's fate, which has the element of free will. Kyo's father is French and his mother Japanese, and in his parentage he represents the larger world's involvement with 1927 Shanghai. Kyo will not follow the party discipline of Katov; he leads the Shanghai party in rebellion to take over the city in advance of the KMT onslaught. He has a private side to his life as well—his love for his wife, May, a physician in the party's women's union. Kyo decides that party discipline and the inexorable course of history as seen in Marxism are not enough. He chooses to resist.

Tchen is the third figure at the center of the novel. Terrorism is built into the Communist ideology (the class enemy, the counterrevolutionaries, must be eliminated), and Tchen takes to it as a dedicated Marxist. The thought that he might have private desires or needs apart from the great cause of the revolution is agonizing to him. But in fact, Tchen is one of those near-pathological human beings who cluster around any political movement, intellectually incorporating and thereby legitimizing terroristic cruelty and killing. When ideology authorizes terrorism, killers will come forward. Tchen has made the Communist coup possible when he crept into a Shanghai hotel room after midnight to stand silently at the bedside of a sleeping man. Should he lift the mosquito netting or strike through it? He strikes through the net "with a blow that would have split a plank." He gathers up the papers needed to gain control of a shipment of arms. When the coup has gained power and the Nationalists move into Shanghai to liquidate the Communists, Tchen throws a bomb at Chiang Kai-shek's car, but the car is empty. He then turns himself into a bomb in another attempt to kill Chiang, but that attempt fails too, and Tchen dies in agony. His death is not a revolutionary act; he simply destroys himself, because for him and those like him, terrorism is erotically irresistible, blurring metaphysics, politics, and sex.[9]

Malraux's Kyo prefigures Pasternak's Yury Zhivago. His May is, like Yury's Lara, another person, someone to whom he is humanly committed. Love between two individuals is something the party cannot tolerate, because it puts something above the necessity to sacrifice one's all for the revolution.

Chiang's KMT takes Shanghai. He has selected an exquisite way to destroy the Communist leaders; throw them one by one, alive, into the boiler of a steam locomotive. Here is terrorism with no reference to ideology or individual commitment, just barbarism unleashed. As prisoners, Katov and Kyo, who have reached the mouth of the boiler from different paths and principles, can hear the locomotive whistle whose sound signals that another one of their comrades has been shoved into the steam boiler. Katov then breaks his own poison tablet in two and gives it to two terrified young Chinese boys who are next in line—the ultimate revolutionary sacrifice, as a KMT officer summons him to the fiery furnace.

Kyo's recognition of the difference between his acts and his being is the heart of the book. *The Human Condition* is the better title, for it is set against Man's Fate as defined by the party. The human condition is love with and for another. At one point May is unfaithful to Kyo. For revolutionaries, this means nothing, and Kyo shrugs it off, but within, both he and May know of the wrong and seek to set it right.

Kyo at one point listens to a recording of a man's voice. He is shocked when he is told it is his own voice. Kyo is assured that this often happens the first time one hears a recording of one's voice. But he is affected by the recognition that, as in Rimbaud's famous line, "Je est un autre" ("'I' is another"). One is another; there must be another. The collectivity must not be, cannot be, the all.

Chiang Kai-shek's 1927 destruction of the Communist Party in Shanghai launched political, military, and intellectual changes that would reshape Chinese and world communist ideology. With the urban proletariat base devastated, Mao established Communist bases in Chingkangshan, the almost impenetrable, steep-sided mountains inland from the coastal cities. To go with his geostrategic shift, Mao reformulated the ideology to feature peasants rather than urban workers. This was a radical shift from Marx and Lenin, both of whom viewed the peasantry as conservative and backward-looking, without the proletariat's revolutionary consciousness.

In the early 1930s Chiang's Nationalist army launched one "encircle-ment" campaign after another to try to destroy Mao's bases; each failed as the Communists simply evaded the assault's spearhead and then returned to their base once the Nationalists withdrew. Mao was perfecting a guer-rilla strategy drawn from the ancient Chinese *Art of War* by Sun Tzu: "The enemy attacks, we retreat; the enemy halts, we harass; the enemy retreats, we pursue."

But the Fifth Encirclement Campaign, of 1934, succeeded. Chiang Kai-shek had changed his strategy. He drew on another ancient Chinese strategic source: the game of *wei ch'i,* also called "Go." The Nationalists pushed fortified lines of communication into Chingkangshan, held them, and secured the territory inside the gridline. Mao had no answer for this (nor did the Vietcong when U.S. General Creighton Abrams used a similar strategy in Vietnam between 1969 and 1973).[10] Mao's forces set out on their epic "Long March," moving into Szechuan province in the west and then north to Yenan, where a new communist base was set up and Mao gained time to further refine his "Thought."

After Japan's defeat by the Allies in 1945 and the flight of Chiang's Nationalists to Taiwan in 1949, Mao established the People's Republic of China. For more than a decade he sought to build true communism on Marxist lines throughout China. This meant transforming the economic structure of society, for in Marx's materialistic doctrine, every aspect of life follows from the economic base; change that and everything else would change.

It didn't work. Mao changed the economic base of China, but social transformation did not follow. So Mao turned Marxism on its head and launched the "Cultural Revolution." Culture—what was in people's heads—must change. Until it did, society as a whole could not accept the perfected form of human life that was communism. Mao therefore called for every aspect of traditional, bourgeois, intellectual Chinese culture to be destroyed. Peking Opera was abolished, and entirely new operas were written—revolutionary works like "Taking Tiger Mountain by Storm."

In this campaign the Marxist-Leninist doctrine of terrorism was expanded. In the Soviet ideology, the proletariat was the authentic class, the possessor of the revolutionary consciousness. Other classes would have to accept "the Dictatorship of the Proletariat" or suffer the consequences, as when Stalin ordered the liquidation of the entire class of landed peasants, the kulaks. Under Mao, anyone suspected of retaining any shred of bourgeois mentality or counterrevolutionary sentiment might be "struggled" against or eliminated.

This approach was carried out more thoroughly by the Khmer Rouge in the genocide it inflicted upon Cambodia in the late 1970s. To wear glasses or carry a ballpoint pen was evidence of a bourgeois education; the consequence was to be sent to the countryside and worked to death, or to be executed at once. The Khmer Rouge made careful records, with photographs and detailed explanations of each individual it eradicated. Under the doctrine of justified, indeed required, terror, Khmer Rouge members were proud to be able to prove what good Communists they were.

As the People's Republic of China was violently promoting a world order to replace the Westphalian state system, the "overseas Chinese" leader of Singapore was prodding that Asian people swiftly into statehood. When George Kennan pointed out that the memoirs of statesmen had become a genre of literature, he was thinking of Britain and America; few examples can be found in Asia. But Lee Kuan Yew, the man who put tiny Singapore on the world's economic and diplomatic stage, and the greatest Asian statesman of the twentieth century, wrote a classic in the field, *The Singapore Story*.

At 10 AM, the pop tunes on the radio were cut off abruptly. Stunned listeners heard the announcer read out a proclamation—90 words that changed the lives of the people of Singapore and Malaysia:

Whereas it is the inalienable right of a people to be free and independent, I Lee Kuan Yew, prime minister of Singapore, do hereby proclaim and declare on behalf of the people and the government of Singapore that as from today, the ninth day of August in the year one thousand nine hundred and sixty-five, Singapore shall be forever a sovereign, democratic and independent nation founded upon the principles of liberty and justice and ever seeking the welfare and happiness of her people in a more just and equal society.

Two hundred and fifty miles to the north, in peninsular Malaysia, Tunku Abdul Rahman was making his own proclamation, declaring that "Singapore shall cease to be a state of Malaysia and shall forever be an independent and sovereign state and nation separate from and independent of Malaysia, and that the government of Malaysia recognizes the government of Singapore as an independent and sovereign government of Singapore and will always work in friendship and cooperation with it."[11]

Here was the Westphalian moment: a new state comes into being, enters the international system as a member state of the United Nations, and is given diplomatic recognition as legitimate, even permanent, and sovereign, with commitments by all to adhere to the norms of the established world order.

In his memoir, Lee tells of his boyhood, first under the British Empire, then under the occupying power of Imperial Japan, then after World War II under the reimposed British Empire until independence for Malaysia-Singapore. As a new state, Lee's Singapore would struggle desperately to avoid being taken over by the Communist Party backed by the People's Republic of China.

In 1970 Prime Minister Lee visited Harvard. About twenty faculty members invited him to dinner at the Faculty Club. As a Foreign Service officer then doing a fellowship at Harvard, I attended too. The intellectuals were in a jolly, self-satisfied mood, for the American war in Vietnam was going badly. The "New Left" had arrived on American campuses—new because the student left had turned to Mao's China and Red Guards as models, Stalin's Soviet crimes having been denounced in Khrushchev's 1956 "Secret Speech." Mao's Cultural Revolution was inspiring student activism in Europe and the United States. At Harvard, I watched in horror as students "struggled" (in the Maoist sense of the term) against the distinguished China scholar John King Fairbank, viciously condemning him for his "counterrevolutionary" views. The campus was in its second year of upheaval, with students "on strike"; the faculty members present at the dinner supported "the kids" and were ready to acquiesce in their demands that classes, papers, and examinations—but not grades—be canceled.

A professor of sociology helpfully wanted to clear something up at the start of the dinner. There had been some talk that perhaps the prime minister was not entirely opposed to the war in Vietnam: "But I'm sure that's a gross canard, is it not?" the professor asked rhetorically, or perhaps suggestively.

Lee was having none of it. He lit into them with blistering rhetoric: "What America has done and is doing by helping the Republic of Vietnam survive the Communist attack is buying time for other Southeast Asian people to consolidate their independence as legitimate sovereign states. If the U.S. were not fighting in Vietnam, Singapore would be gone by now!" Lee meant that the American decision to support South Vietnam's resistance to Communist takeover was necessary for Singapore as well as Malaysia, the Philippines, Indonesia, and Thailand to battle communism in their own lands and consolidate their young states. The professors called an early end to the evening. Not many years later, the emergence of the "Asian Tigers" as successful states in the global economy would prove Lee correct.

A half-century ago, Asia was the most violent, turbulent region of the world. Communism, the deadly enemy of the international state system, was making it so. At the turn of the twenty-first century, Asia is firmly and for the most part comfortably ensconced in the Westphalian system. Singapore—Hindu, Malay, and Chinese in makeup—has been one of the exemplars. And no member of the international system is more assiduous in asserting the importance and inviolability of the privileges and immunities of the sovereign state than the People's Republic of China, though this may in part stem from Beijing's awareness that it in some sense remains an empire (with boundaries not much changed since the Ch'ing Dynasty) in the clothing of a state. Overall, Asia is now as Westphalian as they come. The progress of Asian societies has demonstrated that despite decades or even a century or more of war, turbulence, and injustice, when a state is established and functions as a good citizen of the international system, things quickly improve for its people.

Singapore undeniably was shaped by Lee Kuan Yew as a hybrid: economically open but politically closed, an authoritarian-capitalist model. When the model is copied on a gargantuan scale, as it was in the People's Republic of China, powerful contradictions emerge.

When I was assigned to Hong Kong as a "China watcher" as the madness of Chairman Mao's Great Proletarian Cultural Revolution was bursting out, we paid close attention to Shanghai as a pivotal point in the upheaval.[12] From Hong Kong I was assigned to Harvard University for a year and then to the American embassy in Saigon. When I left Vietnam in 1973 after the Paris Peace Accords were signed, I returned to Washington, D.C., where, within hours, I was ordered to return to Asia.

Communist China was suddenly open to Americans. I escorted a group of seventeen teenagers, most of them black, from Chicago's inner city. Mayor Richard Daley had offered them as a delegation, and Premier Chou En-lai had accepted, apparently believing they would be "urban revolutionaries" and pro-communist in spirit.

They were not. They were American high school kids, and the overarching interest they had in the People's Republic of China was to find a basketball court. They nagged and pestered the "minders" assigned to accompany us, but no courts were to be seen. Suddenly, in Shanghai one evening, we were informed that it was time to play basketball, after we had all finished a massive Chinese dinner in a hostel. The lights of the hostel and all the surrounding area were turned off by some municipal switch, and the lights at the recreation-sports field were turned on. (Later, when the authorities wanted "the masses" to go home, the lighting would be reversed.)

We were taken to a big outdoor stadium and led to the basketball playing surface. On all four sides of the court, every seat was filled. Thousands of spectators were packed together, quietly waiting for us. Everyone in the stands wore white cotton short-sleeved shirts, dark blue cotton trousers, and black *busye,* cotton and rubber shoes. Our side was in every color and style of the times, bedecked with jewelry, and all, boys and girls alike, wearing heavy clogs or high-heeled shoes.

We took the court against the Shanghai no. 3 Tramways team, who wore regular basketball shoes and uniforms. The American girls instantly formed themselves into a cheerleading squad and cavorted to the center of the court to shout at the crowd, doing a brightly choreographed routine as they did:

They ain't no flies on us!
They ain't no flies on us!
They may be one or two on you! [all point to the Chinese crowd]
But they ain't no flies on us!

We won the game.

Following the death of Mao, the People's Republic of China became an assiduous member of the international state system. Nothing could be more symbolically Western than the Olympics, with the 2008 Beijing Olympiad staged as a coming-out party for China's rise to the first rank of states. Yet many works of modern Chinese literature defy identification with the modern Chinese state because of its place in "the language of the Westphalian international order, a set of European concepts exported to the East with European imperialism and sustained by the continuing Euro-centrism of international relations discourse."[13] Here Chinese literature and the Chinese regime are starkly at odds. The novel *Beijing Coma,* by Ma Jian, attempts an epic treatment of contemporary China from the Tiananmen massacre to the devastating construction projects for the Olympics, all strung along a series of excerpts from an ancient Chinese mythological text.

Beijing Coma is a book about books. The student Dai Wei carries with him the *Shan Hai Jing* (*The Classic of Mountains and Seas*), an ancient source book for Chinese literature. Dai Wei's father's copy of the *Selected Works of Mao Zedong* had not saved him from political ruin when he was denounced as a "rightist." Reading Kafka's *The Castle* causes Dai Wei to turn to his father's journals to try to understand why he, like K, had no control over his fate.

Beijing Coma interweaves two stories, demarcated by quotations from *The Classic of Mountains and Seas.* One concerns the student movement, culminating in the Tiananmen massacre of 1989, in which Dai Wei is struck a devastating blow: "My head exploded. . . . My hand reached out to touch my head, but couldn't find it." Dai Wei, "a vegetable" unable to move or talk, can hear and think about everything going on around him in the years of wild capitalism leading to China's successful bid for the Olympics. Tiananmen Square is the physical site of this first story, representing traditional China, Mao's Cultural Revolution, and the students' valiant but doomed erection of the white "Goddess of Democracy" bearing the "torch of liberty," which brings on the murderous crackdown by the People's Liberation Army: "In the distance, we heard the Goddess of Democracy crash to the ground."

The physical symbol of Dai Wei's other story is the national stadium, the "Bird's Nest" to be built for the Olympics. His mother, deteriorating amid increasingly squalid conditions, is the last holdout of her apartment building, condemned for demolition.

The scene is a version of the Tiananmen massacre of a decade before, as "the bulldozer charges into the building like an army tank. . . . The covered balcony and most of the outer walls and windows of the rest of the flat have fallen down. All the flats to our left and right have been demolished, as have the stairwell and landing behind us. Our flat is now no more than a windy corridor. It's like a bird's nest hanging in a tree. I can feel it shaking in the wind."

At the end of the book, Dai Wei comes out of his coma, his visit to the Underworld, without any understanding of what he is to do next: "Once you climb out of this fleshy tomb, where is there left for you to go?"

The fourth-century poet-recluse T'ao Ch'ien—somewhat like Machiavelli many centuries later—wrote, in "On Reading the Classic of Mountains and Seas," about working all day in the field, then coming home to write:

> The time has come
> > to return and read my books.
> The narrow lane—
> > deep ruts on either side—
> Rather deters
> > the carriages of friends!
> Contentedly I sit
> > and pour the new spring wine. . . .
> A gentle shower
> > approaches from the east
> And a pleasant wind
> > comes along with it.
> I read at length
> > the story of King Mu
> And let my gaze wander
> > over pictures of hills and seas.

Thus with a glance I reach
the ends of the Universe—
If this is not a pleasure
where could I ever find one?

No scene could be more unlike Dai Wei's reading in *Beijing Coma* of the *Classic.* The first half of the *Classic* is filled with leisurely descriptions of a harmonious land in which ritual sacrifices are carefully performed to maintain the favor of the gods. Then suddenly, order and well-being are gone, and the narrative style becomes fragmented and tense with hideous dangers when China encounters foreign ways and thoughts. Surely Ma Jian chose to hang the horrors of *Beijing Coma* on the structure of the ancient *Classic* for just this reason, a contribution to modern Chinese literature's portrayal of modernity as a crisis, and an opposition to China's identity as a state in the international system.[14]

Twentieth-century Chinese literature abounds with references to beheading and cannibalism as representative atrocities of China's failure to find a humane accommodation with modernity.[15] Ma Jian's *Beijing Coma* offers a clear, compelling explanation of what Montaigne was driving at in "Of the Cannibales." Ma describes the actual killing and eating, under political orders in the Cultural Revolution, of a sixteen-year-old girl, symbolizing the vast societal forces that in the new authoritarian capitalist China are consuming the nation's young.

Recalling Kafka's parable, messages from China's emperor today do get through to the people, instantly and incessantly. Has the Great Wall provided the foundation for a new Tower of Babel—China as a "Propaganda State"? Traditional China was the "thesis"; the antithesis can be seen in China's adoption of foreign ideas in three vast phases: missionary Christianity, leading to twenty million to thirty million killed in the Taiping Rebellion; communism, with an equally horrendous death toll by the end of Mao's Cultural Revolution; and capitalism, which voraciously possesses China today. The synthesis has not yet been found. The Chinese Revolution, begun in the Opium War of 1839 and renewed periodically ever since, is not yet over.

As he was dying in 1924, Kafka dreamed of moving to Palestine, thinking it a refuge from the modern predicament. Forty years before the Balfour

Declaration of 1916 called for "the establishment in Palestine of a national home for the Jews," and ten years before the term *Zionism* was coined, Mary Ann Evans, under her pen name George Eliot, intuited the modern state of Israel in her novel *Daniel Deronda.* Theodore Herzl, the handsome and charismatic founder of political Zionism, seemed to step from those pages into life. His own book *The Jewish State,* published in 1897, led to the founding of the World Zionist Organization. Israel might not exist were it not for *Daniel Deronda.*

George Eliot was, after Dickens, the second most popular writer of the Victorian age. *Daniel Deronda* is her most perplexing work, weaving two seemingly different stories: one about Gwendolen Harleth, a romantic English country house girl, the other about Deronda's emerging awareness of his Jewish identity and purpose. *Daniel Deronda* relates spiritual questions to world affairs on an epic scale.

The sickly, impoverished haunter of a London East End bookshop, Mordechai Lapidoth, introduces Eliot's hero to "the Masters who handed down the thought of our race—the great Transmitters," the Talmudic scholars, rekindling in him the fire of ancient Jewish nationalism and inspiring him to the cause of creating a new Judea, "founded on the old, purified, enriched by the experience our greatest sons have gathered from the life of the ages." Eliot likens this new founding to the creation of the United States, where "the people grew like meeting waters—they were various in habit and sect—there came a time, a century ago, when they needed a polity. And there were heroes of peace among them."

Deronda tells Gwendolen, who loves him, "the idea that I am possessed with is that of restoring a political existence to my people, making them a nation again, giving them a national centre, such as the English have, though they too are scattered over the face of the globe. That is a task which presents itself to me as a duty: I am resolved to begin it, however feebly. I am resolved to devote my life to it. At the least, I may awaken a movement in other minds."

Daniel sets out for the Middle East. Mordechai, his visionary guide, dies on the day of the departure, like Moses, who did not live to cross over into the Promised Land.

Sensing, preternaturally, that Jews of the Diaspora were about to take up a modern concept of nationality and claim "admittance to the community of nations as a legitimate member," Eliot makes these themes universal.[16] Her novel reveals much about statecraft in the late nineteenth century, particularly the preoccupation of the chancelleries of European great powers with the territories of the disintegrating Ottoman Empire—"the Eastern Question." Britain viewed German and Russian ambitions in the Middle East as a threat to its passage to India; Palestine was strategically important.[17] Eliot sees that a series of texts has preserved her hero's Jewish identity. Meanwhile the English characters in the novel, secure in England's green and pleasant land, are in danger of losing their national sense of a shared literature. Yet Diaspora Jews are poised to exchange their "homeland" of text for "a more conventionally national, landed form of identity" in the Middle East.[18] *Daniel Deronda* is a modern version of Malory's *Morte d'Arthur,* with Daniel as Arthur, raised in obscurity, unaware of his lineage, yet destined to inherit and refound his kingdom.

As Deronda set out for the Middle East, the Arab peoples were evolving from one form of political identity to another. The Ottoman Empire, which had imposed Turkish-led governance across the region for centuries, was crumbling. Most unwisely, the Ottomans allied with the kaiser's Imperial Germany in 1914 to wage the Great War, declaring "jihad" against the West. Arab nationalism seemed ready to throw off Turkish hegemony.

T. E. Lawrence had been reading T. S. Eliot when he was writing *Seven Pillars of Wisdom,* which would echo *The Waste Land* as "a vast modernist experiment."[19] The detritus of modern, urban, industrial life made an ugly contrast to the clean, romantically antique purity of the desert. Lawrence visited Cairo, Jerusalem, and Damascus but could not bear to describe them in more than a perfunctory, dismissive way. The term *waste land* had reversed its usual meaning.[20] Lawrence's title, an image of a roofless, ruined palace in the desert recalling "Ozymandias," suggests the lost greatness of Arab civilization as well as the possible collapse of Western civilization. Winston Churchill would call it a "treasure of English literature" ranking with *Robinson Crusoe* and *Gulliver's Travels.*[21] *Seven Pillars* is about the making of the modern Middle East and the Arab people's relation to international order. The wisdom of the pillars remains elusive.

In a 1922 letter, Lawrence wrote of his shelf of "titanic" books: *The Brothers Karamazov, Thus Spake Zarathustra, Moby-Dick;* his ambition was to write a fourth. He later would add to his list of titans Cervantes, Tolstoy, and Whitman. When under way with Arab warriors, Lawrence carried Homer's

Odyssey and Malory's *Morte d'Arthur* in his camel's saddlebags, and scenes from Xenophon's *The March Up Country* (*Anabasis*) in his head.

Along with these classics, consciously or not, *Seven Pillars* also follows Machiavelli's *The Prince.* The greatest endeavor is the founding of a polity; the selection of a worthy and able prince to advise and serve; the necessity for the "armed prophet"; and the genius to defy tradition, adjust to circumstances, employ deception, and inflict clarifying acts of violence at key moments; and a compendium of guidelines for getting and keeping power under conditions favorable or unfavorable.

The Ottoman Empire's decision to side with the kaiser's Germany "was by far the single most important decision in the history of the modern Middle East, and it was anything but inevitable."[22] The act jeopardized both the empire and the Caliphate it held over the Islamic world.

The Ottoman Empire was "the sick man of Europe," and power in Constantinople-Istanbul had been seized by "the Young Turks." The future of its region had long been debated and negotiated. In 1916 a secret exchange of notes among Britain, France, and Russia, known as the Sykes-Picot Agreement, described how the Middle East would be partitioned after the war: the Arabian Peninsula would be independent. Palestine west of the Jordan River would be under an international regime. A French sphere would stretch from the Mediterranean to Damascus to Mosul in Mesopotamia. A British sphere would run across the south from the Negev Desert to east of the Jordan River into central Mesopotamia, with a northern arm reaching into Persia, a southern arm to the Persian Gulf and Baghdad under direct British control. Tsarist Russia agreed to all this in return for the right to annex lands along its southern border.

The Sykes-Picot deal was discovered and published by the Bolsheviks after the Russian Revolution. Both Arabs and Zionists harshly criticized the agreement as contrary to promises made by the Allies. Although the French and the British envisioned semiautonomous Arab states coming into being within their spheres, the plan clearly was for Western dominance of all the Middle East formerly under the Ottoman Empire and Caliphate.

With the Middle East at its turning point within the international system, Lawrence aimed to enter history by propelling the Arabs to cast off Ottoman rule. Once liberated, what form of Arab polity would follow? Lawrence is less than clear, but he seemed to envision a single, independent Arab state, nearly equivalent in territory to the Ottoman Empire, and perhaps a new Caliphate under which Islam would be Arab-ruled and guided from Damascus, seat of the first, long-gone Arab Caliphate.

Lawrence analyzed the Arab political mind: "Their idea of nationality is the independence of tribes and parishes, and their idea of national union is episodic, combined, resistance to an intruder. Constructive politics, an organized state, and an extensive empire, are not only beyond their capacity, but anathema to their instincts. . . . Unless we, or our allies, make an efficient Arab empire, there will never be more than a discordant mosaic of provincial administrations."[23]

Britain had been ignominiously defeated at each end of the Ottoman Empire: at Kut in Mesopotamia and at Gallipoli in the Dardanelles. They were thus open to, if not hopeful about, raising an Arab revolt against the Turks alongside their conventional military campaign to be waged by General Allenby south-to-north along the coastal plain.

Lawrence had a grander vision: "I mean to make a new nation, to restore to the world a lost influence, to give twenty millions of Semites the foundation on which to build a dream-palace of their national thoughts."

Whatever polity Lawrence had in mind, it is clear from letters exchanged in 1915 and 1916 between the sharif of Mecca, Hussein bin Ali, and the British high commissioner in Egypt, Sir Henry M. McMahon, that in return for allying with the British against the Ottomans, the Arabs sought support in reestablishing an Arab Caliphate. This the British could accept, but they did not accept the Arab idea of the territory to be covered. Hussein wanted all of Arabia plus the Fertile Crescent. Such a vast, unified Arab state was inconceivable to British officials.

So Lawrence's idea of a Great Arab Revolt was based not on Arab nationalism or anti-Ottoman fervor but on Sharif Hussein's ambition to replace the Ottoman Empire and Caliphate with his own Arab version.[24] In awareness of this, Lawrence would at times condemn himself for foisting a double-dealing fraud on the Arabs and at other times convince himself that by leading them to a signal victory in taking Damascus, he could eliminate the objections of all parties to true Arab national liberation.

Lawrence's modern version of epic prose begins with his overview of the geostrategic situation and "the Foundations of Revolt." As the Ottomans decided to enter the Great War on the side of Imperial Germany, "a Holy War was proclaimed [to give the Turkish government] something of the traditional sanctity of the Caliph's battle-order in the eyes of the old clerical elements; and the Sharif of Mecca was invited—or rather ordered—to echo the cry." But Sharif Hussein refused.

Like Niccolò Machiavelli choosing Lorenzo de Medici as the prince he would guide, T. E. Lawrence surveys likely candidates for his Arab Revolt. Sharif Hussein was too old. His son Abdullah was too foolish. Son Ali was too "clean," trusting and naïve. Seid, too "cool" and blasé. In book I, Lawrence provides an essay on Arab leadership which he later parallels in book VI with a survey of British Army commanders, all evaluated as though they were battle characters in the *Iliad*. The key to leadership lies in temperament and judgment.

Lawrence settles on Feisal, son of the Sharif. In the Hejaz, west of Mecca and Medina, Lawrence is led to an inner court where "framed between the uprights of a black doorway, stood a white figure waiting tensely for me. I felt at first glance that this was the man I had come to Arabia to seek—the leader who would bring the Arab Revolt to full glory." They sat in a shaded room with many silent figures staring intently at the two:

Feisal: And do you like our place here in Wadi Safra?
Lawrence: Well; but it is far from Damascus.

"The word had fallen like a sword in their midst. There was a quiver. Then everybody present stiffened where he sat, and held his breath for a silent minute. . . . Feisal at length lifted his eyes, smiling at me, and said, 'Praise be to God, there are Turks nearer to us than that.'" Lawrence knew that he had found his man. "Feisal seemed to govern his men unconsciously: Hardly to know how he stamped his mind on them, hardly to care whether they obeyed. It was as great art as [Sir Reginald] Storrs'; and it concealed itself, for Feisal was born to it." He possessed both fire and reason.

When Feisal raised the Arab flag, "the pan-Islamic supra-national State, for which [the Ottoman Sultan-Caliph] Abdul Hamid has massacred and worked and died, and the German hope of the cooperation of Islam in the world-plans of the Kaiser, passed into the world of dreams."

A dream world indeed. Lawrence told himself he was leading the Great Arab Revolt to end the Ottoman Empire and Caliphate and establish an independent Arab state. Feisal and his father Sharif Hussein saw themselves as successors to both Empire and Caliphate, which would be Arab instead of Turk, with Damascus, not Istanbul, as the imperial capital. The British High Command aimed to defeat the Turkish army by conventional warfare and saw Lawrence's Arabs as at most a sideshow. And Lawrence, within, knew it was all a concoction. Feisal was the chosen prince, but the story from here is Lawrence on Lawrence.

Next comes an essay on war-fighting. Turkish forces overwhelm the Arab positions. A new plan is needed for a campaign of "dervishes against conventional troops." Lawrence reconsiders the books on strategy he read "like any other man at Oxford": Clausewitz and Jomini, Mahan and Foch, Napoleon's campaigns, Hannibal's tactics, and the wars of Belisarius. He finds little of use.

The focus is on Medina. Lawrence believed that taking the city from Ottoman control was necessary to any further progress of the Arab Revolt and to carry the war to the conquest of Damascus. But in pondering how to defeat the Turkish garrison at Medina, the thought dawned on Lawrence, what was the good of Medina? "We were in occupation of 99 per cent of the Hejaz. The Turks were welcome to the other fraction until peace or doomsday showed them the futility of clinging to our windowpane. . . . The answer flashed out from reflection—'why bother about Medina?'"

So he goes around Medina. In *Seven Pillars,* Lawrence sets forth a guidebook to insurgent war-fighting under the chief principle that "Battles in Arabia were a mistake."

Lawrence thinks about "the whole house of war." Structure is strategy. Arrangements are tactics. The sentiments of the people are psychology. The commander is responsible for all these at once. Strategy and tactics must be conducted as one. All the elements of war are in things, lives, and ideas. "Most wars were wars of contact. . . . Ours should be a war of detachment."

So Lawrence hit upon the uses of irregularity in an age of regularity; of mobility in an age of immobility (think of the Great War's Western Front). Only in the desert, it seemed, where the front was nowhere, could such a concept be tested. As George Bernard Shaw noted, even Lawrence's camels were not fed according to regulations.[25]

As he leads the Arab expedition first to capture Aqaba at the head of the Red Sea and then northward, Lawrence returns again and again to the integrity of his mission. His Arab Revolt had begun on false pretenses, because Britain and France had all along determined to serve their own interests and ambitions for influence in the region. As for the Arabs, they still clung to "the dim glory of the early Caliphate, whose memory endured among the people through the centuries of Turkish misgovernment," and Feisal pretended to seek to revive "the glories of the Ommayad or Ayubid" caliphates. These were dreams, Lawrence told himself.[26] The answer would come through his vow to win the war in a way that would make Arab claims for independent nationhood undeniable. On this basis Lawrence figured he would "win the later battle of the Council Chamber."

References to religion are scattered through the text, but they never add up to a major theme. The Arabs want Lawrence to convert, but he is openly a confirmed Christian. There are references to this or that Muslim fanatic, but this is a book about statecraft; religion is extraneous to great world affairs, more a cultural characteristic than a strategic consideration.

Once Lawrence's epic is complete, its high point in retrospect comes in book V, halfway through his narrative. At Wadi Musa, between Petra and the Jordan Valley, Lawrence sets a trap for the enemy. The Ottomans consider the Arabs regular troops, but they are not. Their forces are so dispersed that their extent cannot be estimated. But the Arabs have excellent intelligence on the size of the attacking force. They let the Turks into the Wadi and then strike them on both flanks. The Turks "never again attacked a prepared Arab position." Lawrence's irregulars have defeated a regular army on its own terms.

Wadi Musa, named for Moses, commemorates the farthest place reached by the leader of the Israelites. He led his people to the Promised Land but did not cross over Jordan with them.

From this point onward, it all goes wrong for Lawrence of Arabia. By November 1917 Allenby is ready to launch a general attack across his entire Gaza-Beersheba front. To disrupt the expected Ottoman retreat, Lawrence tries to cut the Yarmuk Valley railway, but fails.

Then comes the most famous—or infamous—episode in *Seven Pillars,* at Deraa, the junction of the rail lines, the "navel" of the Turkish armies in Syria. Expert and scholarly opinion holds that Lawrence's Deraa incident never happened; its dates do not accord with Lawrence's known movements, and the story itself does not quite cohere.[27] Why is the Deraa story there?

Every classic epic involves a visit by the hero to the Underworld, where the experience will reveal to him his true, fated mission. Reaching the nether region requires contact with a vegetation symbol, like Virgil's golden bough, and a guiding companion. Lawrence and his men are in rainy winter quarters. In the evening,

There arose a strange, long wailing round the towers outside. Ibn Bani seized me by the arm and held to me, shuddering. I whispered to him, "What is it?" and he gasped that the dogs of the Beni Hillal, the mythical builders of the fort, quested the six towers each night for their dead masters.

We strained to listen. Through Ali's black basalt window-frame crept a rustling, which was the stirring of the night-wind in the with-ered palms, an intermittent rustling, like English rain on yet-crisp fallen leaves.[28]

Then comes, unheralded, the outlaw, deadly, swaggering Talal el Hareidhin, Sheik of Tafas, a sinister Mephistopheles-like figure. "When a day had made me sure of him, I took him secretly to the palm-garden, and told him my ambition to see his neighborhood." The hero and his guide then ride through lava fields to "the hollow land of Hauran" and its chief town, Deraa.

There a voice calls out in Turkish and a sergeant takes Lawrence roughly by the arm. "The Bey wants you." Lawrence is then led through nightmarish urban squalor reminiscent of *The Waste Land:* through a tall fence, into a compound of huts, to a mud room, a guard room with men in dirty uniforms sprawled about, across six tracks of a railway yard, near an engine shop, through a side gate, down a street, past a square, to a house where men loll about a dark entry. There Lawrence is taken, flogged, and sodomized. In Deraa that night, "the citadel of my integrity had been ir-revocably lost." His physical debasement depicts his moral condition. As in all epics, in the Underworld his mission is made entirely clear: "I must take up again my mantle of fraud in the East."

From this point on, Lawrence's efforts are thoroughly subsidiary to Allenby's, and his narrative is hastened and truncated until "our united forces entered Damascus unopposed" and the old Arab capital "went mad with joy."

In my capacity as deputy for Feisal, I pronounced [the Ottoman] civil government of Damascus abolished. . . . Our aim was an Arab Government, with foundations large and native enough to employ the enthusiasm and self-sacrifice of the rebellion, translated into terms of peace. . . . When I left Damascus on October the Fourth the Syrians had their de facto government, which endured for two years, without foreign advice, in an occupied country, wasted by war, and against the will of important elements among the Allies.

In his epilogue, Lawrence strangely refers to the Biblical Hebrew yearning for a state and land: "Super Flumina Babylonis, read as a boy, had left me longing to feel myself the node of a national movement. We took Damascus, and I feared."[29] Lawrence's saga bears out Machiavelli's perception that the manner in which a polity is acquired will affect one's ability to keep it.

Seven Pillars of Wisdom strangely intertwines the ancient epic of the Israelites on the march to the Promised Land with Lawrence's modern tale of the Arabs on their way to liberation. In 1940 an American traveler in the Jordan Valley encountered an Arab whose father had fought alongside Lawrence. They spoke of Deraa: "Deraa was pretty much the climax in this show, wasn't it. The last big show before Damascus. It was the same as the Israelites' campaign, when Og and all his people went out to Edrei. Same place as Deraa, of course. But the Israelites were making for Jerusalem, so to speak, not Damascus."[30]

Like Moses, Lawrence sees himself as a founder, and like Moses, he does not get to go forward with his people to see what they would do after being led to the threshold of liberation and state foundation. Moses stopped short of the Promised Land so that the Israelites could make their own history, free of his overwhelming presence.[31] The Israelites in search of a polity faced a choice between emulating the tyranny they had left behind in Egypt and anarchy in the wilderness. Lawrence's Arabs would face the same choice.[32] What Moses had heard from God and passed on verbally would emerge as a book. Moses disappeared into the book. The Prophet Muhammad would do the same. And so Lawrence disappears into his book. Leaders understand that their purpose is to make themselves unnecessary.[33] Only the book endures.

The postwar distribution of the former Ottoman Empire's territories partially reflected the Sykes-Picot Agreement between Britain and France but was modified by the League of Nations' Mandate System, which forbade any direct rule of the Middle East by the Allied powers yet left them in de facto control. In effect, when the Ottoman Caliphate collapsed in 1924, the map of the Middle East went blank. No regular, recognized boundary lines appeared other than "zones" of control to be exercised by the European powers that had won the Great War, primarily Britain and France. Through various forms—mandates, protectorates, zones of influence—a grid of "future states" was dropped on the map that would eventually bring the entire region into the international state system.

By 1960 a leading scholar of world affairs would note: "It is a paradoxical yet obvious fact that the new Muslim nations are more nearly in accord today claiming the political legacy of Western Europe than in demanding a resuscitation of the political traditions of Islam. Occidental ideals of the state have inspired their national movements and independence, and the Western vocabulary of constitutionalism is generally employed today in most Muslim societies."[34]

In the mid-twentieth century, Muslim scholars found ways to adapt Islamic law to their states, and their societies to changing modern realities. They embraced the ideas of state sovereignty, international law and organization, and the requirements of professional military and diplomatic practice.[35]

But the Middle Eastern states were not democracies. The new states that emerged in the post-Ottoman decades were governed by hereditary monarchies, false parliamentary systems under autocratic control, or military dictatorships. Muslim societies traditionally have been deeply suspicious of formal political authority and inclined instead to trust family, tribal, and religious connections. Bad governance of the states created after the Ottoman collapse, typically with the complicity of major world powers, deepened such suspicions and tainted the concept of the state.

The collapse of the Ottoman Caliphate raised the question of succession, with Egypt under King Fuad and the sharif of Mecca the chief claimants. Neither could accept the other. In 1936 a conference was called for the purpose of determining the next caliph, but it failed to produce agreement. The vision of a restored Caliphate, stirred in Lawrence's time, would excite many in the Muslim world thereafter.

Lawrence prophetically sensed the danger of those who would use terror to realize their apocalyptic vision. He called them "daytime dreamers": "All men dream: but not equally. Those who dream by night in the dusty recesses of their minds wake in the day to find that it was vanity: but the dreamers of the day are dangerous men, for they may act their dream with open eyes, to make it possible."

In 1648, the year of the Treaty of Westphalia, Cossacks murdered more than one hundred thousand Jews, and they killed thousands more thereafter as the Russian Empire expanded into Poland. The scale of the killing of Jews would not be exceeded until the Holocaust.[36]

When I, as a junior American diplomat posted to Israel, first engaged Israeli officials, military strength for the defense of the Jewish people dominated their work, as they urgently sought recognition for Israel as an independent, legitimate, sovereign state. Late one blustery afternoon, I sat with Abba Eban in his modest villa near the Mediterranean beach at Herzliya Petuach. Once the fabulously articulate young diplomatic face of the new state of Israel at the United Nations, now a sidelined elder statesman, he poured glassfuls from a huge pitcher of orange juice and made the usual Israeli joke about the orange crop having once been the mainstay of the Israeli economy.

In 1947 a resolution of the United Nations General Assembly partitioned the old League of Nations Mandate for Palestine into two states, one Arab, one Jewish. The Arabs rejected it, the Jews accepted it, declared their independent state, and entered the United Nations as a member state. Thereafter, Israel has had constantly to strive for wider diplomatic recognition, for a peace agreement to provide it with secure and recognized borders, for acceptance of Jerusalem as its capital, and for acceptance of its rights in international organizations. To Israelis and all Jews, this was far more than a matter of due respect, it was essential for survival. As Eban put it starkly on the first Israeli official visit to Auschwitz: "Our state and our flag have come too late."

Muriel Spark's *The Mandelbaum Gate* seems at first to be a typical English lady's novel, a drawing room comedy of genteel, slightly dotty characters who chatter through a coincidence-rich, intricately plotted tale that should conclude with all the characters paired off and properly accounted for. The "middle registers of experience" are played out here, but in a context of extremes. This is Spark's only long novel, in the tradition of George Eliot. It is as though the author of *Daniel Deronda* had gone to the Jewish State a century later to see for herself. Spark's novel is set in Jerusalem, sharply divided between the State of Israel and an Arab population under Jordanian control but lacking any international legal status.

The Mandelbaum Gate is shaped around a border crossing—"no man's land"—between the new Jewish state of Israel and the Hashemite Kingdom of Jordan (also a new state, carved out of the old British mandate). Israel's paramount goal is to become diplomatically recognized as a legitimate state in the international system. Jordan's role, on behalf of the entire Arab-Islamic world, is to prevent the achievement of this goal, even to the extent of denying Israel's very existence.

Barbara Vaughan, Jewish, British, and a Catholic convert, is a modern cross-category seeker for a place and clear identity that always is just beyond reach. The gate allows her to move from one version of herself to another and back again.

Read today, after the turbulent *intifada,* terrorism, security barriers, air strikes, and rocket barrages, Spark's novel seems perfectly civilized, even charming. The violent history that separates 1961, the year in which the novel is set, from today does not obscure Spark's intuition that statecraft cannot escape the increasing power of religion and that mixed identities add volatility to their intersection.

As other works of English literature in the lineage of Jane Austen and George Eliot might hang their narratives on country-house proprieties or vicarage jealousies, Spark's novel superficially is in the genre of a post–World War II tourist story: an educated lady traveler finds herself amid a set of new acquaintances, some exotic, some pedestrian, and her presence creates a round of rivalries and affections that produce a fresh twist or surprise every few pages.

Not until the final sentence of the novel are we told just how banal the Mandelbaum Gate is as a symbol in the Arab-Israeli conflict. It was "hardly a gate at all, but a piece of street between Jerusalem and Jerusalem, flanked by two huts, and called by that name because a house at the other end once belonged to a Mr. Mandelbaum."

> The intensity at the Gate was quite absurd. One could understand the border incidents where soldiers would flare-up an incident suddenly and unaccountably. But there at the Gate the precautions and suspicions of the guards were quite absurd. No Israeli money allowed into Jordan, no Israeli postcards. The Jordanian police almost biologically unable to utter the word "Israel." The Israeli police were inordinately dramatic: "Safe crossing," they would say as one left the immigration hut. The Israeli porter would run and dump one's baggage half-way and run for the life of him back to his post. The Jordanian porter would wait till the path was clear; he would run the few seconds' space

to pick up the bags and run for the life of him back to his post. They dramatized everything. Why did people have to go to extremes, why couldn't they be moderate? Freddy bumped into a man in European dress, rushing out of a shop as they all did. The man said something in Arabic. Freddy had thought that he was a Jew. You couldn't tell the difference sometimes. Some of them had extremely dark skins, almost jetters. Why couldn't people be moderate?

The speaker is Freddy Hamilton, a British diplomat. His charming but querulous yearning for "moderation" sets a deeper matter before the reader. Moderation and compromise may be the diplomat's stock in trade, a necessity if any hope is to be held out for maintaining international peace and security. But Freddy's approach cannot comprehend, let alone affect, the bitter passions of the Arab-Israeli conflict. Britain's exasperated and exhausted failure to control Palestine led it, in 1947, to give up the League of Nations mandate over Palestine it had assumed after the First World War. This mandate was an international obligation to assist the peoples of Palestine achieve the foundation for eventual statehood within "the international community." Hopes for moderation were dashed again and again, especially after the upsurge in Jewish immigration after the Holocaust propelled the cause of a Jewish State, and the Arab world furiously dedicated itself to "driving the Jews into the sea."

Freddy is the epitome of the old-school diplomat, the delight of hostesses, for whom he composes clever verses of thanks for their gracious hospitality. As a representative of the Foreign Office he moves easily around Jerusalem, both the eastern Jordanian old city and the western Israeli side. What he observes is not moderation but passion, and he declares it to be "absurd," his stock epithet. He sees Orthodox Jewish boys:

> Freddy was rather sorry for the boys with their sausage side-curls and black knickerbocker rigout. . . . He was convinced that the boys with ringlets were going through some sort of hell. . . . The ringlets, like the [Mandelbaum] Gate, were quite absurd.
>
> "Quite absurd!" On the strength of this phrase he had struck up friendships all over the place.

The heroine of *The Mandelbaum Gate* is Barbara Vaughan, an English girls' school teacher, whose background—half Jewish, half Gentile—signals that her touristy visit to "find her true self" in the Holy Land will situate the book in the genre of "ladies' novels." But this is Muriel Spark's own heritage, and she is able to create an authentic depth as Barbara, a convert to Catholicism who recognizes that her Jewishness is somehow essential to her selfhood, moves from being "Gentile and Jew" to being a "Gentile Jew."

Freddy's litany, that every action or thought other than bland moderation is "quite absurd," is confronted fiercely by Barbara; she alone of Jerusalem society will not be charmed by Freddy's supercilious ways.

> "Do you know," said this passionate spinster in a cold and terrifying voice, "a passage in the Book of the Apocalypse that applies to your point of view?
>
> "It goes like this," she said, enunciating her words slowly, almost like a chant:
>
> I know of thy doings, and find thee neither cold nor hot. . . . Being what thou are, lukewarm, neither cold not hot, thou wilt make me vomit thee out of my mouth.
>
> Freddy did not reply. People should definitely not quote the Scripture at one. It was quite absurd.

The Arabs have their own version of this dynamic in the Ramdez family: Yusef, the father, a scurrilous con man, pimp, and classic entrepreneur in the shadows of postcolonial, prerevolutionary, crime-rich modernity; the slickly sexy daughter Suzy, dark-haired but blue-eyed, representing some crusader or Western imperial moment past; and her brother Abdul. "It would be a waste of time to rely on any statement about himself and his life spoken from the lips of Abdul Ramdez."

But Abdul nonetheless states clearly his version of the great strategic issue in the novel. "I'm a man of passion and enthusiasms," he says to Freddy: "That is to say, I'm passionate in general, but I don't get worked up about any particular thing for long. In this way I avoid the great Arab mistake, as we have obsessions that leave us exhausted and incapable of action when the time for action comes."

Abdul Ramdez sees some civilizational merit in Freddy's fussing about moderation. He finds on Freddy's table a letter he has been writing to a friend at Oxford, remarking that Freddy had just found a rhyme for the word *Capricorn*. Abdul dwelt on the glamour of the name "All Souls" which he knew to be that of an Oxford College. . . . He was fascinated by the entire vision of that state of heart in which one wrote to a Fellow of All Souls about a rhyme for Capricorn. It could not result in any large benefit to Hamilton or his friends, nor could this piece of information damage Hamilton's enemies. It was disinterested and therefore beautiful, even if it was useless to the immediate world. And this was something Abdul could never make his middle-class Arab acquaintance understand—how it was possible to do things for their own sake, not only possible but sometimes necessary for the affirmation of one's personal identity. The ideal reposed in their religion, but somewhere in the long trail of Islam, the knack of disinterestedness had been lost, and with it a large portion of the joy of life. His father would never accept that Hamilton's activities were as meaningless as they looked. What is his motive? Is it political? Why does he write those verses to send to the Cartwright house? Are they in code? Why does he spend so much time in Jordan? Have you found out why he is learning Arabic? Have you read any of his private correspondence? . . . Why does he stay on at a hotel, this Hamilton? This Hamilton, why does he walk everywhere instead of taking a taxi? There must be a reason, everything means something.

Readers of *The Mandelbaum Gate* a half-century after its setting will bring to the text an awareness of what has grown out of the seeds that Spark located in the Jerusalem of that time. Israel was then still a new state, the "Modern State," it called itself, to affirm the ancient Hebrew presence and ownership of the land. It was in 1961 an accepted member state of the United Nations, but it sought—and still seeks—as its overriding political goal, full diplomatic recognition with permanent and legitimate international borders. The 1967 Six-Day War would make Israel the paramount military power of the region. Faced with this, the Arab world would silently abandon the conventional military option; there no longer existed any possibility of driving the Jews into the sea. Instead, the Arab states would urge Palestinian Arabs to become the sole front-line enemy of Israel and provide them with the ideology, the techniques, and the religious justification for using terrorism as the weapon of first resort. A major theme of *The Mandelbaum Gate* is that a person, or a people, can come to feel "all of a piece" though made up of disparate parts. From the seeds displayed here would emerge the first clear Palestinian national identity, and on top of that, an Islamist politico-faith, a communion of believers in death over life. On the Israeli side, nationalist and somewhat secular Zionism, in parallel with a radical religious fervor for *Eretz Yisrael,* would spread settlements across Judea and Samaria of the West Bank and southward into Gaza, which never in antiquity was integral to any Jewish kingdom. Some decades after the settlement movement sprang up, some Israeli scholars would revise their view of the founding of the modern state, and political-military leaders would abandon their once nonnegotiable refusal to cross certain "red lines" (never negotiate with the Palestine Liberation Organization, for example; never accept a Palestinian state; never permit an official Arab presence in Jerusalem; never give up the right to settle anywhere west of the Jordan River). It was, as it still is, a narrative of moderation and passion, and as in *The Mandelbaum Gate,* religion is the key.

Freddy Hamilton is studying Arabic, as every good diplomat assigned to the Middle East should. The sentences he is given to translate in his Arab grammar book provide a sense of the problem:

"Your speech was delightful, but you did not mention the blood which flowed in the Arabs' battles."

"The affairs of our nation became secure after the murder of the author of that harmful book."

Muriel Spark could not have made those up.

The Mandelbaum Gate is set in 1961, the year that Adolf Eichmann was put on trial in Israel for his part in Nazi Germany's genocidal Holocaust against the Jews. Spark touches on the trial only here and there, but Eichmann's hovering presence hinges the question of good and evil, moderation and fanaticism, in the story. Hannah Arendt would famously address these issues in *Eichmann in Jerusalem* and coin the phrase "the banality of evil" to describe the defendant's "ordinariness." Spark's conception in *The Mandelbaum Gate* is greater than Arendt's in placing the Eichmann example at the center of a wider, more universally human conundrum. Moderation can be essential for the good, and passion can be devastatingly bad. But moderation can also be wholly in the service of evil, and passion can be indispensable for the success of a rightful cause. In this sense, Spark's narrative is an extended examination of W. B. Yeats's dark observation, "The best lack all conviction, while the worst are full of passionate intensity." In this modern world of uncertainty and indeterminate identity, Eichmann has welcomed categorization by an oppressive regime. A malignantly, falsely integrated being, Eichmann is the antithesis of Barbara Vaughan in her search for identity.

Barbara's Jerusalem days play out these themes to a satisfying resolution, yet one that leaves the great strategic questions—national and personal—to be answered by her readers. There are two stories at work on Barbara. First, she is engaged to marry an archaeologist who works on the Dead Sea Scrolls. But she is a devout Catholic and he is divorced. So while she is in Jerusalem, he is in Rome petitioning the Rota for an annulment of his first marriage. At first they reject him, which means that Barbara must either break the engagement or marry outside the church and be shorn of peace of mind. Ricky, a spiteful enemy to Barbara—a spurned lesbian, we suspect—seeks to ensure that the Rota will deny Barbara's fiancé's petition by researching his family records for some evidence that will wreck the case. But Ricky's knowledge of Catholic marriage doctrine is flawed. The document she has found would, she thinks, *favor* Barbara; in fact it would have doomed her case. Ricky destroys it and has a document forged expressing the opposite set of facts. This, Ricky believes, will ensure a negative decision by the Rota; in fact it does the opposite. Barbara's fiancé's earlier marriage is annulled.

Second, Barbara decides upon a secret visit, a pilgrimage, to the major Christian shrines, nearly all of which in 1961 were in East Jerusalem: inside Jordan. Her friends urge her not to go. As a Jew, even a half-Jew, she could get into real trouble. A mob might seize her. Barbara goes anyway, disguised as the wholly covered servant of her tour guide Suzy Ramdez. While she is there, an item in an Israeli newspaper mentions her as the cousin of a British Jewish lawyer who has come as a consultant to the Eichmann trial: "While in Jerusalem, Mr. Aaronson was able to spend some time with his cousin, Miss Barbara Vaughan, who has been spending a vacation in Israel. Miss Vaughan, who teaches school in England, is a Roman Catholic Convert. She claims that her new religion is not in conflict with her Jewish blood and background, and is enthusiastic about Israel and the Israelis. Miss Vaughan left Friday for a tour of Jordan."

With this story out in public, Barbara becomes a target. Her disguise may be taken as proof that she is a spy. Her first attempt to get back across the Jordan-Israel hillside frontier is stopped when shooting starts. Her second attempt succeeds: disguised in a traditional nun's black habit, she is escorted by Abdul, his head shaved and his body garbed as an Arab Franciscan friar. They pass through the Mandelbaum Gate.

All this to present-day readers seems delightfully, operatically melodramatic. Yes, there was danger back then, but not so savagely murderous as it is today. *The Mandelbaum Gate* in this sense is more entertainment than epic. Nonetheless, the seeds of a far more serious international confrontation are in Spark's book, and the moderation-or-passion theme places this work in the first rank of literary statecraft.

The Mandelbaum Gate is a nonlinear text that uses flashbacks to reveal the truth. The book is structured by unbalanced chapters, frequent page breaks, narrative gaps, and deliberate repetitions—statements reported more than once, but not by the same actors. These physical markers evoke the novel's swirling conception of time. Spark's text reflects the way statecraft between Arabs and Israelis is performed, with each cast of characters having a different script, different lines, different intentions. Its disorienting structure is an introduction to Middle East diplomacy.

The Bible which binds the Old and New Testaments together, building the new on the foundation of the old, represents the unity Barbara seeks. Jerusalem is the *omphalos* of the world, "the core and paradigm of God's plot."[37] The totality of the place, like the Bible, is a book that binds together multiple, even infinite parts. The division of Jerusalem into states makes no eternal sense to Barbara. The city reminds her of Dante in *Paradiso,* comprehending the world—and God—as one great book. A world of states and the Book of Jerusalem seem fundamentally incompatible, yet Spark tries to bridge the two. The outcome is darkened by Barbara's furious prophetic quoting from the book of Revelation. Those who do not succeed in comprehending and managing somewhere between cold and hot, moderation and passion, may find themselves staring in the face of the apocalypse.

As Abba Eban wrote in his autobiography, in theory the state, as a concept and as the fundamental entity of world affairs, ought to be in eclipse. The multiplicity of states in a world where sovereignty has lost much of its meaning is "the central political anomaly of our age. . . . There is no sign that the individual nation-state is about to be superseded as the focus of allegiance and social pride."

Israel's vulnerability is much increased by the fact that we have not won any degree of international legitimacy for the present territorial and administrative structure. The realistic school of diplomacy held that military power was the dominant theme of interstate relations. It has now been proved that the eclipse of legitimacy is a more potent issue.

After the Six-Day War, Arab regimes sought the most potent way to strike at Israel. They declared at Khartoum "The Three Nos": no peace (that is, no secure and recognized borders), no negotiation (no diplomacy), and no recognition (no legitimacy)—a rejection of all of Israel's claims to statehood. A fourth "no" was to refuse to utter the name of "the Zionist entity." A decade later, Egypt signed a treaty of peace with Israel. In 1981 President Anwar Sadat was assassinated as payback for his apostasy.

Since then, the "peace process," disrupted by wars and profoundly endangered by ideologically driven Islamist terrorists, has struggled toward a "two-state solution." Across the entire Middle East region, every one of its many conflicts is centered on the question of the state: will failed states be reconstituted? Will "rogue states" return to responsible statehood? Will a State of Palestine join the State of Israel in mutual recognition and peace? If so, the international state system would gain renewed vitality.

At the start of *Seven Pillars of Wisdom,* Lawrence of Arabia wholly adopts a Bedouin identity. Over the course of the book, however, he gradually pulls back, accepting that he cannot really become a nomadic Arab tribesman. "In my case, the efforts for these years to live in the dress of Arabs, and to imitate their mental foundation, quitted me of my English self, and let me look at the West and its conventions with new eyes: they destroyed it all for me. At the same time I could not sincerely take on the Arab skin: it was affectation only."

Rudyard Kipling's *Kim* takes the matter of identity to another dimension. The greatest novel of India in the English language—and perhaps the greatest novel of India—opens in Lahore, which, inconceivable to Kipling, is today not in India but in Pakistan. India itself was not a state when Kipling wrote, and there is no hint of the right of self-determination in the book.

Arnold Toynbee, in his magisterial and now neglected twelve-volume work *A Study of History,* described the rugged mountains and valleys strad-dling Afghanistan and British India as a "roundabout," a place which drew in armies and migrations from all directions, spun them around, and sent the mixture out every which way. *Kim*'s first paragraphs depict a jumble of identities. Kim, defying the rules, sits drumming his heels astride the great cannon Zam-Zammah outside the city museum. He has just kicked off all the other boys in a game of "king of the hill." Who holds Zam-Zammah holds the Punjab, the saying goes; the English hold the Punjab and Kim is English. Only he is not: he is Kimball O'Hara, Irish, or half-Irish, raised by a "half-caste" woman who pretends to be his aunt. He's burned black by the sun and jabbers the same bazaari lingo as the urchins who cavort with him. Depending on the opportunities available, Kim has at hand Euro-pean clothes, Mohammedan garb, and "a complete suite of Hindu kit, the costume of a low-caste street rascal, which Kim has stored in a secret place under some baulks in Nila Ram's timber-yard, behind the Punjab High Court." Disguised—and real—identity is a major theme of the novel. Kim is not merely a master of disguises, he is a master of identities; he infiltrates a community by joining it.[38]

> "Off! Off! Let me up!" cried Abdullah, climbing up Zam-Zammah's wheel.
>
> "Thy father was a pastry-cook, Thy mother stole the *ghi*," sang Kim. "All Musselmans fell off Zam-Zammah long ago!"
>
> "Let me up!" shrilled little Chotalal in his gilt-embroidered cap. His father was worth perhaps half a million sterling, but India is the only democratic land in the world.
>
> "The Hindus fell off Zam-Zammah too. The Musselmans pushed them off. Thy father was a pastry-cook—."

Thus was Kim's potted history of South Asia, justifying British sovereignty by Hindu and Muslim inability to hold on to their lands. Kim is not taunt-ing, he is playing with friends: all through *Kim,* until the very end, conflict will be turned into play.

Much of the novel is strung along the Grand Trunk Road, a British engineering marvel, providing a secure and productive route for all sects, classes, and races under the Raj. In this setting, Kim acquires a companion and mentor in adventures ahead, an old, half-mad Tibetan lama on pilgrim-age to India to see the four Buddhist holy places before he dies. Kim will become his *chela,* or disciple; the lama will become a father to Kim. The lama's conviction that the world is an illusion fits Kim's assumption that it is a world of play.

Also a father to Kim will be Mabub Ali, a Punjabi horse trader and a secret agent in the service of the British Raj as C.25.1B. They will play a spy-story role in the Great Game, the Russian-British contest for Eurasian influence in which India was the magnificent prize. It is a "game," but it is deadly serious as well, a Hobbesian war of all against all epitomized when Russian and French agents viciously beat up the lama. The empire must be protected, by espionage in the first instance, by war if it must come to that.

At the end of Kim's adventures, his boyhood just over, he has been tested in spycraft, statecraft, sexual temptation, and spiritual questing. He comes exhausted to the point where he must decide on his life's mission:

> There stood an empty bullock-cart on a little knoll half a mile away, with a young banyan tree behind—a look-out, as it were, above some new-ploughed levels; and his eyelids, bathed in soft air, grew heavy as he neared it. The ground was good clean dust—no new herbiage that, living, is half-way to death already, but the hopeful dust that holds the seeds of all life. He felt it between his toes, patted it with his palms, and joint by joint, sighing luxuriously, laid him down full length along in the shadow of the wooden-pinned cart. And Mother Earth was as faithful as the Sahiba. She breathed through him to restore the poise he had lost lying so long in a cot cut off from her good currents. His head lay powerless upon her breast, and his opened hands surrendered to her strength. The many-rooted tree above him, and even the dead man-handled wood beside, knew what he sought, as he himself did not know. Hour upon hour he lay deeper than sleep.
>
> Towards evening, when the dust of the returning kine made all the horizons smoke, came the Lama and Mabub Ali, both afoot, walking cautiously, for the house had told them where he had gone.

Mabub Ali and the Lama discuss Kim's mission as he sleeps under his "Bodhi Tree": either the Lama's way of contemplation, or Mabub Ali's way of action needed by the state. Kipling's ending to the book has defied critical consensus. The choice returns to one of the great questions of statecraft, classically put forward by Polybius in the lineage of Thucydides. Must historians or other thinkers on strategy have experienced war or diplomacy in the field in order to pronounce credibly on it? The classical answer was yes, certainly; Churchill exemplified it in our time. Kim does as well; he will take the road of action, although he will temper it with the contemplative wisdom of the lama, whose influence will last throughout his life. On the last page, Kim is still the lama's chela and still an agent of the Raj.

The lama in *Kim* is the archetype of Tibet in the world's imagination: spiritual, otherworldy, a kind of human wildlife in need of protection. But the international state system recognizes Tibet as part of the People's Republic of China and as such disqualified from statehood. Within the People's Republic, Tibet supposedly possesses the rights of political autonomy and cultural-religious protections; in reality Beijing has despised Tibetan lamaism as feudal and congratulated itself on programs to eradicate it thoroughly. With world pressure on China in its Olympic year, "negotiations" between the PRC and Tibetan authorities began anew. In the literature of statecraft, the contradictions between the two sides are reminiscent of the last book of Virgil's *Aeneid*, when Juno intervenes with a solution for the future of Trojan relations with the Latins in Italy: the Trojans are accepted as overlords, but they must be subsumed by the culture they will rule. Under the *Aeneid*'s formula, Tibetans would keep the name Tibet, would maintain their language and their dress; in the union of China and Tibet, the former would be recessive in culture but dominant in power. All in all, perhaps less than the Tibetans already have on paper, but more than they have in reality.

Only a novel in English can encompass all Indian reality; books in one or another of the subcontinent's sundry languages, even Hindi, are bound to a regional part. When Kipling wrote *Kim*, incipient nationalist and religious movements were under way which would lead to the departure of the British in 1947 and the partition of the subcontinent into two states, which would enter the international system. Salman Rushdie would write a postindependence version of *Kim*.

Kim's heir is Salman Rushdie's *Midnight's Children*, a series of escapades exacerbating the problems of individual and national identity in a postmodern world, as well as a novel consciously self-placed in reference to the canon of English literature. The hero, Saleem Sinai, takes 129 pages to be born, a feat directly comparable to that of Laurence Sterne's Tristram

Shandy. Rushdie also set out to create an epic of modern South Asia in the lineage of classical Greece and Rome, by including a "descent into the Underworld" as the fulcrum on which the narrative swings.

An epic has to be about the forging of a nation through war as told by an extraordinary yet somehow representative hero. Saleem Sinai is born at the stroke of midnight August 15, 1947, the exact moment when the British Raj gave way to independence for the peoples of South Asia, partitioned between India as a predominantly Hindu state and the predominantly Muslim areas of Pakistan. A huge Muslim population remained resident in India, however, including baby Saleem. He was also one of "midnight's children," the "strangely literary" number of one thousand and one born in the hour after midnight. All were to have special talents and powers; those at the far end of the hour rather disreputably so, but Saleem—and his rival Shiva— born on the hour itself, heroes-to-be for Muslims and Hindus, respectively. Saleem's ability to look into the "hearts and minds" of the people is Whitmanesque: he comprehends and becomes one with the masses.

Saleem, like Sterne's Tristram, contains multitudes; all of the bizarre, delightful, brilliant, and scurrilous characters of the book are simultaneously present in Saleem. Like the picture of the sovereign in the frontispiece to Hobbes's *Leviathan,* Saleem's body seems to reflect, or even be made up of, the tiny figures of "the people." In Hobbes's social contract, the people ceded their rights to the sovereign in return for security for their lives and property. Rushdie's "body politic," embodied in Saleem, is in a search for the meaning of the concepts of sovereignty, state, and nationhood.

Saleem begins, as he moves toward adulthood, by identifying, though a Muslim, "with the state that Nehru and the Congress Party wrested from the British."[39] But Saleem's family moves to Pakistan, "The Land of the Pure." While they should feel more "at home" in the thoroughly Muslim state, Saleem is tugged in different directions. The existence of the state border interferes with his telepathic contacts with others in the midnight's children contingent. He broods over the fact that he has "invaded" Pakistan from "the wrong direction"; all the great Muslim conquerors of history came down from the northeast. And he laments that "I never forgave Karachi for not being Bombay." On the other hand, his family contacts give him access, even as a boy, to high military circles. As General Zulfikar describes how the army will take charge of the new state, Saleem moves pepper pots around the family table to demonstrate revolutionary operations.

When the Indo-Pakistan War breaks out in 1965, Saleem feels that its entire purpose is "to eliminate my benighted family from the face of the earth." Six years later a greater war opens and Saleem is swept up in it. East Pakistan—the "other wing" of the country, separated from Pakistan proper by the huge bulk of India—begins to move toward secession and its own independent statehood as "Bangladesh." Saleem, now in the Pakistan army as a tracker with a canine unit, is sent to the East as part of Pakistan's effort to put down the separatists. The Indian Army intervenes. Saleem and his unit flee into a "dream forest," this epic's version of the Underworld of Odysseus or Aeneas. There he is struck in the heel by a serpent, is embraced by "daughters of the forest," comes upon a monumental Hindu temple, and becomes translucent or transparent. The reader recalls Emerson becoming a "transparent eyeball." Once again, Saleem encompasses all South Asian humanity. His Underworld experience is not so much a rebirth as a reconception, enabling him to return to India.

The war has reconceived South Asia as well. India is the winner. Pakistan will turn ever more Islamist. East Pakistan enters the international state system as Bangladesh. The United States "tilts" toward Pakistan, whose regime arranges for Henry Kissinger secretly to fly to Beijing to "open" China. Pakistan turns to the People's Republic of China for patronage, and India seeks the support of the Soviet Union. Saleem has been the epicenter of tectonic shifts in world affairs.

Saleem's project is now "nation-saving," the redefinition of the nation. A nation validates itself by gaining international recognition as a state. But what was formerly one nation in South Asia has split into three states, none perhaps fully legitimate because their nation-to-state linkage is somehow problematic.

At the end, Saleem reencounters the rival of his midnight birth-moment Shiva, now a major and the most decorated hero in the Indian army. But the reader knows that Saleem the Muslim and Shiva the Hindu were switched at birth—another epic, fairy-tale, "changeling" touch—when the wrong tag was tied to Saleem's toe. The Muslim would have been brought up Hindu, the Hindu a Muslim. Yet Saleem is also of mixed parentage, his father the Englishman Methwold. *Midnight's Children* is an epic of a people's struggle to find a foothold when modernity and the international state system impose themselves on a non-Western culture.

Rushdie's *The Satanic Verses* caused book burnings, riots, and murders and aroused diplomatic, political, and religious tensions around the globe. The book was published in Britain in September 1988. In February 1989, shortly after the American edition appeared, Iran's Ayatollah Khomeini issued a *fatwa,* an Islamic legal teaching, calling for Rushdie to be killed. A reward of one and a half million dollars, later doubled, was posted for the author's assassin.

Salman Rushdie's novels, brilliantly witty, verbally exuberant, and deeply informed by layers of high culture and relevant intellectual history, denounce, mock, rage, and sneer at every political leadership, government, power, or authority the author has ever encountered. Rushdie's novels attack modern India, Pakistan, Britain, and the United States. Only in Marxist-Sandinista Nicaragua of the 1980s did he find a regime worthy of his praise.

The Satanic Verses brought this approach to a world-scale perspective. Rushdie's novel became a matter of state, even international, security. In it, the state as the international unit seems already to have been done away with, or—in the case of Britain—is far advanced in doing away with itself. The new, emerging source of world authority is religion, and Rushdie addresses it frontally. He does so in the context of a global scene that is postnational, disaggregated, even postethnic; everything is mixed, caught in a globalized maelstrom. Individuals search for a fixed point, for a center that will hold, even as they are on the move in a *Völkerwanderung:* a vast movement of peoples, signaling a time of far-reaching upheaval.[40] Above all, *The Satanic Verses* is about writing and power.

Gibreel Farishta, a living legend, the biggest star in the history of Indian movies, so evocatively portraying Hindu gods that fans have begun to see him as being one, boards Air India flight 420, *Bostan* (one of the perfumed gardens of Paradise). Also boarding is Mr. Saladin Chamcha, an expatriate, love-struck for all things English, returning to his adored London—although for him, the recent debasing of Englishness by the English is too painful to contemplate.

Chamcha, waking from a troubled sleep on flight 420, recognizes among his fellow passengers the woman of his dreams, walking calmly up and down the aisles of *Bostan.* The dream-woman is so loaded down with explosives that she is not so much a bomber as a bomb. The woman walking the aisles holds a baby that Chamcha sees as a bundle of dynamite sticks. He catches himself just on the verge of crying out in alarm.

Chamcha is drifting back to sleep when four armed, shouting figures come running down the aisles. The hijackers will hold the passengers on the seized aircraft for 111 days on a sheik's private desert airstrip at the oasis al-Zamzam.[41] One of the terrorists is a woman.

In order to prove to her captives, and also to her fellow-captors, that the idea of failure, or surrender, would never weaken her resolve, she emerged from her momentary retreat in the first-class cocktail lounge to stand before them like a stewardess demonstrating safety procedures. But instead of putting on a lifejacket and holding up a blow-tube whistle, etcetera, she quickly lifted the loose black djel-labah that was her only garment and stood before them stark naked, so that they could all see the arsenal of her body. The grenades like extra breasts nestling in her cleavage, the gelignite taped around her thighs, just the way it had been in Chamcha's dream. Then she slipped her robe back on and spoke in her faint oceanic voice. "When a great idea comes into the world, a great cause, certain crucial questions are asked of it," she murmured. "History asks us, what manner of cause are we? Are we uncompromising, absolute, strong, or will we show ourselves to be timeservers, who compromise, trim and yield?" Her body had provided her answer.

On the 110th day the hijackers conduct their first "sacrifice," shooting a passenger in the back of the head and pushing him out to fall on the tarmac. Their demands not met, they take off for London. "*Bostan* circled over England's shore like a gigantic seabird. Gull. Albatross. Fuel indicators dipped towards zero." Then the woman pulls "the wire that connected all the pins of all the grenades beneath her gown. . . . And the walls came tumbling down." So, "Just before dawn, one winter's morning, New Year's day or thereabouts, two real, full-grown living men fell from a great height, twenty-nine thousand and two feet, towards the English Channel, without benefit of parachutes or wings, out of a clear sky."

Mulciber in *Paradise Lost,* cast out of heaven, "Dropped from the zenith like a falling star" to become the Fallen Angel architect of Pande-monium. Gibreel (Gabriel) Farishta (angel) falls out of the sky to create pandemonium on earth in his own Muslim way.[42]

"To be born again," sings Gibreel Farishta, tumbling from the heavens, "first you have to die. Ho ji! Ho ji! To land upon the bosomy earth, first one needs to fly."

Both survive, and landing on a snow-covered English beach, memories, escapades, and metamorphoses begin. Gibreel becomes Gabriel the archangel. He will later become—or Salman Rushdie will appear as—the seventh-century Salman al-Farsi, Persian scribe and the first non-Arab convert to Islam. *The Satanic Verses* is significantly a Mughal (Persian-Indian Muslim) encounter with the Arabic empire of Islam.

Rushdie's novel is a text about the text of the Koran, and as Cervantes displayed every trick in the author's books to undermine the stability of the text of *Don Quixote,* Rushdie does the same to undermine the Koran, and his own novel as well. *The Satanic Verses* is the anti-Koran, offering in place of the sacred text's absolute certainty a rival narrative of doubt.[43]

An authoritative statement on the Koran declares it to be "a record of the exact words revealed by God through the Angel Gabriel to the Prophet Muhammad. It was memorized by Muhammad and then dictated to his companions and written down by scribes, who cross-checked it during his lifetime. Not one word of its 114 suras has been changed over the centuries."[44] Rushdie's novel sets out to undermine the authority of the Koran through three main episodes, all of which are presented as dreams or delusions: "The author could hardly have gone further on distancing [his book] from any pretensions to historical realism."[45]

First, the "satanic verses" of the title: In Rushdie's narrative, the Prophet's new revelation of the one and only God would ruin the exploitative tourist trade of Jahilia, the polytheistic center that would later become Mecca. When urged by greedy locals to incorporate verses referring to three pagan goddesses into the new faith so that their intercession would attract more pilgrims, the Prophet agrees. The verses are Satanic in origin and have to be expunged. In the Koran the temptation to incorporate the goddesses is firmly rejected, but as presented by Rushdie, the Prophet himself can be led to corrupt the authentic text.[46] Nothing could be more subversive of Islam than the acceptance of words that would negate its foundation stone of monotheism.

Second, the scribe Salman al-Farsi, whose name makes him the novelist's alter ego, begins in a seemingly trivial way to play games with the text, to substitute his own words for those of the Prophet:

Little things at first. If Mahound recited a verse in which God was described as all-hearing, all-knowing, I would write, all-knowing, all-wise.[47] Here's the point. Mahound did not notice the alterations. So there I was, actually writing the Book, or rewriting, anyway, polluting the word of God with my own profane language. . . . So the next time I changed a bigger thing. He said Christian, I wrote down Jew. He'd notice that, surely; how could he not? But when I read him the chapter he nodded and thanked me politely.

But the prophet does catch on: "Your blasphemy, Salman, can't be forgiven. Did you think I wouldn't work it out? To set your words against the words of God." About to be beheaded, Salman swears loyalty, begs, and makes an offer—to tell the Prophet who is his true enemy: Baal the poet-satirist. The Prophet lets Salman live.

Then begins the third episode, most blasphemous of all, the tale of the curtain (*Hijab*), the most popular brothel in Jahilia, where prostitutes take the names of the wives of the Prophet. There Baal is disguised as a djinn eunuch assigned to the harem, and writes his finest poetry. Soon the fiction becomes indistinguishable from the reality. The twelve whores no longer can recall their real names; all is disrupted.

Baal begins to sing his odes as the voice for all versifiers. He takes off his disguise and declares, "I recognize no jurisdiction except that of my muse; or, to be exact, my dozen muses." Guards seize him. Baal tells his story to the people, who are delighted. Sentenced to be beheaded, he shouts to the Prophet, "Whores and writers, Mahound. We are the people you can't forgive." Mahound replies, "Writers and whores. I see no difference here."

All this was a dream of Rushdie's fictional character Gibreel Farishta.

Across these literary works, in George Eliot, Charles Dickens, T. E. Lawrence, Muriel Spark, is the theme of split identity, even of the fragmented self, and of the search for wholeness. *The Satanic Verses* depicts a shift toward finding a way to live, exuberantly, within a multiple, disconnected, and impermanent context—even to reject unity or oneness-with-oneself.

As an Indian Muslim, lapsed from the faith, Rushdie derives his Islamic identity from the Persian-influenced Mughal Empire. His novel can be read as an intellectual rebellion against the Arab-centric empire of Islam, and the sole authority asserted by the "untranslatable" Arabic-language Koran. *The Satanic Verses* is, in volume, primarily a novel of *Völkerwanderung,* of migration, rootlessness, multiple identities and fractured entities, of post-modernity's shattering effect on traditional cultures and national bonds. Its emblematic character is Saladin Chamcha, the Britain-smitten Indian heartbroken in his realization that there won't "always be an England."

The disorienting effects of globalization have caused peoples to turn, in search of certainty, to traditional religion. To the absolute changeless and unchangeable authority of Islam. Rushdie, who in early books deconstructed cultures and states, here goes directly at the foundation stone of the faith, the impermeable Koran, and casts doubt on its messenger, its transmission, and its message. The writer will not put up with any authority. The only fixed point in the universe is the writer and the writer's "muse."

Shortly after the fatwa was issued, Rushdie, under the protection of state authorities, went into hiding from people for whom his death would be a divine mission. Nineteen years after the publication of *The Satanic Verses,* Britain conferred a knighthood upon him. He is now Sir Salman.

The Arab-Israeli conflict has emerged as only one dimension of a war against the international state system. The defenders of the international system are those states that are members of it in good standing, such as the Gulf States, Israel and Jordan, and those that seek to move in that direction, like Lebanon, Yemen, Egypt, and Iraq. Its enemies are oppressive regimes which have seized state power for their own enrichment and set themselves against the international state system. Saddam Hussein's Iraq was such a state until overthrown. Qaddafi's Libya was such an enemy too until recently. Most ideologically virulent are the nonstate, antistate Islamists, the jihadists who oppose and would overthrow and replace the international state system. The Middle East is the main battleground of this world-spanning confrontation. It has been, and is, a matter of moderation or passion in the best or worst forms of each of those qualities.

Throughout most of the modern age, the worry about the state has been its exaltation, even deification, in its ceaseless drive to expand its powers. After the Cold War, another assessment has pointed to globalization, electronic communications, migration, and the devolution of power downward along with the voluntary transfer of power upward—new and centrifugal forces, possibly heralding the end of the sovereign state. Yet the state, and the Westphalian international system of which it is the basic entity, remain the only working mechanism for world order.

9

THE WRITER AND THE STATE

The grave of Hermann Broch, in a cemetery in the pleasant southern Connecticut town of Killingworth, is a strange yet fitting symbol of a life in the ravaged twentieth century. The author of "one of the major literary works of the century," the "last great achievement of European literary modernism," Broch, born in Vienna in 1886 and at one time "a captain of industry," fled the Nazi rise in 1938.[1] Coming to the United States an impoverished outsider, he would search unsuccessfully for an academic place to continue his work until Henry Seidel Canby, a Yale professor and a founder of the *Saturday Review of Literature,* gave Broch a place at Yale and a room in Canby's Killingworth home. Broch's wanderings and troubles would be given a central place in Hannah Arendt's *Men in Dark Times.*[2]

The Death of Virgil is a tone poem, a "500-page psalm" about Virgil, dying of consumption on board the ship carrying the Emperor Augustus on his way to Rome in the year 19 B.C. As the ship comes into harbor at Brundisium, Virgil receives a strange command: "Burn the *Aeneid!*" The epic poem represents many things. Written, polished, and refined at the pace of one line a day for some twelve years, it is as close to aesthetic perfection as literary art can be. At the same time, it is not yet perfected, not yet finished; with Virgil's death it would never stand as he intended it to be.

The *Aeneid* is regarded as a paean to Augustus, an epic giving the new Roman order a genealogy of grandeur and legitimacy. The emperor and his Rome can take from the poem a sense of being at one with history and destiny. Yet the Aeneid, as some will read it, has its dark side, conveying that the founding of Rome, the republic, and the empire have all come at a vast human cost.

Does Virgil, the author, have a right to destroy his own poem? Or does the creation of a work of art provide humanity with a right to its existence?

All this takes place at a time of "no longer and not yet," when the old order, though still persisting, cannot continue as in the past, yet a new dispensation has yet to arrive—a time like Broch's and like our own.[3] Augustus appears, "standing palpably before [Virgil], a familiar sight with his slightly undersized figure, which although almost foppish succeeded in being very majestic, with his face still boyish beneath the already graying shortcut hair, and he said: 'As you did not feel like taking the trouble to come to me, I had to seek you out; I greet you on Italian soil.'"

They then engage in a dialogue in the Platonic style; Augustus speaks of the *Aeneid*'s lines about himself and the great turning point of the Battle of Actium. Virgil agrees with the emperor, "For that day at Actium marked the victory of the Roman spirit and its customs over the evil forces of the East, to whose dark secrets it had almost succumbed. This was your triumph, Augustus."

Augustus has been informed that Virgil intends to destroy his poem, and calls the act criminal. Virgil replies, "That which happens by the command of the gods cannot be criminal."

Augustus is entirely a man of the state. The *Aeneid,* to him, because of its greatness, is public property: "Even the work of art has to serve the needs of the people and, in so doing, of the state. . . . The state itself is a work of art in the hands of one who has to build it up."

Virgil disputes this: the state may be a work of art, but it has to remain open, unperfected. Poetry is otherwise, and must be kept by the poet until it reaches its consummation; better to destroy the work than to release it before it reaches perfection. The poetic work can be misused, can be used to obscure the truth, can deceive us into finding satisfaction in the aesthetic alone. "The emperor is impatient: You have interpreted Rome and therefore your work belongs to the Roman people and the Roman state which you serve, even as we all must serve it. Only what is unfinished remains our possession, perhaps also the failures and all those deeds which were un-successful; but what has actually been accomplished belongs to everyone, and to the whole world."

For the reader, who knows how much of the culture of Western civilization will derive from Virgil's "universal classic," the idea that it would not exist to be drawn upon raises the vision of an almost unrecognizable contemporary culture.[4] To burn the *Aeneid* would leave unborn much of the literature and civilization yet to come. A Virgilian shiver is felt.

The emperor and the poet go on, in an extensive exploration of art and statecraft. Which is more real, Rome the State of Augustus, or Rome the Poem of Virgil? Clearly Augustus has the power and the will simply to seize the manuscript. But he does not; more is at stake. Is Augustus arguing for the *Aeneid,* or for his own work?

> *Augustus:* No longer exists? No longer? You sound as though we were standing at the end of something. . . .
>
> *Virgil:* Perhaps it would be better to say, not yet! For we may assume that a time for artistic tasks will dawn again.
>
> *Augustus:* No longer and not yet . . . —and between them yawns an empty space.

They debate time, perception, power, the gods, architecture. Augustus delivers his greatest speech, saying "the state is the supreme reality" because it is where the intellectual and the physical meet to work through the highest questions of philosophy and existence.

Thus, says Virgil, the state is only a metaphor. Its genuine reality and real stature will be won only in the future.

> The Caesar wrapped himself in his toga: "I have placed my life at the service of my work, at the service of public welfare, at the service of the state. In doing so my sacrificial need found satisfaction enough. I recommend the same to you."
>
> What passed back and forth between them now amounted to nothing, just empty words, or not even words any more, racing across an empty space that was no longer even space. Everything was an unbelievable nothingness, cut off and bridgeless.

The two then flare up in a shouting match, each revealing emotions beyond statesman and poet. Suddenly Virgil says: "Octavian, accept the poem," a personal gift, an act of love to Augustus, not a tribute to the emperor. They then fall into bantering reminiscence, arguing like peasants over the color of a horse they once picked out together. Augustus accepts the *Aeneid* "only insofar as I am the advocate of the Roman people; others possess private property, not I, as you know."

Augustus becomes the state again. And Virgil, dying, becomes the poem: "Floating beyond the expressible as well as the inexpressible . . . he floated on with the word. . . . He could not hold fast to it and he might not hold fast to it: incomprehensible and unutterable for him: it was the word beyond speech." The reader now must consider why Broch did not contemplate burning *The Death of Virgil,* or perhaps he did.

Early on the dark, cold evening of January 12, 1986, Secretary of State George Shultz was escorted up the grand staircase between Patience and Fortitude, the famous inquiring lions of the New York Public Library. Shultz was greeted by Norman Mailer, then the president of PEN (Poets, Playwrights, Editors, Essayists, and Novelists). This was the first meeting of PEN International in the United States in twenty years; the topic was "How Does the State Imagine." "PEN's chief business," said the novelist Richard Stern, "is rescuing the world's writers from the political and social consequences of their work. The world is older than the state. Words form and reform states. Those who run states know the powers of words and attempt to control them. PEN, as much as any group, not only stands for the liberty of the word but does something about it. It gets international petitions to parliaments and heads of state. Frequently it helps to unlock prison doors."

Shultz was surprised and pleased, if apprehensive, to have been invited to speak to the meeting. He surely had been asked, although it was never openly admitted, to represent "the state." In the library hall, a letter of protest against Shultz's presence was being handed out along with an article from the *Nation* by the novelist E. L. Doctorow, sneering at Shultz and asserting that the American chapter of PEN "has put itself in the position of a bunch of obedient hacks in the writers' union of an Eastern European country gathering to be patted on the head by the Minister of Culture." The American secretary of state was being equated by an American writer with a Cold War Communist-bloc commissar. As Shultz rose to speak, protesters all over the densely packed north wing reading room ostentatiously walked out.

Shultz began with a lighthearted salute to the gathering for having invited him as a decision in favor of free speech. Grace Paley jumped up to shout that the petition against his presence be read aloud from the podium. Shultz persevered. He praised

the creative literary writer as an individual of primary importance for the entire range of thought, culture, and human existence. . . . America is proud to have you here. Diversity, debate, contrast, argumentativeness, are what we as a people thrive on. . . . Freedom—that is what we are talking about and why we are here. And the writer is at the heart of freedom.

No government or ideological system has ever yet succeeded in stopping the writer. . . . There are countries in which writers know that if their art appears to threaten the political fortunes of their rulers, they may be silenced, imprisoned, or even killed. . . . By contrast, there are other countries—and I am proud to say that the United States is one of them—where writers can speak, write, and publish without political hindrance.

"So," Shultz concluded, as a kind of joking jab, "Don't be so surprised that Ronald Reagan and I are on your side."

The hall erupted in outrage. Mailer rose to speak. Hoots and catcalls. "Read the protest!" "Up yours!" Mailer shouted.

Shultz later noted the strange extent to which some writers "rebuked the open society's state while expressing both fear of and a thrilling attraction to the totalitarian state—even on artistic grounds." He quoted George Steiner's "haunting paradox" that "historical evidence goes a long way to suggest that great literature flourishes under political-social repression." But in an open society where everything can be said, "the writer is not, as Tolstoy proclaimed him to be, 'the alternative state.' . . . The censorship of the free and mass-market economies is wonderfully light. . . . But it corrodes, it trivializes."[5]

At a PEN panel the next day, January 13, 1986, John Updike gave a different view. Updike spoke of being born into "a tribe," the United States, with its Stars and Stripes and other national symbols. "I never see a blue mailbox without a spark of warmth and wonder and gratitude that this intricate and extensive service is maintained for my benefit," Updike said. "Now, what do these hollow blue monuments on street corners from here to Hawaii tell of how the state imagines? It desires, we must conclude, its citizens to be in touch with one another; the tribe seeks interconnection and consolidation."

Updike continued his genial approach to the state but concluded that "the writer's imagination and the imagination of the state have opposite tendencies and should keep a respectful distance from one another." Keep the mails operating and safeguard freedom of expression. For a writer, "this is plenty, and this is enough."

Looking back on that PEN panel, Updike found that his brief speech "sticks in my mind as an epitome of discomfort in its delivery."

> The audience—writers and workers in the literary vineyard, assembled from many countries but predominantly New Yorkers—seethed with barely suppressed anger. . . . What seemed fabulous to me was the goblin air of fevered indignation and reflexive anti-Americanism. . . . If, for most of those citizens present, the United States had proved to be a land of educational and economic opportunity, with almost unparalleled guarantees of free expression, there was, once my mouth shut, not a whiff of acknowledgement, let alone gratitude.

The question of the writer and the state hangs heavily over the twenty-first century. Alexandr Solzhenitsyn's *Gulag Archipelago,* as George Kennan said, was "the most powerful single indictment of a political regime ever to be levied in modern times." Solzhenitsyn, Mandelstam, Pasternak, and other writers in the time of Soviet totalitarianism may strive to enter the ranks of great literature, but their topic must be the repression that enveloped them. Post-Soviet Russia has produced little work of literary merit. Post-Maoist China has a vibrant literature, but the best work seems fixed on the outrages of authoritarian capitalism. As one survey concluded, "Authoritarian places nurture a class of recognized intellectuals whose utterances are both carefully listened to and strictly controlled. Democracies produce a cacophony, in which each voice complains that its own urgent message is being drowned in a sea of pap. . . . The cacophony is the lesser evil. Ideas should not be suppressed, but nor should they be worshipped."[6]

The Foreign Service of the United States trained me to be a close reader of communist texts, as one of the best ways available to fathom what was going on in the minds of those at the top of the Soviet Union and the People's

Republic of China. The speeches and "toasts" were prepared with utmost care, far more than even the multiple-drafted products of White House or State Department speechwriters. In the Kremlin, each sentence was numbered, and within each sentence the numbering sequence was refined. In this way "86.4" would take you directly to the point in question, should some member of the Politburo raise an issue of doctrine. All this was necessary in a culture where commissars and cadres—and Kremlinologists and Dragonologists—would scrutinize each text with the intensity of medieval scholastics searching for signs of ultimate meaning.

My brief second diplomatic career came at the invitation of the newly elected U.N. Secretary General Boutros Boutros-Ghali. As his "special counselor on policy," I was no longer an American diplomat but a member of the United Nations staff.

In preparing for the visit of Pope John Paul II to New York for the fiftieth anniversary of the United Nations, I read recent texts of the Vatican and Holy See and found them, unsurprisingly, characterized by excruciating care in setting out a comprehensive, coherent argument. Even a reader wholly at odds with Roman Catholicism would admire the way these documents attempt to cover all bases, anticipate objections, state fundamental principles with the utmost clarity, and set out a fully formed philosophy of religion and life.

The pope's most important address, to the Special Commemorative Session of the General Assembly of the Fiftieth Anniversary of the United Nations, was not printed in full by either the *New York Times* or the *Washington Post,* and their excerpts omitted some of the most intriguing and revealing references. Taken as a major statement at a symbolically important international occasion, the pope's speech, despite a lead editorial in the *Wall Street Journal,* was not closely analyzed.

John Paul II's theme stressed an unmistakable, if not specifically cited, reference to Immanuel Kant's definition of the Age of Enlightenment, our modern era. Kant declared, "Enlightenment is man's emergence from his self-incurred immaturity. . . . The motto of Enlightenment is therefore: *Sapere Aude!* Have courage to use your own understanding!"[7] John Paul replied directly: "It is one of the great paradoxes of our time that man, who began the period we call 'modernity' with a self-confident assertion of his 'coming of age' and 'autonomy,' approaches the end of the twentieth century fearful of himself, fearful of what he might be capable of, fearful for the future."[8]

At the United Nations, the world organization of states, the concept of the state, under fire, has been pointedly reaffirmed: "The foundation-stone [of human security] is and must remain the State," declared Boutros Boutros-Ghali in his first major document after taking office as secretary-general. "Respect for its fundamental sovereignty and integrity is crucial to any common international progress."[9] During the 1990s the sovereign nations of the world made more ringing assertions of the essentiality of the state than had been made for generations. Institutions in decline are often zealously guarded.

In this context, the appearance of the pope in New York to mark the fiftieth anniversary of the United Nations was remarkable, for the pope came there to reject the fundamental unit of the international state system. For any pope, especially since the unification of Italy in 1870, the state as the primary entity in world affairs is contrary to God's plan as set forth in centuries of church doctrine. John Paul II, addressing delegates of the world's states in the General Assembly of the United Nations, dismissed the concept of the state.[10] Stressing his awareness that he was addressing "the whole family of peoples living on the face of the earth," the pope offered a logic chain intended to stand on its own. Not until the end of his speech did he say "we Christians."

John Paul's argument stemmed from the quest for "freedom" around the world, a quest based on "universal rights" reflecting a "universal moral law" that was "written on the human heart." He then paid tribute to the United Nations for formulating, "barely three years after its establishment, the Universal Declaration of Human Rights which remains one of the highest expressions of the human conscience of our time." The universal moral law, the pope said, is a kind of "grammar" for the world's people. But "no similar international agreement has yet adequately addressed the rights of nations." This, he said, raises urgent questions about justice and freedom in the world today. The United Nations, John Paul seemed to be saying, really should be the world organization of nations, not of states.

This declaration of nations' rights, derived, like human rights, from a universal moral law, was astonishing. Nationalism had not been warmly received in the twentieth century. Toynbee called it the cause of modern wars, the most horrible of wars—"a struggle between nationalities equally blind, haphazard, and non-moral, but far more terrific, just because the virtue of self-government is to focus and utilize human energy so much more effectively than the irresponsible government it superseded."[11] Kenneth W. Thompson echoed Toynbee's sentiments: "Nationalism unites the self-sacrificial loyalty to a given nation-state with the frustrated aggression of the masses who seek through their nation to achieve the supremacy denied them as individuals in mass societies."[12]

Others see nationalism as a force on its way out in a world of supranational associations, a future world order "in which nationalism and the nation-state principle will have forfeited their absolute validity."[13] To some it is a European invention that will give way to new inventions, to others a world program from previous centuries that has little historical importance today.[14] Most imaginatively, it is viewed as numerous parts of a single global cultural network in local disguise.[15]

To clarify his position, John Paul stated his recognition that nationalism can take the unhealthy form of teaching contempt for other nations. Patriotism is fine, the pope said, for that is love of one's own country. He warned against extreme nationalism, which can give rise to new forms of totalitarianism. And religion, in the form of fundamentalism, can be dangerous. Despite these qualifications, the pope seemed very much at ease with the idea of the renaissance of the nation and therefore of nationalism. John Paul's profound distinction between *nation* and *state,* as the *Wall Street Journal* put it, offered "broad scope for reflection as we ponder over what kind of future world order will be most hospitable to freedom and democracy."[16] To take the pope's argument as contemporary political philosophy, we are being told that the nation, the old, often disparaged concept, must emerge once again to become perhaps the fundamental building block of world order—as a matter of universal moral law.

Is the nation to become the new "intelligible field" of political life? Are nations to be preferred as entities of coherent culture, language, history, and ethnicity? Was the pope correct in seeing the nation playing an increasingly crucial role as mediator and bearer of meaning for the individual adrift in an impersonal and frightening sea of globalization? And what of the United States and other multiethnic, multicultural states? Should its constituent cultures be transformed into "nations," with rights under universal moral law, a kind of twenty-first-century version of early-twentieth-century American states' rights?

Much of this seems far-fetched and obviously not feasible. But John Paul put down a major challenge to the established system. Must the state remain the fundamental building block of international order simply because there is no other concept or system in sight? Or has the pope given us the seeds of some other system?

The pope provided hints, lodged in sentences in the middle of a paragraph that the press did not include in its excerpts:

> I am reminded of the debate which took place at the Council of Constance in the fifteenth century, when the representative of the Academy of Krakow, headed by Pawel Wlodkowic, courageously defended the right of certain European peoples to existence and independence. Still better known is the discussion which went on in that same period at the University of Salamanca with regard to the peoples of the New World. And in our own century, how can I fail to mention the prophetic words of my predecessor, Pope Benedict XV, who in the midst of the First World War reminded everyone that "nations do not die," and invited them "to ponder with serene conscience the rights and the just aspirations of peoples" (To the Peoples at War and Their Leaders, 28 July 1915).

By referring to the Council of Constance, held from 1414 to 1418, John Paul offered a new base point for the start of the modern international era. Rather than the Treaty of Westphalia, which ended the Thirty Years' War in 1648 and is generally considered the incubator of the modern state system, Constance is where nations first were recognized, at a time when the previous world system of Latin-speaking Christendom had effectively come to an end.

In the recognition that the old order had ended but a new order had not yet been born, the chancellor of the University of Paris, with the oddly modern name of John Gerson, proposed the council as a way of returning to the conciliar foundations of the church. According to commentators, it was the University of Paris's established practice of categorizing its students by their place of origin that led to the practice at Constance of registering the leaders of the church as representatives of one of the five nations: Italy, France, Germany, England, and Spain.

The pope's reference to Constance calls forth a parallel with the present, when the bipolar Cold War system and the unipolar post–Cold War system are both gone, but their replacement has not yet been settled upon.[17] John Paul's address suggested that at least one major part of the new order should be a return to the United Nations as the kind of world organization envisioned a half-century ago.

In referring to the "discussion" at Salamanca—the debate between Bartolomé de las Casas and Juan Ginés de Sepúlveda in 1550, in which it was concluded that Native Americans possessed souls—John Paul II looked back to a world-transforming period, in which human rights and rights of nations were linked as part of the fundamental nature of human life on earth. The international system, the pope seemed to be saying, must rest on these conceptual foundations and, to the extent that it has not done so, it must return to this base point. "Nations do not die," he said, quoting his predecessor.

This address to the General Assembly was drafted with great care in order that its arguments might be accessible, and perhaps acceptable, to non-Christians. The pope was appealing to a transconfessional sense of universal human solidarity, to a "natural" quality of reason and plain sense. No scripture was cited, and John Paul did not "confess" to being a Christian himself until the very end of his address.

The question of the rights of nations, John Paul said, is an urgent one, with implications for justice and freedom today. It is also an ancient question that "has presented itself repeatedly to the conscience of humanity, and has also given rise to considerable ethnic and juridical reflection." Looked upon in this way, the papal speech, as the *Wall Street Journal* editorial writer said, provides a profound basis for searching reflection on the foundations of international order and interactions.

EPILOGUE:
TALLEYRAND AND EVERYTHING ELSE

Robert Calasso's *The Ruin of Kasch* is an attempted epic of literature and statecraft, a *summa* that touches upon much that is spread across the pages of this book: diplomacy, the state, and statecraft. The consensus of reviewers has been that there is "no take-away thesis," but this misses the logic chain of *Kasch.* Like Joyce's *Ulysses,* Calasso's *Kasch* is meant for a reader's lifetime of concentrated effort, so any clear-sounding line of thought extracted from it must be a distortion. Nevertheless, *Kasch* suggests that Westphalian structures have been hollowed out by the corrosive rationalism of modernity and that the example of Talleyrand, "the last man to know anything about ceremonies," holds the door open to renovating the foundations of world order. At a critical moment in world affairs, Talleyrand recognized one of those rare occasions when an idea can shape the fate of nations—the concept of "legitimacy," so severely damaged today.

The international world of states and their modern system is a literary realm; it is where the greatest issues of the human condition are played out. A sacral nature must infuse world order if it is to be legitimate. That order is not to be identified with a particular social system, but to be legitimate, the system at least must hint at the underlying divinely founded order. The modern Westphalian system was conceived when such was the case, but with the

Enlightenment's addition of secularism, science, reason, and democracy, the system increasingly spurned, then forgot, its legitimizing sources of authority. This is what John Paul II strove to convey at the United Nations' fiftieth anniversary. Revolutionary ideology radicalized secularism, science, and reason into the task of erasing original sin, of perfecting humanity— all requiring terror to create "the New Man." Modern efforts to create a sovereignty potent enough to fill the void produced the statist monstrosities of Stalin and Hitler. America became an empire but never gained the understanding to go with it. China is now on its own misguided course.

Kasch is a rewriting of, or addendum to, primal literature of statecraft: the *Rig Veda, The Classic of Mountains and Seas,* Frazer's *The Golden Bough,* anthropologists' tales of precivilizational rites in which "The King Must Die," illustrated in ancient Dar Fur, and in Calasso's hands a vast elaboration of T. S. Eliot's *The Waste Land.* The ruin of Kasch ends the rite; it is the origin of literature and the start of the state.

Italo Calvino said that *Kasch* is about two things: the first is Talleyrand; the second is everything else. Talleyrand is the key to comprehending the modern predicament because he was born in a cyclical ceremonial age and lived to stage-manage a linear experimental age. Sent into the church by his family because of a lame foot, Talleyrand rose to become a bishop under Louis XVI. When the French Revolution erupted, he proposed that the church's wealth be confiscated and, Calasso points out, was responsible for article 6 of the Rights of Man and the Citizen: each is equal to all others. Thus he grasped the great modern dilemma: how to describe and manage equality when equality does not exist in nature. When the guillotine fell too often and indiscriminately, Talleyrand fled to the United States, where, always a gifted accumulator of wealth, he dabbled in land speculation. In Connecticut, Talleyrand found the new American man, woodsmen and fishermen, indifferent to history and nature and not at all like his counterparts in Europe. Following the statesman's maxim to sense the course of change and work to bring it about as swiftly and smoothly as possible, Talleyrand helped Napoleon rise to power and became Bonaparte's foreign minister. "When he saw that the Emperor's conquests were doomed to failure, he plotted to restore the Bourbon monarchy; and at the Congress of Vienna, though the representative of a defeated country, he helped to draw a new map of Europe, based on the principle of legitimacy, which now became his own."[1]

"L'état, c'est moi," the Sun King had said. Calasso describes Talleyrand in 1814 as himself the state:

> At that moment all Europe seemed suspended from a single point—
> namely, his bedroom on the mezzanine of his palace on the rue
> Saint-Florentin. By then, Talleyrand was already the flotsam of three
> different tides: bishop of the ancien régime, sacrilegious drafter of
> revolutionary texts, minister of Napoleon. But no one dared to say
> this—and Alexander I slept in safety a few meters above him. Vi-
> trolles, who observed Talleyrand with blatant curiosity (though also
> with devotion, because he still sensed in him the presence of "myster-
> ies that the uninitiated can never penetrate"), notes: "It is difficult
> to form an idea of what the provisional government was. It was all
> contained in Monsieur de Talleyrand's bedroom, on the mezzanine
> of his palace. Some clerks who had been gathered under the direction
> of Dupont de Nemours, the last and best of the economists, made up
> the office staff, and Roux-Laborie was the assistant secretary-general.
> Monsieur de Talleyrand kept the room open to all his acquaintances,
> men and women, and the conversations of the many people who came
> and went were the real deliberations on the affairs of state. . . . All the
> cumbersome liturgy of power is here dissipated in continuous chatter,
> which is open to anyone who passes through. Yet sovereignty remains,
> like an intact crystal, even if now it is hidden under the many pillows
> of the Prince. It will be a long time before Europe sees it again in
> so bold a form—so close to aura and miasma, its primordial state.
> A few months later, at the Congress of Vienna, sovereignty already
> seemed corroded by a certain lack of inner substance. A morganatic
> kinship links the monarchs of the Congress of Vienna and the depu-
> ties of the Weimar Republic. And soon thousands of people will light
> torches in the Nuremburg stadium to summon from the darkness the
> vanished essence of sovereignty, before bathing it in blood to enliven
> its ghostly pallor.

Diplomacy, says Talleyrand, is a branch of theology. Talleyrand would
rise to consider himself one of the greatest of history's "theologian-diplomats,"
the highest form of the art because religion is required for "that duality of
consciousness that is the ineradicable mark of humanity." Only Talleyrand-
style diplomacy can comprehend and manage the statecraft of the interna-

tional system. This is because, as Calasso writes at the opening of *Kasch,* Talleyrand was the last man who understood ceremony. Every ceremonial event recapitulates—or should recapitulate—all the history of its subject. This is the message of Confucius's *Analects.* Protocol, the proper conduct of ceremony because it protects abandoned symbols, is the first literary genre.

All through *The Ruin of Kasch,* works of modern literature, art, philosophy, and political economy are turned over, taken apart and reassembled, placed in juxtaposition with one another to create novel patterns of understanding. The anamorphosis of the skull of Holbein's *The Ambassadors*—a message of silence from the two envoys—is linked by *Kasch* to the skull as inspiration for the silence of the Trappist order. "Glosses on Marx" makes up a major section of *Kasch;* Marx got it wrong, but he brilliantly recognized the modern power of production without limits for a world market, reintroducing the fate that the Enlightenment supposedly abolished. Calasso uses Walter Benjamin's *Arcades Project* to ally *Kasch* with a literary theme of the arcades of Paris:

> Benjamin's perceptive eye would have seen those mouths [arcades of Paris] as entrances to the Hades of the new world, *facilus descensus Averni.* "In ancient Greece, people knew of places that gave access to the Underworld. Our whole waking life is a land where at certain points we descend into the Underworld—a land full of scarcely visible places out of which dreams flow. During the day we pass by them, suspecting nothing; but once sleep comes, we quickly head back to them." In the day, the streets resemble consciousness; but at night the blackness of the arcades stands out, frighteningly.

The Underworld is located and described. Richelieu chose the spot, with his gift for finding the center of gravity. Here in the Palais-Royal you can hear, see, know everything. In Richelieu's time it was known as the Palais-Cardinal, then the Palais-Royal, then the Palais-Marchand, then the Palais-Egalité, then the Jardin de la Revolution, then once again the Palais-Royal. As Talleyrand spanned regimes, so did this place, which swarmed with ghosts, "a locus of rumors and 'profound idleness,' a universal storehouse, a promise of perpetual availability, a no-man's land where the police never set foot (such is the power of the Orleans), a park of the Son of Heaven, a *paradisus inversus,* a 'vast flesh-market.' A herald of the industrial phantasmagoria that Benjamin will find in the arcades."

And on into a catalogue of its denizens, like other great indexes of names, such as those recorded by Saint-Simon and Proust. "Any reader of the *Iliad* who is unwilling to linger over the list of ships' names is unlikely to be a good reader."

Literature is supreme because "the Word was willing to do anything and could cover anything." Writing is a sacrificial offering, and the play of sacrificial ceremony identical with the cosmos. This stands against Goethe's Faust, who will not accept that "In the beginning was the Word." No, Faust cries, "In the beginning was the Act!"; that is, modern revolution and its terror. Only literature can deal with the world market and universal history whose achievements and disasters reawaken "all the archaic categories"; only the word can heal the ravages of the Faustian modern age. Everything is a pageant, a mystery in this "unnameable present" which began, Calasso says, in 1945. So the call is for the theologian-diplomat, the comprador of ceremonies. The choice in each age, says *Kasch,* is between Talleyrand and terror.

Talleyrand's last negotiating table was his deathbed. "I'm afraid of only one thing," he said: "impropriety." He feared the impropriety of being denied church burial because of his immoral life (but it was, true to Machiavelli, a higher kind of *morality* because in the service of the state). He postponed his recantation until, at the last moment, he signed an *aide-mémoire:* "Charles-Maurice, Prince de Talleyrand," the name which had appeared at the bottom of the great treaties of the age.

> But when the document reached Rome, the Holy See deemed it insufficient. If Talleyrand had survived for a few more days, he would have had to undergo the humiliation of signing again—and of signing a far more stringent text. Now it was too late. . . . Yet the Church never publicized the fact that the Pope considered Talleyrand's recantation inadequate. For a long time, those pages remained on the desk of Gregory XVI among his most precious documents. Then they vanished. The maternal Vatican archives contain no trace of them.

Such is Calasso's intensely literary effort to salvage world order. Sir Lewis Namier, the relentlessly fact-based diplomatic historian, writing on the eve of the Second World War, saw something not dissimilar in Talleyrand, who saw at a critical moment in history "one of those rare occasions when an idea can shape the fate of nations," and so became "the apostle of *légitimité.*"[2]

* * *

Legitimacy in governance remains a concept too esoteric for mere politicians to grasp. Literature and the book may be required.

Henry Kissinger, who wondered at Mao's addiction to books, and George Shultz, who defended literature and the state in front of the cat-calling international assembly of writers, sat in a seminar room recently to consider a new phenomenon. As described by Kissinger:

> I put a proposition to you all: we have entered a time of total change in human consciousness of how people look at the world. Reading books requires you to form concepts, to train your mind to relationships. You have to come to grips with who you are. A leader needs these qualities. But now we learn from fragments of facts. A book is a large intellectual construction; you can't hold it all in mind easily or at once. You have to struggle mentally to internalize it. Now there is no need to internalize because each fact can instantly be called up again on the computer. There is no context, no motive. Information is not knowledge. People are not readers but researchers, they float on the surface. Churchill understood context. This new thinking erases context. It disaggregates everything. All this makes strategic thinking about world order nearly impossible to achieve.

The restoration of literature as a tutor for statecraft has been the aim of this book.

NOTES

1. CLASSICAL ORDERS

1. J. Peter Euben, *The Tragedy of Political Theory: The Road Not Taken* (Princeton: Princeton University Press, 1990). Also see J. Peter Euben, "Creatures of a Day: Thought and Action in Thucydides," in *Political Theory and Praxis: New Perspectives,* ed. Terrence Ball (Minneapolis: University of Minnesota Press, 1977), 28–56.

2. Simone Weil, "The *Iliad* or the Poem of Force," in *The Proper Study of Mankind: Essays on Western Classics,* ed. Quentin Anderson and Joseph Mazzeo, eds. (New York: St. Martin's, 1962), 3–29.

3. Siep Sturman, "The Voice of Thersites: Reflections on the Origin of the Idea of Equality," *Journal of the History of Ideas* 65 (April 2004): 171–189.

4. Seth Benardete, *Achilles and Hector: The Homeric Hero* (South Bend: St. Augustine's, 2005), 102.

5. Joseph B. Strayer, *On the Medieval Origins of the Modern State* (Princeton: Princeton University Press, 1970), 3.

6. Henry Sumner Maine, *Ancient Law* (London: Dent, 1917), 100.

7. Genesis 2:24.

8. Nowhere does Homer call the Greeks by that name: they are Achaeans,

Argives, Danaans, the names of different tribes. Those who later took the name of "Greeks" were too dispersed to feel a collective identity before the Trojan War. See Thucydides, *History of the Peloponnesian War.*

9. On the jury trial of Orestes, see Norma Thompson, *Unreasonable Doubt: An Ordinary Murder in New Haven* (Columbia: University of Missouri Press, 2006).

10. Note the rejections of this assertion by Hugh Lloyd-Jones: "The cliché we have heard repeated all our lives, that the Eumenides depict the transition from the vendetta to the rule of law, is utterly misleading"; *The Justice of Zeus* (Berkeley: University of California Press, 1971), 94–95. Professor Lloyd-Jones refers to evidence that the blood feud existed side by side with the administration of law by ancient regimes. This is a classicist's inability to understand the importance of untenable theories as presented by political philosophers or in literature.

11. See Daniel Hoffman, *Form and Fable in American Fiction* (Charlottesville: University Press of Virginia, 1994), 328.

12. Adda B. Bozeman, *Politics and Culture in International History* (Princeton: Princeton University Press, 1960), 81.

13. Amery to Wavell, July 24, 1946, Wavell to Amery, August 2, 1946. These documents are found in AMEL 2/3/13, Leo Emery Papers, Churchill Archives Centre, Cambridge. References provided by Kate Epstein, Ohio State University.

14. *The Works of John Ruskin,* ed. E. T. Cook and Alexander Wedderburn, 23: 163, quoted in Maurice Mather and Joseph William Hewitt, eds., *Xenophon's "Anabasis" Books I–IV* (Norman: University of Oklahoma Press, 1962), 23.

15. Simon Goldhill, *How to Stage Greek Tragedy Today* (Chicago: University of Chicago Press, 2007).

16. Jacob Howland, "Xenophon's Philosophic Odyssey: On the *Anabasis* and Plato's *Republic,*" *American Political Science Review* 94 (2000): 875–889.

17. Simon Hornblower, "This Was Decided (*edoxe tauta*): The Army as *Polis* in Xenophon's *Anabasis*—and Elsewhere," argues that other Greek (but not Roman) armies on campaign had a tendency to take the form of political entities. In *The Long March: Xenophon and the Ten Thousand,* ed. Robin Lane Fox (New Haven: Yale University Press, 2004), 243–263.

18. A. E. Housman, "Epitaph on an Army of Mercenaries," in *The New Oxford Book of English Verse,* ed. Helen Gardner (New York: Oxford University Press, 1972), 805.

19. Lord George Gordon Byron, *Childe Harold's Pilgrimage,* 4: 160; Percy Bysshe Shelley, *Works in Verse and Prose,* ed. Harry Buxton Forman (London: Reeves and Turner, 1880), 7: 44.

20. Mark Griffith, "What Does Aeneas Look Like?" *Classical Philology* 80 (1985): 309–319.

21. Robin Sowerby, ed., *Dryden's "Aeneid"* (Bristol: Bristol Classics, 1986), 65.

22. Charles Hill, "A Herculean Task: The Myth and Reality of Arab Terrorism," in *The Age of Terror,* ed. Strobe Talbott and Nayan Chanda (New York: Basic, 2001), 81–112.

23. Robert Seymour Conway, *Makers of Europe* (Cambridge: Harvard University Press, 1931).

24. Jonathan Sherman-Presser, "From Personal Relationship to Political Phenomenon." Yale College paper, October 26, 2002, unpublished.

2. CREATIVE DISORDER

1. Selma al-Radi, *The "Amiriya in Rada": The History and Restoration of a Sixteenth-Century Madrasa in the Yemen,* Oxford Studies in Islamic Art, vol. 13 (Oxford: Oxford University Press, 1997).

2. Erich Auerbach, *Dante: Poet of the Secular World,* trans. Ralph Manheim (New York: Review Books, 2001).

3. Ibid., 178.

4. For Gandhi's role playing see the introduction to Mary Gordon, *Joan of Arc* (New York: Viking Penguin, 2000).

5. Liah Greenfeld, *Nationalism: Five Roads to Modernity* (Cambridge: Harvard University Press, 1992), 91. See also Graham Robb, *The Discovery of France: A Historical Geography from the Revolution to the First World War* (New York: Norton, 2007); William Pfaff, *The Wrath of Nations* (New York: Simon and Schuster, 1993).

6. W. H. Auden, *Lectures on Shakespeare* (Princeton: Princeton University Press, 2000), 4.

7. Isaiah Berlin, *The Roots of Romanticism* (Princeton: Princeton University Press, 2001), 87.

8. Mark Twain, *Personal Recollections of Joan of Arc by the Sieur Louis de Conte* (New York: Harper and Brothers, 1896). See introduction vi–ix.

9. Ibid.

10. Ibid. See the afterword, by Susan K. Harris, 9–10.

11. Brian Tyson, *The Story of Shaw's Saint Joan* (Montreal: McGill-Queen's University Press, 1982), 16–17.

12. Susan Foister, Ashok Roy, and Martin Wyld, *Holbein's Ambassadors* (London: National Gallery, 1997), 13.

13. Ibid., 57: "The whole painting then may be read as a meditation on Dinteville's melancholy and misery, and of de Selve's despair at the condition of Europe. Standing on a floor which may allude to the cosmos, and placed between objects including astronomical instruments, perhaps arranged to simulate heaven and earth, and which certainly allude to a world of chaos, both men think of the brevity of life and their end, but also of the hope of the life to come."

14. For a postmodern interpretation, confused about the painting and about diplomacy in general, see Costos M. Constantinou, *On the Way to Diplomacy* (Minneapolis: University of Minnesota Press, 1996), 3–26.

15. Erich Auerbach, *Mimesis* (Princeton: Princeton University Press, 1953), 285–311.

16. See J. I. M. Stuart, introduction to Montaigne, *Essays,* trans. John Florio (New York: Modern Library, 1933), v.

17. Donald Frame, *Montaigne: A Biography* (New York: Brace and World, 1977), 146.

18. Heinrich Mann, *Young Henry of Navarre: A Novel,* trans. Eric Sutton (Woodstock, NY: Overlook, 2003), 300 ff.

19. Ralph Waldo Emerson, "Montaigne; or, The Skeptic," in *The Portable Emerson,* ed. Mark van Doren (New York: Viking, 1946), 13.

20. Bertrand De Jouvenel, *Sovereignty: An Inquiry into the Political Good* (Chicago: University of Chicago Press, 1957), 291–292.

21. Claude Rawson, *God, Gulliver, and Genocide: Barbarism and the European Imagination, 1492–1945* (New York: Oxford University Press, 2002), 21 ff.

22. Ian Watt, *Myths of Modern Individualism: Faust, Don Quixote, Don Juan, Robinson Crusoe* (Cambridge: Cambridge University Press, 1996), 54.

23. Donald Kuspit, "A Mighty Metaphor: The Analogy of Archeology and Psychoanalysis," in *Sigmund Freud and Art: His Personal Collection of Antiquities,* ed. L. Gamwell and R. Wells (Binghamton: State University of New York Press, 1989), 133–151.

24. Plato, *The Republic,* 8: 514–517; Yulia Ustinova, *Caves and the Ancient Greek Mind: Descending Underground in the Search for Ultimate Truth* (New York: Oxford University Press, 2009).

25. Carlos Fuentes, introduction to *Don Quixote,* trans. Tobias Smollet (New York: Noonday, 1986), xxii.

3. SOURCES OF MODERN WORLD ORDER

1. Paul Kennedy, "On the Thirty Years' War," unpublished paper, 2002.

2. Grotius, *De Jure Belli ac Pacis,* trans. Louise Loomis (New York: Black, 1949). See Corbett, introduction xvii–xx: "Strange as it seems to us, Grotius found his data not in his existing society of nations, but in the society of the men, gods, and peoples presented by Homer, Plato, Thucydides, Polybius, Livy, Plutarch, Cicero, Caesar, and Tacitus. . . . From these materials Grotius compiles a righteous guide for the rulers of states and the commanders of armies."

3. David Stacton, *People of the Book* (New York: Putnam, 1965), 69. He continues: "Grotius fell in a sumptuously bound paper splash beside his field cot. Mercy and justice are irreconcilable, the former a pragmatic thing and therefore subversive of order, though, true, without it no order could for long be maintained. Shoot whom? And for the matter of that, how many? It is customary to consider great men as being amoral. And so they are, but this does not mean they do not have principles. . . . He is neither good nor bad. He is merely that epitome of the nation which is strong enough to hand it back its orders. Whether he saves them or destroys them depends on them, not him, for no man ever imposed a will that was not wanted. The state is not a charismatic body. For the golden age, or for the nightmare, one needs always the act of one man."

4. Louis Auchincloss, *Richelieu* (New York: Viking, 1972), 192.

5. Stacton, *People of the Book,* 45, continues: "As a result, when he walked, France walked. When he sat, France sat. When he moved, France was moved. . . . Nobody liked him and he did not care. No more would a field care. It was impossible in his presence or out of it to see this star-spangled prince of darkness was only a feeble man with a bad cough. . . . He loomed as large as Lucifer, had the same plans, and fell just as majestically through all eternity."

6. Otto George von Simson, "Richelieu and Rubens: Reflections on the Art of Politics" in *The Image of Man: A "Review of Politics" Reader,* ed. M. A. Fitzsimons, Thomas T. McAvoy, and Frank O'Malley (South Bend: University of Notre Dame Press, 1959), 92.

7. The most vivid portrayal of the silent, fearsome political power of the éminence grise is the painting by Gerôme in the Boston Museum of Fine Arts. The scene is the palace of Cardinal Richelieu. The gaunt figure of the friar, utterly absorbed in his missal, is slowly descending the grand marble staircase. Coming up the steps is a crowd of richly dressed courtiers, each pausing to doff his hat

and make a sweeping reverential bow to the Capuchin and then, from the gallery above, looking back at him with expressions of awe and fear.

8. Jean Orieux, *Talleyrand: The Art of Survival,* trans. Patricia Wolf (New York: Knopf, 1974), 37.

9. Deborah Guth, *George Eliot and Schiller: Intertextuality and Cross-Cultural Discourse* (London: Ashgate, 2003), 112.

10. See the editor's introduction to *Schiller's "Wallenstein,"* ed. Max Winkler (New York: Macmillan, 1911).

11. C. V. Wedgwood, *A Coffin for King Charles: The Trial and Execution of Charles I* (New York: Time-Life, 1981), 68.

12. In his vast personal capacities, self-absorption, and sense of transnational vision, he recalls the portrayal of Alcibiades by Thucydides and Plato. In his ambition, individualism, flirtation with the demonic, to powers of the cosmos, he resembles Faust. (Schiller makes clear that astrology is a creation of man's mind which has credence only because man is frail enough to believe it.) Classic, romantic, and modern are all here.

13. Theodore K. Rabb, "At 27° to the Universe," *Times Literary Supplement,* December 6, 2002, 27.

14. William Lecky, *History of the Rise and Influence of the Spirit of Rationalism in Europe* (New York: Appleton, 1867), quoted by Adrian Wooldridge in *World Affairs,* Spring 2008, 48.

15. John Lukacs, *The Hitler of History* (New York: Knopf, 1997), 247n; Claudia Schmölders, *Hitler's Face: The Biography of an Image* (Philadelphia: University of Pennsylvania Press, 2006).

16. Grass's *Simplicissimus* is his novel *The Tin Drum.*

4. WHAT KIND OF STATE?

1. Leo Strauss, *The Political Philosophy of Hobbes: Its Basis and Genesis* (Chicago: University of Chicago Press, 1962), 110.

2. See James Boyd White, *When Words Lose Their Meaning* (Chicago: University of Chicago Press, 1983).

3. Horst Bredekamp, "Thomas Hobbes's Visual Strategies," in *The Cambridge Companion to Hobbes's Leviathan,* ed. Patricia Springborg (Cambridge University Press, 2007), 30.

4. Certainly Hobbes's social contract is a literary fiction. There never was a moment when "the people" decided to trade their rights for a sovereign's guarantee

of security. But the idea took hold, an example of the importance of untenable theories in international relations.

5. Cicero, *Pro Murena*. From A. J. N. Wilson, "On 'An Horatian Ode'" in *Andrew Marvell: Poems, A Casebook,* ed. Arthur Pollard (London: Macmillan, 1980), 179.

6. Ibid., 180.

7. The first English Horatian was Ben Jonson. Translators and imitators have included Pope, Kipling, and Auden, each emulating Horace's uncanny ability to meld the intimate moment with mighty, historic undertakings. Horace's *Odes* 1.14 enshrined the ancient image of "the ship of state" as a metaphor for all time.

8. The great Marc Antony does not appear in Horace's *Actium Ode.* Why not? Antony's presence, a man whose infatuation causes his lapses from classic Roman virtues, might be interpreted as the tale of the fall of one mighty figure through personal weakness rather than the general decline of the Roman people.

9. Frank Kermode, *The Classic: Literary Images of Permanence and Change* (New York: Viking, 1975), 31–32, 65–79.

10. "It is from [Cromwell's] own words well read," Thomas Carlyle later wrote, "that the world may first obtain some dim glimpse of the actual Cromwell, and see him darkly face to face." Peter Gaunt, *Oliver Cromwell* (New York: New York University Press, 2005), 13.

11. Oliver Cromwell's letter to the General Assembly of the Church of Scotland, August 3, 1640.

12. Antonia Fraser, *Cromwell: Our Chief of Men* (London: Weidenfeld and Nicolson, 1973), 213.

13. Linda Colley, *Britons: Forging the Nation* (New Haven: Yale University Press, 2005).

14. Cromwell, speech of January 22, 1655. See Maurice Ashley, ed., *Cromwell* (Englewood Cliffs, NJ: Prentice Hall, 1969), 17–18.

15. Marvell expurgated his Cromwell ode and other pro-Puritan pieces from his editions and went on to flourish in the Restoration.

16. Robert Thomas Fallon, *Milton in Government* (University Park: Penn State University Press, 1993), ix.

17. Sigfried Giedion, *Mechanization Takes Command* (New York: Oxford University Press, 1948).

18. Ephesians 6:11.

19. In the late 1630s Milton visited Italy, where in Florence he called upon the

elderly Galileo, who was still living under a form of "house arrest" for his heretical astronomical views. Galileo let Milton look through his telescopes.

20. In literary works across centuries, the changing portrayal of leaves reveals the religious character of the time. In a sermon at Yale's Battell Chapel in the late autumn of 2006 I tried to bring some of these images together. The warrior Glaukos in the *Iliad* depicts leaves as meaningless symbols of man's life in endless generational cycles. Virgil in the *Aeneid* writes of leaves as individuals; death is not so easily accepted as part of the natural cycle. Dante's leaves, in autumn, detach themselves by free will, and fall one by one. There is a progression across these texts from life's end as withered nothingness to life in possession of an eternal soul. But in twentieth-century literature, leaves as symbols have no souls. Ernest Hemingway saw "wet, dead leaves on the paving of the courtyard where the firing squad carried out its orders."

We are back to a world that is cyclical, meaningless, and dead, from *the* generation of leaves in the *Iliad* to Santayana's "You are like *a* generation of leaves." Robert Frost was even more bleak: "We think of the tree. . . . / The tree has no leaves and may never have them again . . . / But if it is destined to grow, / It can blame the limitless trait in the hearts of men."

What is this "limitless trait"? Man's innate drive to go wrong. In several of the works taken up here, the author finds the answer in his book, or *the* book: God as a book.

21. God foreknows but does not foreordain. Thus free will and choice exist.

22. Another threshold is crossed at this time. Milton's poem is the last epic. As Adam and Eve leave the garden, the *vertical* transactions between Heaven and earth—as with those angels going up and down Jacob's ladder—become the *horizontal* field of history. Literature moves from the epic to the novel, which will be as digressive and wandering as the steps taken by Adam and Eve when they leave Paradise and enter history. And the novel, of course, will be all about love and marriage and adultery and the travails of men and women.

23. Martin J. Evans, *Milton's Imperial Epic: Paradise Lost and the Discourse of Colonialism* (Ithaca, NY: Cornell University Press, 1996).

24. William C. Spengemann, *A New World of Words: Redefining Early American Literature* (New Haven: Yale University Press, 1994).

25. To track Milton's grand strategy, turn to American novels. Nathaniel Hawthorne's *The Scarlet Letter* is a sequel to *Paradise Lost* in New England: an American Eden, an American Adam, an American Eve, an American serpent. And an American consequence: little Pearl. And then perhaps F. Scott Fitzgerald's *This*

Side of Paradise and John Steinbeck's *East of Eden.* R. W. B. Lewis brought this idea together in *The American Adam.*

26. Edmund Wilson, *Letters on Literature and Politics 1912–1972* (New York: Farrar, Straus and Giroux, 1977), 265.

27. Quotation from Harold Bloom, editor's introduction to *Jonathan Swift's "Gulliver's Travels"* (New York: Chelsea House, 1986).

28. Lord Acton, *Cambridge Modern History* (Cambridge: Cambridge University Press, 1908), 5: 2.

29. Clifford Geertz, *Negara: The Theatre-State in Nineteenth-Century Bali* (Princeton: Princeton University Press, 1980).

30. James Boswell, *The Life of Samuel Johnson,* ed. R. W. Chapman (Oxford: Oxford University Press, 1998), 921.

31. "It was Temple . . . whose theories and experiences moulded Swift's ideas at this formative stage. Swift's early works abound with borrowings from Temple, and although many are ironic, they demonstrate clearly that it was through analyzing his patron's attitudes that Swift arrived at his own"; David Nokes, *Jonathan Swift: A Hypocrite Reversed* (New York: Oxford University Press, 1997), 17–18.

32. Rawson, *God, Gulliver, and Genocide.*

5. ENLIGHTENMENT

1. Kenneth Rexroth, *Classics Revisited* (New York: Avon, 1968), 249.

2. Elizabeth Horodowich, *Language and Statecraft in Early Modern Venice* (Cambridge: Cambridge University Press, 2008), 5.

3. Bozeman, *Politics and Culture in International History,* 468.

4. Although Montaigu was determined to sign all dispatches to Versailles himself, he was indifferent about dispatches to other ambassadors. See Madeleine B. Ellis, *Rousseau's Venetian Story: An Essay upon Art and Truth in "Les confessions"* (Baltimore: Johns Hopkins University Press, 1966), 83–84.

5. Maurice Cranston, *Jean-Jacques: The Early Life and Work of Jean-Jacques Rousseau, 1712–1754* (London: Lane, 1983), 179–180.

6. Horodowich, *Language and Statecraft in Early Modern Venice,* 201.

7. At a political science conference a few years ago, I heard a well-known professor, when Rousseau's "forced to be free" came up, reply, "Of course, you don't think Rousseau was serious about that, do you?" Among intellectuals, what one thinks of Rousseau seems to be a signpost for one's politics. Most regard him as a sublime cultural hero who gave the world a way to believe that human nature

is good, that people yearn to cast off their individual interests and merge in a collectivity, with equality and prosperity held in common. When, at a pleasant lunch on Chapel Street in New Haven, I argued to one of the great Rousseau scholars of our time that Rousseau's design had been used to impose the most odious totalitarian tyrannies in history, he replied with a sweet smile, "Yes. True. But if his ideas had been carried out in the proper spirit, wouldn't it be lovely?" For more on my side of this issue, see Robert Nisbet, "Rousseau and Totalitarianism," *Journal of Politics* 5 (1943): 93–114, and Louis Halle, *The Ideological Imagination* (London: Chatto and Windus, 1972), 30–41.

8. Peter Gay, lecture in Directed Studies, 1997, Yale University.

9. Immanuel Kant, *Perpetual Peace,* ed. Lewis White Beck (New York: Bobbs-Merrill, 1957). See the editor's introduction ix–xiv.

10. Some years ago, at another university, I was talking to a professor who had just completed an important book on Edward Gibbon's *Decline and Fall of the Roman Empire.* I remarked that Gibbon had made a statement about global warming when he mentioned the reindeer. My friend frowned. "There's no reindeer in Gibbon," he said. I pulled down his copy of volume 1 and read the passage to him: "The reindeer, that useful animal, from whom the savage of the north derives the best comforts of his dreary life, is of a constitution that supports, and even requires, the most intense cold. He is found on the rock of Spitzberg, within ten degrees of the Pole; he seems to delight in the snows of Lapland and Siberia; but at present he cannot subsist, much less multiply, in any country south of the Baltic. In the time of Caesar, the reindeer . . . was a native of the Hercynian forest, which then overshadowed a great part of Germany and Poland."

Gibbon was noting that the climate had warmed considerably in the past two millennia. Writing at about the same time as Gibbon, Immanuel Kant also noted the significance of the reindeer, but for a different reason. The reindeer is the starting point of the chain of argument that Kant will make on the questions of "Why are there wars?" and "How can we achieve peace?"

11. Immanuel Kant, *Political Writings,* ed. Hans Reiss, trans. D. B. Nisbet (Cambridge: Cambridge University Press, 1994), 310.

12. Ibid., 114.

13. The question was still alive in the twenty-first-century controversy over whether the European Union Constitution should refer to Christianity's place in Western (European) civilization.

14. G. M. Young, *Gibbon* (New York: Appleton, 1933), 93–94.

15. The choosing of an epic topic always is a mighty and perplexing business.

Milton wavered between King Arthur and Adam and Eve, choosing the latter. Gibbon was drawn to, of all things, the history of Switzerland, apparently discerning in it an epic of liberty. Fortunately for us, he changed his mind, and in his *Memoirs* he describes when, where, and how the idea came to him. He was suddenly struck by the visible evidence of the displacement of Roman grandeur by Christianity. The famous passage about this, as Claude Rawson has shown, was worked over many times by Gibbon, through many drafts until he captured just the tone he wanted: "It was at Rome, on the fifteenth of October, 1764, as I sat musing amidst the ruins of the Capitol while the barefooted Friars were singing Vespers in the Temple of Jupiter, that the idea of writing the decline and fall of the City first started to my mind." See Claude Rawson, "Musing on the Capitol: The Subject and Sources of Gibbon's 'Grave and Temperate Irony,'" a review of David Womersly's edition of *The Decline and Fall, Times Literary Supplement,* July 14, 1995, 3–5.

16. Leslie Stephen, *History of English Thought in the Eighteenth Century* (New York: Harcourt, Brace and World, 1962), 449.

17. Lewis P. Curtis, "Gibbon's Paradise Lost," in *The Age of Johnson: Essays Presented to Chauncey Brewster Tinker,* ed. Frederick W. Hilles (New Haven: Yale University Press, 1949), 79.

18. These sentiments are central to *The Decline and Fall.* Cicero's concept of right reason is found in the chapter on Roman Law, where Gibbon says that Cicero "labours to deduce from a celestial origin the wisdom and justice of the Roman constitution. The whole universe, according to his sublime hypothesis, forms one immense commonwealth; gods and men, who participate of the same essence, are members of the same community; reason prescribes the law of nature and nations; and all positive institutions, however modified by accident or custom, are drawn from the rule of right, which the Deity has inscribed on every virtuous mind."

19. Kenneth Setton, *Western Hostility to Islam, and Prophecies of Turkish Doom* (Philadelphia: American Philosophical Society, 1992), 55.

20. Gibbon and Washington Irving both used the archaic "Mahomet."

21. Bernard Lewis, *Islam and the West* (New York: Oxford University Press, 1993), 236.

22. G. E. von Grunebaum, "Islam: The Problem of Changing Perspective," in *The Transformation of the Roman World: Gibbon's Problem After Two Centuries,* ed. Lynn White (Berkeley: University of California Press, 1966), 167.

23. Johann Wolfgang von Goethe, *Selected Verse,* ed. David Luke (New York: Penguin, 1964), 233. "Talismane" is a hymn to the hundred names of Allah.

24. Ruth ApRoberts, *The Ancient Dialect: Thomas Carlyle and Comparative Religion* (Berkeley: University of California Press, 1988), 101.

25. Gustav Weil, *Mohammed der Prophet, sein Leben und seine Lehre* (Stuttgart: J. B. Metzler, 1843).

26. George Bush (1796–1859), a distant relative of President George W. Bush, wrote *The Life of Mohammed* in 1831. Not so much a biography as an abstract consideration of theology, the book is firmly Christian in its orientation, yet its author is clearly impressed by the Prophet's religious genius and worldly achievement.

27. Washington Irving, *Mahomet and His Successors,* ed. Henry A. Pochmann and E. N. Feltskog (Madison: University of Wisconsin Press, 1970), 190–199.

28. Fukuyama later seemed to recant his "end of history" thesis in a series of lectures at Yale, published as *America at the Crossroads: Democracy, Power, and the Neoconservative Legacy* (New Haven: Yale University Press, 2006).

6. AMERICA

1. James Boswell, *The Life of Samuel Johnson,* ed. R. W. Chapman (Oxford: Oxford University Press, 1998), 321.

2. Quoted in Lewis Hanke, *All Mankind Is One: A Study of the Disputation Between de Las Casas and de Sepulveda in 1550 on the Intellectual and Religious Capacity of the American Indians* (DeKalb: Northern Illinois University Press, 1974), 82.

3. Max Savelle, *The Origins of American Diplomacy: The International History of Angloamerica, 1492–1763* (New York: Macmillan, 1967), 195.

4. The ship's master orders the boatswain to summon all hands on deck; they are about to run aground. The boatswain does so, transmitting the master's order by providing his own details of expertise in handling a ship in distress. Then the passengers appear: Alonso, the king of Naples; his brother Sebastian; Alonso's son Ferdinand; Antonio, the usurper duke of Milan; and Gonzalo, their counselor. The grandees begin to instruct and bother the boatswain, who tells them to go below and get out of his way. This rejoinder raises hackles among the elite. The boatswain tells them to use their hierarchical authority over the forces of nature if they are so powerful. Furious, the aristocrats curse the mariner, "A pox o' your throat, you bawling, blasphemous incharitable dog!" The boatswain challenges them to work the ship even as he demonstrates that they possess none of the skills that he now employs: "Lay her a-hold, a-hold! Set her two courses; off to sea again; lay her

off." The once-powerful nobles continue to curse the boatswain, even though he is their only hope of avoiding shipwreck.

5. Joyce A. Rowe, *Equivocal Endings in Classic American Novels* (Cambridge: Cambridge University Press, 1987).

6. Harold Bloom, ed., *Daniel Defoe's "Robinson Crusoe"* (New York: Chelsea House, 1988), 12.

7. Michael Seidel, "Crusoe's Island Exile," in *Robinson Crusoe,* ed. Harold Bloom (New York: Chelsea House, 1988), 123–131.

8. William Rooson, *Daniel Defoe and Diplomacy* (Selinsgrove, PA: Susquehanna University Press, 1986), 34–40.

9. Remarkably, Karl Marx himself analyzes *Robinson Crusoe* in *Das Kapital:* "Our friend Robinson, having rescued a watch, ledger, and pen and ink from the wreck, commences like a true-born Briton, to keep a set of books. His stock-book contains a list of the objects of utility that belong to him, of the operations necessary for their production; and, lastly, of the labour time that definite quantities of those objects have, on an average, cost him"; trans. Samuel Moore and Edward Aveling (Chicago: Kerr, 1909), 1: 88–91.

10. Hendrik Spruyt, *The Sovereign State and Its Competitors* (Princeton: Princeton University Press, 1994), 151–189.

11. A shipboard rebellion led by the captive Cinqué took command of the *Amistad,* which was intercepted off Long Island by the *USS Washington.* A court case brought in New Haven reached the U.S. Supreme Court, where Justice Joseph Story, a fervent adherent of property rights, ruled that the mutinous slaves were not property and must be freed. The episode is commemorated in New Haven by a sculpture near the town green, and in the harbor by a replica of the *Amistad.*

12. Joseph Cardinal Ratzinger, *A Turning Point for Europe? The Church in the Modern World* (San Francisco: Ignatius, 1994), 49–53.

13. Adam I. P. Smith, "All Men," *Times Literary Supplement,* June 8, 2007, 9; David Armitage, *The Declaration of Independence: A Global History* (Washington: Howard University Press, 2007).

14. Carl J. Richard, *The Founders and the Classics: Greece, Rome, and the American Enlightenment* (Cambridge: Harvard University Press, 1994), 234.

15. Ibid., 128.

16. Ibid., 132.

17. Washington's message on private virtue and character would be echoed in King's 1963 "I Have a Dream" address. See also John Patrick Diggins, *Eugene O'Neill's America: Desire Under Democracy* (Chicago: University of Chicago Press,

2007), 6: "Neither the French philosopher [Rousseau] nor the American playwright [O'Neill] believed that the future of the United States depended on its political institutions."

18. Quotation from George Kateb, *Emerson and Self-Reliance* (Thousand Oaks, CA: Sage, 1995). Yale's Harold Bloom said "The Mind of Emerson Is the Mind of America." See *Times Literary Supplement,* July 21, 1995, 6.

19. Thoreau's neighbor Emerson, the owner of the woodlot on which Henry was putting up the house, had memorialized the battle of the Minute Men and Redcoats in a fiftieth-anniversary poem: "By the rude bridge that arch'd the flood, / Their flag to April's breeze unfurled, / There the embattled Farmers stood / And fired the shot heard round the world."

20. A revivalist assertion of *The Great Awakening,* quoted by Gordon S. Wood, "American Religion: The Great Retreat," *New York Review of Books,* June 8, 2006, 61.

21. Robert F. Sayre, *Thoreau and the American Indians* (Princeton: Princeton University Press, 1977), 60, 147–150.

22. Robert B. Richardson, *Henry Thoreau: A Life of the Mind* (Berkeley: University of California Press, 1986), 370.

23. Sean Wilentz, "Homegrown Terrorist," *New Republic,* October 24, 2005, 23–30.

24. Louis A. De Caro, *"Fire from the Midst of You": A Religious Life of John Brown* (New York: New York University Press, 2002), 235.

25. Edwin H. Cady, *Young Howells and John Brown: Episodes in a Radical Education* (Columbus: Ohio State University Press, 1985), 45.

26. Janet Kemper Beck, *Creating the Brown Legend: Emerson, Thoreau, Douglass, Child, and Higginson in Defense of the Raid on Harper's Ferry* (Jefferson, NC: McFarland, 2009), 164.

27. Quoted in Perry Miller, ed., *The American Transcendentalists: Their Prose and Poetry* (New York: Doubleday Anchor, 1957), 368–370.

28. For the quotation, see the translator's introduction to Alexis de Tocqueville, *Democracy in America,* trans. Harvey C Mansfield (Chicago: University of Chicago Press, 2000).

29. Roger Asselineau, "Nationalism and Internationalism in *Leaves of Grass,*" in *Critical Essays on Walt Whitman,* ed. James Woodress (Boston: G. K. Hall, 1983), 320–329. Asselineau is quoting from "On the Beach at Night Alone" in Walt Whitman, *Leaves of Grass,* ed. Michael Moon (New York: Norton, 2004), 218–219.

30. Walt Whitman, preface to *Leaves of Grass,* 1872 ed., in *Leaves of Grass and Other Writings,* ed. Michael Moon (New York: Norton, 1973), 648.

31. Donald Pease, *Visionary Compacts: American Renaissance Writing in Cultural Context* (Madison: University of Wisconsin Press, 1987), 126.

32. Lawrence Lipking, *The Life of the Poet: Beginning and Ending Poetic Careers* (Chicago: University of Chicago Press, 1981), 139.

33. My sense of Whitman goes back to my South Jersey boyhood when aged heads in the town conveyed that there had been a great poet who lived not so far away, in Camden. Later came the controversy over naming the new bridge across the Delaware River after Walt Whitman, which was done over complaints that he was a "dirty" poet. The bridge would end South Jersey's quiet, road-dusty, shore-lined peninsular life, one much like that of Whitman's Long Island *Paumanok.* In graduate school, my student job was to go to the Gotham Book Mart to scout out first editions for Sculley Bradley, whose 1965 critical edition of *Leaves of Grass* is still the established one. As with democracy and statecraft itself, Whitman never regarded *Leaves of Grass* as complete; the work of constant revisions and additions must go on until death. And the free verse means the subject is freedom, free first of all from the meter-making of English literature.

34. In a class at the University of Pennsylvania, Robert Spiller, the first great historian of American literature, told of questioning Carl Sandburg about his six-volume biography of Lincoln, which was a publishing phenomenon in midcentury America. Spiller was puzzled by the work, finding it unlike a scholarly work of biography. Sandburg brushed the remark away. "It's not a biography," he said, "it's a poem; a poem about a poet."

35. Daniel Mark Epstein, *Lincoln and Whitman: Parallel Lives in Civil War Washington* (New York: Ballantine, 2004), 14.

36. Ibid., 22.

37. Abraham Lincoln, *Speeches and Writings, 1832–1858* (New York: Library of America, 1989), 431; Duncan Faherty, *Remodeling the Nation: The Architecture of American Identity, 1776–1858* (Durham: University of New Hampshire Press, 2007), 1–7.

38. C. A. Bayly, *The Birth of the Modern World, 1780–1914* (London: Blackwell, 2004), 165.

39. Roger Thompson, "Ralph Waldo Emerson and the American *Kairos,*" in *Rhetoric and* Kairos: *Essays in History, Theory and Praxis,* ed. Phillip Sipiora and James S. Baumlin (Albany: State University of New York Press, 2002), 187, 197.

40. Harold Bloom, *The American Religion* (New York: Simon and Schuster, 1992).

41. This was coined by John Updike.

42. Allen Grossman, "The Poetics of Union in Whitman and Lincoln: An Inquiry Toward the Relationship of Art and Policy," in *The American Renaissance Reconsidered,* ed. Walter Benn Michaels and Donald E. Pease (Baltimore: Johns Hopkins University Press, 1985), 183–204.

43. Helen Vendler, *Invisible Listeners: Lyric Intimacy in Herbert, Whitman, and Ashbery* (Princeton: Princeton University Press, 2005), 56.

44. Quoted in Len Gougeon, "Emerson's Circle and the Crisis of the Civil War," in *Emersonian Circles,* ed. W. Mott and R. Burkholder (Rochester: University of Rochester Press, 1977), 29–51.

45. No less a personage than the great orator-parliamentarian Edmund Burke had described the vast cultural gap that had opened between Americans and Britons, comparing the globe-spanning dynamism of Yankee whalers to their sluggish British counterparts. There was no possibility, Burke argued, of holding such people under the British crown's power.

46. Richard Weaver, *The Southern Essays of Richard Weaver,* ed. George M. Curtis III and James J. Thompson, Jr. (Indianapolis: Liberty, 1987), 185, 235–236, 240.

47. Edmund Wilson, *Patriotic Gore* (New York: Oxford University Press, 1962), 164.

48. Lincoln had already given away this point in terms of international law when he declared a blockade of southern ports. This gave an internal rebellion the status of a conflict between two belligerent parties.

49. Quoted in Gougeon, "Emerson's Circle and the Crisis of the Civil War," 41.

50. John Wheeler-Bennett, "The Trent Affair: How the Prince Consort Saved the U.S.," in *A Wreath to Clio: Studies in British, American, and German Affairs* (New York: Macmillan, 1967), 110–127.

51. In Talleyrand's original: *"Surtout, pas trop de zèle"*—Above all, not too much zeal!

52. *Proceedings of the Massachusetts Historical Society, 1888* (Boston: Massachusetts Historical Society, 1888), 150.

53. Thomas A. Bailey, *A Diplomatic History of the American People* (New York: Appleton-Century-Crofts, 1995), 376.

54. Amy Dunagin, "Foundational Principles: Henry Adams and British Diplomacy in the American Civil War," unpublished paper, Yale College, 2005.

7. DISORDER AND WAR

1. Charles Dickens writes in *A Tale of Two Cities:* "The hangman, ever busy and ever worse than useless, was in constant requisition; now, stringing up long rows of miscellaneous criminals; now, hanging a housebreaker on Saturday who had been taken on Tuesday; now, burning people in the hand at Newgate by the dozen, and now burning pamphlets at the door of Westminster Hall, to-day taking the life of our atrocious murderer, and to-morrow of a wretched pilferer who had robbed a farmer's boy of sixpence."

2. Dickens writes: "It was the sign of the regeneration of the human race. It superseded the Cross. Models of it were worn on breasts from which the Cross was discarded, and it was bowed down to and believed in where the Cross was denied."

3. Simon Schama, *Citizens: A Chronicle of the French Revolution* (New York: Knopf, 1989), 579, 649.

4. Micheline R. Ishay, *Internationalism and Its Betrayal* (Minneapolis: University of Minnesota Press, 1995), 54.

5. George Rudé, ed., *Robespierre* (Englewood Cliffs, NJ: Prentice Hall, 1967), 198–199.

6. Quoted ibid., 199.

7. David P. Jordan, *The Revolutionary Career of Maximilien Robespierre* (New York: Free Press, 1985), 66.

8. Patrice Gueniffey, "Robespierre" in *A Critical Dictionary of the French Revolution,* ed. François Furet and Mona Ozouf (Cambridge: Harvard University Press, 1989), 312.

9. Quoted ibid., 304.

10. Marcel Aymé, *The Green Mare* (London: Bodley Head, 1955), 101.

11. Henry James's early novel *The American* is set within this international melodrama of brutal military-political power. *The American* portrays a guileless American's romantic adventure in a European swirl of high political drama that is beyond the innocent hero's New World powers of comprehension. It is high international drama seen from the individual perspective, from low to high. Bismarck's literary invention portrays the scene from the top down, with the great statesman manipulating and replotting the story as though its characters were figures in a dollhouse. See John Carlos Rowe, "The Politics of Innocence," in *At Emerson's Tomb: The Politics of Classic American Literature* (New York: Columbia University Press, 1997).

12. William L. Langer, "Bismarck as Dramatist," in *Studies in Diplomatic History and Historiography in Honor of G. P. Gooch,* ed. A. O. Sarkissian (London: Longmans, 1961).

13. Bismarck's later narrative of the events in Ems and Berlin in July 1870 were as imaginatively crafted in his memoirs as had been his rewriting of the telegram from Ems. A "statesman," Bismarck supposedly said, "can only listen carefully for an echo of the steps of God through world events and then seize the hem of His robe and walk a few steps with Him." This describes perfectly Bismarck's role in the matter of the Ems telegram.

14. Andrei Sinyavsky, *Soviet Civilization: A Cultural History* (New York: Arcade/Little, Brown, 1988), 5.

15. Cited in François Furet, *Marx and the French Revolution* (Chicago: University of Chicago Press, 1988), 82–84.

16. Peter Lancelot Mallios, "Reading *The Secret Agent* Now," in *Conrad in the Twenty-first Century,* ed. Carola Kaplan, Peter Mallios, and Andrea White (New York: Routledge, 2005), 155–172.

17. For a discussion of the rhetoric of capitalism in Conrad's work see Stephen Ross, *Conrad and Empire* (Columbia: University of Missouri Press, 2004), 155.

18. E. M. W. Tillyard, "The *Secret Agent* Reconsidered," in *Conrad: A Collection of Critical Essays,* ed. Marvin Mudrick (Englewood Cliffs, NJ: Prentice Hall, 1966), 105.

19. John Carey, *Pure Pleasure* (London: Faber and Faber, 2000), 13.

20. Mallios, "Reading *The Secret Agent* Now."

21. Emphasis added.

22. Henry A. Kissinger, *Diplomacy* (New York: Simon and Schuster, 1994), 258–259.

23. Lazar Fleischman, *Boris Pasternak: The Poet and His Politics* (Cambridge: Harvard University Press, 1990), 284.

24. Quoted ibid., 290.

25. American attention to the book continued into the next decade and was heightened by David Lean's extravagant film production of 1965. For years thereafter women would, when commenting on an attractive man, say, "he has eyes like Omar Sharif," the actor who played Yury Zhivago. The film's theme music, "Lara's Song," was heard at every high school prom. In the midst of the Vietnam War my language teacher insisted that I go with her to see *Doctor Zhivago,* then showing in Saigon's only movie theater. I agreed, and shivered through hours of watching vast wastes of snow in Siberia as the theater manager accompanied the projections

with ultrafrigid air-conditioning. Today, *Doctor Zhivago* seems wholly to have disappeared. No Yale freshman class I have asked has ever heard of Pasternak, the novel, or even the film.

26. Ronald Hingley, *The Russian Mind* (New York: Scribner's, 1977), 208–209.

27. Ibid., 213.

28. Ibid., 213.

29. Karl Marx, "On the Jewish Question," in *Selected Writings,* ed. Laurence H. Simon (Indianapolis: Hackett, 1994), 1–26.

30. Marx, "Toward a Critique of Hegel's *Philosophy of Right*" (1844) in *Selected Writings,* 28.

31. Hingley, *The Russian Mind,* 210.

32. Miriam H. Berlin, "Visit to Pasternak," *American Scholar* 52 (1983): 327–336.

33. Stephen Stepanchev, "Whitman in Russia," in *Walt Whitman and the World,* ed. Gay Wilson Allen and Ed Folsom (Iowa City: University of Iowa Press, 1995), 300–312.

34. Italo Calvino, *Why Read the Classics?* trans. Martin McLaughlin (New York: Pantheon, 1999), 180.

35. Stuart Hampshire, "As from a Lost Culture," *Encounter,* November 1958, 3, 129.

36. Sinyavsky, *Soviet Civilization,* 138.

37. V. I. Lenin, *The State and Revolution,* trans. Robert Service (New York: Penguin, 1992), 41–43.

38. Sinyavsky, *Soviet Civilization,* 190–225.

39. Mann's writing is flecked with glancing references, only slightly explained if at all, to great international events. His short novel *Death in Venice* begins, "On a spring afternoon in 19__, a year that for months glowered threateningly over our continent . . . " This was 1911, the year when the story was written, a time of diplomatic crisis which would move the world closer to war. Mann intended *The Magic Mountain* to be a companion piece to his novella, but the work grew to vast proportions. Published in 1924, it, like Proust's final volume, deals with how war came, from retrospective knowledge about what war brought.

40. Thomas Mann, "Extracts from Essays," in *Death in Venice,* ed. and trans. by Clayton Koelb (New York: Norton, 1994), 101.

41. Friedrich Nietzsche, *The Birth of Tragedy,* trans. Douglas Smith (Oxford University Press, 2000), 28.

42. Henry Hatfield, "The Magic Mountain," in *Thomas Mann's "Magic Mountain,"* ed. Harold Bloom (New York: Chelsea House, 1986), 97.

43. Hans Blumenberg, *The Legitimacy of the Modern Age,* trans. Robert M. Wallace (Cambridge: MIT Press, 1985).

44. The Islamist view of the state is similar to Naphta's.

45. Kenneth Weisinger, "Distant Oil Rigs and Other Erections," in *A Companion to Thomas Mann's The Magic Mountain,* ed. Stephen Dowden (Rochester, NY: Camden House, 1998), 177–220.

46. John Farrenkopf, *Prophets of Decline: Spengler on World History and Politics* (Baton Rouge: Louisiana State University Press, 2001), 112.

47. Helmut Koopman, "The Decline of the West and the Ascent of the East: Thomas Mann, the Joseph Novels and Spengler," in *Critical Essays on Thomas Mann,* ed. Inta M. Ezergailas (Boston: G. K. Hall, 1988), 238–266.

48. William C. Carter, *Marcel Proust* (New Haven: Yale University Press, 2000), 3, 50–51.

49. Malcolm Bowie, *Proust Among the Stars* (New York: Columbia University Press, 1998), 101, 105.

50. Milton Hindus, *A Reader's Guide to Marcel Proust* (Syracuse: Syracuse University Press, 2001), 13.

51. René Girard, "Deceit, Desire, and the Novel: Self and Other in Literary Structure," in *Marcel Proust's "Remembrance of Things Past,"* ed. Harold Bloom (New York: Chelsea House, 1987), 84–85.

52. Paul Eidelberg, *A Discourse on Statesmanship: The Design and Transformation of the American Polity* (Urbana: University of Illinois Press, 1974), 312–362.

53. Gaddis Smith, *Woodrow Wilson's Fourteen Points After 75 Years* (New York: Carnegie Council, 1993), 6.

54. Akira Iriye, *The Globalization of America, 1913–1945,* vol. 3 of *Cambridge History of Foreign Relations* (New York: Cambridge University Press, 1993).

55. Nathaniel Berman, "Modernism, Nationalism, and the Rhetoric of Reconstruction," *Yale Journal of Law and Humanities* 4 (1992): 351–380.

56. Mylae, in Sicily, was the site of the first sea battle of the Punic Wars, in 260 B.C. See Polybius, *History,* 1: 22–23.

57. Give. Sympathize. Control. Peace, Peace, Peace.

58. Berman, "Modernism, Nationalism, and the Rhetoric of Reconstruction."

59. Jahan Ramazans, "Modernist Bricolage, Postcolonial Hybridity," *Modernism/ Modernity* 13 (2006): 445–463.

60. Frederick R. Karl, *Franz Kafka: Representative Man* (New York: Ticknor and Fields, 1991), 261.

61. Ibid.

62. Martha Robert, *The Old and the New: From Don Quixote to Kafka* (Berkeley: University of California Press, 1977), 199.

63. Quoted in Robert W. Hill, Jr., *Tennyson's Poetry* (New York: Norton, 1971), 82n1.

64. E. J. Chiasson, "Tennyson's 'Ulysses': A Reinterpretation," *University of Toronto Quarterly* 23 (1953–1954): 402–409.

65. Matthew Connolly, ed., *The Selected Works of Cyril Connolly,* vol. 2, *The Two Natures* (London: Picador, 2002), 135.

66. Cyril Connolly, *The Unquiet Grave: A Word Cycle by Palinurus* (New York: Viking, 1957), 145–146.

8. THE IMPORTED STATE

1. Franz Kafka, *Shorter Works,* trans. Malcolm Pasley (London: Secker and Warburg, 1973), 1: 66.

2. This message, in the final paragraph of the tale, was deleted from the text by Kafka.

3. Maurice Collis, *Raffles* (London: Faber and Faber, 1966), 164.

4. Ibid., 177.

5. The outrageously imaginative, ribald novel *Flashman and the Dragon* (1985) by George McDonald Fraser, gives a feeling for the personal drama in this clash of systems.

6. I came across the novel when I first went to China in the 1960s. Thirty-four chapters were serialized in the *Tientsin Daily News;* Liu apparently wrote them to deadline, much as Dostoevsky wrote his novels. *The Travels of Lao Ts'an* was published in book form in 1925 with an introduction by Hu Shih, the most notable Chinese noncommunist intellectual of the twentieth century. Hu Shih's imprimatur gave the novel immediate standing. I have carried around the translated *Travels* on my own travels for decades. Its photographs of pavilions, *yamens,* and such village scenes as "women pounding clothes by the moat in Tsinan" give a vivid sense of what Lao Ts'an saw in his peregrinations around a China in ever-growing crisis. The translator's introduction gives a sense of the book's standing in the mid-twentieth century: "The literary merits of the book, its masterly use of the vernacular, and its descriptive power became recognized; it has now achieved a

secure place of honor among the novels of China. It is hardly possible to open one of the school anthologies published during the last twenty years without finding several excerpts included as models of style." See the translator's introduction to Liu T'ieh-yün (Liu E), *The Travels of Lao Ts'an,* trans. Harold Shadick (Ithaca, NY: Cornell University Press, 1952), xvii.

7. While writing *The Travels of Lao Ts'an,* Liu, through one of his numberless public schemes, ran afoul of the warlord (later to be president of the republic) Yüan Shih-k'ai. He was arrested and banished to Sinkiang Province in the far west. He died in 1909.

8. André Malraux, *Man's Fate,* trans. Haakon M. Chevalier (New York: Modern Library, 1934). Malraux became world famous as an intellectual and man of action in the 1920s. He explored, and looted, Angkor Wat. He denounced French colonialism in the Far East and elsewhere. He fought in the Spanish Civil War and in the French resistance to Hitler. When Charles de Gaulle returned to power in France in the late 1950s, Malraux was his close adviser, known to Americans when he escorted the *Mona Lisa* to Washington in 1963, where he also squired Jacqueline Kennedy around town. A self-promoter, Malraux nonetheless was legitimately close to authority in his many adventures. The French intellectual Raymond Aron called Malraux "one-third genius, one-third false, one-third incomprehensible."

9. Leo Bersani, *The Culture of Redemption* (Cambridge: Harvard University Press, 1990); Nathan A. Scott, Jr., *The Poetry of Civic Virtue: Eliot, Malraux, Auden* (Philadelphia: Fortress, 1976), 63–69.

10. Scott A. Boorman, *Protracted Game: A Wei-ch'i Interpretation of Maoist Revolutionary Strategy* (New York: Oxford University Press, 1969).

11. Lee Kuan Yew, *The Singapore Story* (Singapore: Prentice Hall, 1998), 1–10.

12. More immediate for me were the rowing boats on the racks of the Royal Hong Kong Yacht Club's Rowing Section boathouse on Middle Island near Repulse Bay on the China Sea side of Hong Kong's Victoria Island. They were heavy lap-straked fours and eights that had been evacuated from the old Shanghai Rowing Club on Soochow Creek just across from the Astor House Hotel with its once-famous Long Bar. We took out the eights and raced them on the Fourth of July, Oxford-Cambridge versus Harvard-Yale. I later noted that the earliest nineteenth-century prints of the Shanghai riverfront show, among the junks and merchant ships on the Huangpoo River, four- and eight-oared shells being raced.

13. Yomi Braester, *Witness Against History: Literature, Film, and Public Dis-*

course in Twentieth-Century China (Stanford: Stanford University Press, 2003), 207–208.

14. Braester, *Witness Against History,* 207–208.

15. Ibid., 12.

16. Quotation from David Kaufman, *George Eliot and Judaism,* trans. J. W. Ferrier (New York: Haskell House, 1970), 94. This is in contrast to Gotthold Ephraim Lessing's play *Nathan the Wise* (1779), a document of the age of Enlightenment, which placed German Jewry within a tolerant, progressive humanism.

17. Eitan Bar-Yoseph, *The Holy Land in English Culture, 1799–1917: Palestine and the Question of Orientalism* (Oxford: Oxford University Press, 2005), 223.

18. Irene Tucker, *A Portable State: The Novel, the Contract, and the Jews* (Chicago: University of Chicago Press, 2000), 121. George Steiner's anti-Zionist essay "Our Homeland, the Text" puts the written corpus above and at odds with the state and its landed location.

19. Angus Calder, introduction to T. E. Lawrence, *Seven Pillars of Wisdom* (Ware, Hertfordshire: Wordsworth, 2007): "*Seven Pillars of Wisdom* in its various forms straddles different genres—history, autobiography, travelogue and fiction. There is a lot to be said for reading it as a novel, for certainly there is much in it that is fictitious" (ix, xi). Also see Robert Irwin, "Ecstasy in the Desert: Betrayal in the 'Oxford Text' of T. E. Lawrence," *Times Literary Supplement,* April 2, 2004, 3.

20. Stephen E. Tabachnick, ed., *The Lawrence Puzzle* (Athens: University of Georgia, 1984), 115–123.

21. Charles McMoran Wilson, Lord Moran, *Churchill at War, 1940–1945* (New York: Carroll and Graf, 2002), 126.

22. Efraim Karsh and Inari Karsh, *Empires of the Sand: The Struggle for Mastery in the Middle East, 1789–1923* (Cambridge: Harvard University Press, 1999), 3.

23. T. E. Lawrence, *Secret Despatches from Arabia,* ed. M. Brown (London: Bellew, 1991), 72.

24. Karsh and Karsh, *Empires of the Sand,* 206, 228, 349–354.

25. Cited in A. W. Lawrence, ed., *T. E. Lawrence by His Friends* (Leipzig: Paul List, 1938), 132–133.

26. Lawrence's publisher pressed him to be consistent in the spelling of Arab names. He refused, saying Arabic was unsuited for any orderly practice: "I spell my names anyhow, to show what rot the systems are."

27. Calder, introduction to Lawrence, *Seven Pillars,* xvi.

28. "Leaves" are significant images in epic poetry from the *Iliad* onward. Milton's leaves "strow the ground" at Vallombrosa, the entrance to the Underworld.

29. This seems to be Lawrence imagining himself as Ezra, who led the Jews back from captivity in Babylon to Israel, a leader second only to Moses.

30. Louis Golding, *In the Steps of Moses* (Philadelphia: Jewish Publications Society, 1943), 490.

31. Waller Newall, "Moses Revealed," *New Republic,* October 17, 2005, 39–40.

32. Aaron Wildavsky, *Moses as a Political Leader* (Jerusalem: Shalem, 2005). See foreword by Yoram Hazony, xviii.

33. Wildavsky, *Moses as a Political Leader,* 174, 188.

34. Bozeman, *Politics and Culture in International History,* 359.

35. Abdeslam Maghraoui, "American Foreign Policy and Islamic Renewal," U.S. Institute of Peace, Washington, D.C., 164 (July 2006): 7.

36. Martin Gilbert, *Atlas of Russian History* (New York: Oxford University Press, 1993), 31.

37. Frank Kermode, *Puzzles and Epiphanies: Essays and Reviews, 1958–1961* (New York: Chilmark, 1962), 180–183.

38. Priya Satia, *Spies in Arabia: The Great War and the Cultural Foundations of Britain's Covert Empire in the Middle East* (New York: Oxford University Press, 2008), 115.

39. Neil Ten Kortenaar, *Self, Nation, Text in Salman Rushdie's Midnight's Children* (Montreal: McGill-Queen's University Press, 2004), 136.

40. Arnold J. Toynbee, *A Study of History* (Oxford: Oxford University Press, 1934), 1: 52–59.

41. The 111 days approximate the number of verses (114) in the Koran; Zamzam is the well at Mecca.

42. Mulciber is the Greek Hephaestus and the Roman Vulcan.

43. Malise Ruthven, *A Satanic Affair: Salman Rushdie and the Rage of Islam* (London: Chatto and Windus, 1990), 17.

44. Islamic Affairs Department, Embassy of Saudi Arabia, Washington, DC. Cervantes's description of the story of Don Quixote as received and recorded by Cide Hamete Benengeli and translated from the Arabic echoes the textual lineage of the Koran.

45. Ruthven, *A Satanic Affair,* 187.

46. Rushdie is telling an apocryphal story, oft repeated. See Phillip K. Hitti, *Islam: A Way of Life* (New York: Regency, 1987), 24.

47. Rushdie uses a medieval Christian name for the Prophet, an insulting term.

9. THE WRITER AND THE STATE

1. Quotations from Theodore Ziolkowski, *Hermann Broch* (New York: Columbia University Press, 1964), 33; Malcolm Bull, introduction to Hermann Broch, *The Death of Virgil,* trans. Jean Starr Untermeyer (New York: Penguin, 2000), x.

2. Hannah Arendt, *Men in Dark Times* (Harcourt, Brace and World, 1968), 111–152.

3. *Noch nicht, und doch schon.*

4. Theodore Ziolkowski, *Virgil and the Moderns* (Princeton: Princeton University Press, 1993), 203–239.

5. George P. Shultz, *Turmoil and Triumph* (New York: Scribner's, 1993), 697–698.

6. "Speaking Truth to Power: Solzhenitsyn's Example and the Failure of His Heirs," *Economist,* August 9, 2008, 9.

7. Immanuel Kant, *Political Writings,* 54.

8. Address of His Holiness Pope John Paul II to the Fiftieth General Assembly of the United Nations Organization, New York, October 5, 1995, 18. A similar reference and rebuttal to Kant's *Sapere Aude!* appeared in the works of Cardinal Joseph Ratzinger, later to become Pope Benedict XVI.

9. Boutros Boutros-Ghali, *An Agenda for Peace* (New York: United Nations, 1992), paragraph 17.

10. George Melloan, "John Paul's World Order Demotes the State," *Wall Street Journal,* October 9, 1995.

11. Arnold J. Toynbee, *Nationality and the War* (London: J. M. Dent, 1915).

12. Kenneth W. Thompson, *Institutions and Values in Politics and Diplomacy: Theory and Practice* (Baton Rouge: Louisiana State University Press, 1992), 89.

13. Peter Alter, *Nationalism* (London: Edward Arnold, 1989), 182.

14. Respectively, Elie Kedourie, *Nationalism* (London: Hutchinson, 1966), 9; and E. J. Hobsbawm, *Nations and Nationalism Since 1780: Programme, Myth, Reality* (Cambridge: Cambridge University Press, 1990), 181.

15. Frederick Buell, *National Culture and the New Global System* (Baltimore: Johns Hopkins University Press, 1994).

16. Melloan, "John Paul's World Order Demotes the State."

17. See "The Cold War as an International System," in Gordon A. Craig and Alexander I. George, *Force and Statecraft: Diplomatic Problems of Our Time* (New York: Oxford University Press, 1994).

EPILOGUE

1. Theodore Zeldin, "A Master Opportunist," *New York Times Sunday Book Review,* April 28, 1974.

2. Lewis Namier, *Vanished Supremacies* (London: Peregrine, 1962), 23.

BIBLIOGRAPHY

The Primary Texts section of this bibliography lists books, poems, and essays that are principal topics of discussion in the book, and the Secondary Sources listed have informed my work in a more general way. Specific citations of these works have been omitted from the endnotes of the book, but the reader can find the edition I have used for each text by consulting these lists.

PRIMARY TEXTS

Achebe, Chinua. *A Man of the People.* New York: Penguin, 2001.

Adams, Henry. *The Education of Henry Adams.* New York: Oxford University Press, 1999.

Aristotle. *Politics.* Trans. Benjamin Jowett. New York: Random House, 1941.

Broch, Hermann. *The Death of Virgil.* Trans. Jean Starr Untermeyer. New York: Penguin, 2000.

Calasso, Roberto. *The Ruin of Kasch.* Trans. William Weaver and Stephen Sartarelli. Cambridge: Harvard University Press, 1994.

Cervantes, *Don Quixote.* Trans. John Rutherford. Penguin, 2000.

Classic of Mountains and Seas (Shan Hai Jing). Trans. Anne Birrell. London: Penguin, 1999.

Conrad, Joseph. *The Secret Agent.* London: Penguin, 1990.

Dante. *Inferno.* Trans. Michael Palma. New York: Norton, 2002.

Defoe, Daniel. *Memoirs of a Cavalier; or, A Military Journal of the Wars in Germany and the Wars in England from the Year 1632 to the Year 1648.* Oxford: Oxford University Press, 1991.

———. *Robinson Crusoe.* New York: Norton, 1994.

Dickens, Charles. *A Tale of Two Cities.* Oxford: Oxford University Press, 1988.

Dostoevsky, Fyodor. *Demons.* Trans. Richard Pevear and Larissa Volokhonsky. New York: Vintage, 1994.

Eliot, George. *Daniel Deronda.* New York: Barnes and Noble, 2005.

Eliot, T. S. *The Waste Land and Other Poems.* New York: Harcourt, Brace, Jovanovich, 1962.

Gibbon, Edward. *The Decline and Fall of the Roman Empire.* New York: Modern Library, 2003.

Grass, Günter. *The Meeting at Telgte.* Trans. Ralph Manheim. New York: Harcourt, 1979.

Grimmelshausen, Hans Jakob Christoffel von. *The Adventures of Simplicissimus.* Trans. George Schulz-Behrend. Columbia, SC: Camden House, 1993.

Grotius. *De Jure Belli ac Pacis.* Trans. Louise Loomis. New York: Black, 1949.

Hamilton, Alexander, John Jay, and James Madison. *The Federalist Papers,* ed. Clinton Rossiter. New York: Mentor, 1961.

Hobbes, Thomas. *Leviathan.* New York: Penguin, 1968.

Homer. *Iliad.* Trans. Robert Fagles. New York: Penguin, 1991.

Huxley, Aldous. *Grey Eminence.* New York: Harper and Brothers, 1941.

Jian, Ma. *Beijing Coma.* Trans. Flora Drew. New York: Farrar, Straus and Giroux, 2008.

Kafka, Franz. *The Castle.* Trans. Anthea Bell. New York: Oxford University Press, 2009.

Kant, Immanuel. "Perpetual Peace." In *Kant: Political Writings.* Trans. H. B. Nisbet. Cambridge: Cambridge University Press, 1991. Pp. 99–130.

Kipling, Rudyard. *Kim.* Maire Ni Flathuin, ed. Ontario: Broadview, 2005.

Lawrence, T. E. *Seven Pillars of Wisdom.* New York: Penguin, 1962.

Lincoln, Abraham. *Speeches and Writings, 1832–1858.* New York: Library of America, 1989

Liu T'ieh-yün (Liu E), *The Travels of Lao Ts'an.* Trans. Harold Shadick. Ithaca, NY: Cornell University Press, 1952.

Locke, John. *Two Treatises of Government.* Ed. Peter Laslett. Cambridge: Cambridge University Press, 1990.

Mann, Golo. *Wallenstein: His Life Narrated.* Trans. Charles Kessler. London: Andre Deutsch, 1976.

Mann, Thomas. *The Magic Mountain.* Trans. John E. Woods. New York: Vintage Books, 1929.

———. *Stories of Three Decades.* Trans. H. T. Lowe-Porter. New York: Knopf, 1941.

Mao Tse-tung. *The Poems of Mao Tse-tung.* Trans. Willis Barnstone. New York: Harper and Row, 1972.

Marvell, Andrew. *The Poems of Andrew Marvell.* Nigel Smith, ed. London: Pearson Longman, 2003.

Milton, John. *Paradise Lost.* Ed. Alastair Fowler. 2d ed. New York: Addison Wesley Longman, 1998.

Montaigne, *Essays.* Trans. John Florio. New York: Modern Library, 1933.

O'Neill, Eugene. *Three Plays: Desire Under the Elms, Strange Interlude, Mourning Becomes Electra.* New York: Vintage, 1995.

Pasternak, Boris. *Doctor Zhivago.* Trans. Max Hayward and Matya Hariri. New York: Ballantine, 1981.

Proust, Marcel. *In Search of Lost Time.* Vol. 6, *Time Regained.* Trans. Andreas Mayor and Terence Kilmartin. New York: Modern Library, 2003.

Ralegh, Sir Walter. *Selected Writings.* New York: Penguin, 1986.

Rousseau, Jean-Jacques. *The Confessions.* Trans. J. M. Cohen. New York: Penguin, 1953.

Rushdie, Salman. *Midnight's Children.* New York: Penguin, 1991.

———. *The Satanic Verses.* New York: Picador, 1989.

Schiller, Friedrich. *Die Jungfrau von Orleans.* New York: Henry Holt, 1887.

———. *Maid of Orleans.* Trans. M-G. Maxwell. London: Walter Scott, 1882.

———. *"Mary Stuart" and "The Maid of Orleans."* Trans. Charles E. Passage. New York: Frederick Ungar, 1961.

———. *"Wallenstein" and "Mary Stuart."* Ed. Walter Hinderer. New York: Continuum, 1991.

Shakespeare, William. *King Henry VI, Part 1.* London: Arden, 2001.

———. *The Tempest.* London: Arden, 2001.

———. *Troilus and Cressida.* London: Methuen, 1982.

Shaw, George Bernard. *Saint Joan.* New York: Penguin, 1968.

Spark, Muriel. *The Mandelbaum Gate.* New York: Knopf, 1965.

Stacton, David. *People of the Book.* New York: Putnam, 1965.

Thoreau, Henry David. *Essays.* Ed. Lewis Hyde. New York: North Point, 2002.

———. "A Plea for Captain John Brown." In *Political Writings,* ed. Nancy L. Rosenblum. Cambridge: Cambridge University Press, 1996.

———. *"Walden" and "Civil Disobedience."* New York: Penguin, 1986.

Thucydides. *The Peloponnesian War.* Trans. Thomas Hobbes. Chicago: University of Chicago Press, 1989.

Tocqueville, Alexis de. *Democracy in America.* Ed. J. P. Mayer. Trans. George Lawrence. New York: Harper and Row, 1969.

Twain, Mark. *Adventures of Huckleberry Finn.* New York: Oxford University Press, 1999.

Updike, John. "How Does the Writer Imagine?" In *Odd Jobs.* New York: Knopf, 1991. 122–136.

Virgil. *Aeneid.* Trans. John Dryden. Penguin, 1997.

———. *Aeneid.* Trans. Allen Mandelbaum. Berkeley: University of California Press, 1982.

Whitman, Walt. *Leaves of Grass.* Ed. Michael Moon. New York: Norton, 2004.

Xenophon. *The Persian Expedition.* Trans. Rex Warner. London: Penguin, 1978.

SECONDARY SOURCES

Abulafia, David. *The Discovery of Mankind: Atlantic Encounters in the Age of Columbus.* New Haven: Yale University Press, 2008.

Adamson, Jane. *Troilus and Cressida.* Brighton, Sussex: Harvester, 1987.

Adler, Eve. *Vergil's Empire: Political Thought in the Aeneid.* New York: Rowman and Littlefield, 2003.

Ahmed, Akbar S. *Postmodernism and Islam: Predicament and Promise.* New York: Routledge, 1992.

Anand, Dibyesh. *Geopolitical Exotica: Tibet in Western Imagination.* Minneapolis: University of Minnesota Press, 2008.

Anderson, Benedict. *Imagined Communities: Reflection on the Origin and Spread of Nationalism.* London: Verso, 1991.

Anderson, Susan C. *Grass and Grimmelshausen: Günter Grass's "Das Treffen in Telgte" and "Rezeptionstheorie."* Columbia, SC: Camden House, 1987.

Arendt, Hannah. *Men in Dark Times.* New York: Harcourt, Brace and World, 1968.

———. *Reflections on Literature and Culture.* Ed. Susannah Young-ah Gottlieb. Stanford: Stanford University Press, 2007.

Armstrong, David. *Revolution and World Order: The Revolutionary State in International Society.* Oxford: Clarendon, 1993.

Arnold, T. W. *The Caliphate.* Oxford: Oxford University Press, 1924.

Ashe, Laura. *Fiction and History in England, 1066–1200.* Cambridge: Cambridge University Press, 2007.

Ashley, Maurice, ed. *Cromwell.* Englewood Cliffs, NJ: Prentice Hall, 1969.

Auchincloss, Louis. *Reading Henry James.* Minneapolis: University of Minnesota Press, 1975.

Auden, W. H. *New Year Letter.* London: Faber and Faber, 1941.

———. *Selected Poems.* Ed. Edward Mendelson. London: Faber and Faber, 1979.

Bacon, Francis. *The Essays.* London: Penguin, 1987.

Badie, Bertrand. *The Imported State: The Westernization of Political Order.* Stanford: Stanford University Press, 2000.

Bagby, Laurie M. Johnson. "Father of International Relations? Thucydides as a Model for the Twenty-First Century." In *Thucydides' Theory of International Relations,* ed. Lowell S. Gustafson, 17–41. Baton Rouge: Louisiana State University Press, 2000.

Bailyn, Bernard. *To Begin the World Anew: The Genius and Ambiguities of the American Founders.* New York: Vintage, 2004.

Bar, Shmuel, "Deterring Terrorists: What Israel Has Learned." *Policy Review,* no. 149 (2008): 29–42.

———. *Warrant for Terror: The Fatwas of Radical Islam and the Duty to Jihad.* New York: Rowman and Littlefield, 2006.

Bartelson, Jens. "The Trial of Judgment: A Note on Kant and the Paradoxes of Internationalism." *International Studies Quarterly* 29 (1995): 255–279.

Beck, Lewis White, ed. *Perpetual Peace.* New York: Bobbs-Merrill, 1957.

Beer, Gillian. "George Eliot: Daniel Deronda and the Idea of a Future Life." In *Darwin's Plots: Evolutionary Narrative in Darwin, George Eliot, and Nineteenth-Century Fiction,* 169–195. London: Ark, 1985.

Begley, Louis. *The Tremendous World I Have Inside My Head: Franz Kafka, a Biographical Essay.* New York: Atlas, 2008.

Belkin, Kristen Lohse. *Rubens.* London: Phaidon, 1998.

Benét, Stephen Vincent. *John Brown's Body.* New York: Rinehart, 1928.

Berkowitz, Peter. "The Ambiguities of Rawls's Influence." *Perspective on Politics* 4 (2006): 121–127.

Bernard, G. W. *The King's Reformation: Henry VIII and the Remaking of the English Church.* New Haven: Yale University Press, 2005.

Bernard, J. F. *Talleyrand.* New York: Putnam, 1973.

Bhabha, Homi. *The Location of Culture.* New York: Routledge, 1994.

Birch, Cyril, ed. *Anthology of Chinese Literature.* London: Penguin, 1967.

Blanning, Tim. *The Pursuit of Glory, Europe, 1648–1815.* New York: Viking, 2007.

Bloom, Allan. *Love and Friendship.* New York: Simon and Schuster, 1993.

Bloom, Harold, ed. *George Bernard Shaw's "Saint Joan."* New York: Chelsea House, 1987.

———, ed. *George Eliot.* New York: Chelsea House, 1986.

———, ed. *Michel de Montaigne.* New York: Chelsea House, 1987.

———, ed. *Rudyard Kipling's "Kim."* New York: Chelsea House, 1987.

Boar, Frederick S. "Joan of Arc in Shakespeare, Schiller, and Shaw." *Shakespeare Quarterly* 2 (1951): 34–45.

Bobbitt, Philip. *The Shield of Achilles: War, Peace, and the Course of History.* New York: Knopf, 2002.

Boehmer, Elleke. *Colonial and Postcolonial Literature: Migrant Metaphors.* New York: Oxford University Press, 2005.

Boesche, Roger. *Tocqueville's Road Map: Methodology, Liberalism, Revolution, and Despotism.* Lanham, MD: Lexington, 2006.

Booker, M. Keith. *Critical Essays on Salman Rushdie.* New York: G. K. Hall, 1999.

Boswell, James. *Life of Johnson.* Oxford: Oxford University Press, 1998.

Boutros-Ghali, Boutros. *Unvanquished.* New York: Random House, 1998.

Bowersock, G. W., John Clive, and Stephen R. Graubard, eds. *Edward Gibbon and the Decline and Fall of the Roman Empire.* Cambridge: Harvard University Press, 1977.

Bowra, C. M. *From Virgil to Milton.* New York: Macmillan, 1957.

Brann, Eva. *Homeric Moments.* Philadelphia: Paul Dry, 2002.

Brantlinger, Patrick. *Rule of Darkness: British Literature and Imperialism, 1830–1914.* Ithaca, NY: Cornell University Press, 1988.

Broch, Hermann. *Geist and Zeitgeist.* New York: Counterpoint, 2002.

Brown, L. Carl. *Religion and the State: The Muslim Approach to Politics.* New York: Columbia University Press, 2000.

Buchan, John. *Augustus.* London: Chatto and Windus, 1937.

———. *Greenmantle.* New York: Penguin, 1956.

Bull, Hedley, Benedict Kingsbury, and Adam Roberts, eds. *Hugh Grotius and International Relations.* Oxford: Clarendon, 1990.

Butler, E. M. *The Tyranny of Greece over Germany: A Study of the Influence*

Exercised by Greek Art and Poetry over the Great German Writers of the Eighteenth, Nineteenth, and Twentieth Centuries. Cambridge: Cambridge University Press, 1935.

Casanova, Pascale. *The World Republic of Letters.* Trans. M. B. DeBevoise. Cambridge: Harvard University Press, 2004.

Cassirer, Ernst. *The Myth of the State.* New Haven: Yale University Press, 1946.

Caws, Peter, ed. *The Causes of Quarrel: Peace, War, and Thomas Hobbes.* Boston: Beacon, 1989.

Charles I (John Gauden). *Eikon Basilike.* Peterborough, Ontario: Broadview, 2006.

Chew, Ernest C. T., and Edwin Lee, eds. *A History of Singapore.* Singapore: Oxford University Press, 1991.

Chou, Min-chih. *Hu Shih and Intellectual Choice in Modern China.* Ann Arbor: University of Michigan Press, 1984.

Clapham, Christopher. *Africa and the International System: The Politics of State Survival.* Cambridge: Cambridge University Press, 1996.

Clausewitz, Carl von. *On War.* Trans. Michael Howard and Peter Paret. New York: Knopf, 1993.

Clowes, Edith W. *"Doctor Zhivago": A Critical Companion.* Evanston: Northwestern University Press, 1995.

Cocking, J. M. *Proust.* Cambridge: Cambridge University Press, 1982.

Coetzee, J. M. "Diary of a Bad Year." *New York Review of Books,* July 19, 2007, 20.

Commager, Steele, ed. *Virgil: A Collection of Critical Essays.* Englewood Cliffs, NJ: Prentice Hall, 1966.

Connecticut Humanities Council. *The Amistad Incident: Four Perspectives.* Middletown, CT, 1982.

Conrad, Joseph. *Nostromo.* Oxford: Oxford University Press, 1995.

Conway, Robert Seymour. *New Studies of a Great Inheritance.* London: John Murray, 1921.

Coroneos, Con. *Space, Conrad, and Modernity.* New York: Oxford University Press, 2002.

Cragg, Kenneth. *The House of Islam.* Belmont, CA: Dickenson, 1969.

Creel, Herrlee G. *The Origins of Statecraft in China.* Vol. 1. Chicago: University of Chicago Press, 1970.

Crèvecoeur, Hector St. John de. *Letters from an American Farmer.* New York: Penguin, 1981.

Cronin, Richard. *Imagining India.* London: Macmillan, 1989.

Davenport, Guy. *Every Force Evolves a Form.* San Francisco: North Point, 1987.

Davie, Donald, and Angela Livingstone, eds. *Pasternak.* London: Macmillan, 1969.

Davies, Stevie. *Images of Kingship in "Paradise Lost": Milton's Politics and Christian Liberty.* Columbia: University of Missouri Press, 1983.

Dawson, Christopher. *The Dynamics of World History.* New York: Sheed and Ward, 1956.

Dowden, Stephen D., ed. *A Companion to Thomas Mann's "Magic Mountain."* Rochester, NY: Camden House, 2002.

Doyle, Michael W. "Kant, Liberal Legacies, and Foreign Affairs." *Philosophy and Public Affairs* 12 (1983): 205–235.

Drucker, Romy. "Spaces of Diplomacy in *The Mandelbaum Gate.*" Unpublished paper, Yale College, 2005.

Du Bois, W. E. B. *John Brown.* New York: Modern Library, 2001.

Dunn, Francis M. *Present Shock in Late Fifth-Century Greece.* Ann Arbor: University of Michigan Press, 2007.

Dyck, J. W. *Boris Pasternak.* New York: Twayne, 1972.

Eban, Abba. *Personal Witness: Israel Through My Eyes.* New York: Putnam, 1992.

Eco, Umberto. *On Literature.* Trans. Martin McLaughlin. New York: Harcourt, 2004.

Emerson, Ralph Waldo. "Montaigne; or, The Skeptic." In *The Portable Emerson,* ed. Mark van Doren, 488–512. New York: Viking, 1946.

Empson, William. *Milton's God.* London: Chatto and Windus, 1965.

Epstein, Daniel Mark. *Lincoln and Whitman: Parallel Lives in Civil War Washington.* New York: Ballantine, 2004.

Epstein, Joseph. "A Literary Education." *New Criterion,* June 2008, 12–13.

Erlich, Victor. *Pasternak: A Collection of Critical Essays.* Englewood Cliffs, NJ: Prentice Hall, 1978.

Fairbank, John King. *The Chinese World Order: Traditional China's Foreign Relations.* Cambridge: Harvard University Press, 1968.

Falk, Richard. "World Order After the Lebanon War." August 24, 2006. http://www.reformwatch.net/fitxers/203.pdf.

Fontana, Biancamaria. *Montaigne's Politics: Authority and Governance in the "Essais."* Princeton: Princeton University Press, 2008.

Forsyth, Neil. "Saint and Martyr: *Eikon Basilike.*" *Times Literary Supplement,* August 4, 2006, 23.

Foster, John Burt, Jr. "Nabokov on Malraux's *La Condition humaine:* A Franco-Russian Crisscross." In *Nabokov at Cornell,* ed. Gavriel Shapiro. Ithaca, NY: Cornell University Press, 2003.

Fowler, Elizabeth. "The Ship Adrift." In *"The Tempest" and Its Travels,* ed. Peter Hulme and William H. Sherman. Philadelphia: University of Pennsylvania Press, 2000.

Frank, Joseph. *Dostoevsky: The Mantle of the Prophet, 1871–1881.* Princeton: Princeton University Press, 2002.

Franklin, David. "The Importance of T. E. Lawrence." In *Against the Grain: The New Criterion on Art and Intellect at the End of the Twentieth Century,* ed. Hilton Kramer and Roger Kimball. Chicago: Ivan Dee, 1995.

Frazer, James George. *The Golden Bough.* Vol. 1, *The Magic Art and the Evolution of Kings.* New York: Macmillan, 1935.

Freeman, James A. *Milton and the Martial Muse: "Paradise Lost" and European Traditions of War.* Princeton: Princeton University Press, 1980.

Friede, Juan, and Benjamin Keen, eds. *Bartolomé de las Casas in History: Toward an Understanding of the Man and His Work.* DeKalb: Northern Illinois University Press, 1971.

Fukuyama, Francis. *State-Building: Governance and World Order in the Twenty-First Century.* Ithaca, NY: Cornell University Press, 2004.

Fussell, Edwin. *Lucifer in Harness: American Meter, Metaphor, and Diction.* Princeton: Princeton University Press, 1973.

Gikandi, Simon. *Reading Chinua Achebe.* London: James Currey, 1991.

Gilbert, Felix. *To the Farewell Address.* Princeton: Princeton University Press, 1961.

Goethe, Johann Wolfgang von. *Selected Verse,* ed. David Luke. New York: Penguin, 1964.

GoGwilt, Christopher. *The Invention of the West: Joseph Conrad and the Double-Mapping of Europe and Empire.* Stanford: Stanford University Press, 1995.

Gong, Gerritt. *The Standard of Civilization in International Society.* Oxford: Oxford University Press, 1984.

Gougeon, Len, and Joel Myerson, eds. *Emerson's Antislavery Writings.* New Haven: Yale University Press. 1995.

Grant, Damien. *Salman Rushdie.* Plymouth: Northcote House, 1999.

Greenaway, Peter. *Prospero's Books.* Filmscript. New York: Four Walls Eight Windows, 1991.

Grene, Nicholas. *Shakespeare's Serial History Plays.* Cambridge: Cambridge University Press, 2002.

Grieve-Carlson, Gary. "John Brown's Body and the Meaning of the Civil War." In *Stephen Vincent Benét: Essays on His Life and Work,* ed. David Garrett Izzo and Lincoln Ronkle. Jefferson, NC: McFarland, 2003.

Griffiths, F. T., and S. J. Rabinowitz. "*Dr. Zhivago* and the Tradition of National Epic." *Comparative Literature,* 32 (1980): 63–79.

Gustafson, Lowell S., ed. *Thucydides' Theory of International Relations: A Lasting Possession.* Baton Rouge: Louisiana State University Press, 2000.

Halkett, John. *Milton and the Idea of Matrimony.* New Haven: Yale University Press, 1970

Hall, John A., and G. John Ikenberry. *The State.* Minneapolis: University of Minnesota Press, 1989.

Halle, Louis. *Civilization and Foreign Policy.* New York: Harper and Brothers, 1952.

Halliday, Fred. *Revolution and World Politics: The Rise and Fall of the Sixth Great Power.* Durham: Duke University Press, 1999.

Hardman, John. *Robespierre.* London: Longman, 1999.

Harrison, James. *Salman Rushdie.* New York: Twayne, 1992.

Hart, Jeffrey. "Our Literature of Extremes." *Claremont Review of Books* 6, no. 2 (2006): 32.

Hecht, Anthony. *Melodies Unheard.* Baltimore: Johns Hopkins University Press, 2003.

Heilbut, Anthony. *Exiled in Paradise: German Refugee Artists and Intellectuals in America.* Boston: Beacon, 1984.

Held, David. *Political Theory and the Modern State.* Stanford: Stanford University Press, 1989.

Heller, Eric. *The Artist's Journey into the Interior.* New York: Random House, 1965.

Henrie, Mark C. "Thomas Pangle and the Problems of a Straussian Founding." *Modern Age,* Winter 1994, 128–138.

Herodotus. *The History.* Trans. David Grene. Chicago: University of Chicago Press, 1987.

Hironaka, Ann. *Neverending Wars: The International Community, Weak States, and the Perpetuation of Civil War.* Cambridge: Harvard University Press, 2005.

Holoch, Donald. "The Travels of Laocan: Allegorical Narrative." In *The Chinese Novel at the Turn of the Century,* ed. Milena Dolezelova Velingerova. Toronto: University of Toronto Press, 1980.

Howard, Michael. "Ethics and Power in International Policy." In *Herbert Butter-*

field: The Ethics of History and Politics, ed. Kenneth W. Thompson. Lanham, MD: University Press of America, 1980.

———. *The Invention of Peace: Reflections on War and International Order.* New Haven: Yale University Press, 2000.

Hsia, C. T. *A History of Modern Chinese Fiction.* New Haven: Yale University Press, 1961.

Hughes, Ted. *Shakespeare and the Goddess of Complete Being.* London: Faber and Faber, 1992.

Huizinga, Johan. *Men and Ideas: History, the Middle Ages, the Renaissance.* New York: Vintage, 1959.

Hyman, Stanley Edgar. "Henry Thoreau in Our Time." *Atlantic Monthly,* November 1946, 137–146.

Innes, C. L. *Chinua Achebe.* Cambridge: Cambridge University Press, 1990.

Innes, C. L., and Bernth Lindfors, eds. *Critical Perspectives on Chinua Achebe.* Washington, DC: Three Continents, 1978.

Izre'El, Shlomo. "The El-Amarna Letters from Canaan." *Interdisciplinary Bible Scholar* 1 (1979): 14–22.

James, Harold. *The Roman Predicament: How the Rules of International Order Create the Politics of Empire.* Princeton: Princeton University Press, 2006.

Johnson, W. R. *Darkness Visible: A Study of Virgil's "Aeneid."* Berkeley: University of California Press, 1976.

Johnston, Kenneth R. *The Hidden Wordsworth: Poet, Lover, Rebel, Spy.* New York: Norton, 1998.

Jones, Dorothy V. *Code of Peace: Ethics and Security in the World of the Warlord States.* Chicago: University of Chicago Press, 1991.

Jones, James. *The Merry Month of May.* New York: Delacorte, 1971.

Kafka, Franz. *Shorter Works.* Trans. Malcolm Pasley. Vol. 1. London: Secker and Warburg, 1973.

Kagan, Robert. *Dangerous Nation.* New York: Vintage, 2006.

Kahn, Victoria. "Machiavellian Rhetoric in *Paradise Lost.*" In *Rhetorical Invention and Religious Inquiry,* ed. Walter Jost and Wendy Olmstead, 223–253. New Haven: Yale University Press, 2000.

Kant, Immanuel. *Political Writings.* Ed. Hans Reiss. Trans. D. B. Nisbet. Cambridge: Cambridge University Press, 1994.

Keay, John. *Sowing the Wind: The Seeds of Conflict in the Middle East.* New York: Norton, 2003.

Kedourie, Elie. *The Chatham House Version and Other Middle-Eastern Studies.* Hanover, NH: University Press of New England, 1984.

Keens-Soper, Maurice. "The Practice of a States-system." *Studies in History and Politics* 2 (1981–1982), special issue, *Diplomatic Thought, 1648–1815:* 15–36.

Kelly, William P. *Plotting America's Past: Fenimore Cooper and "The Leatherstocking Tales."* Carbondale: Southern Illinois University Press, 1983.

Kennan, George F. *American Diplomacy, 1900–1950.* Chicago: University of Chicago Press, 1951.

———. *From Prague After Munich: Diplomatic Papers, 1938–1940.* Princeton: Princeton University Press, 1968.

Kennedy, Richard S. *The Window of Memory: The Literary Career of Thomas Wolfe.* Chapel Hill: University of North Carolina Press, 1962.

Kermode, Frank. *Shakespeare's Language.* New York: Farrar, Straus and Giroux, 2000.

———, ed. *Shakespeare's "The Tempest."* London: Methuen, 1954.

Kinbrough, Robert. *"Troilus and Cressida" and Its Setting.* Cambridge: Harvard University Press, 1964.

The Koran. Trans. N. J. Dawood. New York: Penguin, 1999.

Kupchan, Charles A. *The End of the American Era: U.S. Foreign Policy and the Geopolitics of the Twenty-First Century.* New York: Knopf, 2004.

La Feber, Walter. *The American Age: United States Foreign Policy at Home and Abroad Since 1750.* New York: Norton, 1989.

Lafont, Bertrand. "International Relations in the Ancient Near East: The Birth of a Complete Diplomatic System." *Diplomacy and Statecraft* 12 (2001): 39–57.

Landau, Jacob M. *The Politics of Pan Islam: Ideology and Organization.* Oxford: Oxford University Press, 1994.

Leatherbarrow, W. J. *Dostoevsky's "The Devils": A Critical Companion.* Evanston: Northwestern University Press, 1999.

Lepenies, Wolf. *The Seduction of Culture in German History.* Princeton: Princeton University Press, 2006.

Levin, Michael J. *Agents of Empire: Spanish Ambassadors in Sixteenth-Century Italy.* Ithaca, NY: Cornell University Press, 2005.

Lewis, Bernard. *The Shaping of the Modern Middle East.* Oxford: Oxford University Press, 1994.

Lewis, C. S. *A Preface to "Paradise Lost."* New York: Oxford University Press, 1961.

Lewis, R. W. B. *The American Adam.* Chicago: University of Chicago Press, 1955.

Lim, Walter S. H. *The Arts of Empire: The Poetics of Colonialism from Ralegh to Milton.* Newark: University of Delaware Press, 1998.

Liu, Lydia H. *The Clash of Empires: The Invention of China in Modern World Making.* Cambridge: Harvard University Press, 2004.

Livingstone, Angela. *Pasternak's "Doctor Zhivago."* Cambridge: Cambridge University Press, 1989.

Longfellow, Henry Wadsworth, trans. *Dante's Divine Comedy.* Boston: Houghton Mifflin, 1895.

Löns, Hermann. *Harm Wulf: A Peasant Chronicle.* New York: Minton, Balch, 1931.

Lughod, Janet Abu. *Before European Hegemony: The World System A.D. 1250–1350.* New York: Oxford University Press, 1989.

Lüthy, Herbert. "Montaigne, or the Art of Being Truthful." In *The Proper Study,* ed. Quentin Anderson and Joseph Mazzeo. New York: St Martin's, 1962.

Lützeler, Paul Michael. *Hermann Broch.* London: Quartet, 1987.

Machiavelli, Niccolò. *The Prince.* Trans. Harvey C. Mansfield, Jr. Chicago: University of Chicago Press, 1985.

MacIver, R. M. *The Modern State.* Oxford: Oxford University Press, 1926.

Maier, Pauline. *American Scripture: Making the Declaration of Independence.* New York: Vintage, 1997.

Makovsky, Michael. *Churchill's Promised Land: Zionism and Statecraft.* New Haven: Yale University Press, 2007.

Malia, Martin. *History's Locomotives: Revolutions and the Making of the Modern World.* New Haven: Yale University Press, 2006.

Manent, Pierre. *A World Beyond Politics? A Defense of the Nation-State.* Princeton: Princeton University Press, 2006.

Mann, Heinrich. *Young Henry of Navarre: A Novel.* Trans. Eric Sutton. Woodstock, NY: Overlook, 2003.

Mann, Thomas. "Extracts from Essays." In *Death in Venice,* ed. and trans. by Clayton Koelb. New York: Norton, 1994.

Maritain, Jacques. *Man and the State.* London: Hollis and Carter, 1954.

Martindale, Charles. *John Milton and the Transformation of Ancient Epic.* London: Croom Helm, 1986.

Marx, Karl. *Selected Writings.* Ed. Laurence H. Simon. Indianapolis: Hackett, 1994.

Maser, Werner. *Hitler's "Mein Kampf": An Analysis.* Trans. R. H. Barry. London: Faber and Faber, 1970.

McBratney, John. *Imperial Subjects, Imperial Space: Rudyard Kipling's Fiction of the Native-Born.* Columbus: Ohio State University Press, 2002.

McCullough, David. *John Adams.* New York: Simon and Schuster, 2001.

McDiarmid, Lucy. *Auden's Apologies for Poetry.* Princeton: Princeton University Press, 1990.

———. *Saving Civilization: Yeats, Eliot, and Auden Between the Wars.* Cambridge: Cambridge University Press, 1984.

McKenna, George. *The Puritan Origins of American Patriotism.* New Haven: Yale University Press, 2007.

McPherson, James. "Days of Wrath." *New York Review of Books,* May 12, 2005.

Mehring, Walter. *The Lost Library: The Autobiography of a Culture.* Trans. Richard Winston and Clara Winston. Indianapolis: Bobbs-Merrill, 1951.

Merli, Frank J. *The "Alabama," British Neutrality and the American Civil War.* Bloomington: Indiana University Press, 2004.

Meyers, Jeffrey. *The Wounded Spirit: A Study of "Seven Pillars of Wisdom."* London: Martin Brian and O'Keefe, 1973.

Miller, James E., Jr. *The American Quest for a Supreme Fiction: Whitman's Legacy in the Personal Epic.* Chicago: University of Chicago Press, 1979.

Morson, Gary Saul, ed. *Literature and History: Theoretical Problems and Russian Case Studies.* Stanford: Stanford University Press, 1986.

Mowat, Barbara A. "Knowing I Loved My Books": Reading *The Tempest* Intertextually." In *"The Tempest" and Its Travels,* ed. Peter Hulme and William H. Sherman. Philadelphia: University of Pennsylvania Press, 2000.

Munk, Linda. *The Devil's Mousetrap: Redemption and Colonial American Literature.* Oxford: Oxford University Press, 1997.

Nappa, Christian. *Reading After Actium: Virgil's "Georgias," Octavian, and Rome.* Ann Arbor: University of Michigan Press, 2005.

Nicholl, Charles. *The Creature in the Map: A Journey to El Dorado.* Chicago: University of Chicago Press, 1997.

Nicolson, Harold. *Peacemaking, 1919.* London: Constable, 1933.

Noll, Mark. *America's God.* New York: Oxford University Press, 2002.

North, John. *The Ambassador's Secret: Holbein and the World of the Renaissance.* London: Hambleton and London, 2002.

Okechukwu, Chinwe Christiana. *Achebe the Orator: The Art of Persuasion in Chinua Achebe's Novels.* Westport, CT: Greenwood, 2001.

O'Loughlin, Michael. *The Garlands of Repose: The Literary Celebration of Civic and*

Retired Leisure: The Traditions of Homer and Virgil, Horace, and Montaigne. Chicago: University of Chicago Press, 1978.

Osiander, Andreas. *Before the State: Systemic Political Change in the West from the Greeks to the French Revolution.* New York: Oxford University Press, 2007.

Pagden, Anthony. *European Encounters with the New World.* New Haven: Yale University Press, 1993.

Parkinson, R. N. *Edward Gibbon.* New York: Twayne, 1973.

Pearce, Roy Harvey. *Savagism and Civilization: A Study of the Indian and the American Mind.* Baltimore: Johns Hopkins University Press, 1953.

Pipes, Daniel. *The Rushdie Affair: The Novel, the Ayatollah, and the West.* New Delhi: Voice of India, 1990.

Pippin, Robert B. *Henry James and Modern Moral Life.* Cambridge: Cambridge University Press, 2000.

Plato. *Republic.* Trans. G. M. A. Grube. New York: Hacket, 1992.

———. *Republic.* Trans. R. E. Allen. New Haven: Yale University Press, 2006.

Plutarch, *Lives of the Noble Grecians and Romans.* Trans. John Dryden. Vol. 2. New York: Modern Library, 1992.

Pocock, J. G. A. "The Historiography of the *translatio imperii.*" In *Barbarism and Religion,* J. G. A. Pocock, vol. 3. Cambridge: Cambridge University Press, 2003.

Poggi, Gianfranco. *The State: Its Nature, Development, and Prospects.* Stanford: Stanford University Press, 1990.

Pollard, Arthur, ed. *Andrew Marvell: Poems, a Casebook.* London: Macmillan, 1980.

Price, Kenneth M. *To Walt Whitman, America.* Chapel Hill: University of North Carolina Press, 2004.

Pritchett, V. S. "Midnight's Children." In *Complete Collected Essays.* New York: Random House, 1991.

Prose, Francine. "Casting a Lifeline." Review of Ma Jian, *Beijing Coma. New York Review of Books,* June 26, 2008, 52.

Prud'homme, Richard. "Walden's Economy of Living." *Raritan* 20 (2001): 118–121.

Quint, David. *Cervantes's Novel of Modern Times: A New Reading of "Don Quixote."* Princeton: Princeton University Press, 2003.

Rainey, Lawrence. *The Annotated Waste Land, with Eliot's Contemporary Prose.* New Haven: Yale University Press, 2005.

Raubitschek, A. E. "The Speech of the Athenians at Sparta." In *The Speeches in Thucydides,* ed. Philip A. Stadter. Chapel Hill: University of North Carolina Press, 1973.

Reed, J. D. *Virgil's Gaze: Nation and Poetry in the Aeneid.* Princeton: Princeton University Press, 2007.

Rexroth, Kenneth. *More Classics Revisited.* New York: New Directions, 1989.

Reynolds, David S. *John Brown, Abolitionist.* New York: Knopf, 2005.

Richardson, R. C., ed. *Images of Oliver Cromwell: Essays for and by Roger Howell, Jr.* Manchester: Manchester University Press, 1993.

Rippy, J. Fred. *Latin America: A Modern History.* Ann Arbor: University of Michigan Press, 1968.

Roberts, Adam. "Revolutionary Challenges to the Anarchical Society of States." *Diplomacy and Statecraft* 5 (1994): 394–400.

Ronda, Bruce A. *Reading the Old Man: John Brown in American Culture.* Knoxville: University of Tennessee Press, 2008.

Rorty, Richard. *Contingency, Irony, and Solidarity.* Cambridge: Cambridge University Press, 1989.

Rose, Natalie. "The Englishmen of a Gentleman: Illegitimacy and Race in *Daniel Deronda.*" In *Troubled Legacies: Narrative and Inheritance,* ed. Allan Hepburn. Toronto: University of Toronto Press, 2007.

Rosecrance, Richard N., and Arthur A. Stein. *No More States?* Lanham, MD: Rowman and Littlefield, 2006.

Rousseau, Jean-Jacques. *The Basic Political Writings.* Trans. Donald A. Cress. Indianapolis: Hackett, 1987.

———. *Emile.* Trans. Barbara Foxley. New York: Dutton, 1957.

Rudova, Larissa. *Understanding Boris Pasternak.* Columbia: University of South Carolina Press, 1997.

Ruland, Richard, and Malcolm Bradbury. *From Puritanism to Postmodernism: A History of American Literature.* London: Routledge, 1991.

Saad-Ghorayeb, Amal. *Hizbu'lah: Politics and Religion.* London: Pluto, 2002.

Said, Edward. *Culture and Imperialism.* New York: Knopf, 1993.

Schama, Simon. "Mr. Europe: Peter Paul Rubens and the Universalist Ideal." *New Yorker,* April 28–May 5, 1997, 207–220.

Schlant, Ernestine. *Hermann Broch.* Chicago: University of Chicago Press, 1986.

Schmidt-Nowara, Christopher. *The Conquest of History: Spanish Colonialism and National Histories in the Nineteenth Century.* Pittsburgh: University of Pittsburgh Press, 2006.

Schroeder, Paul W. "A Papier-Maché Fortress." *National Interest,* Winter 2002, 125–132.

Schwartz, Benjamin. *In Search of Wealth and Power: Yen Fu and the West.* New York: Harper and Row, 1964.

Scott, H. M. *The Birth of a Great Power System, 1740–1815.* London: Pearson Longman, 2006.

Sharpe, Lesley. *Schiller and the Historical Character: Presentation and Interpretation in the Historiographical Works and in the Historical Dramas.* Oxford: Oxford University Press, 1982.

Sherwood, Roy. *The Court of Oliver Cromwell.* London: Croom Helm, 1977.

Simons, John D. *Friedrich Schiller.* Boston: Twayne, 1982.

Smigelskis, Daniel J. "Cultivating Deliberating: Mindfully Resourceful Innovation in and Through the *Federalist Papers.*" In *A Companion to Rhetoric and Rhetorical Criticism,* ed. Walter Jose and Wendy Olmstead. London: Blackwell, 2004.

Smith, Richard Norton. *Patriarch: George Washington and the New American Nation.* Boston: Houghton Mifflin, 1993.

Sofer, Sasson. "The Diplomat as Historical Actor." *Diplomacy and Statecraft* 12 (2001), 107–112.

Spender, Stephen. "Elbe Swans and Other Poets." *New York Review of Books,* June 1981, 35–36.

Spengler, Oswald. *The Decline of the West.* 2 vols. New York: Knopf, 1950.

Sprinker, Michael. *History and Ideology in Proust: "A la recherche du temps perdu" and the Third French Republic.* Cambridge: Cambridge University Press, 1994.

Stanislawski, Bartosz H., ed. "Para-States, Quasi-States, and Black Spots." *International Studies Review* 10 (2008): 366–396.

Stein, Arnold. "Milton's War in Heaven: An Extended Metaphor." *English Literary History* 18 (1951): 209–220.

Steiner, George. *Language and Silence: Essays on Language, Literature, and the Inhuman.* New York: Atheneum, 1976.

———. "Our Homeland, the Text." *Salmagundi* 66 (1985): 4–25.

Stephen, Leslie. *Hobbes.* London: Macmillan, 1904.

Stetkevych, Jaroslav. *Muhammad and the Golden Bough: Reconstructing Arabian Myth.* Bloomington: Indiana University Press, 1996.

Strachan, Hew. *The First World War.* New York: Viking, 2003.

Sun Tzu. *Art of War.* Trans. Samuel B. Griffith. Oxford: Clarendon, 1963.

Tagliacozzo, Eric. *Secret Trades, Porous Borders: Smuggling and States Along a Southeast Asian Frontier, 1865–1915.* New Haven: Yale University Press, 2005.

Taylor, Charles. *Modern Social Imaginaries.* Durham: Duke University Press, 2004.

Telhami, Shibley. "The Return of the State." *National Interest,* Summer 2006, 109–113.

Thomas, Carol G., and Craig Conant. *Citadel to City-State: The Transformation of Greece, 1200–700 B.C.E.* Bloomington: Indiana University Press, 1989.

Thompson, Norma. *Herodotus and the Origins of Political Community: Arion's Leap.* New Haven: Yale University Press, 1995.

———. *The Ship of State.* New Haven: Yale University Press, 2001.

Tilly, Charles, ed. *The Formation of National States in Western Europe.* Princeton: Princeton University Press, 1975.

Toulmin, Stephen. *Cosmopolis: The Hidden Agenda of Modernity.* Chicago: University of Chicago Press, 1992.

Trevor-Roper, H. R. *Historical Essays.* London: Macmillan, 1957.

Turner, Jack. "Performing Conscience: Thoreau, Political Action, and the Plea for John Brown." *Political Theory* 33,(2005): 448–471.

Twain, Mark. *Personal Recollections of Joan of Arc by the Sieur Louis de Conte.* New York: Harper and Brothers, 1896.

Vickery, John B., *The Literary Impact of the Golden Bough.* Princeton: Princeton University Press, 1975.

Viorst, Milton. *In the Shadow of the Prophet.* Boulder, CO: Westview, 2001.

Wang, David Der-wei. *Fin-de-siècle Splendor.* Stanford: Stanford University Press, 1997.

———. *The Monster That Is History: History, Violence, and Fictional Writing in Twentieth-Century China.* Berkeley: University of California Press, 2004.

Warner, Marina. *Joan of Arc: The Image of Female Heroism.* New York: Knopf, 1981.

Waterfield, Robin. *Xenophon's Retreat: Greece, Persia, and the End of the Golden Age.* Cambridge: Harvard University Press, 2006.

Wawro, Geoffrey. *The Franco-Prussian War: The German Conquest of France in 1870–1871.* Cambridge: Cambridge University Press, 2003.

Weigand, Herman. *Surveys and Soundings in European Literature.* Princeton: Princeton University Press, 1966.

Weil, Eric. *Hegel and the State.* Trans. Mark A. Cohen. Baltimore: Johns Hopkins University Press, 1998.

Weintraub, Stanley, and Rodelle Weintraub. *Lawrence of Arabia: The Literary Impulse.* Baton Rouge: Louisiana State University Press, 1975.

Wells, Lemuel A. *The History of the Regicides in New England.* New York: Grafton, 1937.

Westbrook, Raymond. *Amarna Diplomacy: The Beginnings of International Relations.* Baltimore: Johns Hopkins University Press, 1968.

Weston, Jessie L. *From Ritual to Romance.* Cambridge: Cambridge University Press, 1920.

Willey, Basil. *The Eighteenth-Century Background: Studies on the Idea of Nature in the Thought of the Period.* New York: Columbia University Press, 1953.

Wilson, A. J. N. "On 'An Horatian Ode.'" In Pollard, *Andrew Marvell.*

Winkler, Max, ed. *Schiller's "Wallenstein."* New York: Macmillan, 1911.

Wren, Robert M. *Achebe's World: The Historical and Cultural Context of the Novels of Chinua Achebe.* London: Longman, 1980.

Wright, Andrew. *Fictional Discourse and Historical Space.* London: Macmillan, 1987.

Wright, Robin. *The Last Great Revolution.* New York: Knopf, 2000.

Zeruneith, Keld. *The Wooden Horse: The Liberation of the Western Mind from Odysseus to Socrates.* Trans. Russell L. Dees. New York: Overlook Duckworth, 2007.

Ziolkowski, Theodore. "Historical Analogy." *New York Times Book Review,* May 17, 1981.

ACKNOWLEDGMENTS

My parents, who let me read in the sunroom even when guests came calling. Aunt Alice, always with a book in her hand, and Aunt Elsie with a stock-pile in her attic. The schoolteachers of Cumberland County, notably Mrs. Livingston, who taught Boswell's *Johnson* before the state commandeered the curriculum. Dr. Doherty, the peripatetic veterinarian who gave me *God and Man at Yale.* Tosh Hosoda, who drove us in his red Chevy pickup to the Philadelphia Free Public Library, where I read Daniel Defoe's *Journal of the Plague Year, 1665.* Mary Ann Gbur, who took me to *Bell, Book and Candle.*

"Gentlemen Under the Elms": I. J. Kapstein, Elmer Blistein, Charles Alexander Robinson, and Albert van Nostrand, who made me study, grudgingly, "Manfred," "In Memoriam," the Delian League, and *What Maisie Knew.* Hyman Minsky, who made me read all of *Das Kapital.* Mar-tha Mitchell, who threw my slender volume of verse over the Pembroke College hedge. Robert Frost, who spoke darkly at Alumnae Hall. A.D., a literary circle which demanded a short story—"Roadhoss"—about my work with the International Hod Carriers and Common Laborers Union. The wandering scholars who pursued "Applied Romanticism" with me at the University of London. The *Brown Daily Herald,* which set me to writing headlines, a training in haiku.

George Haskins, who endured my views on the public law of the Massachusetts Bay Colony. Anthony Nicholas Brady Garvan, who put me on his architectural history team to transform the Old Patent Office into the National Portrait Gallery. Joe Evans, who talked of Santayana on the Jersey Shore. Law school wretches H. Beatty Chadwick, who later did fourteen years in the penitentiary, and Rod Henry, who sent him books. The Penn Library, which paid me to shovel the papers of Studs Lonigan's author.

James Hillman, fellow South Jerseyan, who refused me Jungian analysis at Küsnacht. Max Horkheimer, who visited me, his vice consul, in Zürich to worry about the unintended consequences of Reason. The grass-writing, poetry-intoning Chinese sages who taught me Mandarin in the Foreign Service Institute garage in Roslyn and at Taichung, Republic of China.

John Fairbank, Ezra Vogel, Ben Schwartz, and Merle Goldman, Harvardians who coped with Mao's Great Proletarian Cultural Revolution, the Vietnam War, women's liberation, the New Left, the student strike, and me all at the same time. Lionel Trilling and W. H. Auden, who took no note of such happenings when speaking in Sanders Theatre.

Adlai Stevenson, who taught me the first rule of diplomacy during the Cuban missile crisis. Ellsworth Bunker, who followed Fabius Maximus Cunctator in Vietnam. Henry Kissinger, who "read Metternich by candlelight" and threw crumpled speech drafts at me during the day. Phil Habib, who feigned furious anger in order to make friends. Menachem Begin the metahistorian, who made me the prime minister's "shabbas goy" during the Lebanon War. Alexander Haig, who pounded a desk made from "Don't Give Up the Ship" planks. George Shultz, who commissioned me to collect books on diplomacy for a "Secretary of State's library." Joseph Alsop, who said the only volume needed would be the memoirs of the duc de Saint-Simon at the court of Louis XIV. Bernie Kalb, manly reporter, uneasy State Department spokesman, who with me visited Berggasse 19 and other cultural shrines, always humming "I'll take Manhattan . . ." Boutros Boutros-Ghali, gallant magus from the pages of *The Alexandria Quartet.* Fellow foreign policy speechwriter Peter Rodman, who got the secretary of state to say "Thucydides" and "schistosomiasis" in the same speech. Nick Platt, Hong Kong oarsman and China watcher. Sam Lewis, Red Sea diver and peace processor. Jerry Bremer, *chef de cabinet* and patriot.

Departed bookstores: Leary's, Philadelphia; Gotham Book Mart, Manhattan; Savile, Georgetown; Kelly and Walsh, Hong Kong; Librairie

Xuân-Thu, rue Tu-Do, Saigon; Ludwig Mayer Ltd., Shlomzion Hamalka, Jerusalem; Pangloss, Cambridge; Chimera, Palo Alto; Bryn Mawr Books, New Haven. And the British Council Libraries of Zürich and Saigon.

Gaddis Smith, who created "international studies" as one of the humanities at Yale. Bill Foltz, Gus Ranis, Ian Shapiro, and Nancy Ruther, who let me teach in it.

Paul Kennedy and John Lewis Gaddis, colleagues in Grand Strategy, and the greats who accompany them: Keats, Kipling, and Kennan. The economy's bard, Paul Solman.

The masters of Berkeley College from the time of Robin Winks, the last man to understand academic ceremony. The literary executive fellows Fred Robinson and Claude Rawson. Cyndi Erickson, astonished to read about my note taking in the pages of a Bob Woodward book.

Joseph Hamburger, Jane Levin, Howard Bloch, Paul Freedman, Kathryn Slankski, Justin Zaremby, Norma Thompson, and all the directed studies teachers of the best of all students. Maria Menocal and all The Women of the Whitney Humanities Center.

Romayne Ponleithner, foremost in the pantheon of editors. Susan and David Hennigan, Bill Frucht, Lynn Chu, and the readers of the manuscript. Ann Carter-Drier, Monica Ward, Kathleen Murphy. At Hoover, Grace Hawes, Susan Schendel, Juanita Nissley, Phyl Whiting, and the friendship of John Raisian and Fouad Ajami.

Katie, who reads and thinks fairy tales; Emily, who fought reading and reading won. The reading Thompsons.

Generations of close readers and literary commentators who are the real authors of this book, except for my blunders.

And those moral and intellectual bastions of civilization, Don and Myrna Kagan.

INDEX